Punishment and Power
in the Making of Modern Japan

Daniel V. Botsman

PRINCETON UNIVERSITY PRESS

PRINCETON AND OXFORD

Library of Congress Cataloging-in-Publication Data

Botsman, Dani.
Punishment and power in the making of modern Japan /
Daniel V. Botsman
p.   cm.
Includes bibliographical references and index.
ISBN 0-691-11491-9 (cloth : alk. paper)
1. Japan—History—1868– 2. Punishment—Japan—History. I. Title.
DS881.95.B67 2004
364.6′0942′09034—dc22   2004044280

British Library Cataloging-in-Publication Data is available.

This book has been composed in Janson

Printed on acid-free paper. ∞

www.pupress.princeton.edu

Printed in the United States of America

10 9 8 7 6 5 4 3 2 1

For my mother, Barbara Clare Botsman,
and in memory of my father, Peter Bernard Botsman

Contents

Illustrations

Acknowledgments

IN THE COURSE of writing this book I have received guidance and support from many people in many places. At the Australian National University, where this project had its beginnings as an undergraduate thesis, it was my great good fortune to be nurtured in the study of Japanese history by John Caiger and Richard Mason, and to be further encouraged to pursue my interests by Stewart Lone, John Ballard, Gavan McCormack, Geremie Barmé, Tessa Morris-Suzuki, and Shun Ikeda (who shared with me not only his wisdom but also his home). It is now more than ten years since I left Australia, but the example set for me by this remarkable group of scholars has never ceased to be a source of inspiration. At Oxford, where I embarked upon my graduate studies, Avner Offer, Joanna Innes, Margaret Pelling, Paul Slack, and John Stevenson helped me develop a comparative perspective on Japan through the study of British social history, while James McMullen patiently guided my reading of Tokugawa period texts and Ann Waswo generously made time to supervise my initial attempt to rethink the significance of the Stockade for Laborers. Drew Gerstle helped ease my transition to life in England with his kind words and later provided me with an invaluable opportunity to present my early research on Nakai Riken at an important conference on Kansai at the School of Oriental and African Studies in London. I am deeply grateful to Sheldon Garon for the faith he has shown in me since our very first meeting in Canberra and for having encouraged me to make another continental leap, this time across the Atlantic, to Princeton, N.J. There I found a truly congenial environment in which to complete my graduate studies and the doctoral dissertation on which this book is based. While Shel challenged me to deepen my understanding of modern Japan, David Howell, inspired me with his knowledge, rigor, and enthusiasm for the study of Tokugawa history. In spite of his strong interest in questions of status, it is difficult to imagine a more open or accessible font of academic wisdom, and I am proud to have been the first in what will undoubtedly be a long line of his advisees. I am also grateful to Martin Collcutt, Marius Jansen, Nell Painter, Sue Naquin, Ruth Rogaski, and Bill Jordan for their advice, encouragement, and support. In addition to the opportunities for intellectual growth I was afforded, I wish to express my sincere appreciation for the generous financial support that I received at Princeton. Particularly in my fourth year, when all other sources of funding failed, the Princeton Graduate School, together with the Program on East Asian Studies (James Liu Traveling Fellowship), the

Council on Regional Studies, and the Council for International Studies, cobbled together a fellowship to get me to Japan for a much needed year of field research.

Once in Japan, Yoshida Nobuyuki of Tokyo University kindly invited me to join his study group and helped arrange an affiliation at the Historiographical Institute. My time there was made particularly rewarding by my academic supervisor, Miyazaki Katsumi, who did everything in his power to make me feel welcome and guide my research efforts. It was also while I was at Todai that I first met Ronald Toby, whose support over the years since has been invaluable, and whose comments and advice have greatly enriched this book. Tsukada Takashi of Osaka City University, whose work on status and punishment has greatly shaped my own thinking, went out of his way to help and encourage me whenever our paths crossed. Kuchiishi Kumiko, Iyoku Hideaki, Iijima Kishie, Shibuya Yōko, Kaneyuki Nobusuke, Yamaguchi Kazuo, Oikawa Wataru, Sugimoto Fumiko, Yamamoto Hirofumi, Matsumoto Ryōta, and Ōhashi Akiko all provided valuable advice and support.

After a year in Tokyo, it was my privilege to join the ranks of the Faculty of Law at Hokkaido University, which provided me with the time and space I needed to complete my research and begin writing it up. I am grateful to Nakamura Kenichi, Furuya Jun, Kawashima Shin, Matsuura Masataka, Endō Ken, Nomura Maki, Ozaki Ichirō, Nakano Katsurō, Kawasaki Osamu, Hasegawa Kō, Shinkawa Toshimitsu, Yamaguchi Jirō, Shiratori Yūji, Andrew Pardieck, and Fumoto Shinichi for their collegiality and support during my time in Sapporo. I also thank Ishihara Makoto (of the wonderful Sapporo-dō bookstore) and local prison historians Kumagai Masakichi and Misu Tatsuo for their helpful advice.

The transition back to the United States to begin teaching in the history department at Harvard was hectic and often stressful, but the support of my colleagues here has certainly helped make this a better book. Andrew Gordon carefully read through an early version of the manuscript and provided me with detailed comments on every chapter. Harold Bolitho, Akira Iriye, Philip Kuhn, and Sven Beckert offered general comments and encouragement, Rebecca McLennan suggested a number of helpful readings, Carter Eckert kindly looked over the expanded conclusion, and Eileen Chow offered constructive comments and moral support throughout the revision process. The Reischauer Institute for Japanese Studies generously supported my research efforts, and also provided funds to allow me to stay in residence in Cambridge during a year of leave so I could revise the manuscript. While I have benefited from my interactions with all of the graduate students at Harvard, Rustin Gates, Yoichi Nakano, Ann Marie Davis, Joe Wicentowski, Amy Stanley, Marjan Boogart, Chris Hilliard, and Stacie Matsumoto, in particular, have contributed to this book in substantial ways. For their support I also thank Janet Hatch and the staff of the history department, the Reischauer Institute, and the Harvard-Yenching library. Chang Lung-Chih extended me every possible assistance during my visit to Taiwan and kindly arranged for me to present some of my research on flogging at Academic Sinica. Wang Tay-Sheng of Taipei University was generous with both his time and advice.

During the revision process Anne Walthall, Gyan Prakash, Constantine Vaporis, Peter Weiler, Tessa Morris-Suzuki, and Morris Low all offered extremely thoughtful readings of the manuscript, as did Harry Harootunian, long one of my intellectual heroes. Shigematsu Kazuyoshi, Japan's foremost prison historian, offered his warm encouragement and support from afar. For their comments and help I am also grateful to my comrades Annie Reinhardt, Shinju Fujihira, Steve Price, David Ambaras, Alex Vesey, Kevin Uhlade, David Gordon, Umemori Naoyuki, Ben Middleton, Robert Hellyer, Alexis Dudden, Angus Lockyer, Vanessa Ward, Umemura Mitsuhisa, and Cathy Corman. In the final stages of writing, Royall Tyler carefully read through my revised chapters and helped soothe my anxieties with warm reminders of better times. Marcella Bungay Stanier provided much needed editorial assistance early on, and with Michael, always gave me reason to smile. Over the years Miyokawa Norifumi has contributed to this book in innumerable ways and for his enduring friendship, and that of Yuriko, I am truly grateful. I thank Samantha Kent and Brian R. MacDonald for their heroic efforts to bring clarity to my prose and consistency to my footnotes, and Julie Stephens for all of her help in the preparation of the manuscript.

At Princeton University Press I have been extremely fortunate to have the expert guidance and advice of Brigitta van Rheinberg and the helpful support of Alison Kalett. I am also grateful to Ellen Foos for patiently leading me through the production process, and to Tom Broughton-Willet for his assistance with the preparation of the index. Three anonymous readers for the Press provided me with thoughtful comments, and while I fear I have not been able to address all of their criticisms adequately, I hope they can at least agree that this book is better than it would otherwise have been. Whatever errors of fact and interpretation remain are, of course, mine and mine alone. An early version of some of the material in the Tokugawa chapters appeared in my article "Punishment and Power in Tokugawa Japan" (1992). I gratefully acknowledge the permission of *East Asian History* to reproduce parts of that work here. I also thank Shigematsu Kazuyoshi, the National Archive of Japan, Tsukigata Kabato Museum, the Criminal Museum of Meiji University, Seikadō Bunko Art Museum, the Kawanabe Kyōsai Memorial Museum, and the Japanese Correctional Association for permission to make use of the images that appear in the book.

Crystal Feimster, my darling wife, has shared this process with me as no one else could, inspiring me always with her integrity, brilliance, and love. She has rescued me from despair and exhaustion, helped me work through ideas, and contributed in her own way to every page in this book. My brother Peter (who first introduced me to Foucault), and my sisters Lyn and Tara have been a source of support and strength throughout, as have the Johnsons in North Carolina, the Kawases in Kobe, and the Okitas in Kamakura. Although the subject matter is hardly fitting, I dedicate this book to my mother, who has given so generously for so long, and to the memory of my father. I hope it would have made him proud, even as it stands, without his comments and suggestions to complete it.

Abbreviations

HBT — Naikaku kirokukyoku, ed. *Hōki bunrui taizen* [1889]. 88 vols. Reprint. Tokyo: Hara shobō, 1977–81.

Hōreki shūsei — Takayanagi Shinzō and Ishii Ryōsuke, eds. *Ofuregaki Hōreki shūsei*. Tokyo: Iwanami shoten, 1935.

Kampō shūsei — Takayanagi Shinzō and Ishii Ryōsuke, eds. *Ofuregaki Kampō shūsei*. Tokyo: Iwanami shoten, 1935.

KKSK — Hiramatsu Yoshirō. *Kinsei keiji soshō-hō no kenkyū*. Tokyo: Sōbunsha, 1960.

Kyūjishimonroku — Kyū Tōkyō Teikoku Daigaku shidankai, ed. *Kyūjishimonroku* [1889–91]. Tokyo: Seiabō, 1964.

MKK — Tezuka Yukata. *Meiji keihōshi no kenkyū*. 3 vols. Tokyo: Keiō tsūshin, 1986.

NKGS — Nihon keimu kyōkai, ed. *Nihon kinsei gyōkei shikō*. 2 vols. Tokyo: Keimu kyōkai, 1943.

NKT — Takimoto Seiichi, ed. *Nihon keizai taiten*. 54 vols. Tokyo: Shishi shuppansha, 1928.

Reiruishū — Ishii Ryōsuke, ed. *Oshioki reiruishū*. 16 vols. Tokyo: Meicho Shuppan, 1971.

Temmei shūsei — Takayanagi Shinzō and Ishii Ryōsuke, eds. *Ofuregaki Temmei shūsei*. Tokyo: Iwanami shoten, 1936.

Tempō shūsei — Takayanagi Shinzō and Ishii Ryōsuke, eds. *Ofuregaki Tempō shūsei*. 2 vols. Tokyo: Iwanami shoten, 1937.

TKKK — Ishii Ryōsuke, ed. *Tokugawa kinreikō (kōshū)*. 5 vols. Tokyo: Sōbunsha, 1959–61.

TKKZ — Ishii Ryōsuke, ed. *Tokugawa kinreikō (zenshū)*. 6 vols. Tokyo: Sōbunsha, 1959–61.

TSKE — Keimukyoku, ed. *Taiwan Sōtokufu keisatsu enkaku shi*. 4 vols. Taihoku: Taiwan Sōtokufu keimukyoku, 1933–34.

TSKS — Tokyo-to, ed. *Tōkyō-shi shikō shigai hen*. 86 vols. Tokyo: Tokyo-to, 1912–.

Introduction

*The explanation of the very recent in terms of the remotest past,
naturally attractive to men who have made of this past their chief
subject of research, has sometimes dominated our studies to the point
of a hypnosis. In its most characteristic aspect, this idol of the
historian tribe may be called the obsession with origins.*

Marc Bloch, *The Historian's Craft*

*Historicism enabled European domination of the world in the
nineteenth century.*

Dipesh Chakrabarty, *Provincializing Europe*

IF YOU WANDER AROUND the antiquarian bookstores of Tokyo's famous Jim-
bochō district looking for material on the history of punishment, you are
bound to discover copies of an old picture book called *Tokugawa bakufu
keiji zufu* (An Illustrated Guide to the Punishments of the Tokugawa Shogunate).[1] Compiled in 1893 by an artist named Fujita Shintarō, the guide
contains some sixty color drawings, divided into three main sections. The
first section depicts a range of crimes supposedly typical of the Tokugawa
period (1603–1867). There are drawings of thieves and bandits, corrupt
merchants and gamblers, and—in what undoubtedly constitutes evidence
of the ongoing gender anxieties of the Meiji era (1868–1912)—an usually
large number of "poison women": beautiful entertainers who stole money
from their customers, vicious concubines who plotted to kill their masters
and tormented their heirs, conniving members of the shogun's harem who
hatched political intrigues, and so on.[2] This first section ends with an illustration of one of the samurai "patriots" involved in the early stages of the
struggle to overthrow the shogun's regime and "restore" the long-over-
shadowed emperor to his rightful place as ruler of Japan. He sits alone with
a grave look on his face, and in the pages that follow the reasons for his
concern become increasingly clear.

After several drawings showing the rough methods of arrest used by
samurai officials and the deep shame of suspects being led through the
streets of the city in full public view, the second section of Fujita's guide
moves on to present the full horrors of Tokugawa justice in graphic and
gory detail. Suspected criminals (including several of the "poison women"
depicted earlier) are shown being chained up and beaten during their initial interrogations, then thrown into a squalid, overcrowded jailhouse and
tortured mercilessly in the presence of fearsome samurai magistrates until

confessing to the crimes they have been accused of. The guide reaches its climax with a long series of illustrations depicting the broad array of punishments used by the Tokugawa and the bloody, mutilated remains of those subjected to the harshest of them. Then, finally, in a stark and deliberate contrast to these gruesome images, it turns to the new "enlightened" system of justice that had been introduced in the decades following the Meiji Restoration of 1868. This section shows policemen in modern uniforms being carefully supervised by superiors as they conduct an arrest; criminal suspects now appear wearing special masks designed to protect their identities as they are escorted through the city streets. There are also illustrations of the spotless, well-ordered interiors of one of the new prisons and of public trials being conducted in grand-looking courthouses and courts of appeal. The two final pages of the guide show on one side a group of convicts diligently working away under the supervision of uniformed guards and on the other a modern gallows with two nooses hanging ready to inflict clean, bloodless sentences of death.

The Whiggish "before and after" narrative that Fujita's guide outlines will, no doubt, strike readers as a familiar one. A dramatic shift away from brutal methods of interrogation and punishment to a more humane and rational system of justice has, after all, long been understood to constitute an important part of the birth of "modern" civilization, and the same story of sweeping penal reforms has often been told in the context of the emergence of the world's first bourgeois societies. After the American Revolution, we know, leaders of the new republic proclaimed an end to all "cruel and unusual punishment," dramatically curtailed the use of the death penalty, and eventually built the world's first model penitentiaries, all as part of their efforts to create a virtuous, Christian society, distinct from the corrupt European monarchies with which they had so boldly broken.[3] In France too, the great revolution of 1789 quickly led to the abandonment of the old regime's expansive arsenal of punishments and (the excesses of the Terror notwithstanding) to the rise of a new penal system based primarily on fines, imprisonment, and that most scientific instrument of death, the guillotine.[4] The reform process in England may not have taken place in the same context of domestic political revolution, but the changes implemented there in the late eighteenth and early nineteenth centuries were no less dramatic. Figures such as John Howard, the prison reformer, William Blackstone, the jurist, and Robert Peel, the reform-minded politician, have often been seen by historians as secular saints for the roles they played in eradicating the abuses of the old eighteenth-century system of justice and its infamous "Bloody Code."[5]

The example of Meiji Japan as portrayed in Fujita's guide seems to fit with this classic Western model, and it is not difficult to string together "hard facts" from the historical record to further support this view. Within

Figure 1. "Punishment by burning at the stake" from Fujita Shintarō, *Tokugawa bakufu keiji zufu* (An Illustrated Guide to the Punishments of the Tokugawa Shogunate) (1893). The Criminal Museum of Meiji University.

just a year of the Meiji Restoration, Japan's new government had already begun to abolish the harshest of the old Tokugawa punishments, and within a decade efforts to build a national network of modern courts and prisons were well underway. Although there is no denying the revolutionary speed of these changes, however, Fujita's guide also reminds us of one way in which the Japanese path to modernity differed profoundly from that of the Western nations just mentioned. Opening the front cover of the guide, the reader is immediately confronted by a "prefece" (*sic*) written in awkward but nevertheless clearly decipherable English. The illustrations in the book, moreover, all carry English captions alongside the Japanese. The guide was thus intended not just for a domestic Japanese market but also for sale among the foreign community in Japan and probably for export. Profit provides one possible explanation for this. Then (as now) Western audiences had a strong interest in the horrors of "Oriental despotism," and Fujita and his publisher were undoubtedly well aware that a book containing graphic illustrations of exotic tortures and punishments was likely to sell. There was more to it than this alone, however. After all, if a profit-hungry appeal to the "fascination of the abomination" was really the book's main purpose, why include a final section depicting the reforms that had been implemented since the Restoration? And why go to the trouble of composing an English-language preface emphasizing how the "revolution of the first year of Meidi [*sic*]" had ushered in an age of "wonderful Progress" and banished the "cruelties" of the Tokugawa shoguns to a chapter of history that, it claimed, was already a distant memory for most Japanese?

More than just a familiar tale of "progress" told in the context of a different national history, these sections of the guide reveal a deeply felt need to secure Western recognition of Japan's social and political transformation and of its commitment to the project of modern civilization. And it is no coincidence that the example of penal reform should have been taken up for this purpose. Practices of punishment and ideas about them had, from the very outset, played a crucial role in shaping Japan's relations with the Western powers. As we shall see in more detail in chapter 5, the primary objective of Commodore Perry's famous mission to "open" Japan in 1853 may have been to secure access to coaling stations and shipping supplies for transpacific trade, but at a moral level it was initially justified in terms of the need to ensure that shipwrecked American sailors were not thrown into squalid jails and subjected to the horrors of "Oriental" justice for having violated the "unreasonable" laws that kept the country "secluded" from the world.[6] To use the language of today's global power politics, Japan in the 1850s was a "rogue state," and stories of the harsh treatment (i.e., human rights violations) of unfortunate American castaways provided a convenient pretext for using force, or the threat of it, to bring it into line with "international norms." Soon after the conclusion of the Perry treaty, pressure also began being put on the Tokugawa regime to allow the establishment of permanent enclaves of Western traders, and in this context the specter of white men being subjected to Japan's "sanguinary codes" provided the necessary moral justification for imposing a series of "unequal treaties" that confirmed the right of all Westerners in Japan to be tried in special consular courts according to their own laws and practices.

Immunity from Japanese laws was not the only advantage secured under these treaties. They also established terms of trade that were strongly favorable to Western interests and denied Japanese officials the right to change tariff levels without permission from the Western powers. Overall, they established Japan's formal status as a backward, "semicivilized" country, well below the nations of the West on the great evolutionary tree that had rapidly grown to maturity in the soil of European empire. After the Restoration, treaty revision quickly became one of the central goals of the Meiji regime; but so long as the Western powers were able to raise doubts about the suitability of Japanese laws and punishments for citizens of the civilized countries, they would always have a reason to reject changes to the status quo. As a result, penal and judicial reforms in Meiji Japan were never simply matters of domestic concern. They were also intimately connected to larger issues concerning Japan's relations with the West and its place within the new world order that European imperialist expansion had built.

The experience of being categorized as backward and inferior and of having to come to terms abruptly with Western ideas and institutions under the threat of force clearly links Japan's modern history to that of most parts of the non-Western world.[7] Yet this aspect of the Japanese past is often overlooked or forgotten. In large part, of course, this is because we have become so used to thinking of Japan as a unique "success." True, the nation may have been confronted by aggressive Western gunboat diplomacy and experienced the *threat* of colonial subjugation, but in the end, unlike other non-Western societies, it did not succumb to the imperialist aggression visited upon it. On the contrary, under the leadership of the Meiji government a massive effort was launched to unlock the secrets of Western power and use them to strengthen the country from within. By the time that Fujita published his guide in 1893 Japan could boast not only of its police, courts, and prisons but also of its national network of schools, its post offices and trains, its modern conscription army, and, most important, its new system of constitutional government—the first of its kind outside the West. Faced with all of this evidence of "progress," the Western powers, led by Great Britain, agreed in 1894 to accept a timetable for revision of the "unequal treaties" that had been imposed on Japan some forty years earlier. (The publication of Fujita's guide was clearly part of the final push toward the achievement of this "great goal.") Within just weeks of concluding the new agreement with the Western powers, the Meiji leaders also led the country into its first modern war, against Qing dynasty China. Victory over the Qing the following year allowed Japan to claim its first major overseas colony, Taiwan, and a massive reparation payment, which, together with the war effort itself, helped stimulate a wave of industrialization in the decade that followed. By the beginning of the twentieth century, the country was thus already well on its way to becoming a "great power," and in the decades that followed it steadily built up its own empire and influence in East Asia.

In terms of both timing and outcomes (not to mention the eventual slide into fascism), this history would clearly seem to link Japan more closely to the "latecomer" states of Europe (particularly Germany and Italy) than to other parts of the non-Western world, and historians have repeatedly made this comparison. Yet the fact remains that in 1850 Japan had been seen by the West as a backward, Oriental country, far removed from the dynamic achievements of European civilization. How was it then that this society managed not only to stave off colonization and subordination but also to grow into a modern nation with an expansive empire of its own? How was it able to become so powerful that by the middle of the twentieth century it would sweep away the old European empires from Asia and mount a serious military challenge to the United States, single-handedly pulling it into the greatest conflict of the modern age?

In the aftermath of Japan's defeat in the Pacific War, questions like these became the central concern of a generation of historians in the English-speaking world whose own lives had been indelibly touched by both the war and the Allied occupation. Turning their attention to the period immediately preceding the arrival of Perry, scholars in the so-called modernization school suggested that perhaps the key to Japan's subsequent "takeoff" and "development" lay in the fact that it had not been so backward in 1850 after all. A close look at Tokugawa society, they suggested, revealed trends that closely paralleled important developments in the West on the eve of the Industrial Revolution. The paradigmatic example of this approach is Robert N. Bellah's famous 1957 study, *Tokugawa Religion*, which maintained that popular religious beliefs in the late Tokugawa period revealed a spirit remarkably similar to the "Protestant work ethic" that Max Weber had identified as an important factor in the emergence of capitalism in western Europe.[8] Similarly, the pioneering social and economic historian Thomas C. Smith showed that Japan, like western Europe, had experienced significant "pre-modern economic growth" (now commonly referred to as "proto-industrialization") and that peasants in the Tokugawa period had been forced to develop a sense of "work discipline" that prepared them well for the rigors of industrial capitalism.[9] Ronald Dore's *Education in Tokugawa Japan* emphasized the fact that literacy rates in Japan were probably as high as anywhere in the preindustrial world, while John W. Hall's biography of the powerful grand chamberlain, Tanuma Oki-tsugu, suggested that by the second half of the eighteenth century there were already signs that some Tokugawa leaders had begun to explore a more "modern" approach to government and economic policy.[10]

In some important respects, the work of these scholars and others in the modernization school can be said to have had a liberating impact on the field of "Japanese studies." In contrast to classic forms of Orientalist schol-arship, which could view Asians only as people trapped within an essentially unchanging world of "civilizations" and "traditions," the basic point of the modernization school's approach was always to highlight the dynamism and vitality of Tokugawa society.[11] In this sense, it posed an important chal-lenge to the narrow, Eurocentric focus of the historical profession in places like the United States, by boldly asserting that a non-Western nation too could have a real history.[12] As the list of works mentioned earlier have already made clear, it also provided an extremely rich research paradigm, adding greatly to our awareness of many aspects of Japan's past. Yet, in the end, it was a paradigm that carried with it a range of serious problems and limitations.

As T. Fujitani has recently pointed out, the modernization school reached the height of its influence and popularity at more or less the same time that Japanese Americans were first being defined as a "model minor-ity" within the United States.[13] The two sets of ideas, he notes, not only were mutually reinforcing but also paralleled each other in key ways. Do-mestically, emphasis was placed on the way that the unique cultural heri-tage that Japanese Americans brought with them to the United States had enabled them to overcome the obstacles of racism and discrimination and "succeed" in mainstream (white) American society. The implication for other minority groups was that if they were unable to overcome such obsta-cles, ultimately it was not because of their specific situations or because of fundamental problems within U.S. society, but rather because they them-selves lacked the right cultural attributes and values to "fit in" and "get ahead." Similarly, by establishing Japan as a "global model minority," which had been able to "succeed" as a nation because of its unique historical development during the Tokugawa period, the modernization school im-plied that if other non-Western nations were unable to "develop," it was not so much because of the legacies of colonial domination or present-day inequalities and problems within the global system but rather because they were not yet properly prepared as societies.[14] To put it another way, rather than holding up Japan as the example that shattered the mystique of white supremacy and proved that people in other parts of the world could also become strong and powerful (as "third world" nationalists had often done), the work of the modernization school effectively positioned it as the exception that proved the rule of European cultural and historical superiority. Japan had been able to succeed because its past was essentially (and uniquely) similar to that of the West. In this sense, far from being independent of the West, its history was inseparably bound to it. It was an "honorary white" nation with an "honorary white" past.

Eventually, of course, there was always the possibility that other non-Western nations might attain the same kind of attributes that set Japan apart, but, as Fujitani notes, the work of the modernization scholars clearly suggested that they would have to be patient. After all, if the roots of "development" in Japan could be traced back several centuries to the beginning of the Tokugawa period, then it would be unreasonable to expect real improvements and changes to occur elsewhere overnight.[15] In this respect, the modernization school's approach to Japanese history can be linked to precisely the same kind of historicist consciousness that Dipesh Chakrabarty has identified as lying at the heart of European imperialism. Historicism, Chakrabarty points out, was what allowed a classic liberal philosopher such as John Stuart Mill to proclaim, on the one hand, that democratic self-rule was the highest form of government and yet, on the other, to argue forcefully against extending it to Britain's Indian and African subjects. Eventually they would be able to rule themselves, the argument went, but "some historical time of development and civilization (colonial rule and education, to be precise) had to elapse before they could be considered ready for such a task."[16] In response to the continual refrain of "not yet" from the colonial rulers, Chakrabarty notes, anticolonial nationalist movements in the twentieth century learned to "harp insistently on a 'now' as the temporal horizon of action."[17] If all people were born free and equal, as the great European thinkers taught, then it followed that Indian and African peasants were, from the outset, just as entitled to rule themselves as the cleverest of British intellectuals. This kind of insistence on "the urgency of the 'now'" helped give rise to the great wave of decolonization that followed World War II, but in its wake the work of the modernization school allowed the example of Japan and its history to be used to support and reassert the old logic of "not yet." Japan's rapid "development" from the Meiji period on had been possible because the society had been properly prepared for it. Other nations, which were not ready but had rushed to claim their political independence, should not expect (or demand) too much too soon.[18]

In addition to these political considerations, there were also fundamental problems of historical interpretation and representation. To begin with, of course, the modernization school's approach was deeply teleological, highlighting only those aspects of the past that seemed to fit with the notion of a society moving steadily toward "modernity" and downplaying those that did not. Leftist scholars in Japan, who in the aftermath of decades of political repression and disastrous wars of aggression naturally found it difficult to see the nation's history in terms of unadulterated "success," were also quick to point out that the modernization school's approach reduced the complex issue of modernity to the single question of industrialization, thereby avoiding more difficult questions about social and political development. By emphasizing Japan's achievements *as a nation*, moreover, it tended to obscure any sense of internal social divisions, oppression, or struggle. Similar kinds of criticisms also began being articulated by a younger generation of scholars in the United States, particularly after the Vietnam War. In their work on the Tokugawa past, some of these scholars turned specifically to the question of what one important collection of essays called "the neglected tradition" of conflict in Japanese history, focusing on peasant protest and other forms of popular rebellion.[19] Others examined areas of the past that had already been taken up by the modernization school (the history of thought, economic history) but strove to do so in ways that avoided the teleological pull of "the modern," the search for "equivalents" to European developments, and the tendency to celebrate the Tokugawa heritage uncritically.[20] As a result of these efforts, our understanding of the Tokugawa period and of Japanese history more generally is undoubtedly fuller and more sophisticated than ever before.

Yet it would be a mistake to assume that the field has managed to escape fully the kind of historicist assumptions that informed the modernization school's approach. At a superficial level it is striking to note the way in which many historians writing in English continue to fall back on the phrase "early modern Japan," a term that clearly implies both preparation for "the modern" and a sense of equivalency with early modern Europe. More substantively, in focusing so much attention on the Tokugawa past and the complex ways in which it may have shaped Japan's subsequent development (for better and for worse), we have continued to downplay or overlook the fact that modernity in Japan was ultimately *not* homegrown and must be understood, at least in the first instance, as a product of the mid-nineteenth-century encounter with Western imperialism.

One of this book's primary goals is to use the example of punishment and penal reform to restore some sense of the way that forces *external* to the history of "the nation" played a crucial role in its formation. It seeks, in other words, to puncture the neat, self-contained boundaries of national history, and to see the encounter with imperialism not just in terms of an aggressive Western challenge that helped trigger a dynamic Japanese response but rather as something that was itself integral to the making of modern Japan. The history of punishment is, in many ways, ideally suited for this purpose. As Fujita's guide suggests, the changes that were implemented in the decades following the Restoration were both visceral and qualitative: no one in the 1890s had any doubt that a real break had been made with the penal and judicial traditions of the Tokugawa period. There was also no doubt that this break was intimately connected to the issue of the unequal treaties and, more generally, to the new notions of civilization that had been used to justify them.

Yet the history of punishment in Japan has hardly been immune to the logic of historicism. As the humiliation of the unequal treaties began to fade from living memory, and the Japanese state became increasingly conscious of its self-appointed role as "the leader of Asia" in the prewar period, Japanese scholars working in the then highly prestigious subfield of legal history had already begun to uncover "evidence" that some aspects of Tokugawa penal practice had shown clear signs of "progress" toward a more "civilized" approach.[21] Japan in 1868 may not have been as advanced as the Western powers, they implied, but even in the Tokugawa period it had moved further along the path to "enlightenment" than the other peoples of East Asia, whom it was now attempting to "raise up" through its own project of colonial expansion. In the decades following the war this particular strand of nationalist discourse simultaneously fed into and was reinforced by the approach of the modernization school, and as a result legal historians in Japan continued to interpret the history of Tokugawa punishments primarily in terms of a steady movement toward modern forms of penality. In general terms they argued that, although Tokugawa punishments were harsh, there was clear evidence of a gradual amelioration over time. They emphasized the significance of an institution called the Stockade for Laborers *(ninsoku yoseba)*, which had been established in Edo in the late eighteenth century. The stockade, they noted, was used to confine people and put them to work for the sake of promoting "reform"—and from this they concluded that it was an indigenous forerunner of the "modern punishment of deprivation of liberty" *(kindai-teki jiyū kei)*.[22]

The first four chapters of this book lay out an alternative framework for understanding the history of Tokugawa punishment. Drawing inspiration from the methodological insights of Foucault's *Discipline and Punish*, as well as other works produced in the "crime wave" that has swept the Western historical profession since the 1970s, I argue that in order to understand Tokugawa punishments properly we must first suspend our concern with issues of barbarism and humanity (i.e., with "progress") and see them instead as one part of a complex set of strategies for ordering society and exercising power.[23] The first chapter provides an overview of the general nature of punishment in the Tokugawa period, focusing particularly on the shogun's capital, Edo (now Tokyo), which by the end of the seventeenth century had become the standard point of reference for penal and judicial practices all over the country. In addition to describing the particular kinds of punishment used by the warrior regime, it also explores some of the basic principles according to which they were managed and applied. The punishments are, in other words, understood to have formed part of a system, and an attempt is made to show how that system worked.

The second chapter considers Tokugawa penal practices from the perspective of contemporary doctrines about good government and political legitimacy. It begins by asking how a system of unashamedly brutal capital and corporal punishments could have continued to function without undermining the credibility of a regime that claimed to govern in accordance with both Confucian principles of benevolence and Buddhist ideals of compassion. By way of an answer the chapter shows how customary practices, gaps in enforcement, and strategic acts of restraint helped temper the way in which the power to punish was exercised. It also explores the crucial role that outcast groups played in the operation of the Tokugawa penal system and considers how their presence infused acts of official punishment with an added layer of political meaning, protecting and bolstering the position of the warrior lords.

Though important for an understanding of how the punishment system worked, outcasts constituted, however, only one stratum of the complex hierarchy of formally recognized "estates" or status groups around which Tokugawa society was organized. Beginning with a detailed analysis of the internal organization of the shogunate's main jailhouse at Kodenmachō in Edo, chapter 3 shows how the principles of the status system (*mibunsei*) permeated and shaped virtually every aspect of judicial decision making under the warrior state. In this it enhances not only our understanding of the nature of the penal system but also our awareness of the centrality of status to the structures of Tokugawa society and our sense of the ways in which that society was fundamentally unlike the one that emerged in the wake of the Meiji Restoration. In general, the first three chapters are all intended to bolster an awareness of the unsettling strangeness of the past. This, however, is not to suggest that we should lapse back into an Orientalist understanding of Tokugawa society as static and unchanging.

Chapter 4 examines how, from the beginning of the eighteenth century, concerns about the ability of the warrior state to maintain social order gave rise to a new scholarly discourse about penal reform and eventually prompted the decision to establish the Stockade for Laborers. Rather than seeing this new institution as evidence of a shift toward a new, more modern approach to punishment and social discipline, however, I argue that it should instead be seen as part of an effort to bolster and reinforce the basic structures of the status system and the mechanisms that it provided for enforcing order and stability. Its establishment shows, in other words, that the old system was changing, but not in any simple, linear manner.

Having examined in detail the basic principles of the Tokugawa punishment system and the broader social context within which it operated, the book then turns to the question of how and why the old system was dismantled and radically remade in the wake of the Restoration. Chapter 5 begins by showing how, from around the time of Perry's arrival in Japan, idealized descriptions of America's recently established penitentiary system began to catch the attention of a small but influential group of activists and scholars who, confronted by a rising tide of domestic social unease and unrest, became fascinated by its twin promise of human mutability and perfect order. At the same time, the chapter also examines how, in the context of the encounter with the West, older penal practices that had for centuries been equated with warrior power, authority, and control were abruptly transformed into symbols of national backwardness and barbarity.

As already noted, the rupture of these established notions was closely connected to the imposition of the unequal treaties, and in the wake of the Restoration the new politics of civilization that they epitomized created a powerful stimulus for reform. Chapter 6 considers the remarkable speed with which major changes in the penal system were implemented in the first five or six years of the Meiji era and traces the process leading up to the establishment of Japan's first modern prison in 1874. Initially, the direction of reforms was greatly influenced by Chinese models that had first been studied in Japan during the debates over punishment in the early eighteenth century, but by the beginning of the 1870s efforts were already being made to learn more about the Western approach to punishment and criminal justice. Of particular importance in this regard was a mission dispatched to Hong Kong and Singapore in 1871 to study British colonial prisons and courts. Upon his return to Japan, the leader of this mission, a middle-level bureaucrat named Ohara Shigechika, effectively laid the foundations for the modern Japanese penal system, drafting a detailed set of prison rules and architectural plans and specifying a range of other reforms that would bring the country in line with contemporary Western practices.

In an important sense, the Japanese authorities' decision at this time to study the prisons and courts of Britain's Asian colonies (where they were told they would be able to observe fellow Orientals being punished according to Western laws and practices) provides another reminder of Japan's own semicolonial status in the years after the Restoration. The final chapter of the book focuses on the reforms implemented by the Meiji government that eventually convinced the Western powers to reconsider that status and give up the special judicial privileges granted them under the unequal treaties. It outlines the debates surrounding the abolition of judicial torture and the preparation of Japan's first Western-style criminal code; it then examines the proliferation of modern prisons and what might well be termed "the great confinement" of the Meiji era. Ultimately, the chapter suggests, the same ideas about civilization, progress, and punishment that had been used by the Western powers to justify the imposition of the unequal treaties came to serve the Meiji regime's own domestic agenda and bolster its legitimacy and authority. The ideologies of nationalism and imperialism, in other words, had begun to mesh. If this was true in a domestic context, it was to become all the more obvious in Japan's own empire. For this reason, the book concludes with an examination of the way that modern ideas about civilization and progress came to affect penal practices in Taiwan during the first ten years of Japanese colonial rule and explores how this particular aspect of colonialism helped lay the foundations for the view that Japan should be seen as a special case, distinct from and superior to the rest of Asia.

Overall, then, this book covers similar ground to that of Fujita's 1893 guide. It also shares with Fujita the basic view that some aspects of the Tokugawa-Meiji transition must be seen in terms of a genuine *break* with the past. Yet, whereas Fujita presented the reforms of the Meiji period as a clear, unadulterated example of human progress, my aim is to show how that same idea of progress was intimately connected with the global project of empire, and how it has served to obscure certain aspects of the past and keep them hidden from our view.

CHAPTER 1

Signs of Order: Punishment and Power in the Shogun's Capital

ONE OF THE STANDARD TROPES scholars have used to discuss the history of punishment in Tokugawa Japan posits a gradual but steady alleviation of cruelty over a period of several centuries.[1] The height of barbarity, we are told, was reached in the sixteenth century, when the old structures of centralized rule were hacked to pieces by hundreds of local warlords. These men (they were always men) engaged each other in fierce struggles for territory and power, but they also faced continual threats from their own allies and followers. Treachery was rife, and the gap between usurper and lord was often no wider than the blade of a sharpened sword. In addition to their own retainer bands, moreover, successful warlords had to assert control over local populations, coercing them to contribute to their mobilization efforts. In this context, the ability to terrify and intimidate became an important asset both on and off the battlefield, and as the epidemic of instability and destruction spread, so too did horrifying techniques for inflicting torture and death. These techniques were not suddenly abandoned when the country was reunified under the authority of the Tokugawa shogunate, but as the "great peace" of the seventeenth century endured, many of them came to be seen as inappropriate for the new age.

This line of interpretation is powerful for various reasons. It confirms our expectations about the horrors of war and the advantages of peace, and it reassures us that human history can be told as a story of "progress." It also contains a strong element of verifiable truth: Over the first century of Tokugawa rule many horrifying methods of execution and torture from the preceding Warring States period did indeed disappear. Quartering (*gyū-wari; gyūsaki*), impaling *(kushi sashi)*, and boiling alive *(nigoroshi; kamairi)*, for example, all fell out of use by the end of the seventeenth century.[2] Other practices such as beheading with a saw, literally "pulling the saw" *(nokogiri-biki)*, were radically transformed: metal saws were replaced with bamboo ones, and rather than being used to actually saw off living heads (as they once had), they were now simply put on public display next to the condemned person for a period of days prior to his execution by other means.[3] Lesser punishments were also altered by the coming of peace. In the first decades of the Tokugawa period various acts of mutilation, including the severing of ears, noses, and fingers, were used as punishments, sometimes in conjunction with other, more serious punishments such as death or banishment. By the end of the seventeenth century these practices too had become much less common.[4]

The alleviation of cruel practices from the Warring States period was accompanied and sometimes facilitated by a gradual standardization of the punishments used in different parts of the country. As is well known, the "great peace" of the Tokugawa period was not the result of a complete conquest of all rivals by one supreme military power. The Tokugawa shogunate, or Bakufu, had direct control over approximately one-third of the territory of Japan, including the largest cities and many important mines and ports, but the rest of the country was divided among hundreds of lesser feudal lords. The most important of these were the "great warlords" or *daimyo*, whose numbers fluctuated between 260 and 270 for most of the period. In return for their loyalty and compliance with shogunal orders, the daimyo were allowed to retain a large degree of autonomous control over their individual domains. Yet, in some matters, including the administration of punishments, the Bakufu made its power felt everywhere.[5] From 1635 the daimyo were formally required to enforce the shogun's laws in all areas under their control, and from 1667 the special inspectors (*junkeishi*) who toured the country when a new shogun took office were ordered to report any daimyo who employed punishments that differed significantly from those used in Edo, the shogunal capital.[6] Edo's status as the national standard for punishments was established more formally in an order issued to the daimyo in 1697. It recognized the basic right of all daimyo to judge and punish criminals independently in their own domains but required them to follow the practices of the capital when doing so.[7] Compliance with this order varied somewhat, but by the end of the seventeenth century the extent to which domainal practices of punishment conformed to those of Edo is far more striking than the evidence of deviation.

In addition to the alleviation and standardization of punishments, the first half of the Tokugawa period also witnessed a steady systematization of their application. Rather than relying on their own individual discretion to determine appropriate punishments, warrior officials were increasingly expected to refer cases to their superiors before passing final judgment. As a general principle, the more serious the offense, the higher up the warrior chain of command it had to be taken. At the same time, however, as the corpus of Tokugawa laws and regulations expanded, top-ranking officials increasingly ceded the task of determining punishments to a small group of specialist clerks, who had developed expertise in legal matters. Officially, the main task of these clerks was simply to keep records of judicial decisions but, as Hiramatsu Yoshirō has shown, in practice they used their power as petty bureaucrats to ensure that punishments were applied in a manner consistent with existing laws and precedents (*hōki senrei*).[8]

Systematization was taken a step further in the middle of the eighteenth century with the completion of the famous *Kujikata osadamegaki* (Rules for Determining Legal Matters), the second book of which consists of a long list of crimes and their corresponding punishments.[9] Compiled under the direct supervision of the eighth shogun, Yoshimune (1684–1751), this list, known also as the *Hyakkajō*, or One Hundred Articles, was meant to streamline the administration of justice and to check some of the de facto decision-making power the legal clerks had won for themselves over the preceding century.[10] It soon became the first source warrior officials consulted when determining punishments. In this sense it was a kind of penal code.

From the foregoing it would not be unreasonable to conclude that over the course of the Tokugawa period penal practices steadily became more like those of a modern nation-state or, to put this another way, something closer to what we like to think of as "normal." Yet, to overemphasize this aspect of change is, in the end, to misrepresent fundamentally the nature of Tokugawa punishments and, indeed, Tokugawa society. To begin with the most obvious of facts, not all of the old practices of torture and death from the Warring States period were forgotten during the "great peace." Consider, for example, the procedure for a punishment called "stringing up" *(haritsuke)* outlined in an official manual from the early nineteenth century.[11] First, the condemned prisoner was bound to a wooden frame with ropes. If the prisoner was a man, both his arms and his legs were stretched wide apart. In the case of a woman, the legs remained bound together so that her body formed a simple cross. After the prisoner's clothes had been cut away so that the gut and chest were fully exposed, the frame was lifted and planted in the ground. Two executioners carrying spears then took their places on either side of the prisoner. As one lowered his spear in front of the condemned person's face, forcing him to examine its specially elongated tip, the other thrust his spear into the side of the prisoner's gut, pushing it diagonally upward until it protruded below the opposite arm pit. Having twisted the spear once inside the dying body, he pulled it out, making way for the second executioner to attack from the other side. The executioners continued to take turns, thrusting in and out in this way until the prisoner had been skewered some twenty or thirty times. According to one former Tokugawa official the streams of blood and undigested food that poured out of the holes on either side of the prisoner's body were enough to turn even the strongest of stomachs.[12] Finally, when the supervising official gave the signal to stop, one of the executioners exchanged his spear for a barbed pike, which he used to grab the hair on the prisoner's head and hold it steady. The other executioner then applied the official coup de grace *(tome no yari)*, running the tip of his spear through the prisoner's neck from right to left. The bloodied corpse

Figure 2. A Tokugawa period crucifixion as originally depicted by Maruyama Ōkyo (1733–95) and later copied by the Meiji era artist Terasaki Kōgyō (1866–1919). Terasaki Kōgyō, *Ōkyo ga nanfuku zu mosha* (Tokyo: Tōyōdō, 1890). Author's private collection.

was left on display for several days before being taken down and thrown into a shallow grave.

When the first European traders and missionaries reached Japan in the mid-sixteenth century, they immediately identified this method of execution as a form of crucifixion, and it has often been assumed that it was first introduced to the country with the Christian religion.[13] In fact, however, the practice of stringing people up on wooden frames before executing or torturing them can be traced back at least as far as the twelfth century in Japan.[14] Of course, Tokugawa officials were undoubtedly well aware of the symbolism involved when they made use of this punishment in their ruthless campaign to suppress Christianity in the early 1600s, but more than two hundred years after this campaign had been completed "crucifixion" was still in regular use as a punishment for ordinary criminals. One of the few reliable sets of punishment statistics available for the Tokugawa period reveals that in the four years between 1862 and 1865 alone fifteen crucifixions were performed in Edo. The Bakufu also burned ten prisoners at the stake in this four-year period and beheaded an average of more than one hundred each year.[15] This was well over twice the number of hangings conducted annually in London in the late eighteenth century when its population drew equal with that of Edo and the Hanoverians' infamous "Bloody Code" remained in full force.[16]

What then are we to make of Tokugawa punishments? One possibility would be simply to dismiss them as brutal, barbaric, and backward. As we shall see in later chapters, this was precisely the attitude taken by the Western imperialists who forced Japan to open its doors in the 1850s; it was also to become orthodoxy for "enlightened" Japanese reformers of the Meiji era. Yet, if we are to come to a better understanding of Tokugawa society, we must look beyond the brutality. We must also transcend the doctrine of historical progress, which blindly assumes that the punishments of Japan's "old regime" were relics of a Hobbesian state of nature that would eventually succumb to some universal "civilizing process." In fact, Tokugawa punishments were as much products of peace as of war, and while they could indeed be cruel, they did not take the form of arbitrary or unrestrained violence. As we have already begun to see, they formed part of a system governed by its own rules and logic. In the first three chapters of this book we consider some of the basic features of that system. Let us begin by examining in greater detail the nature of official punishments in the shogun's capital.

Signs of Order

In studies of early modern Europe, executions are often described as a form of popular theater in which priests and prisoners gave dramatic speeches and "justice" was (literally) performed in front of large crowds of spectators.[17] It is tempting to imagine that executions in Edo were similar events, staged for the benefit of onlookers who were encouraged to witness and approve the horrible deaths of those whom the authorities condemned.[18] The city did have two public execution grounds (oshiokiba; keijō), and some forms of execution, such as crucifixion and burning at the stake, were conducted there. Far from encouraging people to congregate at these places when executions were being carried out, however, from at least as early as the 1620s the Bakufu began to issue bans on such gatherings.[19] Moreover, while crucifixions and burnings at the stake were conducted at the execution grounds, almost all other executions took place not in the open but behind the closed walls of the Kodenmachō Jailhouse.

It is not difficult to imagine why the Bakufu generally sought to avoid executing people in front of large crowds in Edo. The case of eighteenth-century England makes it clear that, although public executions could serve important ideological functions, they were also potentially unstable and destabilizing events. As Michael Ignatieff has noted, if spectators did not approve of an execution, or if they sensed that the basic rights of a condemned person had been violated, they "were quick to vent their wrath on the authorities." In extreme cases, public executions in London triggered full-scale riots, and this tendency to spark disorder was an important reason for their abolition in the nineteenth century.[20] The fact that the Bakufu's earliest bans on gathering at executions grouped them together with "fights and fires," both of which were well-known triggers for popular disturbances and trouble, suggests that it too was quickly made aware of the risks of conducting public executions in a large urban center.[21] Yet, if these risks were deemed significant enough to discourage people from gathering to witness public executions, why continue to crucify and burn people alive at open execution grounds? The key to answering this question lies with one of the simplest governmental technologies of the Tokugawa period: the signpost.

Textbook accounts of Tokugawa society rarely fail to include some discussion of the famous "tall signs" (kōsatsu) that the Bakufu erected in strategic locations all over the country to communicate basic laws and regulations. In an important sense, punishments such as crucifixion and burning at the stake formed an extension of this system of signs, for although the executions themselves were not generally conducted in front of large crowds, the results, in the form of mutilated corpses strung up on crosses and stakes, were left on display for all to see. Next to these bodies-as-signs were conventional signposts that used the written word to make known the identity of the executed person, the offense committed, and the punishment that had been carried out. This blinkering of public attention to showcase the results of an execution but hide the process enabled the Bakufu to use the bodies of criminals to send and reinforce messages about the social order while simultaneously reducing the likelihood that an angry crowd or defiant criminal would create trouble.

One important corollary of this approach was that creating a horrifying spectacle (a memorable sign) was just as important as inflicting pain on the individual being executed—consequently, death was no limit to punishment. When a person who had been sentenced to crucifixion died before the punishment could be carried out, for example, the dead body was often pickled in salt and then crucified as if he or she were still alive.[22] This procedure was followed in eight of the fifteen crucifixions conducted in Edo between 1862 and 1865.[23] Burning at the stake was only conducted with live bodies, but even so death did not mark the end of the punishment. As soon as the prisoner's life had been extinguished, so too were the main flames. Torches were then used to concentrate fire on the genitals of male bodies and the breasts of female ones, as well as on the nose, in order to produce a grotesque stump of humanity for the explicit purpose of display.[24] Although beheading was almost always conducted behind the walls of the Bakufu's main jailhouse, it did not necessarily end with death either. The headless torsos of those who had been sentenced to the standard Tokugawa death penalty (*shizai*) were routinely used to test the battle-readiness of the shogun's arsenal of swords. This practice, known as "trial cutting" (*tameshi giri*), involved dismembering and hewing corpses to pieces. Like the initial beheading, it too was conducted within the grounds of the jailhouse, and in this sense it is, no doubt, better understood in terms of the peculiar needs of warriors in an age of peace than as part of the production of horrifying public displays.[25] The same cannot be said, however, for the punishment of *gokumon*, the severest form of beheading practiced by the Bakufu.

The term *gokumon* (literally "gate of the jail") dates back to medieval times, when severed heads were sometimes hung above the entrance to the jailhouse in Kyoto, the ancient capital.[26] In the Tokugawa period the severed heads of those sentenced to *gokumon* were instead taken from the jailhouse and transported to one of the official execution grounds, where they were placed on specially constructed stands and left on display for several days before being taken down and "thrown away." This punishment, which exemplifies the Tokugawa strategy of displaying the results of executions while concealing the process, was significantly more common than either crucifixion or burning at the stake. A total of 123 cases are recorded for Edo in the four years between 1862 and 1865, making it clear that severed heads formed another important part of the Bakufu's system of bodies-as-signs. Of course, in order for mutilated bodies and severed heads to be effective as signs, it was not enough for them to be dramatic. They also had to be carefully placed. Where, then, were they to be seen?

The Geography of Penal Display

When Tokugawa Ieyasu first reached Edo in 1590 and began converting the existing settlement there into his new headquarters, there was one execution ground close to the center of town. This location was soon abandoned in favor of two new sites, one to the south, at Honzaimokuchō, and the other to the north, just beyond Asakusabashi, near the Torigoe Myōjin Shrine.[27] As Edo's population expanded over the course of the seventeenth century and its borders moved further out, so too did the execution grounds. In the south, the Honzaimokuchō execution ground was relocated first to Shibaguchi, the location of one of the main city gates (*ōkido*).[28] Mass executions of Christians were carried out here in 1623 and 1638.

Figure 3. *Gokumon* as practiced in the twelfth century. The severed head hanging from the gate of the jailhouse is that of Fujiwara no Michinori (Shinzei) (?–1159). "Heiji monogatari emaki: Shinzei no maki." Seikadō Bunko Art Museum.

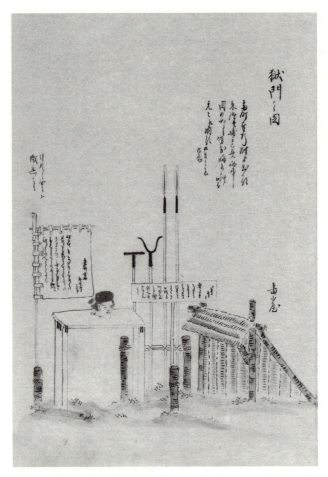

Figure 4. The Tokugawa punishment of *gokumon* as depicted in the "Keibatsu daihiroku." The National Archive of Japan.

Two years later, when another group of Christians was executed, its location had moved again, this time to Shinagawa. For the remainder of the Tokugawa period the southern execution ground was referred to in official documents as Shinagawa, but when its final location was settled, it was in fact just outside Shinagawa proper at a place called Suzugamori. The first executions carried out here came in the wake of the Keian Incident of 1651, when Marubashi Chūya and more than thirty others who had been caught conspiring to overthrow the Bakufu were crucified or had their severed heads put on display.[29] The following year the mutilated corpses of another eleven of their co-conspirators were put on display, this time at the northern execution ground, which was then still located near the Torigoe Myōjin Shrine. At some point before the great Meireki fire of 1657, it too was moved further out of the city to a site in front of Saihōji Temple in the Kondobashi area of Asakusa.[30] Finally, around the time of the great fire it was moved again to Kotsukappara, near Senjū. In 1667 it was put under the control of the Ekōin Temple, which was also made responsible for disposing of unclaimed corpses from all over the city, and in coming centuries the area came to be known among commoners not as Kotsukappara (literally, "field of small hills") but rather Kotsugahara, "field of bones."[31]

This outward movement of the execution grounds may have been related in part to long-held Japanese beliefs about the spiritual pollution (kegare) caused by death and blood. Katsumata Shizuo has argued that in the medieval period crime itself was also seen as a form of pollution: criminals were driven out of their communities and their houses burned to the ground not just to punish them but also to purify and cleanse the place that had been sullied by their actions. He also notes that as the use of capital punishment increased during the tumultuous Warring States period, it became commonplace for lords to pay Shintō priests to perform special rituals of purification (harae) afterward.[32] Thus one of the main reasons for locating the execution grounds on the outermost edges of the city may have been to ensure that the sacred ground of the shogun's capital was not polluted by the "unclean" (fujō) corpses of executed criminals.[33] Their steady outward movement did not mean, however, that the execution grounds disappeared from sight; on the contrary, it allowed them to become key symbolic markers of the main northern and southern entrances to the city.

The Suzugamori execution ground faced directly onto the Tōkaidō highway, the main route linking the shogun's capital to the two other great cities of the period, Kyoto and Osaka, while Kotsukappara was on the Edo side of the bridge at Senjū, where the Nikkō-kaidō, Ōshū-kaidō, and several other smaller highways from the northeast met.[34] These were not the only entrances to the city. The famous "five highways" (gokaidō) to Edo also included the Kōshū-kaidō, which entered the city at Naitō Shinjuku, and the Nakasendō, which entered through Itabashi. Significantly, however, these two entrances led into areas of the city dominated by the residences of the daimyo and the shogun's lesser military vassals, whereas the highways that passed by Suzugamori and Kotsukappara led directly into that area of the city where the houses and shops of commoners were concentrated.

The Tōkaidō was also the route that foreign embassies were required to use when they came to pay homage to the shogun.[35] In 1692 the German physician Engelbert Kaempfer (1651–1716), who accompanied the "captain" of the Dutch trading post in Nagasaki on his journey to Edo that year, wrote the following famous description of the scene that greeted them as they approached the city:

> At the entrance to Shinagawa the execution ground was an ugly sight for the traveler: several human heads and disfigured bodies were lying thrown together with cadavers of dead beasts. A large emaciated dog was rummaging with its hungry snout in a decaying human body. Also many dogs and crows were sitting nearby; they had already satisfied their appetite at this food stall, and would again find a free meal here.[36]

Well over a century later, in 1832, an embassy from the kingdom of the Ryūkyūs was met by an even more gruesome scene at Suzugamori. According to Matsura Seizan (1760–1841), the retired daimyo of Hirado Domain, the Bakufu had specially scheduled a crucifixion to coincide with their arrival and placed an unusually large number of heads out for them to see. Seizan was initially convinced that this was intended simply to intimidate the Ryūkyūan visitors, although Bakufu officials later told him it was done to reassure them that a group of commoners caught throwing stones at a previous ambassador's palanquin had been dealt with appropriately.[37] Either way, there can be little doubt that when furnished with signs of shogunal justice, the execution grounds were unforgettable markers of the approach to his capital.

Needless to say, it was not just foreign ambassadors who passed by the execution grounds. Ordinary people were continually traveling in and out of the capital, and, as with public executions in early modern Europe, their revulsion at the sights that awaited them at Suzugamori and Kotsukappara was often tinged with fascination. Consider, for example, the following note sent by a prostitute working in Senjū, near Kotsukappara, to one of Matsura Seizan's friends: "The rape blossoms are in bloom, there has been a crucifixion, people have come out, and things are lively. You must pop over for a while."[38] The travelers' inns (hatago) around Senjū were well known for the affordable "serving girls" (meshimori onna) in their employ, but judging from this note, their proximity to the execution ground may have provided an important additional attraction. Certainly there is no doubt that some people from the city made special trips to see the severed heads and crucified bodies on display. Matsura Seizan's exalted status as a retired lord prevented him from making such trips himself, but when a daring burglar who had successfully targeted a string of daimyo mansions was finally caught and sentenced to gokumon in 1832, he did not hesitate to send a servant to Kotsukappara to investigate. The servant reported back with a detailed description of the dead man's features and also noted that a sizable crowd of people had been gathered at the execution ground for most of the day.[39] Clearly Seizan was not the only one to have had his curiosity aroused.

The morbid fascination of Tokugawa punishments (and the crimes that had led to them) meant that they were readily incorporated into various forms of popular culture. The stories of tragic figures such as Yaoya Oshichi, who was burned at the stake in 1683, or famous toughs like Hirai Gompachi, who was crucified in 1679, were eagerly taken up by balladeers, woodblock print makers, and writers including the great Ihara Saikaku (1642–93). While the theatricality of actual public punishment was carefully controlled by the Bakufu, the specter of official punishments nevertheless made for good theater. Executions themselves were rarely, if ever, portrayed on the Jōruri or Kabuki stage, but the audience's knowledge of the grisly fate of a famous historical character was often used to add an extra, poignant layer of meaning to a performance.[40] In the early 1820s, for example, the playwright Tsuruya Namboku IV (1755–1829), who became famous for his mastery of the grotesque, used the execution ground at Suzugamori as the backdrop for a scene in which Hirai Gompachi joins forces with another well-known outlaw. No direct reference is ever made in the scene to Gompachi's eventual crucifixion, but the ominous sight of the execution ground, marked on stage, as in life, by an imposing stone obelisk inscribed with a simple Buddhist prayer, made such an impression on audiences that the play quickly came to be known simply as "Suzugamori."[41] All of this, of course, only added to the peculiar mystique of the execution grounds.

Even if a resident of Edo never visited an execution ground or encountered one in popular culture, it would still have been difficult to avoid the spectacle of official punishments in everyday life. The Bakufu was careful to ensure that its bodies-as-signs were visible all over the city, particularly in areas where commoners lived. One of the most effective ways to achieve this was simply to parade (*hiki mawashi*) condemned criminals though the streets on horseback before their executions. The route taken on these parades of death varied somewhat according to the punishment, but it always began at the jailhouse in the middle of the commoners' section of town and generally proceeded in a giant loop around Edo castle.[42] Accompanying the condemned prisoner at all times was a menacing entourage of some thirty men who carried with them the lances, pikes, and other implements used to apprehend armed criminals, as well as a large banner and signpost stating the person's name, crime, and punishment.[43] Similar signs were often placed in strategic places all over the city, including the condemned person's former place of residence and the scene of the crime. In the case of *gokumon*, moreover, it was not only the living, whole body of the condemned person that was paraded through the streets. After he or she had been executed behind the walls of the jailhouse, the severed head was wrapped up in straw matting and hung from a wooden staff. It was then carried through the streets of the city to one of the execution grounds accompanied by a slightly smaller band of men, who brandished the same fearful implements and signs as they went.[44]

The practice of parading condemned criminals and their severed heads through the streets of the capital can in some ways be compared with other public processions of the period. As Ronald Toby and Kuroda Hideo have noted, the parades of the daimyo as they moved between Edo and their domainal capitals, of the foreign embassies that came to pay homage to the shogun, and of the shogun himself as he traveled to the Shrine of the Founder (*Tōshōgū*) in Nikkō all served a vitally important ideological function, impressing onlookers with the power and majesty of their rulers.[45] Edo's parades of death were smaller in scale than these great processions, which often comprised several thousand armed men. Yet, they too were intended to impress onlookers with fearful displays of power. Moreover, whereas the great processions were "special" events, these other parades were probably closer to the everyday lives of the city's residents. They were certainly frequent enough: in 1862 a total of twenty-nine condemned people were paraded through the streets in Edo, followed by sixteen in 1863, nine in 1864, and seventeen in 1865. This is an average of close to eighteen parades per year. Add to this the thirty or so severed heads that were carried to the execution grounds annually in this period, and we reach a total of around fifty parades of death per year in Edo, or just under one a week.[46]

It was not only through these parades that city dwellers came in contact with Tokugawa punishments, however. Even after the old execution ground in the center of town was abandoned in the early seventeenth century, some punishments continued to be administered at Nihonbashi, the famous bridge where the five great highways to Edo converged and which marked the symbolic heart of the commoners' city. Here, for example, people sentenced to "pulling the saw" were put on display. Having been paraded through the city streets for a day, the condemned person would be brought to Nihonbashi and made to sit inside a wooden box buried in the ground. The box was sealed shut with a lid that allowed only the person's neck and head to protrude, and a sword was then used to cut into the sides of his neck so that blood could be smeared on the blades of the bamboo saws. These were put on display on either side of the person's head to serve as a chilling reminder of a time when they would actually have been used to inflict a slow form of death by decapitation. Theoretically, onlookers could volunteer to come forward and pull one of the saws across his neck, although in reality they were rarely willing to do so.[47] In the evening the condemned person would be removed from the box and returned to the jailhouse, only to be put on display again the next day. On the third day he was finally taken to one of the execution grounds and crucified.[48]

This was the severest of all Tokugawa punishments, but even relatively minor penalties often involved some form of public display. The most obvious example is pillorying *(sarashi)*, which involved tying a criminal up with ropes and making him sit for three days in a public place next to a signpost detailing his crimes. It too was usually conducted at Nihonbashi, although in cases involving prostitutes the guilty parties might also be put on display in the licensed quarters. Flogging *(tataki)*, which entailed either fifty or one hundred blows with a cane across the back, was another important form of punishment for minor offenses. Not used on women, it was nevertheless the most common of all Tokugawa period punishments, with between eight hundred and one thousand men flogged in Edo each year between 1862 and 1865.[49] It was conducted in front of the main gate of the jailhouse at Kodenmachō, again in the commoner's section, not far from Nihonbashi.[50] Although the memory of a flogging might eventually fade, it was often combined with tattooing *(irezumi)*, which not only caused still more pain for the person being punished but also indelibly marked him as criminal.[51]

Like flogging, tattooing was officially introduced by Yoshimune in 1720 to replace the older penalties of removing the nose and ears, and for this reason it is often pointed to as evidence of the alleviation of harsh punishments from the Warring States period. Yet, given that the use of these older forms of bodily mutilation had already declined dramatically over the course of the seventeenth century, it is, in fact, better understood as an attempt by the Bakufu (under Yoshimune) to reestablish its power to mark permanently the bodies of petty criminals.[52] Though undoubtedly less painful and dramatic than slicing off a person's nose or ears, tattooing also had the advantage of allowing samurai officials to record additional information directly onto punished bodies. A person caught stealing for a second time, for example, would usually be tattooed with two lines across the forearm to mark them as a recidivist. A third offense would sometimes result in a third stripe. More often it meant death.[53] The authorities in different areas of the country also used their own distinctive tattoos to make it easy to identify where a person had been punished in the past. The Bakufu was generally content to tattoo criminals with relatively nondescript lines on the arm, but in some places a more dramatic approach was taken. In Hiroshima Domain, for example, recidivists had the Chinese character for "dog" tattooed onto the middle of their foreheads. In Kii the character for "evil" *(aku)* was used.[54]

After being tattooed in the jailhouse in Edo, prisoners were held for three days until the ink under their skin had dried and the wound caused by the needles used to implant it there had begun to heal.[55] They were then released back into society, their marked bodies once again serving as signs of the warrior government's power to punish. Not surprisingly, people quickly came to associate tattoos with criminality, and those who had been punished in this way often found themselves being shunned and excluded from their communities. This led to desperate attempts to erase or cover up tattoos.[56] Particularly among the large population of day laborers who formed the bottom stratum of Edo society, it eventually helped give rise to an entire subculture of tattooing, which provided people with a way of transforming the marks inscribed on their bodies by warrior authority into badges of defiant pride.

The intermittent references made here to the Kodenmachō Jailhouse might lead to the assumption that imprisonment was another common form of punishment under the Tokugawa. This, however, was not the case. In addition to providing a space where corporal and capital punishments could be carried out behind closed doors, the main purpose of the jailhouse was to hold suspected criminals while investigations were carried out and an appropriate punishment determined. Imprisonment was used as an official punishment only when there were extenuating circumstances that prevented the application of another penalty. Long-term imprisonment (*nagarō*), a punishment that was not even mentioned in the One Hundred Articles, was occasionally used as a substitute for the death penalty for criminals who had turned themselves in to the authorities, or who were considered worthy of special treatment for some other reason. Short-term imprisonment (*katairō*), for periods of up to thirty days, was somewhat more common. It was used as a substitute for flogging in the case of women, children under the age of fifteen, and occasionally men who were sick or infirm.[57] To be sure, other punishments involved some sort of confinement, ranging from various forms of house arrest to "exile to a distant island" (*entō*), which was considered the harshest of the Bakufu's noncapital sanctions.[58] Banishment (*tsuihō*) from a particular place or area of the country was also common. This form of punishment and its long-term implications for Tokugawa society will be examined more carefully in chapter 4. For now, however, it is worth noting that banishment too was often combined with tattooing, for easy identification.

Some Tokugawa punishments did not involve any form of marking or public display. Fines, for example, were used from the beginning of the period to punish commoners guilty of minor offenses such as gambling. Yet, overall, it should be clear from the discussion thus far, that Edo was a city covered with penal signs. Our next task is to consider what kind of messages these signs were meant to convey.

PATTERNS OF PUNISHMENT, STRUCTURES OF POWER

In the first instance the sight of punished bodies provided evidence that some kind of "order" was being maintained in Tokugawa society. But what exactly did "order" mean in Tokugawa Japan? What particular standards of behavior did the warrior state seek to uphold?

At a general level it might well be argued that many Tokugawa punishments were simply intended to protect people from acts we have little difficulty recognizing as "criminal" today: theft, assault, and murder, for example. Others were clearly intended to deter crimes that constituted a particular threat to society at that time. The best example of this is arson, for which the punishment of burning at the stake was exclusively reserved.[59] In communities where almost all buildings were made of wood, fire was a constant threat to life and livelihood. This was especially true in large urban centers, where the dwellings and shops of townsfolk were densely concentrated, and dancing flames could often move faster than running feet. Yaoya Oshichi's Meireki fire, which claimed more than one hundred thousand lives, was only the very worst of the hundreds of conflagrations that regularly devastated parts of Edo over the course of the period.[60] Not surprisingly, the deliberate setting of fires was generally understood to be the most heinous of crimes, and *being seen* to punish it with the severest of deaths undoubtedly helped to bolster the warrior state's credentials as the legitimate "overseer of public affairs" *(kōgi-sama)*.[61]

Yet, the enforcement of "order" in Tokugawa Japan was about more than just protecting the community from clear sources of harm. Consider, for example, the way in which the crime of murder was understood and punished.

As a general principle the One Hundred Articles (art. 71) stated that anyone responsible for taking the life of another was to be punished with a special form of death penalty known simply as the "penalty for murderers" *(geshunin)*. Those sentenced to it were beheaded within the grounds of the jailhouse, but unlike *shizai*, the standard Tokugawa death penalty, their corpses were not used for "trial cutting," and their property was not subject to confiscation. For these reasons it was considered the least severe of the official Tokugawa death sentences and was, in practice, very rarely used. Whereas the standard death penalty was administered some 285 times in the four years between 1862 and 1865, the "penalty for murderers" was applied only twice. The reason for this was not that murder itself was rare but rather that all murders were not considered equal. Any killing that involved theft, for example, was automatically considered a more serious crime than "ordinary murder" *(tsūrei no hitogoroshi)* and thus required a more serious punishment.[62] The method of killing also mattered: poisonings were considered particularly heinous, as were random attacks in the street *(tsuji-giri)*. The most important factor of all, however, was the nature of the relationship between killer and victim. The "penalty for murderers," predicated on the principle of taking a life for a life, was considered an appropriate punishment only when the social standing of the two parties was roughly equal, that is, when the two lives were considered to be of roughly equal worth. If the victim was of superior standing, a simple execution was not punishment enough; conversely, if he was of inferior standing, it was considered too severe.[63]

The consequences of this basic principle were most extreme when the relationship between killer and victim was defined by one of a few key social institutions. The first of these was feudal service: whereas a master who killed a servant or retainer could expect to be punished relatively lightly, "pulling the saw," the harshest of all Tokugawa death sentences, was reserved for the opposite crime. In fact, under the One Hundred Articles (art. 71), a servant or retainer who so much as caused a serious injury to his master was to be pilloried for three days and crucified. This was also the punishment stipulated for those who killed a former master, while a servant who killed a master's relative was to be paraded through the streets before having his head severed and put on public display.

Hierarchies within families were also given special protection. Under the One Hundred Articles (art. 71) the punishment for parents who killed their own children was banishment. Children who killed a parent, however, were to be paraded through the streets and crucified. Injury of a parent was also punishable with crucifixion, albeit without the added humiliation of parading through the streets. Punishments for older siblings who killed younger ones, for aunts or uncles who killed their nephews or nieces, and even for fathers-in-law who killed sons-in-law were similarly less severe than in the reverse situation.

In total, violent transgressions of service or family hierarchies account for seven of the thirteen acts listed in the One Hundred Articles as punishable with crucifixion. In addition, crucifixion was also the stipulated punishment for pupils who killed their teachers (shishō) (art. 71) and for adulterous wives who murdered their husbands (art. 48). The other, more general regulations concerning adultery in the One Hundred Articles (art. 48) were also clearly intended to protect the rights of husbands over their wives. Infidelity by a husband was not even recognized as an offense, but unfaithful wives and concubines were to be punished with death (shizai); so too were their paramours. In cases where a man actually caught his wife with a lover, moreover, it was his right as a husband to exact vengeance by killing them both on the spot.[64] Tokugawa laws did at least draw a distinction between adultery and rape, but the importance of the rights of husbands is again clear from the fact that rape of a married woman was punishable with death, whereas rape of an unmarried woman was punishable with a severe grade of banishment (omoki tsuihō).[65]

Just as Tokugawa law allowed and, indeed, encouraged husbands to kill unfaithful wives in certain circumstances, it also made special provision for younger brothers or sons who wished to take the law into their own hands in avenging the deaths of older brothers or fathers.[66] In such cases the bereaved person was expected to register his vendetta with the Bakufu, but once this was done, he was free to track down the murderer and challenge him. If he succeeded in exacting revenge, far from being punished for taking another person's life, he stood a good chance of being rewarded by the authorities for his admirable display of bravery and filial piety.[67] Partly for this reason cases of successful "blood revenge" remained fairly common over the course of the period. According to D. E. Mills, there were some thirty-three cases between 1609 and 1703, thirty-five in the century between 1703 and 1804, and the same number again between 1804 and 1865.[68]

One way to explain the emphasis placed on maintaining social hierarchies would be to attribute it to the influence of Confucianism: the notion that the "Five Relationships" of parent and child, lord and retainer, husband and wife, elder and junior, and friend and friend were crucial to social stability and well-being had first entered Japan in the fifth century C.E. and subsequently came to form an important strand of Japanese thought about both morality and government. When the customary laws of the warrior houses began being codified and systematized in the late seventeenth and early eighteenth centuries, moreover, scholars were encouraged to make careful studies of the codes of China's Ming dynasty (1368–1644). This can only have helped to reinforce Confucian influence. Arai Hakuseki (1657–1725), the powerful adviser to the sixth and seventh shoguns, was certainly well aware of the principle of differential punishments laid out in the Ming code. In his autobiography he wrote: "That a man who commits murder should die is the ordinary law of the world (yo no tsune no hō). In the [Ming] codes (ritsu) there are also penalties for crimes committed against one's uncles and parents. . . . It would indeed create a grievous precedent should one who has killed his uncle be punished according to the precedents for geshunin, as if he were an ordinary murderer."[69] Yet, while it would be foolish to discount the significance of Confucian influences, it would also be a mistake to assume that the emphasis given to protecting hierarchies in the Tokugawa period can be attributed to a single source.[70] The patterns of social ordering described here were hardly peculiar to "Oriental" societies. In eighteenth-century England, for example, servants who killed their masters were cut down from the gallows while still alive, disemboweled, and quartered, while women who killed their husbands were burned at the stake. Both of these crimes were considered a "species of treason" because, as one contemporary text explains, they were committed "against a Subject, between whom and the Offender, the Law presumes there is a special Obedience and Subjection."[71]

In the end, far more important than its philosophical underpinnings is the fact that the principle of differential punishments linked the warrior state to the microlevel power structures that formed the basis of everyday social relations in Tokugawa Japan. This link ran two ways, for while the punished bodies of those who violated the "natural" order of things sent a clear message to servants, children, students, and wives that they should submit to their superiors, they also reminded those superiors that their own positions were supported and protected by the power of the shogun. This is not to imply that those in authority were the only ones to see the maintenance of hierarchy as a precondition for social well-being. The power of ideology undoubtedly helped to ensure that it was broadly accepted as both inevitable and good.[72] In the end, however, the system of differential punishments offered real proof of the shogun's commitment to the little kings of everyday life.

This broad alliance with authority figures at all levels of society was certainly valuable to the warrior state; so too was the legitimacy it gained from being seen to protect the general well-being of society. Yet Tokugawa punishments also served to bolster warrior authority in a much more direct way. Indeed, the most obvious message generated by the public display of punished bodies was simply that the consequences of displeasing the shogun and his officials were terrifying and grim. This was true both for those who offended officials indirectly by violating social hierarchies or committing crimes against other subjects, and for those who dared to challenge their authority directly. We have already considered the fate of those arrested in conjunction with the Keian Incident of 1651, but two hundred years later, when Ōshio Heihachirō led his famous rebellion in Osaka to protest official corruption and the plight of the peasantry, the Bakufu's response was similarly severe.[73] In total some eight hundred people were punished in the aftermath of the rebellion, including twenty who were crucified, seventeen whose severed heads were put on display, and three who were sentenced to the standard death penalty.[74] Harsh punishments, including crucifixion, were also meted out to the leaders of hundreds of peasant protests over the course of the Tokugawa period, and, as Anne Walthall has shown, tales of this kind of martyrdom came to form another important strand of popular culture.[75]

Crucially, however, it was not only in dealing with major threats such as rebellions or uprisings that the authorities used the penal system to defend their own position and interests. Anyone whose behavior suggested that they "did not [live in] fear of the overseer of public affairs" *(kōgi o osorezu)* was liable to be punished particularly severely. As Yamamato Hirofumi has noted, this even included petty thieves who made the mistake of targeting the shogun's property.[76] In 1792, for example, a man named Shinroku was arrested for taking a few decorative gold pieces from a damaged drawbridge leading into the shogun's castle in Osaka. In spite of the fact that the value of what he had stolen was only small, the local official responsible for his arrest and interrogation immediately recommended that he be put to death for having dared to steal anything at all from a place that should, by rights, have filled him with fear of the shogun's government. In the eyes of the authorities in Edo even this was insufficient punishment for Shinroku's crime; they ordered that he should not only surrender his life, but also be paraded through the city beforehand to serve as an example to others.[77] The case of a man named Yahei from 1789 is also worth noting. Having discovered that his master was unable to make his yearly tax payment, Yahei broke into one of the Bakufu's granaries in Edo and, with the help of two guards, stole a total of over sixteen hundred bales (hyō) of rice. Because there was clear evidence that he had done this to help his master and not simply for personal gain, the official in charge of the investigation recommended that he be sentenced to "heavy banishment," a relatively lenient punishment. This recommendation was soon overruled by his superiors, however. Breaking into any storehouse was a capital offense, it was argued, but to target one of the shogun's own granaries was especially serious and would ordinarily have been punishable with parading through the streets followed by public display of the severed head. Thus, while some allowance could be made for the fact that Yahei was motivated by a desire to help his master, in the end it was deemed inappropriate to sentence him to anything less than parading through the streets followed by death.[78] Clearly then, when faced with a choice between promoting key social hierarchies, on the one hand, and protecting its own interests and authority, on the other, the warrior state put itself first.

Veiled Laws and Cloaked Procedures

Although printed collections of "Tokugawa law" are now easily available to anyone who wishes to study them, during the Edo period the process by which punishments were determined was cloaked in a veil of secrecy. "Official notices" (ofure) banning or exhorting particular kinds of behavior were widely circulated and posted up on the "tall signs" for all to see, but basic legal texts such as the One Hundred Articles, which indicated how particular crimes would be punished, were not available to the public in any official form. In fact, even within the Bakufu's own bureaucracy, access to official copies of the One Hundred Articles, as well as collections of case law and other key legal texts, was limited to a handful of high-ranking officials. Lower-ranked officials were thus forced to send a continual stream of inquiries (ukagai) to their superiors as to whether a particular punishment was in keeping with the Bakufu's established laws and precedents.[79]

That official access to basic legal texts was restricted in this way did not mean that ordinary people were completely ignorant of the way in which particular crimes were likely to be punished. The punished bodies and wooden signposts that punctuated public space were one obvious source of information. As with other official notices posted by the Bakufu, people often copied down the contents of the sign listing a criminal's identity, crime, and punishment so that they could show others or refer to it later themselves. In some cases, the information posted in public about the punishments meted out to criminals was even collected and circulated in the form of children's copybooks (*otehon*),[80] which were used not only to teach reading and writing but also to instill an awareness of the basic patterns of Tokugawa justice.

In practice, moreover, access to the Bakufu's "secret" legal documents was never as tightly restricted as it was, in theory, supposed to be. As a matter of convenience unofficial copies of the One Hundred Articles and other "secret" legal documents circulated widely within the Bakufu bureaucracy, and others eventually found their way into the hands of private individuals, including commoners.[81] In one fascinating case study, Takahashi Satoshi has described how a wealthy peasant named Gin'emon who was called to Edo in 1850 to represent his village in an official murder investigation was able to make his own private copy of the One Hundred Articles at the "legal inn" *(kuji yado)* where he was staying.[82] In total, there were some two hundred of these inns in Edo, and commoners summoned to the capital for questioning about legal matters were often required to stay in one of them until they received official permission to return home.[83] The masters of the inns gave advice to their guests about what they could expect from the legal proceedings in which they were involved, and Gin'emon was probably not unusual in having been offered an opportunity to make his own copy of the One Hundred Articles. Takahashi suggests that the Bakufu itself may even have encouraged this kind of informal dissemination of legal knowledge: texts such as the One Hundred Articles made it clear that Bakufu judicial procedures were part of a system and this, he suggests, may have made it easier for people to accept them.[84]

Yet, not everyone called in for questioning by the Bakufu was as fortunate as Gin'emon. He was, after all, an official village representative who arrived in Edo with letters of introduction to a number of warrior bureaucrats and enough money to pay for extra information if necessary. Most important, he himself was not suspected of any serious wrongdoing. Otherwise, instead of being allowed to stay in one of the "legal inns" he would have been sent straight to the jailhouse, where there were no opportunities for obtaining such legal advice and information.

Even someone like Gin'emon could get access to copies of the Bakufu's key legal texts only unofficially and in a secretive manner, so he could not be entirely confident that the information therein was reliable or accurate. Nor could he be certain to what extent the written rules and guidelines actually restricted the discretionary power of warrior officials. In this sense, although the official veil of secrecy may have been translucent enough to allow people to see that there was, indeed, a system in place to guide judicial decisions, in the end it still helped to ensure that individual officials were regarded with considerable fear and respect. Just how important this was to the warrior state can also be seen in the process by which the facts of criminal cases were ascertained.

The *formal* process of questioning people in relation to criminal acts (and other legal matters) took place in a special kind of official space known as the "courtyards of white sand" *(shirasu)*.[85] These were located within the grounds of a local administrative official's residence or offices, and anyone who was summoned to appear in them could generally expect to be questioned by that official in person. Well before things got to this stage, however, an initial investigation and interrogation would already have been carried out by lower-level functionaries. In the case of Edo, these generally took place at one of a handful of special guardhouses *(shirabe banya; ōbanya)* located in different parts of the commoners' section of town. The functionaries who conducted these initial investigations were not only expected to ascertain the basic facts of a case but also to make an initial judgment as to the guilt or innocence of the suspect and, if possible, to extract a confession. Torture, usually in the form of beatings with a wooden stick, was often used to loosen prisoners' tongues at this stage of proceedings, and as a result common people came to dread the thought of being called to the guardhouses.[86]

It was important to determine guilt before the process of official questioning on the "white sands" began so as to ensure that proceedings there went as quickly and smoothly as possible. This was not all, however. Officials believed that if large numbers of innocent people began being sent to the "white sands" for questioning, the seriousness with which that step was viewed would be undermined. It would also imply that officials did not *already* know whether a person was guilty or not, and the evidence suggests that fallibility of any kind was something the warrior state was loath to admit.[87]

Of course, the outcome of a case did not rest solely on the findings of the initial interrogation. A suspect would be called to the "white sands" several times before final judgment was passed. At first the prisoner would be asked simply to confirm his or her identity for the official in charge. For commoners in Edo, this was generally one of the two town governors *(machi bugyō)*.[88] After a quick overview of the basic facts of the case, the presiding governor would decide whether the suspect should be sent to the jailhouse or put in the custody of a guardian while further investigations were carried out.[89] Either way, the suspect would then have to wait to be called back to the governor's offices for a second (official) interrogation. This was presided over by one of the governor's officers *(yoriki)*, whose task was to extract a formal statement *(kuchigaki)* from the suspect.[90] When this was done, the prisoner would be called back to the "white sands" to confirm the contents of the statement in the governor's presence.[91] Final judgments, as a rule, were made on the basis of the information contained in the confirmed statement.

If the offense was fairly minor, the governor or other official in charge could sometimes use his independent authority to order a punishment, but in more serious cases, or cases in which there were complicating circumstances, he would propose a punishment to his superiors and then wait for an official response. As we have already seen, it was not uncommon for superiors to overrule the punishment proposed by a subordinate. Once a recommendation for punishment had been received, however, a superior would never overturn a lower-level judgment about a suspect's culpability. In other words, someone found guilty by an investigating official would never be declared innocent by his superiors. The reasoning behind this is laid out in the records of a case of petty theft from 1804:

> If, in the course of an investigation by the appropriate governor, a statement that shows negligent or improper behavior has been compiled under interrogation, and then it is announced [by the governor's superiors] that the matter, which has been recommended for punishment, does not in fact constitute a punishable offense, the fear and respect *(ikei)* felt by the contemptible common people *(hisen no monodomo)* [for the governor] will naturally be diminished.[92]

A united front was to be maintained before the "contemptible commoners," in other words, and nothing done to undermine the aura of official omniscience and infallibility.

The emphasis the warrior state placed on protecting this official aura of omniscience and infallibility can also be seen from the fact that when a final verdict was reached in a criminal case, all those involved were required to place their stamp of approval on the official records, acknowledging the fairness of the outcome. The only exceptions to this rule were where the person was sentenced to death or the heaviest form of banishment.[93] During the official investigation, great importance was also placed on obtaining a formal confession from the accused. In most cases an informal confession of some kind had already been made during the initial interrogation (at the guardhouse), and it was simply a matter of getting the suspect to repeat this earlier statement so that it could be written down and confirmed in the presence of the governor. Sometimes, however, a suspect could not be convinced to repeat an earlier confession, or simply refused to confess at all in spite of clear evidence of guilt. In these relatively rare cases officials could opt to make use of formal judicial torture in order to make the suspect reconsider.[94] Unlike the initial guardhouse interrogation, there were strict rules governing the use of torture at this later stage. It could be applied only when the crime in question was serious and when the "evidence

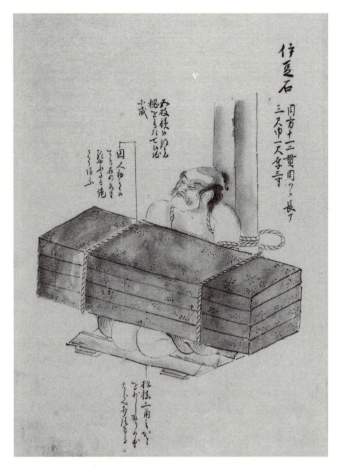

Figure 5. "Hugging the stones," one of four officially sanctioned methods of judicial torture, as depicted in the "Keibatsu daihiroku." Note the "truth board" on which the prisoner is kneeling. The National Archive of Japan.

of guilt was clear" *(zaika no shōko bunmei)*.[95] From the mid-eighteenth century officials who opted to make use of judicial torture were also restricted to four standard techniques.[96] The first, and most commonly applied, of these was beating with a short whip *(muchiuchi)*, but when this proved ineffective, officials could move on to the second technique, called "hugging the stones" *(ishidaki)*. In such cases, the prisoner would be made to kneel on a platform that had sharp triangular grooves cut into the top of it. Two heavy slabs of stone would then be placed on top of his or her thighs. If this failed to yield results, guards would be ordered to push the stones down with their own weight. A total of as many as ten additional slabs of stone might be piled on top of the prisoner, who often had to be revived repeatedly with special smelling salts.[97]

These first two techniques of torture were conducted in a special "drilling room" *(sensakujō)* located inside the grounds of the jailhouse and were often used in combination with each other. If, however, after repeated attempts they failed to produce a satisfactory confession, officials could apply for permission to use two other techniques known as the lobster *(ebizeme)* and suspension methods *(tsurushizeme)*. These were also conducted inside the jailhouse compound, in a separate "torture chamber" *(gōmon kura)*. The lobster method involved tying suspects into a cramped and uncomfortable position with ropes and took its name from the bright red color their bodies turned after they had been tied up. For the suspension method, the prisoner's arms were tied together behind his back with a rope that was then used to suspend his entire body a few feet from the ground. He would be left in this position for several hours, with the rope gnawing away at his skin and the weight of his body pulling his shoulders out of their sockets.[98]

As unlikely as it may seem, some prisoners did manage to survive all four methods of torture without breaking down and confessing to the crimes they were accused of. This was true, for example, of a man named Yoshigorō who endured close to thirty separate sessions of torture in the Kodenmachō Jailhouse after his arrest in 1835.[99] If, in such cases, officials remained convinced of the suspect's guilt, the governor in charge could apply for special permission to order punishment on the basis of his judgment alone *(satto tsume)*.[100] Yoshigorō was eventually sentenced to death in this way in 1836, but his case records make it clear how unusual it was for the Bakufu to take this step. The most recent precedent that officials could find dated from 1801, some thirty-five years earlier.[101]

Punishment on the basis of "judgment alone" was, of course, unusual because few suspects were able to withstand the pain of torture, but officials themselves were also extremely reluctant to make use of it. Not only did it mean accepting a less perfect standard of "proof" than was provided by a confession, it also represented an admission of bureaucratic defeat: if a prisoner who was clearly guilty could not be persuaded to confess using any of the approved techniques of torture, it was thought to cast doubt on the competence of the investigating officials. As a result, by the early decades of the nineteenth century, officials tended to avoid using the lobster and suspension methods.[102] The threat of them was kept in reserve to intimidate suspects, but those who had managed to resist the first two techniques of torture were not generally given the chance to test the system any further. Occasionally they were released without further punishment.[103] More often they were simply held in the jailhouse until they either "broke" or died.[104]

Punishment and Warrior Power

At the beginning of this chapter it was noted that some of the brutality characteristic of punishments during Japan's Warring States period disappeared with the establishment of a sustained peace. Over the first century and a half of Tokugawa rule official punishments were also systematized, standardized, and made subject to a sophisticated system of bureaucratic guidelines and checks. While they may have become less random and arbitrary, however, displays of brutal violence against criminal bodies were never abandoned by the warrior state. At both an ideological and a political level they were simply too useful and important for the maintenance of warrior power. For one thing, they provided a way for the regime to show that in an age of peace, warrior brawn could and did serve a useful purpose—namely, the maintenance of order. Visible punishments, in other words, offered vital support for the Bakufu's claim to be the legitimate "overseer of public affairs." By offering graphic evidence of the shogun's commitment to social hierarchies, moreover, the most dramatic displays of penal brutality (e.g., crucifixions) helped to link the power of the warrior state directly to the power of authority figures at all levels of society.

Tokugawa punishments and the processes by which they were determined also served to bolster the authority of the warrior state in more direct ways. Warrior officials made no secret of the fact that anyone who openly challenged their authority or threatened their property could expect to meet with a particularly severe response. They also sought to enhance the level of apprehension and respect with which they were viewed by cloaking legal procedures and rules in a veil of secrecy and by taking steps to ensure that their decisions projected an aura of infallibility and omniscience at all times. In this regard it is surely no coincidence that the Tokugawa period word for official punishments, *oshioki*, has survived in modern Japanese primarily as a term to describe the punishments parents mete out to their small children. It was precisely this kind of unequal relationship that the warrior rulers of Tokugawa Japan sought to foster between themselves and their subject population, and indeed, the idea that a good ruler should view the people as his children recurs often in the political writings of the day. The importance of avoiding any sense of doubt about the guilt of those they punished meant that warrior officials placed great emphasis on extracting formal confessions from suspects, and this, in turn, meant that the use of torture (albeit with some restrictions) was openly accepted at various stages of the investigative process. This use of torture not only helped to protect the official aura of infallibility; it also added further to the sense of fear with which officials, and official investigations, were generally viewed.

This approach to punishment is clearly in keeping with Mary Elizabeth Berry's recent characterization of Japanese political tradition from the Tokugawa period on as "authoritarian." As she explains, "authoritarianism elevates the state above social control because it is premised on the superiority of rulers to the people."[105] Yet the warrior state's domination of Tokugawa society (perhaps not unlike parental control of small children) was never so complete or secure that it could afford to use its power to punish recklessly or without restraint. We have already gained some sense of this from the Bakufu's reluctance to execute people before large crowds of onlookers in Edo. In the next chapter we explore in more detail some of the dangers and problems associated with the power to punish, and some of the strategies used to overcome or limit them.

CHAPTER 2

Bloody Benevolence: Punishment, Ideology, and Outcasts

VIOLENT EXECUTIONS and dramatic displays of mutilated bodies, veiled laws and brutal interrogations are all things that, at some level, we might expect of a warrior regime. Yet, viewed within the broader context of Tokugawa period ideas about government, they also present us with something of a paradox. While warrior power clearly had its origins in the ability to orchestrate mass slaughter, brute force alone could not guarantee political or social stability over an extended period of time. As the "great peace" of the seventeenth century endured, therefore, the new regime and its supporters began crafting an elaborate ruling ideology in which Buddhist and neo-Confucian notions of "compassion," "benevolence," and "benevolent government" *(jihi, jin, jinsei)* held a central place.[1] Far from dominating or oppressing the common people, the shogun and his allies were presented as figures whose ultimate role was to protect and save *(osukui)* them. Awesome and fearful on the one hand, they were also cast as custodians of the general good—but how was the balance between these two competing elements to be struck?

To the extent that crucified bodies and severed heads were accepted as evidence that warrior brawn was being used to hold back the forces of chaos, it might well be argued that there was no obvious contradiction between the principle of benevolence and the use of harsh punishments. As Herman Ooms has noted, *Tōshōgū goikun*, or, the Founder's Testament, a key text of the ruling ideology elaborated in the seventeenth century, explained that "the way of the warrior" *(budō)* should be understood as an "instrument for killing evil" and that the shogun's task was to use it to "purify the realm."[2] The strict punishment and execution of criminals obviously fit well with this notion of "purification" by the power of the sword and provided one of the most obvious ways for the warrior regime to demonstrate that its power could serve the interests of ordinary people. Certainly, it is no coincidence that to this day one of the best-known executions in Japan's premodern history remains that of Ishikawa Goemon, the legendary robber who reputedly terrorized the ancient capital of Kyoto before being captured and boiled alive with his son in the middle of the city in the 1590s by the great warrior hegemon Toyotomi Hideyoshi.[3] It was, of course, Hideyoshi who laid the foundation for the process of national reunification completed under the Tokugawa, and the story of Goemon's death has been enshrined in Japanese folklore over the centuries, not just because of the gruesome nature of the fate he is supposed to have met (there are, after all, countless examples of brutal executions from this time), but because it is symbolic of the point at which, after a century of turmoil and unrest, warrior lords began to turn their attention away from military conquest and toward the restoration of civil order.

If the enforcement of order could be held up as a collective good, it is also worth noting that the Tokugawa judicial system came to place considerable emphasis on what would today be called "victim's rights." In cases of accidental death, for example, relatives of the deceased were typically given a key role in deciding the fate of the person responsible. By submitting a formal "request for leniency" (oshioki gomen negai) they could have the person's life spared. Otherwise the principle of "an eye for an eye" would hold, and the sentence would almost certainly be the "penalty for murderers."[4] That Tokugawa officials used their power on behalf of those who had been wronged can be seen also from more informal social practices. When a murderer was executed, for example, it was common for the relatives of the victim to visit the official who had presided over the case in order to thank him formally for setting the matter right.[5] And the remarkable popularity that Bakufu officials such as Ōoka Echizen-no-kami (1677–1751), Hasegawa Heizō (1745–95), and Tōyama Kinshirō (1793–1855) continue to command centuries after their deaths (all three remain stock figures in television, film, and fiction today) suggests the extent to which ordinary people at the time came to trust in the benevolence of such figures and the protection they offered.[6]

Yet, even if stern acts of punishment often helped to generate feelings of gratitude toward the warrior state, it was still the case that too much punishment, or punishment that seemed unfairly harsh, always had the potential to throw into question the shogun's credibility as a benevolent ruler (jinkun). This was particularly true given that Japan's own history provided evidence that not all rulers found it necessary to make use of bloody punishments. From the very beginning of the Tokugawa period, older, Buddhist-inspired chronicles such as the Hōgen monogatari spoke to readers of a "golden age," prior to the Hōgen Rebellion of 1156, in which all forms of capital punishment had been abandoned by the imperial court for a period of some three and a half centuries. Beyond just recounting the past, the authors of this text also insisted that "so long as the death penalty is in use there will always be rebels in our country."[7] Implicit in this was a critique of more than the death penalty alone. The Hōgen Rebellion had, after all, constituted the first major intrusion of warriors into the realm of politics and the clear implication was that, far from bringing peace, the warriors themselves were the primary source of strife and instability in the world.

From early in the seventeenth century, those sympathetic to the new warrior regime had begun building a defense against this kind of radical Buddhist critique of harsh punishment. The most important figure in this regard was Suzuki Shōsan (1579–1655), a direct retainer of the Tokugawa family who, in midlife, gave up warrior life to become a Zen monk. Noting that there were many who believed that "it will be hard to bring peace to the world with Buddhism as long as capital punishment continues," Shōsan insisted that, in fact, if it was done for the right reasons, killing could be perfectly compatible with Buddhist principles: "You execute whom you must, you kill whom you must." When motivated by "compassion," he explained, severe punishments actually helped ordinary people escape the "bad karma" that was the source of all their misfortunes. The sight of a crucified criminal warned people who might otherwise be complacent about their own lives to turn away from evil and embrace good. It was also in the spiritual best interests of the criminal himself. Rather than continuing to wallow in his evil ways, thereby condemning himself to an endless cycle of suffering and misery in future incarnations, he instead "meets a sudden end, repents, and cuts off his evil at the root."[8]

The idea that harsh punishments could serve a profound moral purpose by encouraging people to abandon evil and embrace good continued to be expressed in various forms for much of the Tokugawa period. In the mid-eighteenth century the great artist Maruyama Ōkyo (1733–95) included dramatic renditions of a number of gruesome Tokugawa– and Sengoku–period punishments in a scroll commissioned by the head of a Tendai temple in Osaka for precisely this reason.[9] At the level of actual practice, using punishments as a technique for promoting moral reform was taken to an extreme under the fifth Tokugawa shogun, Tsunayoshi (r. 1680–1709). As his grand chamberlain, Yanagisawa Yoshiyasu (1658–1714), explained, Tsunayoshi's infamous Laws of Compassion (*shōrui awaremi no rei*) "initially arose solely out of the shogun's desire to admonish even the slightest lack of benevolence and to perfect the spirit of the common people."[10] The severity of the laws, which included proscriptions against the killing and mistreatment of animals (most famously, dogs), created significant problems for the Bakufu. Reports of people being crucified for killing dogs and other such seemingly minor offenses quickly gave rise to apprehension and resentment among various segments of the population. Far from being seen as a saintly ruler concerned with protecting the sanctity of life and the welfare of the people, Tsunayoshi, "the dog shogun" (*oinu kubō*), has instead been remembered as an eccentric tyrant.

The resentment caused by the Laws of Compassion had serious implications for the stability of Tokugawa authority. Arai Hakuseki, the scholar whose views on differential punishments were mentioned in chapter 1, explained the situation at the time of Tsunayoshi's death as follows:

During the previous reign those in charge of the administration of justice sought to apply the laws as severely as they could. Many people were sentenced to death and their families punished because they mistreated a bird or an animal. Others were exiled or banished from their native regions. The people have lost all sense of security. How many tens of thousands have seen their parents, their brothers, their wives, their children scattered and lost?[11]

The limits of harsh punishment as a tool of social policy had thus clearly been reached, and the Laws of Compassion were quickly repealed after Tsunayoshi's death. For Hakuseki, however, this was still not enough to restore people's faith in the benevolence of the shogun or his government, and Kate Wildman Nakai has noted that as adviser to the new shogun, Ienobu (r. 1709–12), he continued to argue for a further reduction in the overall severity of Tokugawa punishments.[12] In his *Tokushi yoron*, which was based on a set of lectures presented to Ienobu, Hakuseki cleverly pinned the blame for the harshness of Tokugawa punishments on the legacy of Hideyoshi. During Hideyoshi's reign, he wrote,

if a person stole even one penny, he was to be executed. The punishment for ordinary crimes being this severe, those who committed serious crimes were sentenced to things like seppuku and beheading with exposure of the head (*gokumon*). Punishments such as crucifixion and burning at the stake were devised. . . . Today, a hundred years later, when it is time for cruelty to be overcome and killing left behind, should not the continued existence of harsh punishment be reconsidered?[13]

As we have already seen, Hakuseki's suggestion that punishments had changed little since Hideyoshi's time was hardly fair. The first century of Tokugawa rule had seen a significant alleviation of the severity of penal practices inherited from the late Warring States period. As we have also noted, however, punishments such as crucifixion and exposure of severed heads quickly came to play an important role in the Tokugawa era's *peacetime* economy of power—providing regular reminders of the fearsomeness of the warrior lords and their active efforts to enforce order. To have given this up would have required a fundamental rethinking of the strategies of warrior rule. This was not forthcoming, and as a result Hakuseki's calls for the abolition of "harsh punishments" were to go unheeded for the remaining century and a half of Tokugawa rule.

Yet, even as they continued to use harsh punishments, Tokugawa officials were also increasingly aware of the need to establish limits and develop strategies for ensuring that their use would not undermine their claims to provide benevolent government. The moral justifications offered by ideologues such as Suzuki Shōsan were always important in this regard, but as the experience of Tsunayoshi's reign had shown, the actual practice of punishment was also critical. Over the course of the period a range of practical measures designed to balance out the harshness of the harshest punishments, protect the warrior lords from charges of cruelty, and ultimately bolster their reputation for benevolence were developed and implemented.

STRATEGIES OF BENEVOLENCE

One of the simplest ways the warrior regime was able to maintain its reputation for benevolence was by ensuring that certain groups of people who were likely to elicit strong feelings of sympathy from society were not subjected to the full force of official punishments. Most important in this regard were children. Lenient treatment for minors was probably common from the very beginning of the period, but the principle became firmly institutionalized over the course of the eighteenth century. Under the One Hundred Articles children younger than fourteen who committed acts of murder or arson were not executed but were put in the custody of relatives until they came of age and then exiled to a distant island *(entō)*.[14] Children caught stealing were also given punishments one grade less severe than adults, and from at least as early as 1772 minors sentenced to flogging for a first offense were spared corporal punishment and instead were imprisoned in the jailhouse for a short period *(katairō)*.[15] At the level of principle, Tokugawa law insisted that no special consideration be given to women, but in practice, from the last decade of the eighteenth century, they too were exempted from floggings and punished instead with short-term imprisonment.[16] The torture and execution of pregnant women was also prohibited, although once the baby had been born, interrogation and punishment of the mother resumed as usual.[17] Persons judged to be too sick or weak to withstand the pain of flogging might also have their sentences commuted to short-term imprisonment, although in most cases the blows were simply applied with less vigor than usual.[18]

Although the system within which they worked may have been harsh, there is some reason to believe that in their actual treatment of prisoners Bakufu officials were encouraged to be respectful and even compassionate. Consider the instructions regarding interrogations that were passed down to Sakuma Osahiro (1839–1923) when he began training to become an officer of the governor of Edo in the 1850s. These stated that when questioning a suspect, officers should always remember to "hate the crime but not the person" and avoid using "abusive language" even in cases where the prisoner was a person of "low status." New officers were also cautioned against unnecessary shouting and told that the most effective way to conduct an interrogation was always with a "compassionate heart."[19] How consistently such high-minded ideals were maintained in practice is difficult to know, but contemporary accounts suggest that in at least some cases they were. Yoshida Shōin (1830–59), the famous activist and critic of Tokugawa rule, was impressed by the treatment he received from Bakufu officials. After he was arrested for the first time in the 1850s, he noted in his journal how considerate the officials who escorted him to Edo had been, always pausing at rest stops along the way to ask whether he or any of the other prisoners in his group wanted tea, sweets, or something else to eat. According to Shōin this was "standard practice" for Bakufu officials escorting prisoners over a long distance, and in general he claimed to have been "truly moved by their exceeding kindness."[20]

To some degree, the gratitude generated by relatively small acts of kindness can be seen as further evidence of the fear and apprehension with which Bakufu officials were generally viewed. Yet we should not underestimate the extent to which the harshness of the Bakufu's formal legal provisions could be softened at the level of enforcement. One of the best examples of this relates to the rule enshrined in the One Hundred Articles that any theft of goods or money worth more than ten *ryō* was to be punished with death (lesser amounts were punished with a combination of flogging and tattooing). As popular awareness of this official "cut off" point spread, it became customary for those who had larger amounts stolen from them to report the value of their missing goods as exactly nine *ryō*, two *bun*, and three *shu*—that is, the Tokugawa equivalent of 9.99. This practice could not have continued without the acknowledgment and support of Bakufu officials, who routinely recorded this obviously fictional figure in their official reports.[21]

The day-to-day management of the official checkpoints *(sekisho)* maintained by the Bakufu at strategic points along the major highways provides another good example of the way in which officials were often prepared to bend or overlook formal regulations. Officially, evasion of a checkpoint was considered an extremely serious crime, punishable with crucifixion under article 20 of the One Hundred Articles. As Constantine Vaporis has shown in his study of travel along the great highways, however, in practice officials at the checkpoints made a habit of turning a blind eye to the large numbers of people who routinely "took to the bushes" in order to avoid them.[22] Viewed from a modern perspective, this might be interpreted simply as evidence of the comparative weakness of the Tokugawa (i.e., "early modern") state and what James White has characterized as a growing inability to enforce its will.[23] From the point of view of the individual officials involved, turning a blind eye was undoubtedly a way of keeping workloads manageable. Yet, to focus too much on the issue of capacity (as if modern standards of enforcement can be taken as a transhistorical norm) is to miss an important point. Combining the threat of harsh punishment with loose enforcement not only contributed to the sustainability of the punishment system (by making it bearable); it could also serve to promote actively goodwill toward the state and its officials. Thus, as Vaporis points out, the ability to pass around the checkpoints came to be seen by ordinary people at the time not as evidence of weakness but rather of the "benevolence of the realm."

Another example of the way that the letter of warrior law was often softened in practice relates to punishments for accidental fires. As noted earlier, the threat of fire was a major concern throughout the Tokugawa period, and arson was generally punishable with burning alive. In theory, the head of a household from which a fire started accidentally was also liable for (less severe) punishment.[24] In practice, however, it was usually possible for the household head to obtain an official pardon in such cases by taking refuge in his family's Buddhist temple (*bodaiji*) for a short period—an act accepted by officials as an appropriate display of contrition and penitence.[25]

Like the so-called divorce temples (*enkiri dera*) to which women could flee in order to escape the bonds of marriage, this practice of seeking refuge from warrior law is best understood as part of the legacy of Japan's medieval period, when powerful temples had been able to provide a safe haven for persons fleeing persecution by secular authorities for all kinds of reasons.[26] And, while it is true that the destruction of the great centers of ecclesiastical power by Japan's military unifiers in the late sixteenth century severely curtailed the independent role that temples could play in secular affairs, evidence from the study of crime and punishment suggests that a careful reevaluation of their role in Tokugawa society would yield fascinating results. Abe Yoshio has shown that, in spite of Bakufu prohibitions, the practice of fleeing to a temple (*kakeiri*) in order to escape persecution remained alive and well in some regions of the country. In one small corner of Mutsu province more than a thousand people are known to have obtained pardons for various minor crimes in this way in the second half of the period.[27] Even in Edo, where fleeing to a family temple was permitted only in the case of accidental fires, the Bakufu is generally better understood as having co-opted the mediating role of the temples rather than simply destroying it. This can be seen most clearly through a consideration of the Bakufu's system of pardons and amnesties—the most dramatic demonstrations of official benevolence in the Tokugawa period.

Amnesties are a common practice in many premodern societies, and Tokugawa Japan was no exception.[28] In some cases, they were ordered in direct response to specific circumstances. After the death of Tsunayoshi and the repeal of the Laws of Compassion, for example, Hakuseki helped orchestrate what was almost certainly the single largest amnesty of the entire period. According to him, a total of almost nine thousand people were pardoned at this time in a series of ceremonies conducted all over the country by both the Bakufu and the daimyo.[29] While the sheer scale of this particular event is extraordinary, the Bakufu continued to hold smaller amnesties throughout the period.

In general, Bakufu amnesties fell into two basic categories: those held in conjunction with auspicious events, such as the appointment of a new shogun or the coming of age of a shogunal heir, and those held in conjunction with Buddhist funerary or memorial rites for a member of the shogunal family.[30] In the case of the former, the Bakufu's procedures were fairly straightforward: the senior councillors (*rōjū*) simply sent a notice to the governors and other lower officials asking whether anyone currently under investigation or already serving a sentence of exile or banishment should be considered for a pardon. (Because death sentences and corporal punishments were carried out as soon as they were announced, they were not generally subject to any kind of pardon.) The senior councillors then reviewed the list of names submitted to them and informed the governors which ones were to have their sentences lifted.

The amnesties held in conjunction with funerary and memorial rites are more interesting because of the key role played by Edo's two largest Buddhist temples, Kan'eiji and Zōjōji. They were chosen to serve as the official household temples of the main Tokugawa line early in the period, and as a result of the patronage they received, their complexes quickly grew to cover large tracts of land to the north and south of Edo castle. Conducting funeral services and regular memorials for deceased members of the shogunal household was one of their primary responsibilities throughout the period, and this activity linked them to the system of amnesties in a number of ways. Ordinary people could come to the two temples to plead for mercy on behalf of relatives who had been punished by the Bakufu (again, almost always, with either exile or banishment). After first making the appropriate prayers and show of respect to the shogunal ancestors, a person would approach a priest at either temple and ask that the name of the unfortunate relative be entered into a special register of appellants. Eventually, when it was time for funerary or memorial rites to be held, the head priest of the temple would compile a list of names from the register and submit it to the Bakufu, requesting that they be considered for pardon. The final granting of pardons was then announced as a great act of mercy made possible by the particular shogunal ancestor or relative for whom the funerary or memorial services were being held. By cultivating this system of appeals, the Bakufu was able to harness the older, medieval tradition of Buddhist temples providing sanctuary from secular persecution and link it directly to the worship of the shogunal household. Buddhist benevolence and the benevolence of the Tokugawa family were thereby presented as one and the same thing.

This tactical conflation of religious and political authority can also be seen in the special amnesty ceremonies that were performed at the temples from time to time with jailed prisoners who had not yet been sentenced for their crimes. An eyewitness account of one such ceremony conducted at Kan'eiji in 1841 as part of the funeral services for Ienari, the eleventh shogun, makes clear the careful manner in which they were stage-managed. On the seventh day after Ienari's death, a group of some seventy or eighty prisoners was taken from the Kodenmachō Jailhouse and paraded through the city to an area in front of the mausoleum gate at Kan'eiji that had been cordoned off with a giant curtain. After the prisoners had been lined up in front of the gate, Tōyama Kinshirō, one of the legendary governors of Edo mentioned earlier, entered from behind the curtain with a group of his subordinates. Turning to face the prisoners, the governor took a large scroll out of his sleeve and began reading from it, his voice growing steadily louder until, in a climactic burst of volume, he declared that all those assembled were to be pardoned. At that precise moment the gates to the mausoleum swung open, and the head priest of Kan'eiji entered at the head of a long train of lesser priests. Wearing his dramatic purple regalia and sheltered by a special vermilion parasol, the head priest addressed the prisoners, exhorting them to renounce evil and embrace good in their future lives. Then, after saying a short prayer for each of them, he proceeded back through the gates of the mausoleum, and as the gates closed behind him, the prisoners' ropes were cut, and they were set free.[31] The eyewitness who described this event remembered it specifically as an example of the powerful techniques of governance that had been developed by the Bakufu. By the end of the ceremony, he claimed, even the toughest of the prisoners had been reduced to tears.

Overall then, what we have seen in this section provides further evidence of the fundamentally different economy of power that operated in Tokugawa society. Instead of the kind of mechanical application of the letter of the law that we might expect to find under modern states, warrior officials in the Tokugawa period combined relatively lax enforcement and a tendency to turn a blind eye to minor infractions with the use of "flamboyant" displays of their own power—to pardon as well as to punish.[32] This made it possible to bolster warrior authority with the threat of terrifying punishments on the one hand, while also cultivating the goodwill of the general population on the other, with evidence of official flexibility, restraint, and mercy (we return to this point in chapter 4). In addition to the various techniques and strategies described here, however, there was also one other way that the warrior state was able to stop its image as an essentially "benevolent" regime from being undermined by the continued use of harsh punishments: it delegated responsibility for the most unpleasant and visible aspects of those punishments to formally constituted groups of "despised people" (senmin) or "outcasts." The role played by the outcasts is, in fact, one of the most striking aspects of the Tokugawa punishment system and is significant for our understanding of Tokugawa society more generally.

BENEVOLENCE AND BUTCHERY: POSITIONING THE OUTCASTS

The presence of social outcasts, in a general sense, is not a phenomenon unique to premodern Japan. In almost all complex societies there are those who, for a range of different reasons (famine and poverty are undoubtedly the most common), either fall, flee, or are pushed out of their communities and find themselves living a marginal existence. Socially vulnerable and lacking any stable means by which to support themselves, these marginalized people inevitably band together for the purpose of mutual assistance and protection. As Kuroda Toshio has suggested, the formation of recognizable outcast groups in medieval Japan should be understood, at base, as an example of this kind of process.[33] Yet the particular forms and roles that these groups came to assume within medieval Japanese society were also deeply affected by the development of a specific combination of beliefs about death and spiritual pollution (kegare).

From ancient times, members of Japan's imperial court had considered human deaths, births, and sickness to be potentially harmful sources of pollution, requiring various forms of ritual cleansing and purification. With the introduction and spread of Buddhism, however, pollution began to take on a much broader set of meanings.[34] Over the course of the Heian period (794–1185) it came to encompass also dead animals of all kinds and "even the very act of hunting," which had previously been a favorite pastime of court nobles.[35] (The heightened concern with pollution was, no doubt, also one of the main reasons for the three-and-a half-century abandonment of the death penalty by the Heian court, reported in the Hōgen monogatari.) In terms of its impact on outcast groups, such concern naturally exacerbated the tendency for communities to exclude paupers and beggars (whose misfortunes were attributed to bad karma and pollution), as well as the chronically sick or disabled. Indeed, the concern of mainstream communities to avoid the pollution associated with such people was probably a key factor behind the growing stratification of the outcast population, with groups of outcast bosses (chōri) increasingly assuming responsibility for the supervision and control of a lower group of beggars (kojiki hinin), which included lepers.[36]

Over time, different outcast groups began to develop their own specific survival strategies. Some came to specialize in forms of entertainment or petty craft production. Others cultivated a niche for themselves by performing tasks related to the removal or "cleansing" (kiyome) away of pollution.[37] These included such things as sweeping temple and shrine grounds, handling corpses during funerals, and disposing of animal carcasses. The right to collect the carcasses of large animals, such as oxen and horses, in particular, soon became an important form of alms for many outcast groups, who began using them for leather production. Most important for this discussion, by the fourteenth century the pollution-related activities of outcast groups had further broadened to include the guarding of prisoners and, in some cases, the administration of punishments.[38]

Given this background, it is tempting to assume that the Edo period practice of assigning outcasts responsibility for the "unclean" tasks associated with official punishments was simply a continuation or extension of older trends. Yet, there is good reason to question such an assumption. Unlike nobles at the imperial court or members of medieval religious communities who had previously been the primary employers of the "cleansing" services of the outcasts, the men who came to rule Japan in the sixteenth and seventeenth centuries were, after all, warriors, "whose primary function was to engage in acts of killing."[39] When they were not slaughtering foes on the battlefield, they routinely hunted animals to hone their fighting skills, and, although concern about the pollution caused by death and blood did not disappear completely during the Warring States period, they clearly had little reason to use the outcasts to shield them from it.

Warrior lords did, however, have an important reason of their own, separate from the question of pollution, for cultivating ties with outcast groups. The reason was leather. The one commodity that was almost exclusively manufactured and controlled by outcasts was also crucial for the production of such basic military equipment as bow strings, saddles, and armor. In order to secure a steady supply of this vital commodity, many sixteenth-century warlords (*sengoku daimyō*) brought groups of outcast leatherworkers under their direct control, often forcibly relocating them to settlements near their castles.[40] At least in the short term, these changes brought real advantages to the outcast communities involved. Their leaders were often recognized as important vassals and granted a range of special privileges by the warrior lord they served.[41] Even more important, the expansion of commerce in general, and the high demand for their products in particular, seemed to open up the possibility that leatherworkers would be able to escape from the older world of ideas about pollution and purification and assume a place in the newly forming social order roughly on par with ordinary merchants and artisans.[42] By the end of the seventeenth century, however, this possibility had been foreclosed. Increasingly referred to in official documents not as "leatherworkers" (*kawata; kawaya*) but rather as "the polluted ones" or *eta* (literally, "much filth"), they found themselves once again on the bottom rung of a rigid social hierarchy, together with licensed beggars (*hinin;* literally "nonhuman") and other "despised groups" (*senmin*).

In an article that has helped redefine our understanding of the situation of the outcasts within Tokugawa society, Yokota Fuyuhiko has argued that this reinscription of older patterns of discrimination in the early part of the Tokugawa period was closely linked with the emergence of the warrior regime's ideology of benevolent rule.[43] In particular, he pinpoints Tsunayoshi's Laws of Compassion as a crucial turning point, because under them the work of slaughtering horses and cattle for leather production, which had previously been seen as a valuable service, was now repeatedly identified as the epitome of "cruel" and "*un*benevolent" (*fujin*) behavior—the mirror opposite, in other words, of all that the warrior state was supposed to stand for. The trade in sick and abandoned animals that had developed in response to demand for leather became the target of a severe crackdown, and the outcasts who bought such animals to kill and skin were vilified. It was one thing for the outcasts to make use of the carcasses of animals that had already died of natural causes but quite another for them to buy living things in order to kill them for profit. As noted earlier, the Laws of Compassion were eventually repealed after Tsunayoshi's death in 1709. But even after this the ban on the trade in sick and abandoned animals that had been aimed at the outcast leatherworkers was retained and further strengthened. Official records compiled in Kyoto in the late 1710s listed "*eta* who kill cows for commercial purposes" together with "children who kill their parents" as criminals who should be punished with crucifixion. In the early 1730s a new set of decrees were posted up on "tall signs" all over the country condemning the outcasts for mercilessly killing cattle and reiterating the earlier bans in the strongest possible terms.[44]

Whether or not it was consciously planned for this purpose, Yokota argues that the vilification of outcasts for the slaughter of animals was extremely useful for the warrior regime at a time when it was struggling to reinvent its own image and history. Only a generation or so earlier, peasant farmers had used derogatory terms such as "slaughterer" (*tosha*) and "butchering fiend" (*tokai no tagui*) for the warriors who routinely destroyed lives and livelihoods in their vicious struggles for power.[45] In the wake of the Laws of Compassion, these same terms and the image that went with them were now displaced and transferred to the outcast leatherworkers, whose older association with pollution was now overlaid and overshadowed by an even stronger association with inhumanity and cruelty. This, in turn, allowed the warrior state to bolster its own claims to benevolence by presenting itself as a check on outcast excesses. As the outcasts became inhuman "slaughterers," in other words, the warriors became compassionate rulers and protectors of life. This is an important insight. Yet, if Yokota is right to suggest that the image of outcast cruelty owed a great deal to their association with the slaughter of old and sick animals, how much more damning must their role in the Tokugawa punishment system have been?[46]

Although outcasts were already involved in the administration of some forms of punishment before the beginning of the Edo period, that involvement was to become more widespread and systematic than ever before under the Tokugawa.[47] Indeed, by Tsunayoshi's time they had come to play a key role in almost every act of punishment ordered by the warrior state. It is, however, not just the extent of outcast involvement in the Tokugawa punishment system that should be noted but also the specific nature of their role.[48] In some cases outcasts were used simply as assistants to warrior officials. This was true of beheadings, which were carried out by either the shogun's official "sword tester" or a low-ranking samurai functionary (uchiyaku dōshin). As the executioner prepared to lower his sword onto the condemned person's neck, a group of two or three outcasts had the task of holding him in position for a clean cut. Once the head had been severed, they would then push the torso forward and hold the neck down so that the blood spurting from it drained into a hole dug for this purpose. The outcasts were also responsible for retrieving the severed head and washing it, and for cleaning up and disposing of dead bodies.[49] These kinds of tasks were consistent with older views of the outcasts as people who could be used to take care of death-related pollution. Yet the outcasts also came to play a central role in the actual application of some forms of punishment under the Tokugawa. In the case of crucifixions and burnings at the stake, for example, all of the work, including the gruesome task of skewering the condemned prisoner with spears or torching his flesh, was carried out by an outcast headman and his underlings.

One key difference between these two forms of execution and beheadings was obviously the sheer level of horror that they were supposed to generate, but it will also be recalled from chapter 1 that whereas beheadings were almost always conducted behind the closed walls of a jailhouse, crucifixions and burnings alive took place at open execution grounds. Although the warrior authorities in Edo did not encourage large crowds of people to gather at these places, it is nevertheless significant that anyone who did witness the moment of execution would have seen outcasts and not warriors engaged in the act of mutilating criminal bodies. Afterward, moreover, when the mutilated bodies were left out on open display, there was always a group of outcasts on hand to guard them and eventually to take them down from their wooden frames and dispose of them (all in full public view). The same was true of the severed heads of those sentenced to gokumon. After the decapitation had been completed by warrior officials within the jailhouse compound, the outcasts would ferry the head through the city streets to the public execution ground and sit guarding it while it remained on display. The outcasts also guarded live prisoners pilloried at Nihonbashi and paraded condemned prisoners through the streets before their executions. In short, whenever punishments were made openly

Figure 6. A criminal being paraded through the city streets before execution. He is escorted by an entourage of outcast workers carrying signs and the menacing-looking instruments of their official duties to the warrior state. From the "Keibatsu daihiroku." The National Archive of Japan.

visible to ordinary people in Tokugawa Japan, the presence of the outcasts loomed large.[50]

This highly visible outcast involvement in the penal system helped the warriors project and protect their image of benevolence in at least two ways. Most obviously, it distanced them from the most gruesome aspects of the punishments they themselves continued to order. In the public eye the immediate agents of warrior authority were not themselves warriors but a lower kind of human, believed to have no sense of mercy or compassion, and no qualms about inflicting cruel tortures on man or beast. In a sense, these outcasts were held up as an example of exactly the kind of depravity and cruelty that the warriors were supposed to have rescued the country from by imposing order and bringing peace. Given this, it was only fitting that those who rejected warrior authority were handed over to the outcasts to receive their punishments. At the same time, the continual sight of outcasts in the presence of punished bodies also bolstered the view that it was *they* who were the real "slaughterers" and "butchers," and this, in turn, served to draw attention away from the less savory aspects of the warrior rulers' own pasts. After all, in an age of sustained peace, memory of the warriors' capacity for cruelty faded steadily, while every new display of official punishment brought a fresh reminder of the apparent inhumanity of the outcasts.[51]

Viewed in terms of its long-term historical impact, there can be little doubt that the warrior state's policy of systematically using outcasts to perform the bloodiest and most visible tasks associated with the penal system has contributed directly to the widespread discrimination that the so-called *tokushu burakumin* (literally, "special villagers"), who are generally believed to be descendants of Tokugawa era outcasts, continue to face in Japan to this day. Historians clearly have an obligation to decry such discrimination in the strongest possible terms and also to show how the actions of those in positions of power have contributed to its reproduction and intensification over time. Yet, having said that, it would be a mistake to portray the outcasts of the Tokugawa period simply as passive victims of the policies of the warrior state who lacked any historical agency of their own.[52] As Tsukada Takashi's thoughtful work on this topic reminds us, they are much better understood as having been caught up in the same struggles for survival and power as any other social group.[53] In this regard, it is particularly important to recall that social outcasts are always vulnerable to persecution, regardless of the policies of the state. By agreeing to perform various important tasks for the warrior state, however, outcast communities in Tokugawa Japan were able to win a degree of security for themselves. They received formal recognition as a lowly but nevertheless legitimate segment of society, and when problems or disputes arose, they were able to appeal to the warrior state for support on the basis of the faithful service they rendered.

Needless to say, the support and protection the outcasts received was not necessarily equal to that of other social groups. Nor was it given equally to all outcasts. Those outcast communities and leaders to whom the warrior state assigned responsibility for key tasks were able to claim special privileges for themselves and, with the backing of the warriors, assert their authority over others. The right to perform tasks for the warrior state was, in other words, a source of power for outcasts vis-à-vis other outcasts. As a result, far from resenting or rejecting those tasks, Tsukada has shown that outcast communities and their leaders in fact tended to compete with each for the opportunity to perform them.[54] The most successful outcast leaders of the period in this regard were undoubtedly the *eta* chiefs in Edo who, for the duration of Tokugawa rule, took the hereditary name Danzaemon.

The first Danzaemon was one of a handful of outcast headmen in the area around Edo when the Tokugawa established their headquarters there in the late sixteenth century. During the first hundred years of Tokugawa rule his successors not only established their preeminence in the capital itself but also extended their authority over outcast communities throughout the surrounding provinces.[55] We consider the nature of that authority, and its implications for our overall understanding of the Tokugawa polity, in more detail in the next chapter. For now, it is worth noting that when the Tokugawa regime was eventually overthrown in 1868, the last Danzaemon asked the new Meiji government to reaffirm the powers his ancestors had enjoyed over the preceding centuries by pointing specifically to the various services they had performed for the warrior state, "beginning with the administration of official punishments."[56] The clear implication was that if the new government would recognize his traditional authority as lord of the outcasts, Danzaemon would willingly continue to supply labor to help carry out punishments and perform other such tasks for the state.

While the authority of leaders like Danzaemon depended heavily on the backing of the warrior state, Tsukada's research suggests that ordinary outcasts too had reason to see the performance of punishment-related duties as more than just a burdensome task. For people who were used to being marginalized and discriminated against, these duties, after all, provided a rare opportunity to occupy a position of power in the public eye. A set of documents describing the process by which outcasts, peasants, and warriors negotiated the task of putting the severed head of an executed criminal on display in a farming village in Musashi, near Edo, in the middle of the eighteenth century is particularly instructive in this regard.[57] In an interview with the outcasts who were to handle the head and guard it while it was on display, a warrior official sent to supervise proceedings noted that in some areas of the Kantō it was customary to collect a small fee from each person who passed by an execution ground where a severed head or crucified body had been put on display. When asked whether they intended to collect such a fee in this case, the outcasts involved replied that they had "absolutely no intention of taking money." This is of some interest in itself, but, as Tsukada notes, the reasons the outcasts offered are especially important: "Even if it is only a small amount," they explained, "when people in country areas have to pay money in order to pass by, they often take an alternative route, and so the number of people who see [the execution ground] decreases. If this were to happen [in the current case], we would not have fulfilled our duty to the public authority."[58] The outcasts, in other words, wanted as many people as possible to see the severed head and argued that this was an important part of their obligation to the Bakufu. The warrior official, however, expressed doubts about their motives. He noted that "in many areas, when official punishments are carried out, there are stories of [outcasts] using their authority as servants of the shogun (*oyaku no ken'i*) to make things difficult for the peasants in various ways."[59] He ordered them to ensure that no such problems arose in this case. No doubt the order was observed, but even so, the outcast workers who stood on guard with the severed head must have presented a menacing prospect to the peasants who saw them. In a society where weapons of war were a marker of prestige and power, their involvement in the penal system gave them the right to wield spears and other fearsome implements, and given the discrimination they faced in everyday life, it is hardly surprising that they were sometimes tempted to use their "authority as servants of the shogun" to intimidate onlookers and passers-by.[60]

To note that outcasts had their own reasons and motives for wanting to perform punishment-related duties is not to suggest that the policies pursued by the warrior state were irrelevant to their situation, or that they were in any meaningful sense "free" to choose the terms of their relationship with the state. Trapped in a position of weakness and vulnerability, they simply cultivated whatever sources of strength they could find. Ultimately, of course, it was the warrior state that benefited most from the resulting arrangement. The outcasts' involvement in the punishment system certainly did nothing to ease the growing sense of hostility with which they were viewed by most commoners in the latter part of the period. Yet, so long as they were able to maintain their special connection with the state, their situation was never one of total powerlessness. This has important implications for our understanding of the plight of the outcasts and their descendants in the Meiji period and beyond.

The Meiji government effectively brought an end to the old relationship between outcasts and the state in 1871 when it banned the use of derogatory terms such as *eta* and *hinin* and declared that forthwith outcasts would hold the same status in society as commoners. At a time when the new government was still striving to establish its own legitimacy in the eyes of the people, this was held up as an act of "the greatest benevolence, unsurpassed in past or present," and it has often been referred to subsequently as the "liberation order."[61] Yet, as Suzuki Ryō has shown, while the former outcasts were indeed liberated from their various "official duties" and thus their one source of power and independence in the old order, it was not possible (nor did the government try) to legislate away the discriminatory attitudes in society that had built up over a period of centuries.[62] Eventually, in the 1910s and 1920s, modern Japan's "special villagers" would themselves begin articulating a new vision of their rightful place in society. In the meantime, however, they were left to face the hostility and prejudice of their fellow citizens without anything to shield or protect them. To make matters worse, as the Meiji state launched its policy of rapid militarization in the 1880s, it came to rely heavily upon "traditional" structures of rule in rural areas in order to maintain stability. The authority of "local notables" was bolstered, and changes to "old customs" that were considered likely to incite popular opposition were prohibited. As a result, the further subjugation and marginalization of former outcast communities gained the tacit support of a powerful modern state.[63] This situation marked the real beginning of the so-called *burakumin* problem—the bastard child of popular prejudice and the combined "benevolence" of successive regimes.

This chapter began with the argument that dramatic displays of punishment, as useful as they may have been, had to be balanced by various strategies of benevolence in order to protect the warriors' image as virtuous rulers. Any regime that wants to avoid being cast as a tyranny must observe some limits on its use of power and violence, and the central place that notions of benevolence and compassion held in Tokugawa Japan's ruling ideology meant that the warrior state had particular reason to be careful. Yet, from what we have seen, it may also make sense to turn our original argument on its head: in at least some cases the very harshness of Tokugawa punishments opened up opportunities for the warrior state to project its aura of benevolence in ways that would not otherwise have been possible. Relatively small acts of kindness on the part of warrior officials were gratefully accepted as signs of their compassion and concern: when they turned a blind eye to everyday transgressions of formal decrees or accepted false information about the value of stolen goods as if it were true, it was thought to reflect the "benevolence of the realm." In order to take advantage of the system of pardons, people from all over the country journeyed to Kan'eiji and Zōjōji in Edo to pray to the shogunal ancestors and simultaneously to lodge appeals for clemency on behalf of their relatives; and prisoners from the jailhouse were reduced to tears of relief and gratitude in carefully choreographed ceremonies of amnesty. In addition to all of this, the fact that the actual application of harsh punishments came to be associated in the public imagination with the outcasts helped the warriors shed their former image as murderers and "butchers" and reposition themselves as compassionate protectors of the people.

The Power of Status: Kodenmachō Jailhouse and the Structures of Tokugawa Society

GIVEN THE PLACE that outcasts occupied in Tokugawa society and the ongoing discrimination that their descendants have faced, it is not difficult to understand why scholars have sometimes compared their situation with that of African Americans in the United States or to so-called untouchables in India.[1] Yet, just as the full significance of race in an American context, or caste in an Indian context, cannot be understood by focusing solely on the experiences of those who have been most adversely affected by it, so too is it important to acknowledge that the status system in Tokugawa Japan was about more than just an ugly set of prejudices directed against one minority group. Like race or caste, status in the Tokugawa period constituted a set of strategies for ordering human relationships and governing people. As such, it permeated and shaped virtually *every* aspect of the social formation, and punishment was no exception. This chapter examines the concrete ways in which the Tokugawa status system shaped the organization of the Bakufu's main jailhouse at Kodenmachō in Edo and then proceeds to explore its significance for penal practices at all levels of the Tokugawa polity. First, however, it is important to define precisely what we mean by "status."

In textbook overviews of the Tokugawa period, historians have often been content to describe the status system in terms of a neat neo-Confucian vision of a society divided into four estates. According to the routinely intoned *shi-nō-kō-shō* formula, warriors stood at the top of this idealized status hierarchy, followed next by peasants, then artisans, and finally merchants, whose narrow pursuit of commerce was thought to contribute least to the general good. Although this basic schema is indeed important for understanding some aspects of Tokugawa period discourse *about* society, as a tool for understanding the role of status *in* society it is hopelessly inadequate.[2] Not only does it omit a number of small but significant elements of the population (outcasts, priests, court nobles, and so on), it also misrepresents the situation of two of the groups that it purports to describe. In reality, artisans and merchants were never treated as separate estates but instead grouped together under the single category of "townsfolk" *(chōnin)*. Even more important than these problems of omission and inaccuracy, however, is the fact that when it is reduced to the *shi-nō-kō-shō* formula, the Tokugawa status system appears to represent little more than an idealized vision of an impossibly rigid and simple social order. What then is our alternative?

In general, status can be said to describe two distinct, but related, aspects of social organization in the Tokugawa period. First, as Herman Ooms has noted, hierarchies based on status position *within* a community were a basic feature of all levels of Tokugawa social organization. Drawing on the theoretical insights of sociologist Pierre Bourdieu, Ooms has explored the significance this has for our understanding of Tokugawa "village practice." He points to the intense rivalries over status within villages to dismiss the notion that before economic change created rifts along class lines, they were essentially egalitarian and free from significant internal conflict. He also argues convincingly that the overwhelming concern felt by ordinary people about their own position in localized status hierarchies served an important stabilizing function for the Tokugawa regime, by focusing people's attention away from the fundamental division between warrior lords (surplus consumers) and peasant underlings (surplus producers).[3]

What Ooms calls the "fundamental hierarchizing 'imaginary'" of the period is also highly relevant for our understanding of various aspects of the punishment system.[4] At the same time, however, it is important to emphasize that when Japanese social historians write about the importance of status and the status system *(mibunsei)* in the Tokugawa period, it is not just the hierarchical nature of the society to which they refer. Their primary concern is with what John W. Hall correctly identified some three decades ago as a *system of rule* based on the allocation of people into formally constituted "status groups."[5]

Although historians once assumed that this system was more or less imposed from above by the military hegemons who reunified the country at the end of the Warring States period, they now generally agree that its origins actually lay in the self-governing communities that ordinary people formed among themselves following the breakdown of the old structures of centralized rule in the fifteenth and sixteenth centuries.[6] Some of these communities (most notably those associated with the Ikkō Sect of Jōdō Shinshū Buddhism) were eventually crushed for resisting the authority of the ascendant warrior lords, but in general the architects of the "great peace" found it more convenient to incorporate them into the new social and political order of the late sixteenth and early seventeenth centuries. Our earlier discussion of the outcasts and their role in the Tokugawa penal system has already provided one example of how this process worked, but in general, the compromise between forces from above and below resulted in what Hall called a "container" society—that is, a society in which ideally every individual occupied a stable place within an officially recognized social unit. For peasants, the key social container was the village; and for townsfolk, it was the block association *(chō)*.[7] Warriors and nobles were organized into households *(ie)*, the Buddhist clergy into sects *(shū)*, and so on. The warrior state issued directives to help govern the organization of these various units, but the units retained a significant degree of autonomy over their own internal affairs. For the villages, in particular, autonomy was one of the key implications of Hideyoshi's policy of strictly separating peasants and warriors *(heinō bunri)* and forcing the warriors to move off the land into the new castle towns that began to spring up all over the country from the late sixteenth century.[8]

But autonomy came with a price. Throughout the period, each of the many units into which society was divided was required to fulfill certain basic obligations to the warrior lords. The most obvious and important of these was the payment of taxes and levies, but most groups were also expected to perform a range of official duties *(yaku)* for the state. For the outcasts we have already seen that these duties included various tasks related to punishment. For other groups it often meant some form of corvée labor or military service. In general, then, the container units were crucial to the warrior state's ability to harness and mobilize the powers of various segments of the population. This, however, was not their only role: they were also expected to regulate and monitor the activities of their individual members and to ensure that order was maintained within the community. In this sense, the status-based container units played an important *disciplinary* function. Far more than just an informal arrangement, by the middle of the seventeenth century this aspect of the status system had been given a firm bureaucratic basis as a result of the compilation of comprehensive "population registers," which carefully listed the residents of communities all over the country.

Needless to say, in a society in which hierarchical organization was the norm, the various status groups were never considered equal. As a general principle warriors clearly stood higher than villagers and townsfolk, and they, in turn, stood higher than the outcasts. In the end, however, the Tokugawa status system should be understood not simply as a system of hierarchical rankings but, more fundamentally, as a mechanism for determining what kind of "container" a person belonged in. Nowhere was this more obviously and literally true than in the Kodenmachō Jailhouse—an institution that provides a powerful example of the role of status as an organizational strategy in Tokugawa society.

KODENMACHŌ: REALM OF THE RŌNANUSHI

First established in the early 1610s, the jailhouse complex at Kodenmachō was to continue operating in the same location until after the demise of the Tokugawa some two and a half centuries later.[9] Close to the center of

Edo, its grounds were separated from the houses and shops of ordinary townsfolk in the surrounding city by a moat and a high wall crowned with inward-pointing spikes. As a new inmate was escorted in through the main gate, the first building he would have seen in front of him was the main office and interrogation center. To the right stood the official residence of the warden, who carried the hereditary name, Ishide Tatewaki, as well as barracks for his staff, some storehouses, and, in the far corner, an area where executions and "sword testing" were carried out. To the left, behind yet another wall, was the main building. A long, narrow structure running along one full side of the compound, it was given an unmistakable appearance by the rows of wooden bars that formed its outer walls.[10] Inside there were eight main jail rooms—with a central guard post in the middle—and it was here that the principles of the status system found their most obvious expression.

The first two rooms on either side of the guard post were known as the inner and outer *agari-ya* or "upper rooms." Although they were sometimes used for other special purposes, including the imprisonment of women inmates, they were reserved primarily for warriors and other men of relatively high standing. Beyond them were the "great jail" rooms *(tairō)*, where commoner men were held, and then finally at either end of the building were the "lesser" rooms *(nikenrō)*, for male prisoners with no officially registered place of residence.[11] These unregistereds *(mushuku)* were not necessarily "homeless" in the literal sense that we might understand it today but were people who had drifted out of the formal structures of the status system (they were not, in other words, stable members of any container units)—and for this reason they were regarded with considerable suspicion by the warrior authorities.

In addition to these divisions within the main building, still further differentiation of the male inmate population was made possible over the course of the period by the completion of a number of other, freestanding rooms. The first of these were the "upper chambers" *(agari-zashiki)*, built in 1683 to confine warriors and priests of especially high rank.[12] Then, in 1775, a special "peasant jail" *(hyakusho rō)* was added to allow for the separate detention of villagers called to Edo for interrogation and punishment.[13] This meant that for most of the final century of Tokugawa rule there were rooms for five different categories of prisoner at Kodenmachō. Predictably enough, conditions in them varied considerably. Prisoners in the upper rooms and chambers were given better food and more of it, sat on better quality tatami matting, and so on.[14] Yet, what of our earlier assertion that status in Tokugawa Japan was about more than just hierarchies of privilege—that it was also a mode of governance based on semiautonomous "container units"? How did this aspect of the status system manifest itself within the walls of the jailhouse?

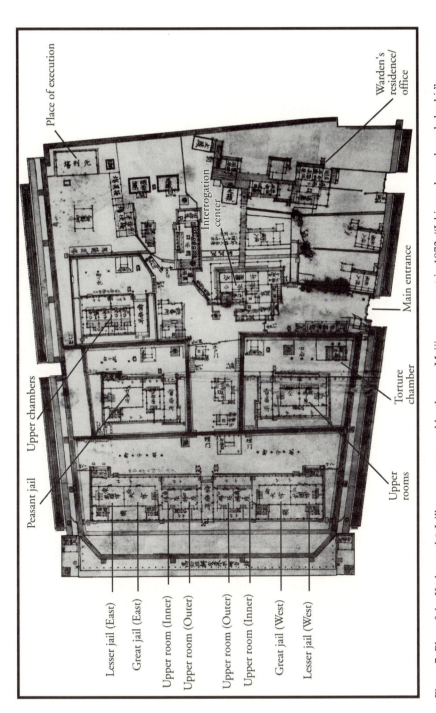

Figure 7. Plan of the Kodenmachō Jailhouse as surveyed by the new Meiji government in 1872. "Ichigaya kangoku enkakushi." Correctional Library of the Japanese Correctional Association.

One of the most remarkable things about the rooms at Kodenmachō was the sheer number of bodies that were routinely crammed into them. The "great" and "lesser" rooms, no more than five and a half meters wide and nine meters long, rarely held fewer than forty or fifty men each, and it was not unknown for the official limit of seventy per room to be exceeded.[15] In spite of this intense concentration of inmates, the number of guards assigned to duty at the main building was never more than six.[16] They, of course, had little chance of imposing order or keeping track of what was going on in the separate rooms and, for the most part, were content to monitor the arrival and departure of inmates. This, however, did not mean that chaos and anarchy were allowed to reign. Just as the villages and city blocks in mainstream society each had their own headman (nanushi) who was responsible for maintaining order, so too did each of the rooms at Kodenmachō have a chief prisoner.

The rōnanushi, or "headman of the jail," is remembered today in Japan primarily as a figure of dread, with good reason.[17] Records from the early nineteenth century describe how new inmates were routinely "welcomed" into the rooms by being stripped naked and beaten with wooden planks. They also list an array of tortures reserved for those who displeased the rōnanushi. In the winter an inmate might be forced to stand for hours in a bucket of icy water or held down while the bucket was dropped repeatedly on his back. Or, he might be deprived of food and water, or suddenly force fed with hot peppers or excrement from the latrines.[18] Some inmates were simply beaten to death or smothered in their sleep. Their bodies were sometimes hidden away for a few days to make it harder to ascertain the cause of death, but in general officials rarely asked questions about those who had died suddenly of "disease."[19]

Greed was undoubtedly one reason for the cruelty of the rōnanushi. The amount of protection money (tsuru kin) that a new inmate was able to smuggle past the guards or arrange to have sent to him generally determined the treatment he received inside, and for those who had no such resources to draw upon, the consequences could be dire. Writing from inside the jailhouse in the 1850s Yoshida Shōin observed bluntly that in the "lesser" rooms particularly, "prisoners without money do not often escape death."[20] Some of the money the rōnanushi collected was used to purchase sake, tobacco, and other items for communal use, and it was also customary for him to distribute small amounts of "sending off" money to inmates who were about to be exiled, or who were being moved to one of the outcast-run hospices (tame) after falling seriously ill.[21] Yet, even with these various expenses, the position of rōnanushi could still be a lucrative one. When Takano Chōei (1804–50), the scholar and physician who was sentenced to "long-term imprisonment" in 1839 for his outspoken criticism of the Bakufu's handling of foreign affairs, rose to become headman of the great

Figure 8. New inmates at Kodemmanchō Jailhouse being "welcomed" by the *rōnanushi* and the other inmate-officials. From the "Rōnai shinhiroku." The Criminal Museum of Meiji University.

jail, he reputedly "earned" enough in the position to be able to send his aged mother a regular stipend. After five years of waiting patiently for a pardon, moreover, he was able to use the cash he had saved to buy his way to freedom: he bribed an outcast laborer (who was later executed for the crime) to set fire to one of the jailhouse buildings so that he could take advantage of the Bakufu's benevolent policy of releasing all prisoners when they were in danger of fire and then escape back into the city.[22]

Clearly then, individual *rōnanushi* were able to use the position to their own personal advantage. But it is important to remember that they also formed part of a larger system. Unlike the informal "prison boss" figures who are a common feature of carceral institutions everywhere, Tokugawa era *rōnanushi* were officially appointed to their positions by the governor of the jail, and their authority over the jail rooms was formally recognized by the Bakufu.[23] If they performed their jobs well, they might receive a monetary "reward" *(gohōbi)* from the warrior officials or even have the severity of their final punishments reduced. If, however, problems arose within their room, they could just as easily be stripped of their position and sentenced to additional punishments.[24] In this sense, the position of the *rōnanushi* was indeed similar to that of a Tokugawa village headman. James Leavell has noted, for example, that because peasants were expected to apprehend anyone who committed petty crimes in their community, it was standard practice for the warrior authorities to blame the headman if they learned that theft or burglary had become a problem for a particular village.[25] This basic principle of "rule by status" helps to explain why harsh practices were sometimes used to discipline people in Tokugawa villages, and it also helps us understand why the *rōnanushi* often resorted to cruelty in order to keep other inmates in line. Of course, the fact that the jail rooms were not generally populated by "honest villagers" only exacerbated this tendency. Looking back on his experiences there, Takano later described the atmosphere in the jailhouse as reminiscent of the Warring States period—with desperate men spurring each other on and learning to laugh in the face of impending doom.[26] Given this, it is hardly surprising that the *rōnanushi*, like the great warlords of that era, found terror to be a useful tool of government.

Yet, while terror certainly helped to keep inmates in line and to establish the authority of the *rōnanushi*, it required more than this alone to run the jail rooms. In addition to ensuring that the official "rules of the jailhouse" were upheld, the *rōnanushi* was also responsible for keeping count of inmates, enforcing sleeping and waking times, checking for signs of disease, obtaining medicine, distributing food, cleaning utensils, and managing the latrines. To assist with these various tasks, an elaborate, formally constituted hierarchy of "inmate-officials" *(rōnai yakunin; yakunin shūjin)* served under him. Their titles and specific responsibilities varied somewhat over time, but the following list of Bakufu-approved positions for the great jail gives some sense of the range of duties they performed:

1. The jail room "deputy" (soeyaku; kashirayaku) had overall responsibility for sick prisoners and any others who required special care or attention.
2. The "corner official" (sumiyaku) supervised all entries and departures and was responsible for keeping track of inmate numbers.
3. The "number two official" (niban yaku) assisted the corner official.
4. The "number three official" (sanban yaku) was responsible for caring for sick inmates and distributing medicine to them.
5. The "number four official" (yonban yaku) was responsible for ensuring that inmates were properly clothed.
6. The "number five official" (goban yaku) was in charge of the bowls used to measure and serve food.
7. The "primary official" (honyaku) served the food and distributed it to the inmates.
8. The "assistant to the primary official" (honyakusuke) was responsible for washing and preparing the bowls and other utensils for use.
9. The "overseer of utensils" (gokiguchiban) distributed and counted the utensils and provided general assistance at meal times.
10. The "overseer of the latrines" (tsume no honban) was responsible for the latrines at the back of the jail room.
11. The "assistant to the overseer of latrines" (tsume no sukeban) helped supervise the latrines and also nursed sick inmates.[27]

Inmates who had served as officials during a previous stay at Kodenmachō or whom the rōnanushi considered worthy of special respect could also be incorporated into the jail room hierarchy as "retired" or "cloistered" officials (inkyo). In spite of the fact that he entered the jail without any money, Yoshida Shōin, for example, found himself appointed to the position of "senior retiree" (kamiza no inkyo) because the rōnanushi in the upper room where he was imprisoned was familiar with his reputation as a thinker and activist.[28]

In addition to ensuring that basic chores were carried out, the elaborate system of prisoner-officials was crucial for the organization of space in the jail rooms. To mark his authority over the other inmates, it was customary for the rōnanushi to perch himself high up off the floor on a stack of ten or more tatami mats. This also allowed him to keep watch over the other inmates, who were divided into four main groups. The two or three highest-ranking inmate-officials were known as "upper seats" (kamiza), and within the perennially overcrowded jail rooms they were usually able to claim space equivalent to one full tatami mat each. Most of the other inmate-officials were either "middle seats" (nakaza), who shared a single mat between two people, or "lower seats" (shimoza), who shared a single mat between three or four. Inmates in these three categories also marked their positions in the hierarchy by elevating themselves on stacks of two or, in the case of the upper seats, sometimes even three or four mats. All of the other inmates were referred to collectively as "small seats" *(koza)*, but they too were further divided up into a number of subcategories. Most squeezed together into a space known as the "far road" *(mukō dōri)* where it was usual for seven or eight people to share a single tatami mat. New inmates who arrived in the jail room with sufficient amounts of money were treated as "guests" *(kyakubun)* of the *rōnanushi* and granted appropriate positions within the jail room hierarchy. Most others spent their first night in the jail room sleeping on the hard wooden or earthen floor from which the mats in the *rōnanushi*'s tower had been taken.[29]

In many ways, this hierarchical allocation of space in the jail rooms formed a neat parallel to the intricate manifestations of rank that played such an important part in the lives of warriors in the Tokugawa period. When the daimyo were called to audiences with the shogun, for example, they too were expected to seat themselves in accordance with a strictly policed hierarchy of power and prestige.[30] Even more striking, however, is the similarity between the physical organization of the jail rooms and the layout of the great urban centers of the Tokugawa period. Just as the jail rooms were organized around the *rōnanushi* seated high up on his tower of tatami mats, so too were most Tokugawa era towns organized around a castle or fort, which served as a constant reminder of the presence and power of the warrior lord inside. And, just as the *rōnanushi* granted extra mats and space to his inmate-officials, so too did the warrior lords set aside large tracts of land near their castles for the residences of their lieutenants and retainers. More than just rewards for service, these residences were always carefully placed, with a lord's closest allies assigned to the most important strategic positions.[31] This too corresponds to the pattern followed in the jail rooms, where the *rōnanushi*'s most trusted officials were always seated around the door in order to prevent escapes. Finally, just as most inmates were crammed into one small corner of the jail room, so too were ordinary townsfolk confined to a tiny portion of available land in Tokugawa cities. According to Andrew Fraser, the town wards of Edo had "the highest population densities ever recorded for regular habitation—67,317 persons per square kilometer," the citywide equivalent of seven or eight men to a tatami mat.[32]

The point here is not to imply that the layout of the jail rooms was ever *consciously* modeled after the castle towns or grand warrior rituals, but rather to suggest that the principles of the status system formed a recurring motif in the fabric of Tokugawa society. It is not my intention to suggest that the jailhouse can stand perfectly for the larger social formation. This was, after all, a closed space, in which conditions could be controlled and the will of those in power imposed with relative ease. Precisely for this reason, however, it has helped us gain a clearer understanding of the fundamental principles and strategies of rule by status, in a situation where they operated in something close to their ideal form.

PUNISHMENT IN STATUS SYSTEM SOCIETY

Layers of Authority

One important consequence of the organization of society into semiautonomous communities was that the administration of punishments in a broad sense was never the exclusive concern of warrior officialdom. We have already noted that village headmen were expected to play a central role in policing their own communities, but in keeping with this responsibility, they were also formally permitted to use a range of minor punishments including fines, ostracism (mura hachibu), and banishment from the village (mura barai) to deal with local troublemakers. In some cases, warrior officials (like the guards at Kodenmachō) were willing to turn a blind eye to far more extreme examples of community justice. Kikuchi Isao has noted that in periods of prolonged famine it was common for authorities in the northeastern part of the country to ignore systematically (and sometimes even to encourage) spates of what were, in effect, lynchings of thieves and beggars.[33] Even when normal social conditions prevailed, it was not unheard of for village leaders to take "justice" into their own hands or to cover up crimes in order to avoid trouble for themselves or other villagers.[34] Officially, whenever a serious crime was committed, village officials were required to defer to the warrior authorities, and those who failed to do so were themselves liable for punishment. Article 59 of the One Hundred Articles stipulated that village officials who failed to report assaults, murders, or suspicious deaths were to be fined and removed from their posts, and from the late seventeenth century there are occasional examples of village headmen who were executed by the warrior state for ordering the deaths of criminals.[35]

Because there was no independent police or judicial system, criminal cases that could not be dealt with at the village level were reported directly to regular administrative officials within the warrior state. Their responsibilities too tended to run along status lines: at the very highest echelons of warrior society, cases involving the daimyo were handled by the Bakufu's great inspectors (ōmetsuke), while matters relating to lesser-ranking shogunal retainers were the responsibility of ordinary inspectors (metsuke). For nonwarrior groups, townsfolk generally fell under the authority of the town governors (machi bugyō); priests, nuns, and others connected with religious institutions were the responsibility of the governors of temples and shrines *(jisha bugyō)*; and peasants were supervised by rurally based intendants *(daikan)* who, in Bakufu lands, answered directly to the governors of accounts *(kanjō bugyō)*.

In practice, of course, things were not always so straightforward. For one thing, because most status groups were tied to particular physical spaces, authority over the group generally also entailed responsibility for certain areas of land. Peasants who lived and farmed land controlled by a large Buddhist temple might thus fall under the authority of the governor of temples and shrines rather than that of the governor for accounts. Physical mobility meant, moreover, that crimes committed in any one place often involved persons from multiple jurisdictions. In such cases, a warrior official's right even to investigate the crime depended entirely on his place within the Bakufu's bureaucratic hierarchy. The rural intendants, who had relatively little independent authority, were automatically required to turn over cases involving multiple jurisdictions to the governor of accounts.[36] By contrast, the town governors of Edo could generally investigate crimes that took place in areas under their control almost regardless of the status and place of origin of the persons involved. Even they were not allowed to venture beyond the limits of their own jurisdiction, however, and as a result they were usually unable to investigate crimes in those large sections of the capital that were assigned to the warrior households and religious institutions.[37]

Separate again from the question of which official had the right to investigate a particular crime was the issue of who could determine how it would be punished. In general, as noted in chapter 1, the more serious the crime, the higher up the warrior chain of command it had to be taken for final judgment.[38] The rural intendants, again, had virtually no independent judicial authority. As a result, when they finished investigating a crime or incident that had taken place within a community in their charge, they were required to turn their findings over to the governors of accounts for judgment. Like the governors of temples and shrines and the town governors of Edo, the governors of accounts had the independent authority to order punishments up to the level of "medium banishment."[39] In cases that seemed to warrant severer measures than this, however, or in which there was some doubt about how to proceed, the governors deferred to the senior councillors *(rōjū)*, who, in the latter half of the period, effectively headed the warrior government. They, in turn, could refer cases to the Deliberative Council *(Hyōjōsho)*, a body consisting of the incumbents of the three governorships mentioned previously, together with the senior councillors, the inspectors, and the great inspectors. If, ultimately, it was determined that a criminal was to be executed or sent into exile, then the formal approval of the shogun himself was also required before a case could be closed.[40]

Overall then, the power to punish was distributed broadly across the various layers of authority in status system society, starting with local community officials and stretching up to the senior councillors and, ultimately, the shogun. No matter which officials ended up passing judgment on a crime, however, the status of the persons involved was always a key factor in determining how it was investigated and punished.

Differential Punishment

From the beginning of any official investigation the principle of differential treatment according to status found concrete expression in the way people were positioned during formal questioning at the "courtyards of white sand." High-ranking warriors were often sentenced without any questioning at all so as to spare them the indignity of having to appear in a space used to interrogate commoners and criminals.[41] Those who did receive a summons were allowed to sit up on tatami matting in the same room as the governor or other presiding official. Others whose status was not quite high enough to merit a place in the same room as the presiding governor sat just outside on the floorboards of a wooden veranda. Several steps below them, on the actual courtyard of white sand, was the area where commoners and, even further away from the governor, outcasts were required to sit.[42]

Of course, status determined far more than just where a person sat during formal questioning. For one thing, there were a number of punishments reserved specifically for members of particular status groups. Commoners, for example, were the only ones who could be fined by the Bakufu. They could also be put in handcuffs for up to one hundred days or, in the case of the townsfolk, ordered to shut down their shops for a fixed period. Priests (in particular those found guilty of lechery) could be sentenced to special forms of public humiliation. There were also various kinds of house arrest specific to particular status groups. By far the best-known example of a status-specific punishment, however, is the notorious *seppuku*, or "suicide by disembowelment" for warrior men. In spite of its name and reputation, when practiced as an official Tokugawa punishment, this was, in fact, little more than a ritualized form of beheading, involving neither genuine suicide nor actual disembowelment; once the condemned warrior had readied himself, he simply reached toward a symbolic wooden sword to signal the executioner to proceed.[43] Like the beheading of commoners, *seppuku* was usually conducted within the grounds of the jailhouse complex or in special cases (including that of the famous "forty-seven samurai") behind the walls of a daimyo mansion. Warriors, however, were also the one group in Tokugawa society who could be sentenced to public beheading *(zanzai)*. This was, in effect, the most serious punishment inflicted on warriors, who were generally spared the indignity of burning alive or crucifixion. As with these other severe forms of capital punishment, it was usually carried out at one of the execution grounds in Edo and was often preceded by a dramatic parade through the streets of the city.[44] The execution itself followed essentially the same procedures used for other forms of beheading, except that a condemned warrior was never blindfolded, and his headless corpse could not be used for sword trials.[45]

Warriors also enjoyed a number of other legal privileges. Article 71 of the One Hundred Articles famously recognized the customary right of warriors to strike down on the spot any commoner who behaved disrespectfully toward them. In practice this right was upheld only under fairly limited circumstances. Even so, the ability to commit legal murder remained an important symbol of warrior power. No commoner could ever be sure that the two swords a warrior wore to mark his status position would not, at some point, be put to use in this way.[46]

In spite of their various privileges, however, the warriors' position atop the status hierarchy was no guarantee of lenient treatment. In fact, as a general rule, they were held to a higher standard of behavior than their social inferiors. Warriors who failed to confess their crimes honestly and directly during interrogations could expect to meet with particularly harsh treatment for having displayed "an attitude unsuitable for a person of [high] status."[47] They were also less likely to receive pardons and more likely to be punished severely for relatively minor crimes.[48] Whereas commoners were executed for theft only if the value of what they had stolen was particularly large, or if there were other aggravating circumstances, for warriors the customary rule was that *any* theft was punishable with death "regardless of the circumstances." This general principle was reiterated clearly in a judgment handed down by the Deliberative Council in 1819: "Because of their high status, members of the warrior houses who commit thefts or other such evil acts are to be handled differently and *punished with considerably more severity* than townsfolk or peasants."[49]

There were, of course, many different ranks of warrior, and in some cases the "foot soldiers" *(ashigaru)* and "lackeys" *(chūgen)*, who filled the lowest rungs of the warrior hierarchy were exempted from these higher standards.[50] A Bakufu judgment from 1807, for example, noted that "even among warrior retainers, when foot soldiers and lackeys commit theft, they are punished in the same way as townsfolk and peasants."[51] Yet, a series of regulations issued during the Kansei Reforms of the 1790s to crack down on gambling make it clear that even the lowliest warrior retainers were sometimes affected adversely by the principle of differential punishment. Under the first set of regulations, issued in 1792, foot soldiers and lackeys who engaged in any kind of gambling were to be automatically banished from the capital.[52] Although this was not as severe as the punishment stipulated for higher-ranking warriors (they were to be exiled to a distant island), it was undoubtedly a heavier penalty than the fines ordinarily used to punish commoners who gambled.[53] In 1795, moreover, the Bakufu supplemented the earlier regulations with a decree stating that all warriors, including foot soldiers and lackeys, would automatically be exiled to a distant island if they were caught gambling within the grounds of their lord's mansion.[54] All of this is highly suggestive of the way in which the warrior mansions in Edo, which were outside the status-based jurisdiction of the town governors, came to form safe havens for criminal activity in the capital, but it also offers clear evidence of how, even for low-ranking servants, the formal status divide between commoners and warriors could have serious consequences.

Further insight into the principle of differential punishment can be gained from a consideration of the treatment of women under Tokugawa law. In stark contrast to male inmates, women at Kodenmachō, regardless of status, were usually held together in one of the "upper rooms" in the main jailhouse. This was partly just a matter of practicality. Women made up a small portion of the overall inmate population, and given the limited space available at Kodenmachō, it simply did not make sense to maintain a series of separate rooms for them along status lines. But it was also indicative of the fact that women were, in some respects, treated collectively as a kind of *trans*-status group under Tokugawa law. There were, for example, a number of official punishments specifically for women, which cut across status lines. One of these punishments, shaving of the head *(teihatsu)*, was commonly used in cases of adultery *(fugi)*, which, as noted in chapter 1, was an offense for married women but not married men.[55] According to Mega Atsuko's analysis of records from Okayama, women of all status groups were more likely to be punished for this crime than any other in the Tokugawa period. Yet her research also suggests that women, like men, were held to different standards of behavior according to their status designations. Adultery accounted for about 39 percent of the criminal cases involving commoner women, but for warrior women the figure was more than twice as high (82 percent).[56] Because of the emphasis that warrior households placed on honor, moreover, warrior women who were caught with their paramours were also far more likely to be struck down on the spot by their husbands. And if they escaped their husband's initial wrath, they were likely to receive far harsher punishments from the warrior authorities than commoner women. Mega cites examples from early in the period of unfaithful warrior wives who were sentenced to such extreme forms of punishment as burning alive and *gokumon*.[57] There are no such examples for commoners.

Unlicensed prostitution was another crime closely (though not exclusively) associated with women.[58] In Edo, those who sold sex without permission could be arrested either directly by warrior officials or, in a slight variation on the principle of "rule by status," by the licensed brothel keepers from the so-called pleasure district of Yoshiwara.[59] They had good reason to carry out their policing duties with some diligence, because an arrest not only protected their official monopoly but also served as a form of labor recruitment: the standard punishment for unlicensed prostitution was a term of three years of service in the pleasure district.[60] For the women involved, of course, three years of service in the pleasure quarters was, in effect, a kind of temporary slavery. And, in fact, women were the only group in Tokugawa Japan who could be formally punished with enslavement (*yakko; nuhikei*).[61] Often this meant a lifetime of menial service in the household of a high-ranking warrior or wealthy townsman, but in cases where there was no "master" willing to take on a woman slave, she would instead be sent to live in the jailhouse, where she would perform menial tasks during the day and sleep in one of the jail rooms at night.[62] In the first half of the period slavery was commonly used to punish the wives and daughters of men who had committed serious crimes such as murder, arson, robbery, kidnapping, and, in some cases, even gambling. With the compilation of the One Hundred Articles in the mid-eighteenth century, however, its use was formally restricted to women who had secretly passed through, or around, one of the Bakufu's checkpoints—and, in practice, its application seems to have declined sharply.[63]

This change was in keeping with a general decline in the practice of extending punishment for serious crimes to the relatives and other close associates of the individual offender. In the early part of the period any person who was sentenced to death by the Bakufu could expect that his or her children would also be severely punished. Sons of the accused were especially likely to accompany them to the grave.[64] In the case of commoners, the Bakufu began to curtail the use of this kind of punishment by association from early in the eighteenth century, and by the time the One Hundred Articles was completed, only the sons of parricides and traitors could still be punished for their parents' crimes. For warriors above the rank of foot soldier or lackey, however, the changes did not go so far. Even at the end of the period, the male heir of a midlevel warrior who had been sentenced to death could expect to be exiled to a distant island.[65] Other blood relatives were expected to relinquish all official duties and posts, and male in-laws were expected to refrain from appearing at audiences with their lord.[66] Warrior lords also were expected to take responsibility for crimes committed by their retainers by withdrawing from all involvement in public life and submitting a formal "inquiry" to the Bakufu about how they should proceed. In some cases a lord might be told that no further "restraint" was required on his part and that he should return to his regular duties, but in more serious cases he too might be stripped of his official posts and duties, or prohibited from appearing at audiences with the shogun.[67]

At one level, the enforcement of harsher punishments for warriors can be seen simply as a mechanism for maintaining discipline in what was, after all, a military organization. Yet, it is also important to recognize the ideological role that the punishment of warriors played in Tokugawa society. Warrior rule and the privileges that went with it were, after all, justified and legitimized in large part through the claim that warriors were morally superior. Harsh punishments served to bolster this notion in two different ways. On the one hand, they created a strong incentive for warrior men and women to maintain high standards of behavior. On the other hand, they provided the authorities with an opportunity to demonstrate to others that warriors who failed to meet such standards were not tolerated; this, no doubt, was the main reason why warriors alone continued to be beheaded at the public execution grounds rather than behind the walls of the jailhouse.[68]

Fuzzy Boundaries

As important as status divisions were for Tokugawa society, the boundaries between different groups were never completely closed. In some cases, people were able to subvert official regulations by "passing" as members of another group, but there were also times when movement between different status groups was formally sanctioned by the warrior regime.[69] Commoners who demonstrated bravery or other virtues considered worthy of a warrior might, for example, find themselves promoted to warrior status and awarded concomitant privileges.[70] Prominent villagers too were sometimes promoted to warrior status so that they could help with the task of governing a particular locality, and in the latter half of the period, as the commercial economy grew, wealthy commoners were increasingly able to buy their way into warrior households.[71] This development has often been taken as evidence of a gradual breakdown of the "static" Tokugawa social order in the face of an increasingly dynamic market economy, but it can just as easily be seen as proof of the ongoing relevance of the status system and its usefulness to the ruling elite as a mechanism for coping with economic and social change. Allowing the occasional commoner to join their ranks not only provided individual warriors with a way of raising funds; it also meant a fresh input of blood and talent into the warrior houses.

Over the course of the period, the semipermeable nature of status boundaries also came to serve the interests of the warrior lords in another way—allowing them to hire commoners to serve as retainers "on contract." This was particularly important in the context of the system of "alternate attendance," under which the lords were required to maintain permanent residences in Edo and to make regular trips back to their own domainal headquarters. By hiring servants and retainers locally in Edo, they were able to reduce the crippling costs involved in traveling to and fro with large retinues of hereditary warrior servants.[72] Already in the early eighteenth century specialist employment agencies called *hitoyado* had sprung up all over Edo to help place commoners in warrior households, and as demands on daimyo finances mounted over time, the importance of the role that hired servants and retainers played in most of the great warrior mansions of the capital steadily increased.[73]

In order for them to be able to fulfill their duties, commoners hired to serve in a warrior household were usually extended the same privileges as hereditary warrior retainers of the same rank, including the right to wear two swords. Once their term of employment expired, however, these privileges were revoked, and the hired retainers reverted to their former status as ordinary townsfolk. In effect, they lived between status groups, traversing the fuzzy boundary that separated low-ranking warriors and commoners. In the context of a system of differential punishments, this kind of multilayered existence gave rise to an interesting question: were hired retainers who committed crimes during their term of employment to be punished as townsfolk or warriors? In 1804 a man named Yasuzō provided the warrior authorities in Edo with an opportunity to provide a clear answer to this question.

Yasuzō was a townsman who had been hired through an employment agency to serve as a valet *(kachi)* in the household of Asahina Yatarō Yasunari, one of the shogun's bannermen.[74] One evening, while waiting for Asahina to return from a visit to his son-in-law, Yasuzō suggested to a fellow retainer that they steal a short sword that had been left sitting near the entrance way they were guarding. According to the Bakufu's case report, the other man refused to go along with the plan, but Yasuzō would not be deterred. He later returned on his own to take the sword and then pawned it for a modest sum (1 *bu* 400 *mon*). He immediately spent the money on food and drink but was arrested for the theft soon afterward, thanks, no doubt, to information provided by the other retainer.

The official investigation of the case was conducted by the office of the town governor, who, in his initial report on the matter, firmly rejected the notion that Yasuzō should be given lenient treatment because he was a hired hand. Starting in the 1770s, the governor's report noted, the Bakufu had repeatedly issued instructions to the warrior houses stating that with regard to illegal or improper behavior even those who had been hired to work for monthly or daily terms were to be held to the same standards as ordinary, hereditary retainers. It had also made a point of punishing hired retainers caught gambling in the warrior mansions in the same manner as other warriors. Given this, the governor concluded, it was only logical that Yasuzō, who had committed theft while serving as a warrior retainer, should be punished in accordance with the basic principle that "all thefts by persons of warrior status are deserving of the death penalty, regardless of the circumstances." When the case was forwarded to the Deliberative Council, the town governor's colleagues there expressed some doubts about his recommendation: his own report had noted a case from 1768 in which a *hereditary* retainer was spared the death penalty after stealing a ladle and a chicken from a *sake* brewer. Yasuzō's crime was admittedly more serious than this. He had stolen a sword from his own lord. Even so, as a *hired* retainer, perhaps he should be treated more leniently. Instead of being punished with death, they asked whether he might not be exiled to a distant island, the normal punishment for commoners who stole from their employers. In response to these doubts, the town governor reiterated what he saw to be the key issue in the case: if hired retainers were not held to the same standards as their hereditary counterparts, they would have no reason to think of their employers as true masters and would inevitably fail to take their responsibilities seriously. Precisely in order to avoid this, he argued, the Bakufu had upheld the right of even *hired* warrior retainers to strike down commoners who behaved improperly toward them. By the same token, they should also be punished according to the same rules as their hereditary comrades. Otherwise a bad example would be set for all the "lowly drifters" who sought occasional employment in the warrior houses. In the end, the other council members concurred with this reasoning, and Yasuzō was sentenced to death.

As in other societies characterized by profound structural inequality, the rebellious and disobedient behavior of retainers and servants was an ongoing source of concern for the warrior elite in Tokugawa Japan, and the problem was made all the more difficult by the relative scarcity of labor in the castle towns.[75] For most of the period, warrior lords simply could not be particular about whom they employed. Understood in this context, the case of Yasuzō suggests that the logic of the status system provided masters of the warrior elite with a valuable weapon in their struggle to maintain order within their own households. It allowed them to insist that commoners who served them meet higher standards than would usually be expected and to threaten those who failed to do so with particularly severe penalties.

Status as Punishment: The Hinin

While even temporary changes in status could thus affect the way a person was punished for a crime, in other cases a change in status could itself serve as a form of official punishment. Warriors could be stripped of their privileges and reduced to commoner status, and commoners could be banished from mainstream society and forced to live as members of the *hinin* outcast group. This punishment, known as *hinin teka* (literally, "under the hand of the *hinin*") is best remembered in Japan today as the penalty for lovers who failed in their attempts to commit double suicide, but it was used also for a range of other crimes, including some forms of incest, gambling, and even assault. In practical terms, being punished with *hinin teka* meant being assigned to one of the special "beggars huts," which served as the basic "container units" for the *hinin* status group. There were at least seven hundred such huts scattered across the city of Edo in the latter half of the period, and each of them was headed by an individual hut boss *(koya gashira)*. They, in turn, fell under the general authority of the capital's four *hinin* chiefs—the most powerful of whom were Kuruma Zenshichi of Asakusa and Matsuemon of Shinagawa.[76] The *hinin* huts were all assigned different areas of the city within which their members were allowed to collect alms from local households at special occasions such as births, marriages, and funerals. They did not beg randomly. Indeed, from the point of view of the townsfolk, one of the *hinin*'s most important functions was to ensure that unregulated, "wild" beggars *(nohinin)* did not bother local residents. They were also responsible for cleaning up unclaimed corpses, animal carcasses, and other "unclean" objects from the areas where they had "begging rights." They collected waste paper and in some cases worked as street performers *(torioi)* or repaired leather sandals *(setta)*.[77]

In addition to these localized duties and services, the *hinin*, like other status groups, were also expected to perform a range of official duties for the warrior state. We have already seen that many of the duties assigned to outcasts generally were related to the administration of punishments, but it is worth noting that the *hinin*, in particular, were always an important presence at the Kodenmachō Jailhouse. Apart from the assistance they provided with the administration of official torture and punishments, *hinin* workers performed a wide range of other tasks: They cleaned the jailhouse and its grounds and disposed of the steady stream of executed and diseased corpses; they escorted prisoners of commoner status to and from the offices of the governors when they were called for questioning; and they worked as firefighters for the jailhouse.[78] Recruiting the workers needed to perform most of these everyday tasks was the responsibility of a *hinin* boss with the hereditary name of Chōbei, whose hut was located right next to the jailhouse on the banks of the moat that surrounded it.[79] Chōbei also sent the wives of *hinin* men in his charge to serve as "attendants" in the women's jail rooms. They took turns living in the jail rooms for periods of a month at a time and performed duties that were in some ways similar to those of the male inmate-officials: they provided general assistance to the officially appointed *rōnanushi* and helped her to maintain order. From the point of view of the jailhouse staff, however, their most important function was to perform official searches of the clothes, hair, and persons of new female inmates, a job considered inappropriate for male guards to carry out.[80]

One other task that the *hinin* provided assistance with was the care of sick inmates. As mentioned previously, prisoners who fell seriously ill in the jail rooms were often removed from Kodenmachō and sent to one of the hospices run by the *hinin* chiefs at Asakusa and Shinagawa. These hospices were originally established in the early eighteenth century to house travelers and others who were found sick in the streets of the capital, but they were soon being called upon to take in increasingly large numbers of sick prisoners.[81] The medical care provided was rudimentary, and death rates high, but by making it possible to remove diseased and dying prisoners they did at least help to ease conditions in the overcrowded jail rooms.[82]

In all of these ways the *hinin* clearly played an important role at Kodenmachō. Yet, it will have been noted from the earlier discussion of the organization of the jailhouse that no mention was made of outcasts being imprisoned there. This is because they hardly ever were.

Outcast as Lord (and Executioner): Danzaemon

By the end of the first century of Tokugawa rule, responsibility for investigating, judging, and punishing almost all crimes that took place within outcast communities in Edo and the surrounding provinces had been given to Danzaemon, the *eta* chief whose rise to power was discussed in chapter 2. In contrast to the *hinin*, whose ranks continued to absorb new members throughout the period, the *eta* were a more strictly hereditary group who, in Edo, lived within the confines of a special walled compound, not unlike the Jewish ghettos of early modern Europe. Within the *eta* compound Danzaemon ruled supreme. His official residence included its own "courtyard of white sands" for questioning outcasts involved in crimes or disputes, and nearby there were a number of special "legal inns" for outcasts who had been summoned from country areas. There was also a special jailhouse adjacent to his residence, and it was here, rather than at Kodenmachō, that *eta*, *hinin*, and all other outcasts suspected of wrongdoing were usually imprisoned.[83]

Within his realm, Danzaemon had the independent authority to order punishments up to the level of the standard Tokugawa death penalty. This meant, in other words, that he had more independent power over the outcasts in his charge than the Bakufu's governors had over the commoners they investigated. Of course, there were some limits on his judicial authority. Most important, Danzaemon did not have the right to investigate or judge any case that involved a person from other jurisdictions or status groups *(taryō tashihai no mono)*.[84] If an outcast was accused of stealing from a townsman in Edo, for example, the matter would have to be turned over to the town governor for adjudication. But if the presiding governor came to the conclusion that the outcast in question should be punished for his crime, in all but the most serious cases he was handed back to Danzaemon for punishment within the confines of the "*eta* village."[85]

The outcasts were not the only group in Tokugawa society whose punishments were administered by a semi-independent figure like Danzaemon. A similar example is provided by the Tōdōza, a guildlike organization originally for blind musicians and performers, which came to function as a special kind of status group for a much broader group of blind people. The head of the Tōdōza in Edo carried the hereditary name Sōroku, and like Danzaemon, his right to punish members of the group was formally recognized in the One Hundred Articles. Katō Yasuaki's detailed research on the Tōdōza suggests that punishments for its members were generally less severe than those used for ordinary commoners, but there were exceptions.[86] Records from the late seventeenth century show that in the first half of the period Sōroku had the power to execute guild members using harsh and unusual methods such as burying alive (*ishikoume, ishikozume*) and drowning (*sumaki*).[87] In 1683, for example, a man named Okitsuichi was drowned in Edo Bay for killing the friend of a man he mistakenly suspected of sleeping with his wife. Following customary practice, he was wrapped up in a straw mat so that he could not move and then dumped over the side of a boat.[88] Just under a century later, in 1779, Sōroku was stripped of his power to order executions after a scandal caused the Bakufu leadership to question the arbitrary nature of Tōdōza justice, but even after this he continued to administer a range of lesser punishments from his official residence in Honjō until the very end of the period.[89]

While Sōroku's position as head of a group that lay outside mainstream Tokugawa society makes it logical to pair him with Danzaemon, the independent punishment rights that both of these figures enjoyed can also be compared directly with those of another set of semi-independent rulers—namely, the several hundred warrior lords with whom the Tokugawa shoguns shared territorial control of the country..

Punishment, Status, and the Tokugawa State

As a general principle, just as Danzaemon was able to investigate, judge, and punish the outcasts who fell under his authority, so too were the warrior lords entitled to investigate, judge, and punish the residents of their "private" fiefs and members of their retainer bands. However, they too were formally prohibited from investigating or judging cases that involved persons from other fiefs or jurisdictions. All such cases were to be turned over to the Bakufu, even when the incident took place in an area that was under the direct control of a warrior lord. In this sense, while the Bakufu's judicial authority may have been spread thicker in some areas than others, it did not simply stop at the borders of the hundreds of private fiefs that spread like patchwork across the country. Of prime importance for this aspect of the Bakufu's "national" authority were the governors of temples and shrines, who handled cases referred to the Bakufu by warrior lords from beyond the Kantō plain, and the governors of accounts, who handled cases from within the Kantō, where an especially complex hodgepodge of small fiefs and fragments of fiefs were concentrated together.[90]

As was the case within the ranks of Bakufu officialdom, in practice the position a lord held within the larger warrior hierarchy helped determine the extent of his punishment powers. The most important and obvious divide lay between the daimyo, whose lands were on record as yielding a total of more than ten thousand *koku* of rice a year, and the shogunal bannermen, whose fiefs were smaller than this. In the early part of the period all bannermen had the authority to sentence criminals from their own fiefs to death, but by the second half of the eighteenth century only the very highest ranking of them retained the ability to authorize punishments more severe than banishment from the fief.[91] In other words, they were generally unable to order any type of death penalty, exile, or serious form of banishment. In the case of most serious offenses, moreover, both the investigations and the administration of punishments came to be handled by the Bakufu.[92]

In contrast to this, at the end of the seventeenth century the Bakufu formally confirmed the right of the daimyo to judge and punish crimes independently in their domains using *any and all* of the punishments administered by the shogun in Edo.[93] Even among the daimyo, however, there were vast differences in terms of domain size, power, and prestige, and as Hiramatsu's research has made clear, this had a direct impact on their willingness to make full use of their formal rights. Of particular importance in this regard were the punishments of crucifixion and burning alive, which the lords of smaller domains were often reluctant to use for fear that they would be seen to be acting above their station.[94] This reluctance was reflected in two ways. First, most small and medium-sized domains went out of their way to double-check with the senior councillors in Edo before proceeding with such punishments. This tendency increased steadily over time, leading the Deliberative Council to recommend in 1811 that the senior councillors simply refuse to entertain all future "inquiries" from the daimyo about matters that were clearly within their established rights to decide independently. The recommendation was rejected in the end, but it is nevertheless significant for what it suggests about the position of the smaller domains vis-à-vis Edo in the latter part of the period.[95]

Even more striking than the practice of double-checking with the Bakufu was the tendency for some small domains to avoid the problem of crucifixion and burning alive altogether by consistently choosing to sentence criminals to less severe punishments. Records from Komoro, a small domain in the Shinano region, are instructive in this regard. Between 1794, when the records begin, and 1871, when the domain was formally abolished, not a single person was sentenced to die by crucifixion or burning alive. This was not for a lack of suitable candidates.[96] In 1844, for example, a Buddhist priest was murdered by one of his disciples. Under Tokugawa law, this was considered a form of treason (*gyakuzai*) and, had it taken place on Bakufu lands, the culprit would almost certainly have been paraded through the streets of the town and crucified. In order to avoid the trouble of sending a formal inquiry to Edo, however, officials in Komoro decided instead to sentence him to the lesser punishment of *gokumon*. In justifying their decision, officials from the domain noted that it was in keeping with "our domain's established practices" (*kahō shikitari*), and they also cited a precedent from 1794 in which an arsonist had been sentenced to the standard death penalty rather than burning alive for the same reason.[97]

Taken in isolation, such decisions to avoid the use of extreme punishments might simply be seen as evidence of benevolence on the part of domain officials. Yet, on closer examination, it becomes clear that the ability to order harsh punishments was an important marker of status among the daimyo in much the same way that the right to bear two swords was for individual warriors in the broader society. Consider the following passage written in the early Meiji period by a proud former retainer of the Aizu domain:

> Under the Bakufu's system each of the great lords had punishments that they could and could not conduct. . . . The lords of small domains could not sentence people to death without the Bakufu's permission, and apart from Owari, Kii, and Mito, all of the other domains needed permission from the Bakufu to carry out crucifixions. The only exception to this rule was our domain. For us it was sufficient to notify the Bakufu after the crucifixion had been completed. Beginning from the time when Lord [Hoshina Masayuki] . . . arrested thirty-six [leaders of the Shiraiwa peasant rebellion] and crucified them without hesitation . . . this [special privilege] became a permanent marker of the rank of all subsequent generations [of Aizu lords].[98]

The three other domains mentioned here, Owari, Kii, and Mito, were the branch houses (*gosanke*) of the main Tokugawa line, and Hoshina Masayuki, founder of the Matsudaira line of Aizu Domain, was half brother of the third Tokugawa shogun, Iemitsu. What this passage implies, therefore, is that only those domains with particularly strong ties to the shogunal household had the independent authority to order crucifixions. Hiramatsu's research shows that this was simply not true. If small domains were reluctant to make full use of their powers, larger domains generally did so with confidence, regardless of the history of their relations with the Tokugawa house. Records from Tottori, one of the large "outside" domains that had not been a formal ally of the Tokugawa during the Warring States period, show that between 1801 and 1848 it conducted at least twelve executions by "pulling the saw" and crucifixion, and eleven by burning alive. In none of these cases was any effort made formally to check with or even notify the Bakufu before the executions were carried out, and according to Hiramatsu, there is not a single example of such a communication being sent to Edo from any large domain for the duration of the period.[99]

All of this clearly has significant implications for our understanding of the structure of the Tokugawa polity. Most obviously, perhaps, it suggests that generalizations about daimyo autonomy should not be based solely on the examples of the large, powerful domains that historians of the period have most often studied. Beyond this, however, it also suggests that rather than resorting to anachronistic terms such as "Bakuhan" or "federal" to describe the nature of the Tokugawa state, we would be better off emphasizing the role of status as the central organizing principle of the warrior regime. This was not a simple two-tier system consisting of a central authority on the one hand and regional statelike entities on the other, but rather a vast and complex arrangement of powers and privileges.[100] In this regard, it was no coincidence that the number of persons crucified and burned alive by the Bakufu at the punishment grounds of Edo in a mere four years in the 1860s was greater than the number subjected to the same punishments in a large domain like Tottori over more than forty. Within the context of a political order in which the administration of extreme punishments was a symbol of power and prestige, the bodies-as-signs that were regularly posted at Suzugamori and Kotsukappara served not only to send warnings to potential criminals but also to mark the position of the shogun and his government at the top of the many layers and pockets of authority that characterized status system society.

If flamboyant displays of brutality and benevolence can both be seen as key points of difference with the "modern" world, then the organization of society around formal hierarchies of status and rank clearly represents another important example of the "pastness of the Tokugawa past." True social equality remains an elusive ideal to this day, of course, but in the Tokugawa period notions of citizenship and formal equality did not exist even as legal fiction. As we have seen, this had wide-ranging implications for almost all aspects of judicial and penal practice. Yet, as we have also seen, status in Tokugawa society cannot be understood solely in terms of hierarchies. It was also a strategy of rule, based on the careful division of society into self-policing "container" units. In this regard, it is useful to recall once more the figure of the *rōnanushi*, seated high up on his pile of tatami mats, and compare him with other authority figures—from village headmen to Danzaemon and the great warrior lords—all of whom were expected to maintain order within their own pockets of society. Of course, to argue that the principles of rule by status were pervasive and influential at all levels of society is not to suggest that they were in any way perfect or complete. The system was more flexible and powerful than many historians have given it credit for; but, like any other strategy of power, resistance and subversion were always present, and new pressures and tensions were constantly forcing responses, adjustments, and innovations. It is to the question of these pressures and the responses they invited that we turn next.

CHAPTER 4

Discourse, Dynamism, and Disorder:
The Historical Significance of the
Edo Stockade for Laborers

THE FIRST THREE CHAPTERS of this book have examined some of the broad principles that governed Tokugawa penal practices in the eighteenth and early nineteenth centuries. In general, these principles remained consistent over time, but Japanese society in the centuries preceding the Meiji Restoration was hardly static. As social conditions changed, new problems and tensions emerged, helping in turn to give rise to new ideas and critical discourses. This chapter begins by examining some of the critiques of the existing punishment system that were developed over the course of the eighteenth century. In addition to the important arguments of Ogyū Sorai (1666–1728) and his disciple Dazai Shundai (1680–1747), particular attention is given to an essay written in the 1780s by Nakai Riken (1732–1817), a scholar closely associated with Osaka's famous merchant academy, the Kaitokudō. Riken's *Jukkei bōgi* (Treatise on Merciful Punishment) is a relatively short piece, but it is of considerable interest, not least because its proposal for the creation of a new kind of jail—in which inmates would be put to work and inured to the habits of industry—may have had a direct impact on the Bakufu's decision to establish a special work camp, the Stockade for Laborers *(ninsoku yoseba)*, on an island in Edo Bay in 1790. As noted in the introduction, Japanese legal historians have often pointed to the Stockade for Laborers as an indigenous "forerunner" of the modern prison. At one level it is easy to understand why. This institution combined elements of confinement, forced labor, and moral exhortation to foster the "reform" of internees. Also, in the context of the Westernizing reforms of the early Meiji period, the grounds of the old stockade were eventually transformed into one of Tokyo's first "modern" prisons. Yet we should not overstate the extent to which it anticipated developments of the Meiji period or moved Japan in the direction of "modernity." While the establishment of the stockade was a significant development that can help us understand the nature of late Tokugawa society, this chapter argues that it must ultimately be viewed within its own historical context—as part of the particular dynamic of status system society rather than as an embryonic version of an institution that developed on the other side of the world in a different social context. Indeed, far from leading to or anticipating the dramatic transformation of the Tokugawa punishment system, the stockade came to function as a support to the existing system, helping to bolster the basic strategies of rule by status at a time when new kinds of disorder were threatening to undermine the Tokugawa order. To put this in more general terms, although important new ideas and institutions were being generated by the changes taking place in late Tokugawa society, there is no need to force them into a model of history that takes Western modernity and its forms as the normal and inevitable outcome of social development.

THE SPECTER OF DISORDER: OGYŪ SORAI AND DAZAI SHUNDAI

The first century of the *pax Tokugawa* had culminated in a period of unprecedented prosperity and cultural flowering, but in spite of this (and perhaps also because of it), by the early decades of the eighteenth century contemporary observers had begun to express concern about the state of various aspects of the society and its government, including the penal system. As noted in chapter 2, the shogunal adviser Arai Hakuseki was one of the first to criticize openly the existing state of Tokugawa punishments, calling for an end to harsh practices such as crucifixion and burning alive on the grounds that they were inappropriate for an age in which cruelty and killing were supposed to have been left behind. Hakuseki was not the last thinker of the period to suggest that Tokugawa punishments could be overly cruel. Yet, whereas the excesses of Tsunayoshi's reign had given him real reason for concern about the shogun's credentials as a "benevolent ruler," later thinkers increasingly took up the question of official punishments in conjunction with another issue: the warrior state's response to what many perceived to be unacceptable levels of social disorder.

Perhaps the clearest and most dramatic expression of the growing concern with social disorder is in the political writings of Ogyū Sorai, aguably the most influential of all Tokugawa thinkers.[1] In the opening sentence of his *Seidan* (Discourse on Government), written and presented to the seventh shogun, Yoshimune, in the mid-1720s, Sorai complained that people's lives and property were simply not safe under Tokugawa rule: "At the present time," he wrote, "houses are being broken into everywhere; criminals murder, steal, and commit arson; and in the middle of the night they lie waiting in deserted places to rob people."[2]

According to Sorai, one of the main reasons for the growth of disorder had been the decision taken at the end of the Warring States period to remove the warriors from the land and force them to live in the castle towns. As important as this policy may have been for the establishment of peace, the pleasures of city life had led to a dramatic decline in the warriors' martial spirit. The days when officials routinely cut criminals down on the spot were now long gone, and as a result, Sorai argued, potential trouble-makers no longer lived in fear of warrior authority. As the cities grew in size, moreover, and rules for conducting investigations became more com-plex, it became increasingly difficult for officials to cope with the sheer volume of disorder and petty crime. In this regard it is worth emphasizing just how few officials were actually involved in "policing" Tokugawa cities. At a time when the population of the capital exceeded a million people, the combined staff of the two Edo town governors consisted of no more than 80 officers and 240 functionaries. Their duties, moreover, were not limited to "policing" alone but included all aspects of urban administra-tion.[3] The Bakufu also appointed special inspectors for arson and theft (*hitsuke tōzoku aratame*) from among the shogun's personal guard (*sakite-gumi*), but as Sorai himself emphasized, their numbers were never sufficient to allow them to deal properly with a city the size of Edo.[4] In order to cope with the situation, Sorai noted that officials had instead come to rely heavily on networks of criminal informants and spies (*meakashi;* literally, "sharp eyes") who often abused their ties with officialdom so they could commit further villainous acts of their own.

Meanwhile, in the countryside, where the peasantry had been left largely unsupervised, conditions were, if anything, even worse. When a crime was committed, Sorai claimed, peasants were reluctant to report it to the proper authorities, in part because they lived in fear of Edo, but also because of the expenses they were likely to incur in the process. Further compounding the problem was the fact that peasants were increasingly lured away from the honest work of agriculture to pursue frivolity and "luxury." "As a result of this," Sorai argued, "the countryside is very much in decline, and gam-bling, theft, and other evil behavior cannot be stopped."[5]

In order to overcome these problems, Sorai urged the warrior lords to follow the example of the ancient sage-kings of China and strengthen the existing mechanisms for permanently fixing people in their proper place within society. In what was essentially an elaboration of one of the basic principles of rule by status, he argued that when people live out their lives within a single community, they are constantly watched by their relatives and friends and are reluctant to commit crimes out of consideration for those around them. So long as the local population remains stable, more-over, "there is no one whom the block or village headman does not know," and the principle of collective responsibility can be easily enforced.[6] It was precisely for this reason, Sorai explained, that China's ancient sages had first developed the system of "household registers" (*koseki*), carefully listing the official residence of every person in the realm. As we have seen, similar registers were already in use under the Tokugawa, but according to Sorai, they were simply not well enough maintained. It was essential, he argued, that every member of every household in the realm should be properly listed and that no one should be allowed to move or change their name without formal permission. Travelers, too, should all be required to carry with them a special road pass *(roin)*, so that even on the highways every person could be properly accounted for. In the capital Sorai suggested that more effective checkpoints be established to restrict people's movements at night, especially in the warrior districts, where the existing guardhouses *(tsujiban)* were largely ineffectual.[7] Most important of all, he argued that the overall population of the capital should be reduced to a more manageable level by repatriating *(hitogaeshi)* recent immigrants to their home provinces and resettling them in stable communities on the land.[8] At the same time, of course, he advocated returning warrior retainers to their individual fiefs in the countryside, so that they could directly govern and supervise the activities of the local peasantry.[9]

The basic thrust of Sorai's proposals for overcoming disorder was thus to strengthen the state's power to police and control people's movements. As he himself summed up, "the difference between good and bad government is the difference between having and not having all the people of the realm under one's control."[10] This belief was also to inform his critique of the Tokugawa punishment system.

In keeping with his reputation as a scholar of the great legal traditions of China, Sorai framed his discussion of Tokugawa punishments in terms of a comparison with Chinese practices from the age of the ancient sage-kings up until the end of the Tang dynasty (618–907).[11] On this basis he pointed to various problems with the existing system in Japan, but the single most important aspect of his critique concerned the widespread use of banishment *(tsuihō)*. According to Sorai, there were no precedents for this punishment in either ancient China or Japan. Instead, its origins could be traced back to the Warring States period, when the country had been divided up among hundreds of feuding warlords concerned only with their own individual territories. For them, the act of expelling criminals and other troublemakers into neighboring areas made good sense. It provided an easy alternative to executions, and in some cases it may also have served a strategic purpose by causing disruption in the territory of a rival lord.[12] In an age of peace, however, the continuation of such a practice was wholly counterproductive. By sentencing a person to banishment, officials were effectively removing him or her from all of the networks of collective responsibility and surveillance that formed the basis of status system society, and which Sorai had already suggested needed to be tightened up. Set free to roam the countryside as "runaways" *(kakeochinin, bōmeisha)*, such persons inevitably drifted toward the capital, and Sorai argued that it was largely because of this that the city had increasingly become "a haven for thieves." In reality, of course, the reasons for the growth of petty crime in Tokugawa cities were more complex than this, but Sorai had clearly pinpointed an important contradiction. Far from discouraging crime, the widespread use of banishment was in fact more likely to contribute to the spread of disorder by forcibly removing people from their communities and setting them on the road to rootlessness and destitution. The problem was exacerbated by the fact that it was not only the Bakufu that made use of banishment; it had also remained a standard punishment in most of the several hundred daimyo domains and bannerman fiefs and even occurred at the local level in the form of "expulsion from the village" *(mura barai)*. Some of those driven out of their home communities each year were, no doubt, eventually able to settle elsewhere, but particularly in times of economic hardship there were inevitably many who could not. Thus, Sorai insisted, the use of banishment had "led to a constant increase in the numbers of criminals."[13]

In order to solve this problem, Sorai argued that banishment should be abolished and replaced with "penal servitude" *(zuzai, tozai)*, one of the "five official punishments" used by successive Chinese dynasties from the sixth century on.[14] The advantages of this punishment were great, he suggested. Prisoners could be used to perform a range of useful tasks (in China they were generally put to work on construction projects or in the salt and iron mines), and by varying the length of time that each individual spent in "servitude," the punishment could be made to fit a wide range of crimes. Also, instead of being set loose to wander the countryside and create new problems elsewhere, criminals sentenced to penal servitude would remain under close supervision in a single place.[15] Eventually, when their terms were up, they would be returned to a stable position within a community, with their names carefully entered into the local household register and their every action monitored by neighbors and elders alike. Although it was never taken up by the Bakufu, the idea of replacing banishment with "penal servitude" was to generate considerable interest in the latter part of the Tokugawa period, particularly in a small handful of the daimyo domains where there was strong interest in Chinese legal scholarship.[16]

Toward the end of the 1720s one of Sorai's most talented students, Dazai Shundai, penned a more extensive and in many ways more radical proposal for reform in his essay, *Keizairoku* (On Political Economy).[17] Shundai agreed with his teacher that the use of banishment was one important "cause of chaos and disorder" in the country, but even more important for him was the fact that Tokugawa punishments had lost their power to strike fear into the hearts of the common people.[18] One of the main reasons for this, he argued, was the proliferation of pardons; would-be criminals were no longer scared of official punishments because they knew that even if they were caught, there was a good chance they would be given a reprieve. As we have seen in chapter 2, the use of pardons and amnesties can be understood as part of the warrior state's strategy for projecting an aura of official benevolence, but like Suzuki Shōsan a century earlier, Shundai insisted that the state's reluctance to execute prisoners was entirely misplaced. After all, he argued, were not China's ancient sage-kings, in their great wisdom, known to have made widespread use of capital punishment on the basis of the principle that "by killing one you allow ten thousand to live"? A squeamish attitude to executions, he noted, was often justified by second-rate scholars who pointed to a passage in Mencius, which stated that a king who takes pleasure in killing will never be able unite his realm.[19] According to Shundai, this passage clearly referred only to the indiscriminate killing of innocent subjects and not to the execution of criminals. And, he argued, while it was true that a ruler should not recklessly kill people, he should not recklessly allow them to live either: "To kill those who would harm the good and disturb the peace, directly and without pardon, is a matter of basic importance for government."[20]

Of course, Shundai did not believe that *all* criminals should be executed. In fact, he argued that another reason why the use of pardons had become so widespread was that death had been made the official punishment for many crimes that clearly did not deserve it. When a benevolent warrior official realized that a criminal was likely to be punished in a manner that was out of proportion with his crimes, it was only natural that he would seek to have him pardoned—but if this meant that the criminal escaped punishment altogether, then the respect that the common people had for the law would inevitably be undermined. The obvious solution was to find good alternatives to capital punishment, but what should these be? Not surprisingly, Shundai, like his teacher, argued that Japanese officials should look to the example of Chinese legal traditions for inspiration. Yet, whereas Sorai advocated the introduction of "penal servitude," a punishment that had only become standard in China after the rise of the great centralized dynasties, Shundai believed that it was the decentralized rule of the ancient sage-kings that provided the best model for Tokugawa Japan, with its complex system of jurisdictions and layers of authority.

Under the ancient sages, Shundai noted, the "five official punishments" had originally been death, castration, amputation of the feet, amputation of the nose, and tattooing. The last four of these had been abolished under the centralized Han dynasty (206 B.C.E.—220 C.E.) on the grounds that they were unnecessarily cruel. Yet, if this were truly the case, Shundai asked, how could the great sage-kings of antiquity ever have condoned their use? The truth of the matter, he insisted, was that the ancients simply had a better understanding of the ways of men than any of their successors: they knew the common folk to be "immature, lowly people" *(shōjin)* who would only commit further crimes if not dealt with firmly, and they also understood that by leaving a permanent mark on the body, punishments such as castration, amputation, and tattooing not only ensured that the culprit himself never forgot his crime but also struck fear into the hearts of those who saw him. In the end, Shundai argued, no matter how severe the law is, if a punishment inflicts only temporary pain without leaving a permanent mark, it will not make a deep impression on the hearts of the common folk, and before long they will once again begin committing crimes.[21] For this reason, he concluded, it was imperative that the Tokugawa authorities introduce a range of punishments involving bodily mutilation, in particular, amputation of the ears, noses, and feet, as well as tattooing.[22]

The overall tenor of Shundai's reform proposals was clearly much harsher than Sorai's.[23] In some ways, however, the two thinkers' proposals were perhaps not as different as they initially seem. Like Sorai, Shundai ultimately saw household registers and self-policing communities as key to maintaining social order. For this reason he endorsed Sorai's proposal to abolish banishment, and in his call for the revival of harsh corporal punishments he was also quick to point out that under the ancient sages criminals sentenced to various forms of mutilation were never simply "discarded" by the state afterward. On the contrary, he stressed, they were always provided with special kinds of work to perform. Those who had been tattooed were given jobs guarding gates around the capital; those who had had their noses cut off were assigned to official checkpoints; those whose feet had been amputated worked in the stables; and the eunuchs, of course, guarded the inner palace, where the king's harem lived. As a result of this arrangement, those who had been punished returned to a stable place in the social order and were able to reflect fully upon their past errors without being pushed into crime again as a result of destitution.[24] This was the ideal that Shundai urged the warrior lords to emulate, and in this regard it is clear that he too was keen to ensure that the punishment system did not contribute to disorder by setting criminals adrift to wander the countryside after they had been punished.[25]

The reform proposals of both Sorai and Shundai ultimately reflected the broader mood of the time in which they were writing, and there can be little doubt that the early direction of Yoshimune's actual reform program influenced their general tone. From as early as 1721 Yoshimune and his advisers had agreed that efforts should be made to curtail the use of banishment, and in 1722 the daimyo were told to avoid expelling criminals into neighboring territories wherever possible.[26] Yoshimune had also been quick to demonstrate his belief in the value of corporal punishments, first by sanctioning a partial revival of amputation of noses and ears in 1718, and then in 1720 by replacing these older punishments with flogging and tattooing.[27] All of this was in keeping with his general determination to restore a sense of the robust warrior ethic that had been eroded by decades of peace and prosperity and to reassert the Bakufu's authority as a government to be feared.

By the end of his period in office, however, Yoshimune's reforms had done much less to address the basic concerns raised by Sorai and Shundai than they had initially promised. In spite of his early efforts to curtail its use, Yoshimune was ultimately unwilling (or unable) to abolish banishment, and when the *Kujikata Osadamegaki* was finally completed in the 1740s, it was given a central place in the Bakufu's list of officially approved punishments. While flogging and tattooing quickly became standard weapons in the warrior state's penal arsenal, Shundai's suggestion that more dramatic forms of corporal punishment be revived was never taken up. Nor were those punished in this way ever provided with special jobs to perform. Commoners who already belonged to a stable community when they were flogged or tattooed were usually handed over to a local headman or relative afterward, but those who had no one to take responsibility for them were simply "driven away" with a warning to stay out of trouble. In this sense, the basic contradiction that both Sorai and Shundai identified in the 1720s still remained: the punishment system continued to encourage rootlessness, and thereby undermined the very order it was supposed to maintain. Sixty years later this same problem would again be taken up, this time by Nakai Riken, who was to argue for a rather different solution.

NAKAI RIKEN AND THE "LONG-TERM JAIL"

Riken was the son of Nakai Shūan (1693–1758), one of the original founders of the Kaitokudō Academy, established in Osaka in 1726 on the basis of the new mercantile wealth generated in the city during the first century of Tokugawa rule. In his important study of the Kaitokudō, Tetsuo Najita notes that, in contrast to his older brother Chikuzan (1730–1804) who, as third head of the academy, actively sought to promote its influence within the broader polity, Riken was something of a recluse, who consciously chose to retreat into the private world of scholarship he referred to as his "kingdom of dreams."[28] This deliberate act of withdrawal, Najita suggests, was motivated by a profound sense of pessimism about the likelihood of meaningful political change under the Tokugawa. Yet, as his *Jukkei bōgi* makes clear, this sense did not preclude him from developing his own proposals for the reform of key aspects of the status quo.[29]

Riken began his treatise by noting that no system of government is ever so perfect that it can survive without occasional adjustments over time.[30] In spite of this obvious truth, he continued, the Bakufu's policies had remained largely unchanged in the centuries since Ieyasu's death, and as a result serious problems had now emerged. The punishment system provided a clear example of this. For Riken, as with Sorai before him, the most obviously anachronistic of all Tokugawa punishments was banishment. In an age in which the entire realm had been united under the authority of the shogun, a measure that simply moved criminals from one area to another without putting a stop to their activities made no sense at all, he argued.

Another serious problem in urgent need of reform was the extensive use of capital punishment. Although Riken stopped short of calling for complete abolition of the death penalty, he urged moderation in both the methods and the frequency of its use. A wise ruler, he argued, should only take the life of a subject with great reluctance, viewing it as an act akin to slicing off one of his own fingers. He also pointed specifically to crucifixion and burning alive as unnecessarily cruel forms of execution, which had their origins in the hateful and violent ways of foreign countries and past ages. In the end, however, it was not the cruelty of these punishments to which he most objected. His real concern was that they were ineffective in stopping crime. As a general principle, Riken insisted that any person not already deterred by the possibility that he might forfeit his life for a crime was no more likely to be put off by the threat of an exceptionally gruesome execution. Instead, these kinds of excessive punishment served only to discourage ordinary people from providing evidence of the crimes committed against them. Riken makes this point by referring to a "royal law" once passed in an unspecified realm that decreed that any person caught stealing from his or her master would automatically be put to death regardless of the circumstances. Far from bringing an end to all theft as hoped, the result was simply that most masters were unwilling to report servants who had stolen from them. In this way, Riken suggested, the threat of overly harsh punishments tended to give criminals a kind of de facto immunity from the law by generating popular sympathy for them. In the case of particularly violent or serious crimes such sympathy was perhaps less likely, but in keeping with his position as a merchant-scholar, Riken's primary concern was clearly with crimes against property and in particular petty theft. "How is it," he asked, "that in this age of peace the cities are full of rogues who, in the full light of day, can pickpocket the things people have [tucked away] in their waists or bosoms?"

In addition to the fact that people were reluctant to cooperate in the apprehension of criminals whose punishments might be disproportionate to their crimes, Riken, like Shundai, believed that another reason why theft had become a problem under the Tokugawa was that officials themselves were often unwilling to arrest the perpetrators: "Though they have a good idea of the [criminals'] names and addresses, their numbers and even their winnings, they turn a blind eye [to their activities]." For Riken, the reason for this was not that officials were softhearted, as Shundai had suggested, but rather that they needed to guarantee the cooperation of petty offenders in order to be able to make the occasional "big" arrest. Even today, there is nothing unusual about police officials promising leniency for lesser criminals in order to gain their cooperation in apprehending or convicting serious offenders. Yet, as Sorai had already suggested in the 1720s, the tendency for Tokugawa officials to rely heavily on networks of underworld spies and informants was greatly exacerbated by the fact that Tokugawa society was not really "policed" at all.

In this regard it is important to note that the "sharp-eyed" informants of the Tokugawa period were not used just to gather information and evidence about other criminals. Much like the infamous "thief takers" of eighteenth-century London, they often also did the work of apprehending them.[31] In Edo the careers of most *meakashi* began after they had been arrested and put in the jailhouse.[32] Having already confessed his own crimes, a fledgling informant would be charged with the task of capturing a group of his former associates and turning them in to the relevant warrior officials. He was not set free to do this on his own, however. In keeping once again with the principles of rule by status, he would be released into the custody of an established *meakashi* boss who was then responsible for supervising his activities on the "outside." If, in the end, the would-be operative failed to do what he had been asked, he was likely to find himself back in the jailhouse facing harsh punishment. But if he succeeded, he would remain under the supervision of his boss and be expected to provide ongoing assistance to the warrior authorities. The *meakashi* bosses and their underlings were paid a small "fee" for their services, but they usually continued to collect additional revenue through involvement in various kinds of illicit activity. This also extended their usefulness to the warrior authorities. Abe Yoshio has noted that from the point of view of the daimyo, in particular, one of the great advantages of using *meakashi* to help apprehend wanted criminals was that the outlaw networks they belonged to tended to transcend official jurisdictional boundaries. This meant, for example, that if a person fled into another lord's domain, a *meakashi* could often use his connections to track him down—thereby avoiding the need for the domain to make a formal request to the Bakufu or the other lord for assistance.[33]

The warrior authorities were not oblivious to the problems that their dependency on networks of criminal informants and spies sometimes created. From as early as the 1680s the Bakufu began issuing public statements stipulating that any *meakashi* who behaved improperly or made a nuisance of himself in Edo was to be reported to the town governors; and from the early 1700s regular attempts were made either to limit or to ban their use entirely.[34] In the end, however, these efforts resulted in a change in nomenclature—*meakashi* was eventually replaced with *tesaki*, a term denoting their role as the "fingertips" on the hand of warrior authority—but not in their importance. Even as late as 1867, on the eve of the Meiji Restoration, an official Bakufu report stated that there were at least 381 *tesaki* bosses in the service of the Edo town governors, with another one thousand underlings in their command.[35]

Clearly, Riken was right to suggest that the need to maintain a network of informers was one of the reasons why Tokugawa officials tended to turn a blind eye to the activities of petty criminals. Yet there was also another, more fundamental factor involved. As we have seen in earlier chapters, the bodies of punished criminals in Tokugawa Japan served as signs, inscribed with political meaning. The point of the system was not purely political, of course. Dramatic public displays certainly did discourage people from committing crimes. Yet, because the most important relationship for officials was, in the final analysis, not that between the criminal and the victim of the crime, or even the lord and the criminal, but rather that between the lord and those who saw what he could have done to a body, it was by no means imperative that every crime be punished. Indeed, according to the overall logic of the system, so long as the occasional body-as-sign was posted, there was relatively little lost and much to be gained by *not* punishing every crime. Too much violent punishment, especially for relatively minor offenders, was, after all, likely to be resented as cruel and oppressive. But by exercising discretion about whom to punish and whom to let go, officials could keep people in fear of *possible* punishment without undermining the lord's image as a benevolent ruler.

In an important sense the relatively haphazard and limited application of harsh punishments was well suited to the political needs of the warrior lords. It promoted an image of them as being at once fearful *and* benevolent and required only a minimum commitment of resources. Moreover, while it may not have been the most effective system for controlling petty crime among commoners, for those who lived behind the walls of the warrior mansions this was not necessarily a matter of great concern, particularly in the first half of the period, when pacifying the warrior clans still constituted the main political challenge of the day. As a merchant-scholar, writing at the end of the second century of the *pax Tokugawa*, however, Riken's perspective was quite different. For him, a system that focused primarily on "major" criminals, while leaving others to pursue petty thievery "exactly as if it were a regular trade," was simply unacceptable. For one thing, he argued, it was from the ranks of petty thieves that more serious criminals tended to rise. Even more important than this, however, was the fact that the damage a thief caused had as much to do with the situation of the victim as it did the actual amount stolen. While there were those who could afford to lose as much as one thousand *kan* without batting an eyelid, Riken noted, there were others for whom the loss of as little as ten *kan* would be enough to force them onto the streets. Petty theft, in other words, was as much a cause of poverty and hardship among the common people as it was a symptom. For this reason, Riken concluded, to ignore the activities of a thief simply because he had not stolen a large sum was entirely unacceptable. Every single thief should, without exception, be rounded up immediately, he insisted.

This approach, however, left Riken with a significant problem: if officials were to begin rounding up thieves in a systematic fashion, how were they then to punish them? He had already ruled out banishment and capital punishment, and although he was presumably well aware of the proposals made by Sorai and Shundai earlier in the century, he showed no interest in them. Instead what he proposed was the creation of a special institution in which those who had caught the "disease" of thievery could be permanently cured of their affliction.

The "long-term jail" *(nagarō)* Riken proposed was to be fundamentally different from the ordinary jails of Tokugawa Japan. Instead of holding criminal suspects while official investigations were carried out, it would serve as a kind of dormitory *(ryō)* to which people were sent for fixed periods of time—six months, three years, five years, ten years, and so on, depending on the severity of the offense. If, at the end of this sentence, an inmate showed signs of having changed his ways *(kokoro aratamarinaba)*, he would be released. Otherwise he would be held until he did or, where necessary, for life. In general, Riken argued that conditions in the long-term jail would be better than in the ordinary jailhouses. Overcrowding was to be avoided and basic standards of hygiene maintained. At the same time, he suggested, the process of reform should be encouraged by a reward system based on the provision of food. Each morning inmates would be served a portion of rice gruel *(kayu)* sufficient to sustain life, but any additional food would have to be earned through hard work. Those with special trade skills would be allowed to use them, while the rest would be put to work making sandals *(zōri)* for a private contractor who would pay inmates for their labor by supplying them with simple meals. Under this system, Riken summed up, "Those who work will be able to eat, those who are lazy will not" *(tsutomuru mono wa shoku o e, okotaru mono wa shoku o ezu)*. Implicit in this aspect of Riken's proposal is the notion that theft was ultimately a problem of morality. Thieves stole because they were lazy and had forgotten how to do an honest day's work. Once they became used to performing steady work again, they could be expected to return to a productive role in society, and the long-term jail would have served its purpose.

Thieves were not the only ones Riken believed could benefit from a lesson in diligence and hard work at the long-term jail. Having introduced the idea for the new institution in the context of his discussion of theft, he quickly went on to list a number of others who might also be interned there. To begin with, he noted that townsfolk and peasants who neglected their duties as productive workers so they could spend time gambling—a characteristic concern of the late Tokugawa period—could be sent there to learn the error of their ways. He also argued that the long-term jail would provide an excellent alternative to all of the different forms of banishment currently practiced in Tokugawa society. Even the parents of troublesome children could be encouraged to send them to the jail, rather than simply disowning them and driving them away from home. Finally, as an act of charity, Riken suggested that all poor and destitute people could be sent there and put to work, regardless of whether they had committed crimes.

By the end of Riken's explanation of the full range of possible uses of the long-term jail then, it is clear that he envisaged it as a measure for dealing with all persons who had dropped, or been pushed, out of a stable place in mainstream society. In this sense, like Sorai's initial call for the abolition of banishment, Riken's proposal can be seen as a response not just to a perceived increase in petty crime but, much more generally, to the growth of a surplus population that was spilling out of the existing networks of social organization onto the highways and city streets of Tokugawa Japan. Needless to say, this was not a matter of concern for scholars alone. The question of how to deal with the proliferation of displaced, marginal people was one the Bakufu had been struggling with from the very beginning of the eighteenth century.

CONTAINING THE SURPLUS: VAGRANTS AND THE BAKUFU

After it had incorporated the established communities of outcast beggars and indigents into its system of rule by status in the first half of the seventeenth century, the Bakufu's main response to the appearance of any new groups of vagrants on the streets of Edo and other cities was simply to order local residents to drive them away.[36] With the end of the boom of the Genroku period (1688–1704), however, it became increasingly difficult for newcomers to find work in the cities, and in 1709, under the sixth shogun, Ienobu, a new two-pronged policy for dealing with the poor was announced. Vagrants who still had registered places of abode (*yūshuku*) were to be sent home and resettled; those who were no longer listed on any local register were to be placed under the authority of a *hinin* boss and made into permanent members of the *hinin* status group.[37] Having slipped out of the status system, in other words, these "unregistereds" (*mushuku*) were to be slotted back into it as members of an officially recognized community of beggars. Predictably enough, this new policy soon led to a noticeable increase in the number of outcasts in the capital, which in the 1720s began to draw widespread criticism.[38] In his *Seidan*, Sorai argued that to reduce unregistereds permanently to the status of outcast beggars not only showed a lack of benevolence but also increased the likelihood of disorder by driving these already marginal people to new lows of depravity and desperation:

> When they come in contact with the dissolute and cruel *(hōitsu muzan)* ways of the established beggars *(hinin)*, instead of changing themselves they become even more evil than before. In performing the official duties of the beggars [moreover] they handle [the corpses of] criminals, sick travelers, and those who are found dead in the rivers, and as a result their hearts become increasingly barbarous and immoral *(bōgyaku mudō).*[39]

Sorai went on to note that in recent years there had been numerous cases of *hinin* involved in arson and other malicious acts, and that because they lived in a separate world *(bekkyōkai)* from that of ordinary commoners, allowing their numbers to increase was "like bringing in a large group of foreigners *(ikokujin)* and setting them loose in the capital."[40] By 1724 even Danzaemon, the outcast chief, had come to believe that the number of people in the charge of the *hinin* headmen was growing too large, and at his request a group of some 226 vagrants were exiled to a distant island rather than made outcasts.[41]

Given all of this, it is not surprising that under Yoshimune the Bakufu began considering other possible solutions to the problem of what to do with unregistereds found loitering around the capital. At the beginning of the 1720s two possible policies were proposed. The first called for unregistered vagrants arrested in the capital to be divided up among a number of daimyo, who would then be encouraged to put them to work clearing new land for cultivation. In particular, it was thought that they could be sent to far-flung domains such as Satsuma and Nambu, where land was plentiful and labor scarce. Far more striking was the second proposal, which called for the establishment of a new kind of outcast hospice *(shinki tame)* to house the unregistereds, who would be put to work at tasks that would help pay for their upkeep until they were ready to support themselves in mainstream society again.[42] This proposed institution was clearly similar to the long-term jail that Riken was to suggest some sixty years later, but neither of the two plans was taken up at this time. By the end of the 1720s the Bakufu had once again decided that the best way to deal with unregistered vagrants was simply to drive them away from the town governors' offices with a warning to stay out of trouble.[43]

This approach was, of course, an easy way to avoid any further increase in the size of the outcast population, but it did nothing to address the problem of vagrancy, and by the end of Yoshimune's reign the outcasts were again being called upon to play a central role in the management of the poor and destitute. In 1742, when the town governors concluded that vagrants were responsible for setting a series of fires around the city, they ordered Danzaemon to begin "rounding up" all of the "wild" beggars *(nohi-*

nin) (i.e., beggars not under the supervision of a *hinin* boss) on the streets of the capital.[44] Within a few months Danzaemon's men had apprehended some 742 such people, and after a year the total stood at just under 1,200. Of these, 4 were put in the care of commoners who were willing to take responsibility for them. The rest were handed over to *hinin* headmen, but with such large numbers to take care of, it was impossible for them to stop many of the newcomers from simply running away. Clearly, there were limits on the extent to which the outcast groups could continue serving as a sponge with which to absorb those who had fallen out of the mainstream of the social system.[45]

In spite of all of this, not until the 1770s was any further attempt made to develop an alternative solution to the problem of vagrancy. By this point, the rapid growth of a commercial economy, encouraged in large part by the policies of the Bakufu's then grand chamberlain, Tanuma Okitsugu (1719–88), had contributed to a significant increase in social tensions and distress.[46] Of course, commercialization of the rural economy did not affect all peasants equally or in the same way. Some gladly capitalized on the new opportunities that resulted from increased integration with regional and national markets and were able to greatly enhance their own wealth by diversifying into various forms of "proto-industrial" activity, moneylending, and so on.[47] More often than not, however, this new wealth came at the expense of less fortunate neighbors, who were forced to become tenant farmers or to abandon the land altogether after falling deeply into debt. Meanwhile, the growth of rurally based proto-industry had an adverse effect on the local economies of many smaller urban centers, with established merchants and artisans finding it increasingly difficult to compete.[48]

By the second half of the 1770s, all of these factors had contributed to a noticeable growth in the number of displaced people on the streets of the shogun's capital, and eventually in 1778 the Bakufu issued a directive outlining a new policy for dealing with the problem. "In recent times," it began, "there have been large numbers of unregistereds loitering around the capital, and as a result of this, arson and theft are common, and there are various other kinds of disturbances."[49] It then decreed that "in order to teach them a lesson" any unregistereds caught in the city would be sent to the island of Sado and put to work bailing water out of the silver mines there. This was no idle threat. Within just a few months of the directive the first group of sixty unregistered men was sent to Sado, and soon after this a walled compound with room for two hundred inmates was completed. Conditions in the mines were harsh, and although some of those sent to Sado were later allowed to return to life as ordinary commoners, for many it was a one-way trip.[50]

The threat of being sent to Sado was, of course, intended to terrify the destitute and deter them from trouble, but there was clearly a limit to the number of paupers the Bakufu could ship off to the silver mines without calling into question the shogun's credentials as a benevolent ruler. It was no doubt for this reason that just two years after the first group of unregistereds was sent to Sado, Tanuma also approved a proposal for an experiment with a second new approach to the problem: the creation of a special "foster home for unregistereds" *(mushuku yōikusho)* not unlike the "new hospice" proposed in the 1720s under Yoshimune.

According to the few relevant documents that have survived, the foster home was the brainchild of the Edo town governor, Makino Seiken. Late in 1780 Makino sent a message to his counterparts explaining that Tanuma had agreed to allow the construction of the new institution and that in future all unregistereds caught in the city were to be sent to him for questioning.[51] Those judged unsuitable for the foster home would continue to be transported to Sado, he explained, but the rest were to be given a chance to redeem themselves in what soon became known popularly in Edo as the "benevolent jail" *(jihirō)*. According to Makino's plan, inmates in the foster home were to be put to work at various tasks and then, after one or two years of this "official support" *(oyashinai)*, resettled in their places of origin. From the outset, however, the institution was plagued by a high incidence of escapes and other problems, and when Makino was promoted out of his position as town governor in 1784, the experiment quickly collapsed. In the middle of 1786, less than seven years after its creation, the foster home was formally abolished.[52]

By the time Riken penned his *Treatise* then, not only had the idea of establishing an institution to confine unregistereds and put them to work been discussed at the top levels of the Bakufu, an attempt (albeit abortive) had been made to put it into practice. In this sense, Riken's proposal for the creation of a long-term jail was not an isolated idea. It clearly reflected a broader moment in the development of official strategies for managing displaced and marginal people. Beyond this, however, there is also good reason to believe that Riken's arguments in particular had a direct impact on the Bakufu's senior councillor Matsudaira Sadanobu (1758–1829) and on his decision to try again to establish such an institution in Edo, this time on a more permanent basis.

Sadanobu, Riken, and the Stockade for Laborers

As Yoshimune's grandson, Sadanobu was of the best possible lineage for leadership of the Bakufu, and he came to office as the representative of a group of lords strongly opposed to the "unorthodox" policies pursued under Tanuma, an infamous parvenu.[53] Tanuma's hold on power began to slip from around 1784, and when his most important supporter, the tenth shogun, Ieharu, died in 1786, he was quickly deposed and put under house arrest. In the middle of the following year Sadanobu was appointed senior councillor, and in 1788 he became special adviser (shōgun hosa) to the new shogun, Ienari, who was just fifteen at the time. With his position at the head of the Bakufu bureaucracy secured, Sadanobu was ready to embark on a program of reforms intended to set right what he and his supporters perceived to be the mistakes of the Tanuma period. Just before launching his reforms, however, Sadanobu left Edo on an official trip to Kyoto and the Kansai region. The trip was a hurried one, allowing him only three days in Osaka, but while he was there Sadanobu spent an afternoon with Nakai Chikuzan, the prominent young head of the Kaitokudō, consulting with him about his views on the state of the country.[54]

During their meeting, Chikuzan made a point of recommending his younger brother as a scholar of superior abilities, and although Riken himself is said to have gone out of his way to avoid an audience with Sadanobu (reputedly fleeing through the back door of his residence when an invitation from the great lord arrived), the text of Chikuzan's famous Sōbō kigen makes it clear that many of Riken's ideas, including his proposal for the long-term jail, were eventually introduced to the Bakufu's new leader regardless.[55] Written specifically in response to the questions put by Sadanobu, the Sōbō kigen is a long, ten-part essay that covers a wide range of contemporary policy concerns. Not surprisingly, it is in a section on theft that the idea of the long-term jail is first introduced.[56] After carefully summarizing the arguments presented in the Jukkei bōgi (which he mentions by name in the text), Chikuzan makes a few additions of his own to Riken's original proposal.

Chikuzan presents the idea of the long-term jail as a variation on the traditional Chinese punishment of "penal servitude" recommended by Sorai earlier in the century. In fact, penal servitude in the Chinese tradition was quite different from what Riken had proposed; it did not involve confinement in a special institution but simply a period of hard labor, usually served in a mine in a distant province.[57] By making this link, however, Chikuzan was able to draw upon the prestige of Chinese legal traditions to bolster his case for the long-term jail and to portray it as an idea fully in keeping with the orthodox Confucian principles of governance that Sadanobu was known to favor.[58] Eventually, the completed text of the Sōbō kigen was presented to Sadanobu in the winter of 1789, and precisely from this time he began seriously exploring the possibility of establishing a new institution for confining unregistereds in the capital. Given this, Hiramatsu is surely right to suggest that Riken's ideas, embellished by Chikuzan to make them seem part of a legitimately Confucian approach to government, had at least some influence on him.[59] The final shape of the institution itself provides further evidence in support of this view.

At the very end of 1789 Sadanobu called upon Hasegawa Heizō (1745–95), Edo's famous inspector for arson and thefts, to draw up plans for the new institution, and at the end of the first month of 1790 he gave him formal permission to proceed with construction of what the two men decided to call the Inspector's Stockade for Laborers (*kayakugata ninsoku yoseba*).[60] Aware, no doubt, of the problems with escapes that had plagued the earlier foster home, Heizō chose the island of Ishikawajima, at the mouth of the Sumida River in Edo Bay, as the site for the new stockade.[61] The work of building the new institution was carried out by unregistereds rounded up from around the city, and within a month enough had been completed for the first group of laborers to begin living in the stockade. The following speech, which was read to all new inmates, provides a good sense of how Sadanobu, its author, hoped the stockade would work:

> Originally, you were to have been transported to Sado, but because you are innocent of crime, you are now, by an act of great benevolence, designated laborers in the custody of the Inspector. You will be sent to the stockade, where you are to work using whatever skills you have learned. You should forsake your former ways, return to your true selves, apply yourselves diligently to your work, and endeavor to raise the resources (*motode*) you need for a new start. When it is judged that you are ready, you will be released from the stockade regardless of how long or short a time you have been held there. Those of you who are of peasant stock will be given an appropriate plot of land, and those of you who were born in Edo will be provided with a shop at your place of birth, and allowed to pursue your family trade. In addition, the Public Authority [i.e., Bakufu] will provide you with the tools needed for your trade and, depending on your conduct, an appropriate payment of money. If, however, you do not keep the lesson of this act of official benevolence in mind, and turning your back on these instructions, fail to work diligently or commit evil deeds, then you shall be severely punished.[62]

In practice, inmates at the stockade were paid wages for their labor, and although most records relating to inmates were lost in fires, in the early years it is clear that many did receive official assistance in establishing shops in Edo after their release.[63] In at least one respect, however, the wording of the speech was misleading: although it suggests that only those who were completely innocent of crimes (*muzai no mono*) would be admitted to the stockade, in reality this was not the case. In order to understand this apparent contradiction, it is necessary to consider once more what usually happened to criminals after they had been punished for petty crimes under the Tokugawa.

In general, it will be recalled that criminals who were sentenced to punishments such as flogging and tattooing were supposed to be handed over to a relative or local headman once their punishments had been completed.

By definition, however, unregistered persons had no such guarantors, and so it became standard practice for them to be simply released and "driven away." Not having any way to support themselves, these people invariably found themselves back on the streets where they often became involved in more serious kinds of trouble.

Sadanobu was particularly concerned about this problem, and soon after taking control of the Bakufu, he ordered that unregistereds no longer be released after corporal punishment but instead be held in the outcast hospices until they could be transported to Sado.[64] This new policy directly contradicted assurances made to the governor of Sado in the 1770s that only "innocent unregistereds" *(muzai no mushuku)* would be transported to the island, and in order to get around this issue, Sadanobu insisted that once a criminal had been punished for his crimes he should be understood as having reverted to the status of an "innocent."[65] As a result, from 1788 on, the phrase "innocent unregistered" *(muzai no mushuku)* came to include not only those who actually were innocent of crimes, but also those who had recently been punished for petty offenses. Proof that the stockade was intended to accommodate both groups is provided also by the following order issued to the relevant Bakufu governors at the time of its opening:

> From now on, when unregistereds are apprehended, all of them, beginning of course with those who have committed evil acts and completed punishments of tattooing and flogging, but also including those who, upon investigation, are found to have committed no evil acts, are to be sent to the Inspector's Stockade for Laborers.[66]

In practice, Tsukada Takashi has shown that the best way to understand the makeup of the stockade's inmate population at any particular time is to focus on the concrete mechanisms by which people were likely to be interned there.[67] In this regard it is important to note that although some initial efforts to "round up" vagrants from the streets of the capital were made after the establishment of the stockade, these lasted for no more than a few months. After this, unregistereds were likely to find themselves being sent to the stockade only if they had already been arrested by the warrior authorities for some other reason—almost always some form of petty crime. Not surprisingly then, two years after the establishment of the stockade an official report noted that the overwhelming majority of inmates had been punished for pickpocketing or some other form of petty theft before being admitted.[68] A small handful of truly innocent vagrants did continue to be admitted to the stockade, as did a small number of juvenile delinquents interned by their parents. But for the most part it soon came to function primarily as a kind of "halfway house" for ensuring that people who had nowhere to go after they had been punished for petty crimes did not simply end up back on the streets causing more problems.

This outcome was, of course, clearly in keeping with the spirit of Riken's original proposal for the long-term jail and the particular emphasis it placed on the need to clear the streets of *known* criminals.[69] Yet, given the fact that petty crime and vagrancy had been a matter of concern since at least the beginning of the century, we are still left with the question of why Riken was inspired to take up the problem at the particular time that he did. Why was it, moreover, that the increasingly cash-strapped shogunate was persuaded to sink its resources into the creation of the Stockade for Laborers—a place where, as one warrior critic put it, petty criminals were "put on stipend"—when a similar institution had proved a failure just a few years earlier?[70] In order to find answers to these questions, it is important that we consider more carefully the social context of the 1780s.

FAMINE, RIOTS, AND POLITICS

By the late 1770s the rapid expansion of new forms of commercial activity had contributed to a marked increase in the number of vagrants and paupers on the streets of Tokugawa cities and towns. In 1783, however, a series of natural disasters and crop failures heralded the beginning of a calamity far greater than any purely man-made troubles that was to last until 1787. What became known as the great Tenmei famine is estimated to have claimed at least one million lives out of a total population of around thirty million.[71]

Many officials at the time were convinced that the main cause of the crisis was the depletion of the peasantry. Contemporary reports do confirm that large tracts of farming land were abandoned in many parts of the country in the 1780s. But rather than seeing this as evidence of economic hardship, officials instead tended to blame it on the moral weakness of the common people, whom they believed were too easily tempted away from the land by the false promise of luxury and an easier life in the cities.[72] When things went badly, it was reasoned, these same people found themselves wandering the streets poor and desperate. Soon they contributed further to the erosion of the productive population by committing thefts and joining gangs that tempted others with the promise of easy money through gambling. As the Edo-based scholar of political economy Honda Toshiaki (1743–1820) was to point out in the late 1790s, however, if they punished ordinary people too harshly, officials would only make the situation worse:

> In years when the harvest is bad and people die of starvation, farmers perish in greater numbers than any other class. Fields are abandoned and food production is still further reduced. As a result there is insufficient food for the nation and much suffering. Then people grow restive and numerous criminals will have to

be punished. In this way citizens will be lost to the state. Since its citizens are a country's most important possession, it cannot afford to lose even one, and it is therefore most unfortunate that anyone should be sentenced to death. It is entirely the fault of the ruler if the life of even a single subject is thereby lost.[73]

The Stockade for Laborers clearly offered a solution to this dilemma, not only by providing a "benevolent" way to deal with petty criminals and other potential troublemakers but also by providing a way to reharness the wasted labor of what were, from the authorities' point of view, idle bodies. In this regard we should note that at the same time the famous Ishikawajima Stockade was established in Edo, the Bakufu also set up a second, smaller stockade in the village of Kamigō in Hitatchi Province, one of the areas of Bakufu territory that had been particularly badly affected by the Tenmei famine. Kamigō was treated as a branch of the Ishikawajima Stockade, and each year a small number of inmates was sent there from Edo and put to work reclaiming abandoned farmland.[74]

Yet, while the combination of abandoned fields in the countryside and unprecedented numbers of vagrants on the city streets was undoubtedly disturbing, there was also another, more important reason why both a merchant-scholar in Osaka and the leader of the Bakufu in Edo would have been particularly concerned about the swelling numbers of people on the margins of society at this time. Vagrants and unregistereds had always been associated with various forms of petty crime and unrest, but in the 1780s poverty and desperation in the cities contributed to a form of trouble that posed a much more direct threat to the position of the warrior authorities and their social allies: large-scale urban riots, or "smashings" (uchi kowashi).

Although there had been a number of similar riots earlier in the eighteenth century, most notably in Edo in 1733, the smashings of the 1780s were both larger in scale and more widespread than ever before.[75] As with the "food riots" described by E. P. Thompson in his now famous article on the "moral economy" of the crowd in eighteenth-century England, the violence unleashed in the Tokugawa period smashings was rarely indiscriminate or undisciplined but almost always targeted the stores and property of merchants accused of rice hoarding and other unfair practices.[76] In 1783, for example, rioters in Osaka concentrated their efforts on the property of one of the city's three most powerful merchants, Kajimaya Kyūzaemon, completely destroying his home and stores in a single day.[77] Crowd anger dissipated once this had been accomplished, but rumors soon began to spread that the next target was to be the house of Masuya, one of the Kaitokudō's major financial supporters.[78] As a result of the rumors, students from the academy were dispatched to help protect Masuya property, and one contemporary diarist places Nakai Riken himself on the barricades, offering to help fight off the angry masses.[79] Riken is also known to have temporarily moved his home closer to the Masuya headquarters at this time, and Yamanaka Hiroyuki speculates that he did this in order to ensure that he would be able to assist in case of a sudden attack.[80] Clearly, the threat of riots and the apparent inability of the Bakufu to prevent them was an issue of more than just academic interest for the Kaitokudō scholars, and their concerns can only have grown in the second half of the decade. When the next major smashing broke out in Osaka in 1787 some two hundred rice stores and merchant houses were destroyed in various parts of the city.[81] The most remarkable aspect of the 1787 smashing, however, was that within the space of just a few weeks similar riots broke out in some thirty other urban centers around the country, stretching from Iwatsuki in the northern Kantō plain to Nagasaki on the southern island of Kyushu.[82]

This widespread rioting itself was clearly a major problem for the Bakufu, but it was soon overshadowed by the rioting that broke out in Edo. For five days and nights at the end of the fifth month of 1787 anarchy reigned in the shogun's capital as thousands of rioters drawn from the lower levels of urban society joined forces to raze a total of close to one thousand rice stores, pawnshops, and sake breweries to the ground.[83] These events were a disaster for the city's merchants, but they were also to have a direct and dramatic impact at the highest levels of the warrior state. After three decades at the head of the Bakufu bureaucracy, the grand chamberlain Tanuma Okitsugu had been removed from office in 1786 upon the death of Ieharu, but many of his supporters remained in positions of power, and they continued to fight a determined rearguard action against Sadanobu and his supporters. Largely as a result of their efforts, Sadanobu's appointment to the senior council was formally rejected in early 1787, and in the ensuing months the Bakufu was effectively paralyzed by the ongoing power struggle. In the end, as Takeuchi Makoto has shown, the eruption of riots in Edo broke this deadlock by providing Sadanobu's supporters with dramatic proof of the need for change.[84] In a submission made to the senior council immediately after the riots had been put down, the lords of the three shogunal branch houses (gosanke) specifically blamed the "uprising in the town" on Tanuma's "bad policies" and urged a return to the practices established by Yoshimune.[85] A week later Sadanobu's appointment had been reconsidered and approved.

To a large degree then, Sadanobu's own rise was made possible by the actions of the rioters, and once he was in power the need to ensure that they did not take to the streets again became a central factor shaping his Kansei Reforms.[86] The most dramatic measure taken by Sadanobu to prevent further uprisings in the capital was the establishment in 1791 of the Edo Town Office (Edo machi kaisho), an institution that used funds collected each year from landowners in the city to provide relief to the poor in times of emergency and low-interest loans to both townsfolk and warriors.[87]

Despite these measures to provide a "safety net" for the urban poor, nervousness about the possibility of further unrest was the main reason why Sadanobu was determined to find a way to limit the number of unregistereds on the streets of the capital. In fact, Sadanobu's decision to proceed with the Stockade for Laborers was made a full year before his plans to establish the Town Office, clearly suggesting that his concern to maintain order among the "lowly people" came prior to his desire to feed them.

BANISHMENT AND THE LATER DEVELOPMENT OF THE STOCKADE

In their accounts of the evolution of the Stockade for Laborers in the late Tokugawa period, Japanese legal historians have tended to emphasize the Bakufu's decision in 1820 to begin sending criminals who had been formally sentenced to banishment there. In many ways this development was not surprising. As we have already seen, thinkers and officials alike had expressed concern about the ill effects of banishment from early in the eighteenth century. Riken, moreover, had specifically suggested that his long-term jail might be used to confine criminals sentenced to banishment, and when Hasegawa Heizō was in the process of building the stockade, he too had proposed to Sadanobu that it should be used for this purpose. In spite of all of this, however, the idea was initially rejected by the Bakufu on the grounds that it would violate the spirit of the law if criminals who were supposed to have been driven out of the city were instead kept in a location so close to its heart.[88] This decision, of course, provides further evidence that the Bakufu's primary motivation for establishing the stockade was to maintain order *in* the capital. By the early years of the nineteenth century, however, Bakufu officials had also grown increasingly concerned about rising levels of crime and unrest in the eight Kantō provinces that surrounded Edo.

Proximity to the capital meant that commercial activity and peasant mobility had steadily increased throughout the Kantō, and efforts to enforce order there were hampered by the fact that the political settlement of the seventeenth century had left most of the region divided up into a hodgepodge of fragmented and ineffectual administrative units. In 1805 the Bakufu attempted to strengthen its hand in this regard by creating a special Kantō Regulatory Patrol (*Kantō torishimari shutsu yaku; Kan hasshū mawari*) with the power to police the entire region, but at the same time, it also began to rethink its position on banishment.[89] It is not difficult to understand why this was the case: although, in theory, there were various official grades of banishment, each of which entailed exclusion from a specific set of areas, in practice, most commoners sentenced to banishment in Edo were simply expected to remain outside a ten-league radius of the capital.[90]

This left them free to roam across most of the Kantō plain, where many were believed to end up in the gangs of gamblers and bandits that were a growing source of trouble. As a partial solution, the Bakufu decided in 1805 to begin sending to Sado and to the Stockade for Laborers in Kamigō village some of those sentenced to banishment. The Kamigō Stockade was well outside a ten-league radius of Edo and was presumably considered a better alternative to Ishikawajima for this reason. From the late 1810s, however, when the Kamigō Stockade began to run out of land for its inmates to cultivate, the possibility of sending banished criminals to the main stockade in Edo was again raised, and in the end it was agreed that so long as they were not permitted to reside in the city after their release it would be acceptable to begin admitting them at Ishikawajima.[91]

This development was important, particularly when understood in the context of the broader discourse on banishment, but Japanese legal scholars have also repeatedly pointed to it as evidence of the stockade's transformation into an institution along the lines of a modern prison, specializing in the confinement of criminals for the purpose of punishment.[92] There are serious problems with this proposition. As we have already seen, most of those admitted to the stockade in its early stages were petty criminals who had been punished with flogging and tattooing. They were sent to the stockade not as an alternative form of punishment but rather to ensure that *after* their punishments had been carried out they did not simply end up back on the streets of the capital again. Similarly, as Hiramatsu has emphasized, confinement at the Edo Stockade after 1820 was never intended to serve as a substitute for the punishment of banishment but as a kind of supplement to it. The idea was to force banished criminals to lead a steady existence in the stockade for a period so that when they were eventually expelled from the capital (as they always were), they would be less likely to become rootless troublemakers.[93] With regard to the overall makeup of the inmate population, moreover, Tsukada has shown that far from evolving smoothly into an institution that specialized in punishing convicted criminals, from the late 1830s the stockade instead began to admit large numbers of genuinely innocent unregistereds for the first time since its establishment. Key to this development was the onset of another major famine, similar in scale to that which had shaken the country in the 1780s.

In 1837, after a succession of major crop failures, droves of displaced peasants began flooding into the capital in search of food. In response the Bakufu ordered the establishment of special "relief shelters" (*osukui goya*) at the main entrances of the city, but at the same time it also decreed that those housed at these shelters were eventually either to be returned to their places of origin or, where this was not possible, sent to the Stockade for Laborers.[94] As a direct result of this new policy, the inmate population of the stockade, which had previously hovered between 130 and 140 persons, quickly skyrocketed to almost 500.[95] This put considerable strain on the stockade's resources, and in order to help it cope with the crisis the Bakufu decided in 1838 to stop sending any more banished criminals there.[96]

This decision clearly underlines the fact that the stockade was still seen primarily as a tool for controlling potential troublemakers in and around the capital. When normal conditions prevailed, banished criminals who would otherwise have been expelled directly into the Kantō plain might be admitted to the stockade, but when famine struck, the Bafuku's first priority was to confine unregistered vagrants judged likely to become involved in petty crime and also in urban riots. There were uprisings in many parts of the country in the 1830s—most notably in Osaka, where Ōshio Heihachirō (1793–1837), a disgruntled Bakufu retainer, led his famous but ultimately short-lived rebellion to "save the people" *(kyūmin)* from the abuses of incompetent officials and greedy merchants.[97] Edo, however, remained relatively calm because of the extra precautions the Bakufu took to protect it.

The dramatic increase in inmate numbers in the late 1830s led to a significant new experiment with inmate labor at the stockade. Originally, it will be recalled, inmates were to have been put to work using whatever trade skills they already had, and early drawings of the Ishikawajima grounds show that there were in fact rows of small workshops set up to cater to a wide range of different trades. In 1841, however, the governor of the stockade came up with the idea of putting inmates to work extracting oil from rape seeds. In contrast to the kind of jobs that inmates had been assigned in the past, the oil extraction enterprise required no skills and was, by all reports, tedious to perform. For this reason its introduction has often been held up as further evidence of the stockade's steady transformation from a "benevolent" institution, intended to ensure that disciplined vagrants found a settled place in society, into a form of out-and-out punishment for an increasingly criminal inmate population.[98] In fact, as we have already seen, the inmate population at this time was far less "criminal" than it had ever been before. The main attraction of the oil extraction enterprise was not that it served a punitive purpose, or even that it provided an easily supervised form of labor for large numbers of inmates, but that it had the potential to become an important source of independent revenue for the stockade at a time when the Bakufu was reluctant to provide it with additional financial support.[99] It was also hoped that former inmates might be given jobs selling and distributing the oil around Edo after their release.[100] But the oil extraction process itself was extremely labor intensive, and with the end of the famine the inmate population had already begun to fall from its earlier peak. In order to ensure the success of the new enterprise, therefore, the governor of the stockade appealed to the Bakufu leadership to round up more unregistered vagrants from the city streets, and in light of this request, the Bakufu also decided to resume the practice of sending banished criminals to the stockade. In the short term, this may well have pleased the governor, but it was not long before the newly expanded capacities of the stockade were once again being strained to the limit by another major shift in Bakufu policy.[101]

Although the various new initiatives launched under Sadanobu in the 1790s had helped the Bakufu cope better with the famine of the 1830s, the combination of widespread suffering, declining tax revenues, and a new wave of uprisings and unrest in many parts of the country gave warrior officials real reason for concern. In Edo, efforts to engineer a comprehensive response to the situation were initially hampered by the long-reigning shogun Ienari, but with his death in 1841 the Bakufu bureaucracy quickly launched a new set of reforms under the leadership of senior councillor Mizuno Tadakuni (1794–1851).[102] Like Sadanobu before him, Mizuno was convinced that in order to prevent further famines and rebuild the warrior state's tax base, every effort had to be made to reverse the depletion of the agricultural labor force. One central part of his plan for bringing this about was to pursue with unprecedented vigor the by then well-established policy of "repatriating" people (hitogaeshi) from the cities to the countryside. Late in 1842 he issued a special "Order for the Return of Unregistereds and Wild Beggars to Their Former Native Places" and launched a full-scale effort to "round up" every vagrant and unregistered person in the capital.

Previously when such roundups had taken place, the Bakufu had sought mainly to repatriate to the countryside those persons who still had registered places of abode there, but under Mizuno's new order all vagrants were now to be sent back to their places of origin, regardless of whether their names still appeared on a local register or not.[103] In particular, those who had come from an area outside the Bakufu's direct control were to be handed over to the local daimyo, as were those who had originally been banished from their home domains. This, however, still left a considerable number of people who were originally from Edo or the surrounding area and who had no one to act as guarantors for them. This group, Mizuno ordered, were to be sent to the stockade, and as a result the inmate population soon began to rise again. Within a month of the order it had grown from around 400 to 460, and by early 1843 the total population exceeded 500 persons. A year later it reached an all-time peak of 600 persons.[104] Even with the oil extraction enterprise fully underway, the stockade was unable to handle this many inmates, and in the third month of 1844 the governor, who had earlier been anxious to increase the inmate population, now formally requested that the Bakufu again stop sending banished persons there until the overall number had halved.[105] Mizuno, however, had long been concerned about the negative effects of banishment on the countryside and would only agree to a partial restriction: banished criminals who had previously lived settled lives with registered abodes need not be sent to the stockade, but those who had been living as unregistereds or who seemed likely to "cause harm to good folks" were to continue being confined there for a period before being driven out of the capital.[106]

Mizuno's efforts to do something about the proliferation of idle bodies were not limited to the capital and the areas around it. In conjunction with his 1842 order he also called for the construction of a network of stockade-like institutions in Bakufu territories across the country and also in each daimyo domain.[107] These new institutions were to be used to hold all unregistereds or vagrants who could not immediately be returned to their places of origin, as well as persons sentenced to banishment from their domain or village. In addition, Mizuno ordered the establishment of a special "stockade for outcasts" (hinin yoseba) in Edo as a response to repeated complaints from Danzaemon that many of the beggars who had been put under the authority of the hinin headmen during the famine of the 1830s had simply absconded and returned to life on the streets.[108] In future, any such wayward outcasts were to be sent to the new stockade.

Overall then, Mizuno would seem to have been intent on clearing the entire country of surplus bodies, whether they were unregistereds, beggars, banished criminals, or wayward outcasts, and his expanded use of the stockade makes it tempting to portray his reforms as something along the lines of a Foucaultian "Great Confinement"—the first step toward a new kind of social order based on networks of "disciplinary institutions" and gray regimes of mass drudgery and drill. In an argument inspired as much by Marx as Foucault, Gary Leupp has suggested that the "workhouses" of late Tokugawa Japan, like those of early modern Europe, came to serve "as the necessary schoolhouse for a work force only gradually acquiring the discipline necessary for wage labor."[109] In this regard, the introduction of large-scale commodity production, in the form of oil extraction, is particularly striking. We might also point to the fact that preachers in the Shingaku tradition of Ishida Baigan, which sociologist Robert Bellah once argued was Japan's version of Weber's "Protestant work ethic," lectured inmates once a month on the importance of upholding the basic moral principles of honesty, diligence, and obedience.[110] Moving beyond the level of surface impressions, however, there are good reasons to reject any suggestion that the stockade played a significant role in the process of "proletarianization" or, more generally, in the formation of a population of disciplined subjects in Japan.

First, at the level of conscious decision making, it is clear that far from wanting to prepare the population for wage labor, Mizuno, like his predecessors, saw the stockade as part of a strategy for resisting any further "freeing up" of the labor force, and for returning people to their proper places within a social order based on feudal economic relations and the principles of the status system. Thus, when vagrants and paupers were rounded up from the streets under Mizuno's orders, the priority was always to try and return them to their place of origin and resettle them on the land. As Tsukada has emphasized, only those who could not be sent home or placed in the custody of a guarantor were confined at the stockade, and even then the basic idea was that after their release they would be slotted back into a stable, productive place within the status system.[111] The confinement of unregistereds and vagrants in the stockade was, in other words, intended to supplement and support the policy of "returning people" to the land, not to serve as a long-term alternative to it. In this regard it is worth noting that in 1842 Mizuno himself rejected a proposal to further expand the capacity of the Edo Stockade on the grounds that inmate numbers there would "naturally decrease once the population registers of Edo have been strictly reviewed and the pleasure-hungry folk [yūmin] who have moved there from the countryside have been removed."[112]

Of course, when considered at the level of structural change, the conscious intentions of leaders like Mizuno would be irrelevant if it could be shown that their decisions had resulted in the establishment of a national network of institutions that served to transform large numbers of marginal people into a disciplined "reserve army" of proletarians. This, however, was almost certainly not the case. Makeshift stockades reportedly operated in Osaka and Kyoto for a few years during Mizuno's period in office, but in the end the only other Bakufu-controlled city to establish a fully fledged stockade was Nagasaki—and this was not until 1860.[113] In the daimyo domains there had already been some experimentation with the creation of small stockade-like institutions from earlier in the nineteenth century, and in the wake of Mizuno's reforms another three or four such institutions were established.[114] Out of a total of more than 250 domains, however, this number is hardly impressive. Even in Edo the effects of Mizuno's reforms were short-lived. By 1845 the intensive roundups of unregistereds and beggars were abandoned, and in 1847 his order was officially rescinded as Bakufu policy. As a result, inmate numbers at Ishikawajima soon began to decline, and the Edo Stockade once again came to serve primarily as a kind of halfway house for unregistereds who had recently been flogged or tattooed, and banished criminals who were considered unlikely to settle in one place if they were immediately expelled from the city.[115] The inmate population at the new Stockade for Outcasts also fell rapidly after 1845, and by the end of 1848 it was officially abandoned.[116] On the eve of Commodore Matthew Perry's arrival to "open" Japan to the West in 1853, Mizuno's vision for a network of stockade-like institutions had largely been forgotten and it is unlikely that his reforms contributed in any significant way to the "disciplining" of the general population.

In spite of all of this, Mizuno's reform efforts are, of course, deeply revealing of significant aspects of the situation in Japan in the middle of the nineteenth century. By the 1840s the warrior state was more concerned than ever about the proliferation of idle bodies outside the structures of the status system and also keen to find some way of dealing with the problem more comprehensively than in the past. The idea of confining people in a special institution and giving them work to perform provided one logical solution and, as we have seen, was first discussed at the upper levels of the Bakufu from as early as the 1720s. Ultimately, however, it took the outbreak of the great Tenmei famine and the urban riots that accompanied it to create the impetus needed to convince the Bakufu leadership to proceed with the actual establishment of such an institution on a permanent basis. In this regard, it makes sense that the Tempō famine and the uprisings of the late 1830s preceded efforts to encourage the construction of similar institutions in other parts of the country. Given more time and more crises, such institutions could perhaps have come to play a more important role in Tokugawa society, and eventually this may have had a significant impact on social organization.

Leaving aside such hypothetical speculation, however, it is important to emphasize once again that the Stockade for Laborers was always seen primarily as a supplement to and support for older strategies of rule, not as part of a new approach to governance. In the 1830s and 1840s the Bakufu's primary response to the presence of growing numbers of paupers and vagrants was to fall back on the old policy of "returning people" to the countryside, which Sorai had advocated so strongly in the early eighteenth century. Only those who could not easily be sent back to the land were put in the stockade, and even then it was expected that after a period of confinement they too would eventually be resettled in a stable community. With regard to the punishment system too, the main purpose of the stockade was not to replace flogging, tattooing, or even banishment, but rather to ensure that their continued use did not contribute further to the growth of a population of rootless, desperate people on the margins of society.

Meanwhile, after more than a hundred years, the system of official punishments codified by Yoshimune in the mid-eighteenth century remained virtually unchanged. Flamboyant displays of the power to punish and pardon were still used to inspire fear, to project benevolence, and to reinforce the "hierarchical imaginary" that informed status system society. Mutilated bodies continued to serve as public signs of order, and warrior officials continued to turn a blind eye to petty violations of the shogun's laws. Yet, as we have seen, some parts of society began to criticize the punishment system and to yearn for a more systematic approach to order. "Order" for the most part still meant the *old* order, but when the Western imperialist powers began to establish a presence on Japanese soil and the weakness of the Bakufu's own position became clear, it did not take long for the accumulated concerns, frustrations, and hopes of the previous century to begin to galvanize behind a comprehensive vision of a fundamentally different kind of society. It was in this context—a context shaped largely by the presence of the Western powers and the new ideas they ushered in— that the Tokugawa punishment system would finally receive its own sentence of death.

CHAPTER 5

Punishment and the Politics of Civilization in Bakumatsu Japan

As THE FORCES of Western imperialism began to make their presence felt in East Asia in the first half of the nineteenth century, criticisms of the existing order of things in Japan were invested with a new sense of gravity. Initially, the Bakufu was able to ensure that the effects of foreign incursions were felt only in limited circles, but with the arrival of Commodore Perry's gunboats in 1853 the parameters of domestic political discourse shifted irrevocably. With the need for some kind of reform widely acknowledged, a range of competing visions (and ambitions) for the future emerged, helping to feed the plots and struggles that eventually culminated in the overthrow of the Tokugawa regime and the restoration of direct rule by the emperor, Meiji , in 1868. The Meiji Restoration has often been characterized as a "new dawn" for a nation arising from its "feudal slumber." This imagery, with its implication of straightforward, unblemished progress out of a "dark age" into an era of "enlightened rule," is clearly inadequate; however, as H. D. Harootunian has noted, the Restoration did serve as "an announcement for a new kind of learning" and, by extension, for a new approach to government.[1]

The emperor's Charter Oath, hurriedly drafted by the leaders of the Restoration in the months after their initial palace coup, famously proclaimed that "evil practices of the past" would be abolished and "new knowledge sought from all over the world to strengthen the foundations of imperial rule." The origins of this call for a radical remaking of society are complex, and clearly cannot be explained solely in terms of a Japanese response to a Western challenge. The rich ferment of ideas in late Tokugawa society and, in particular, the spread of a nativist ideology that fostered faith not only in the emperor but also in the idea of a return to a golden age of Japanese antiquity were vital factors shaping people's expectations and hopes for the future.[2] For a time they also shaped the structure of the Meiji government and the initial direction of the reforms it pursued. Ultimately, however, it was the concern with building national strength in the face of the foreign threat that formed the central imperative for the remaking of Japanese society in the years after the Restoration. This concern, again, was not without significant roots in the late Tokugawa period, but, in the end, the Meiji transformation was to go far beyond anything imagined by Tokugawa thinkers.³ As Makihara Norio has pointed out, one of the realizations made by the so-called men of spirit *(shishi)* during the struggles leading up to the Restoration was that if the country was truly to become strong, then it would not be enough to harness the energies of just a few elite segments of the population.⁴ All members of the society would have to be convinced that they had a stake in (working, mothering, or dying for) the nation.

An important corollary of this conviction was that the social barriers and divisions of the old status system would have to be swept away and, to use the language of the time, "high and low" united as one. The central role of the emperor in the formation of Meiji society can also be understood in this context. More than just a focus of popular devotion and a spur to patriotism, the emperor was key to the creation of a new kind of political community in Japan because, as Fujitani has shown, under "His" *singular* gaze people began to imagine themselves as sharing a destiny and a kind of formal equality as "His" subjects.⁵ In this sense, the reinvention of the emperor as an omniscient and omnipresent monarch went hand in hand with the dismantling of the status system. Yet the creation of the kind of subject-citizens who could build a modern nation-state required much more than just an awareness of the penetrating gaze of a great ruler. Most obvious perhaps, it depended on the establishment of new institutions and structures that could harness, direct, and unleash popular energies—a conscript army, factories, schools, newspapers, and so on. At the same time, it required a state that did not simply rule over the people but also took them as an object of scrutiny and study—a national population—whose capacities and characteristics would be carefully measured, so that their collective strengths could be enhanced and their weaknesses remedied.⁶

One such weakness was, of course, the presence of criminals and "disorderly elements," and in this regard the establishment of a modern criminal justice and penal system was clearly an integral part of the larger process of "nation building." Yet here we must be careful not to reduce the issue of changing modes of penality to a simple matter of increased efficiency (i.e., the replacement of one approach to a problem with a better, more effective one). Particularly in the wake of the social and political upheavals of the final decade of Tokugawa rule, there can be no doubt that the Meiji leaders understood the need to ensure that mechanisms were in place to maintain order and enforce (their) laws. But whereas we have learned to believe that a system of mass incarceration is a "rational" way to achieve this end, in 1860s Japan the attraction of using precious resources to house and feed large numbers of criminals for extended periods of time was hardly obvious. Nor, for that matter, was it clear that the effort to enforce order would be well served by abandoning all public displays of the power to punish. Such changes required a fundamental shift in attitudes, and in order to understand this shift properly, we must begin by examining the new ideas and meanings that came to surround different practices of punishment within the context of Japan's encounter with Western imperialism.

CAPTIVATING TALES: EARLY INTEREST IN WESTERN PENAL PRACTICES

From well before the Restoration the Tokugawa tradition of Dutch studies *(rangaku)* provided Japanese thinkers with an important source of information about developments in the Western world. As is well known, Protestant representatives of the Dutch East India Company had been spared the fate of the Catholic traders and missionaries, who were expelled from Japan in the seventeenth century, and were allowed to maintain a small trading post at Nagasaki throughout the Tokugawa period. Initially, knowledge of the Dutch language was strictly limited to a small number of official translators, but from the 1720s, under Yoshimune's rule, restrictions on the importation of books were eased, and scholars began being encouraged to study Dutch military and scientific works that might be of some use to the Bakufu. Broader interest in Dutch studies was ignited in the latter part of the eighteenth century after the publication of the *Kaitai shinsho*, a European anatomy text translated into Japanese by the physicians Sugita Gempaku (1733–1817) and Maeno Ryōtaku (1723–1803). Although they themselves were initially unable to read what the book said, Sugita and Maeno became convinced of its usefulness after comparing the drawings in it with the insides of an executed criminal dissected for them at Kotsukappara by an elderly outcast man. The drawings were so accurate and complete that they set about translating the entire text with the aid of a single dictionary.[7]

Another scholar who developed an early interest in the study of Dutch astronomy and medicine was Nakai Riken. Najita notes that in 1773, a full year before the appearance of the *Kaitai shinsho*, Riken had already published his own study of human anatomy based on experiments in vivisection that he and the physician Asada Gōryū (1734–99) had conducted using Dutch medical texts as a guide.[8] Given this background, it is worth acknowledging the possibility that Riken's critique of Tokugawa punishments and his call for a long-term jail may also have been influenced by some knowledge of contemporary European developments.

By the time Riken wrote his *Jukkei bōgi*, Europe was awash with the arguments of the Enlightenment philosophes. Montesquieu's *Spirit of the Laws* was completed in 1748, and by the 1760s Cesare Beccaria had taken the critique of harsh and arbitrary punishments even further in his famous essay *On Crimes and Punishments*. Like Riken, Montesquieu and Beccaria both stressed the importance of certainty over severity in punishment. "The certainty of even a mild punishment," Beccaria argued, "will make a bigger impression than the fear of a more awful one which is united to the hope of not being punished at all."[9] Beccaria also called for the abolition of all forms of capital punishment, not on humanitarian grounds, but rather because he was convinced that "the terrible but fleeting sight of a felon's death" was not a real deterrent. A far more "powerful brake on crime," he insisted, would be provided by "the long-drawn-out example of a man deprived of freedom, who having become a beast of burden, repays the society which he has offended with his labor."[10] What Beccaria had in mind, in other words, was a form of "penal slavery," which would be continually visible to others and thus serve as a reminder of the costs of breaking the law.

Beccaria's writings had a significant impact all over Europe, but in England particularly they meshed with another important current of critique, helping to give rise to the idea of the modern "penitentiary."[11] In the early 1770s an Englishman named John Howard undertook a detailed survey of conditions in jails in England, Wales, and, eventually, parts of western Europe. He published his findings in *The State of the Prisons*, a book that shocked the English public with its carefully documented evidence of squalid conditions and mismanagement and the stark contrast it drew between English jails and a small number of well-run institutions that Howard had inspected on the continent.[12] In particular, Howard was impressed by Amsterdam's famous Rasp House, established at the end of the sixteenth century to put idlers and petty criminals to work, and most of all by the Maison de Force built at Ghent in 1771 as part of the Flemish elite's "offensive" against "vagabondage and petty theft" in the wake of the Seven Years' War.[13] Howard came to believe that by copying and combining the methods used at these institutions to maintain discipline and order, it would be possible to build new, large-scale prisons that would not only serve to confine criminals but also facilitate their reform and salvation. He won support for his ideas from a number of influential jurists who had already been converted to the general cause of penal and judicial reform by Beccaria, and at the end of the 1770s two of these men, William Blackstone and William Eden, joined with him in drafting England's first "Penitentiary Act." It envisioned the construction of two large prisons in London, in which inmates would spend up to two years, wearing uniforms, sleeping in solitary cells, and becoming inured to the "habits of industry" through a steady diet of hard labor.[14]

There is no evidence that Riken had any knowledge of Howard or the Penitentiary Act. Even in England, the idea of the penitentiary would not take root for several more decades. The act itself was passed by Parliament in 1779, but the resources needed to put it in to effect were never secured, and transportation of convicts to Australia was soon embraced as an attractive alternative to costly experiments with prison construction.[15] It is, however, significant that the main sources of inspiration for Howard's ideas came from the Low Countries. As Simon Schama has suggested, the Rasp House had long been a source of civic pride for Amsterdam's ruling classes, and the attention it received in the late eighteenth century from Howard and his followers in England only increases the likelihood that some word of it may also have been carried to Japan by Dutch traders around the time Riken was writing.[16] Certainly by the beginning of the nineteenth century information about various other Western carceral institutions was available to those in Japan who cared to know. In 1805, for example, the painter Shiba Kōkan (1738–1818) published a book on everyday life in Holland that included brief descriptions of orphanages *(yōin)*, hospitals *(byōin)*, pest-houses *(shippei-in)*, and poorhouses *(gesuto hausu)*.[17]

At an official level too the early nineteenth century saw renewed efforts by the Bakufu to gather information about the West. In 1808 the shogun's Dutch books were all collected into a single library, and three years later a permanent translation office was established. Initially, the personnel in this office focused on translating dictionaries and reference works, but as F. B. Verwayen has shown, in the wake of the crisis sparked by the unexpected arrival of an American merchant ship (the *Morrison*) on Japanese shores in 1837 and news of Chinese losses in the first Opium War (1840–42), Mizuno Tadakuni ordered that official translations of various "Dutch military and governmental works" be made.[18] The Dutch Criminal Code and Code of Criminal Procedure were among the first batch of documents for which rudimentary translations were completed in 1848, and the small circle of scholars who prepared them must certainly have gained some sense of the Dutch penal system. In the end, however, the first description of contemporary Western penal practices and prisons to have been widely read in Tokugawa Japan came not from the Dutch but from Qing dynasty China.

From the late 1830s a small group of Qing officials had begun making their own efforts to learn more about the Western powers and their rapidly expanding empires. At the center of these efforts was the Qing dynasty's special commissioner in Canton, Lin Zexu (1785–1850), who had been appointed to stamp out the illegal opium trade that was making British merchants along the South China coast wealthy at Chinese expense. Lin's initial success in stopping the flow of narcotics into China was the main trigger for the outbreak of hostilities in the Opium War, and after the string of military disasters that followed he was dismissed from his post in disgrace in 1841. On his way into exile, however, he turned over the material on the West that he had collected to a friend named Wei Yuan (1794–1857), who subsequently incorporated it into a book titled *Haiguo tuzhi*, or in Japanese, *Kaikoku zushi* (An Illustrated Treatise on the Maritime Countries).[19] This work was read widely in China in the late 1840s, and by 1851 the first copies had begun to reach the docks at Nagasaki, where a vigorous trade in Chinese books had continued throughout the Tokugawa period.[20] Wei Yuan's work was soon in high demand in Japan, not only because of his suggestions for improving coastal defenses but also because of the new perspective it provided on the Western world.

Unlike the Japanese, who relied exclusively on the Dutch, Wei and Lin's information about the outside world came mainly from English-speaking missionaries, most notably the American, Elijah Coleman Bridgman (1801–61).[21] As a result, the book's description of the United States was especially detailed, including an extended discussion of the country's history and geography, an overview of the republican system of government, and a detailed survey of each of the twenty-six individual states then in the union. Even before 1853 this kind of information may well have been of interest to readers in Japan, but with the arrival of Perry's gunboats the motivation to learn something about the Americans increased exponentially, and by 1854 a group of publishers in Edo and Osaka, keen to profit from the crisis, had already begun printing vernacular translations of Wei's chapters on the United States under titles such as *Amerika sōki* (A General Account of America).

Although there is no explicit discussion of Christianity in the chapters on the United States (or for that matter anywhere else in the *Haiguo tuzhi*), Wei's text was clearly shaped by the agenda of its missionary informants. Banned from preaching but still eager to introduce Protestant ideas, Bridgman and his colleagues consciously set out to impress Chinese officials by highlighting the "God-inspired humanitarianism" of the American people.[22] As a result, Wei's text included an extensive discussion of various worthy causes promoted by Christian "benevolent societies" in the United States, from the relief of poverty to care for the disabled and even temperance. It was also in this context that the question of punishment and the history of prison reform in America were introduced.

In the United States, Wei explained, "there are only three methods of punishment: death by strangulation [i.e., hanging], imprisonment, or fines. There is no public display of severed heads, criminals are not forced to serve in the army, and there are no punishments involving flogging and the like."[23] Wei also emphasized that death was reserved for particularly serious crimes, and that even in the case of crimes such as arson, rape, or robbery, life imprisonment was often used as an alternative. Lesser crimes were punished with shorter terms of imprisonment, and every town in every region of the country had its own prison made of stone. Prisoners were housed either with a few others, or else entirely on their own, but all rooms were kept "exceedingly clean" and had small windows to allow fresh air to circulate. There was also an area within the prison grounds where inmates were allowed to take walks. The prison officials provided inmates with food and clothing and, using "good words," encouraged them to see the error of their ways. They also gave the prisoners work to perform, which helped offset running costs and generate revenue. According to Wei, in just one year the state of Massachusetts had managed to generate a net profit of more than seven thousand dollars from its use of prison labor.

After setting out this general description, Wei went on to note that American prisons had not always been so well run. Until fairly recently they had, in fact, been "ridden with evil customs." Inmates mixed freely with each other, and because "they had nothing to do all day but learn from the bad examples" they saw around them, most ended up "committing even worse crimes than before" after they were released from prison. Only after special charitable societies were formed to do something about this situation did new prison rules begin to spread throughout the twenty-six states. Under these new rules "good" and "bad" inmates were kept strictly separated at all times. Those who behaved well were rewarded with more comfortable living conditions, whereas the bad were forced to stay in cramped and unpleasant rooms. In addition, all inmates were kept constantly busy with work and encouraged to read from the "good book" on the "day of prayer." As a result of these changes, Wei noted, convicts in America now came to "feel remorse for their past crimes, changed their ways, and became good people." That prisoners received wages for their labor was also important. In the past the various charges incurred as a result of imprisonment had been enough to bankrupt most people, but under the new system, he explained, even those who entered prison with nothing could count on leaving with enough to build a home for themselves.

This account of the American prison reform movement and its achievements in the early nineteenth century was not without a firm basis in historical reality. As Louis Masur and David Rothman have both shown, following the conclusion of the War of Independence penal reform quickly became one of the areas in which Americans sought to forge an identity for themselves as citizens of a virtuous new republic, distinct from the "corrupted monarchies" of Europe.[24] Inspired partly by Beccaria and the Enlightenment, and partly by their hopes for a truly Christian approach to government, influential leaders such as Benjamin Rush, the Pennsylvania physician and signer of the Declaration of Independence, argued forcefully for radical changes to the system of punishments inherited from the British. Initially most criticisms were leveled at the widespread use of the death penalty (which Rush called "the natural offspring of monarchical governments"), and by the turn of the century they had succeeded in convincing most states to reduce radically their rosters of capital crimes. This also meant, however, that some alternative form of punishment had to be found. Lacking the British option of transportation to overseas colonies, the American states soon turned to incarceration as a solution, and from the latter half of the 1790s new state prisons were built everywhere, from Vermont in the north to Kentucky and Virginia in the south.

By the early decades of the nineteenth century it was already clear that this first wave of reforms had not been as successful as hoped. Far from eradicating crime and unrest, the new prisons had themselves quickly "become the scene of rampant disorder."[25] Escapes, riots, and disease were commonplace, and critics charged that prisoners spent most of their time scheming, drinking, and teaching each other new ways of making trouble. Rather than abandoning the prison, however, reformers were stimulated by these early setbacks and a growing sense of apprehension about social order in the new republic, to embark upon a new, more determined round of experimentation with prison design and management. Results came in the form of the "silent system," developed at the Auburn State Prison in New York, and the "separate system," developed in Pennsylvania, and closely associated with the Eastern State Penitentiary built in Philadelphia in 1823. Advocates of the two new systems argued fiercely about their relative merits and faults, but as Rothman has noted, their basic principles were remarkably similar: while the "separate system" kept prisoners isolated from each other at all times, making them work, eat, and sleep in solitary confinement, the "silent system" required them to work and eat together in total silence during the day before being returned to individual cells at night to sleep. Both systems "emphasized isolation, obedience and a steady routine of labor," and both were based on the belief that a combination of strict discipline and time alone to reflect upon their past sins would lead prisoners to repent and save themselves from further wrongdoing.[26]

In an important sense the new American approach to prison management and the institutions associated with it represented a concrete realization of Howard's earlier vision of a "penitentiary," and by the 1830s it had begun to attract considerable attention from European reformers. The official purpose of Alexis de Tocqueville's famous 1831 tour of the United States was, in fact, to assess whether the American penitentiary system would be appropriate for adoption in France, and in Britain, too, Philadelphia's "separate system" provided the main inspiration for London's famous Pentonville prison, which, in turn, "excited emulation" across England and western Europe after its completion in 1842.[27] Ignatieff notes that, "by 1850, ten new prisons had been built on the Pentonville model [in England alone], and ten more had been converted to the separate system."[28] All of this coincided with the rapid decline of transportation of convicts to Australia, so that by 1860 incarceration in cellular prisons was, for the first time, unrivaled as the main method of punishment in the British judicial system.[29]

The remarkable international attention garnered by Jacksonian America's bold experiment with prisons certainly helps explain why Wei's account included an extensive discussion of them, but it is important to note that his description did not fully reflect the realities of the new institutions. The *Haiguo tuzhi* makes no mention of the harsh physical punishments (the whip in New York and the "iron gag" in Pennsylvania) that were used to force inmates to accept prison rules and submit to the authority of the guards.[30] Nor does it consider the harmful psychological effects that the combination of extreme discipline and prolonged periods of solitary confinement routinely had on prisoners. Charles Dickens, who visited the Eastern State Penitentiary in the early 1840s, was perhaps the most dramatic critic of the new American prisons. He described what he saw at Philadelphia as "immeasurably worse than any torture of the body" and argued that "those who have undergone this punishment MUST pass into society again morally unhealthy and diseased."[31] Particularly in the early years, when reformers were at their most zealous in their enforcement of silence and isolation, insanity and suicide were commonplace in the new prisons. Not all inmates were destroyed by the system, of course, but not all were "reformed" by it either. Some continued to undermine or resist prison discipline. Others waited patiently for their sentences to end but were soon back in prison for new crimes. Contrary to Wei's claims, moreover, the strict regime of labor enforced in the new prisons did little to offset the substantial costs involved in running them.[32]

Overall then, the *Haiguo tuzhi* presented the new American prison system as it was ideally supposed to operate, not as it ever actually did. It was a deliberately utopian vision, planted by Wei's missionary informants in order to stimulate people's interest in the achievements of Christian civilization—and in the context of Bakumatsu Japan it did exactly that.

One of the first to take note of the miraculous institutions described in the *Haiguo tuzhi* was Yoshida Shōin, the activist and scholar from Chōshū Domain who provided early inspiration for many key figures in Bakumatsu and Meiji Japan, and who has been mentioned briefly in earlier chapters. As is well known, when Perry returned to Japan in 1854 to negotiate the first official treaty with the United States, Yoshida and a companion attempted to smuggle themselves on board one of his gunboats in the hope that they would be able to travel to America and observe conditions there firsthand.[33] Both men were soon caught, but while being held in Chōshū's Noyama Jailhouse to await trial and punishment, Yoshida obtained a copy of the *Haiguo tuzhi* and was immediately struck by the contrast between what he himself had now seen of Tokugawa jails and the idealized description of American prisons that he read in Wei's text.[34] "During my long stay in jail," he wrote in a short essay on the subject, "I have observed the emotional state of my fellow prisoners closely, and although there are those who pick up evil ways as a result of long periods of imprisonment, I have never yet seen a person who came to have good thoughts [as a result of the experience]."[35] Yet the example of the American jails *(Meriken no gokusei)* showed that things did not have to be this way. Quoting almost verbatim from the *Haiguo tuzhi*, Yoshida explained that in America too there had once been a time when those who were sent to jail generally came out even worse than before. Now, however, they were given "good books" and "instruction," and as a result they "changed their ways and became good people."[36] Under such circumstances, he suggested, it would indeed make sense to call the jails "halls of blessing" as had been the case under the Chinese emperors of old.[37]

Having made these initial observations about the American prison system, Yoshida went on to lay out a ten-point plan for the creation of a new "hall of blessing" in Japan. In the 1930s this plan would win praise from the historian Osatake Takeki as a pioneering vision of modern Japan's prison system, but a close reading of the text soon reveals that it was, in fact, deeply rooted in Yoshida's own political moment.[38] In general, it is clear that Yoshida had very little interest in common thieves and criminals. The institution he envisaged would instead be strictly for delinquent samurai. Rather than exiling wayward warriors to distant islands and wasting their talents forever, he argued that the authorities should build a large new jailhouse where inmates would spend a term of three years "reading, writing, and pursuing other scholarly activities."[39] When this term had expired, the prisoners would be set free or, if they had not yet made amends for their past crimes, held for another three-year term. If, after six full years, a prisoner still failed to demonstrate a change of heart, there would be little choice but to strip him of warrior status and send him into permanent exile. Before such a drastic decision was reached, however, Yoshida was adamant that all warriors should be given every opportunity to demonstrate their potential usefulness to the country. This, of course, included himself, and it is important to note that although the new "hall of blessing" was to be subject to regular inspection by officials and watched over by a small staff of samurai guards, Yoshida imagined that overall responsibility for running the institution would be given to "a resolute and learned person" chosen from among the inmates. This person would be in charge of teaching the other prisoners and evaluating their progress—and lest there be any doubt about his intentions, at the end of the essay (which he presumably intended to present to domainal officials) Yoshida specifically proposed that he himself might be considered for this position so that he could begin repaying his "great debt to the nation."

What Yoshida had in mind, in other words, was something much closer to a private academy, in which he could play the role of teacher to disaffected warriors, than a modern prison. In this sense, if his plan for a "hall of blessing" was an early vision of anything, it was surely the Shōkasonjuku Academy, which he established after being released from the Noyama Jailhouse and put under house arrest. It was here that he devoted himself to training a group of "grass-roots patriots" *(sōmō no shishi)*, who included such important figures in the Restoration movement as Takasugi Shinsaku, Inoue Kaoru, Itō Hirobumi, and Yamagata Aritomo. Yet, while Yoshida had his own particular uses for the idea of the American prison, he was not the only one in Bakumatsu Japan to take note of it. Another important figure in this regard was Hashimoto Sanai (1834–59).

Hashimoto was a student of Dutch learning who had risen to some prominence as a domainal bureaucrat and reformer under Matsudaira Shungaku, the influential daimyo of Fukui. In 1859, after supporting the losing party in a bitter struggle for leadership of the shogunate, Shungaku was ordered to withdraw from political life, and Hashimoto, his lieutenant, was arrested and sent to the Kodenmachō Jailhouse in Edo. He was executed at Kotsukappara less than a week later, becoming one of the first victims of the great Ansei purge, but while he was being held at Kodenmachō, he lectured his fellow prisoners on the need to reform the jails. We know of this from Kusaka Genzui (1840–64), a close disciple of Yoshida Shōin, who was impressed to learn that someone other than his own mentor had become interested in the question of jails: "Our ancient sage-kings carefully investigated the situation of prisoners," he wrote, but "because they are filthy and polluted, today we do not go near [the jails], or even discuss them."[40] Kusaka's account of Hashimoto's views makes it clear that he too had been inspired directly by the *Haiguo tuzhi*: describing the existing jails in Japan as breeding grounds for evil, where inmates had nothing to do but learn from the example of the villains and rogues around them, Hashimoto reputedly argued that the first step to improving the situation was to put all prisoners to work. As in America, those who were diligent could then be rewarded with comfortable rooms, while those who were lazy would be forced to live in cramped quarters. According to Kusaka, Hashimoto argued that a teacher should be appointed in each jail room to give lessons from "sacred books of wisdom," and that prisoners who were released from jail should be paid for the labor they had performed so that they would have some money with which to start a new life. To conclude his summary, Kusaka noted that he too had been deeply impressed to learn about American prisons from Wei's account. If the "barbarians" *(iteki)* of the West had already achieved so much in this area, he concluded, how could "the great and virtuous country" of Japan continue to neglect the question of reforming the jails?

It was, of course, no coincidence that people such as Yoshida, Kusaka, and Hashimoto developed a vocal interest in penal reform after they themselves had been imprisoned. And it is worth remembering that, as a result of the struggles and purges of the Bakumatsu period, many of the activists who would later become leaders of the Meiji government were forced to take a closer look at Tokugawa jails than they might otherwise have done. But not everyone who pointed to the West as a model for reform at this time had firsthand experience of life inside a Tokugawa jail. By far the most impressive Bakumatsu proposal for reform of the jails was written in 1864 by a scholar named Yamada Hōkoku (1805–77) from Matsuyama Domain in the Bitchū region.[41] As a youth, Yamada had studied in Edo with the Yōmeigaku scholar Satō Issai (1772–1859), whose disciples included such prominent students of the West as Watanabe Kazan (1793–1841) and Sakuma Shōzan (1811–64), and who had himself studied under Nakai Chikuzan at the Kaitokudō. After returning to Matsuyama, Yamada was appointed head of the domain school and later came to play a key role in efforts to reform the domain's dilapidated administration. Perhaps partly as a result of the influence of Riken's ideas, his achievements as a reformer included the establishment of a workhouse-like institution for the confinement of gamblers and other itinerants, but it was only after retiring from active involvement in domainal affairs that he turned his attention specifically to the question of jails. In this area, he wrote in a memorandum on the subject, "neither China nor Japan can compare with the West."[42] In the past, he added, the Bakufu had occasionally expressed concern about the state of the jails, but its efforts to improve them had always amounted to nothing. Surely then, it made sense for the authorities to consider the example provided by the Western countries.

Specifically, Yamada argued that reform efforts should focus on four main areas. First, guards should be taught to maintain the highest moral standards and learn from the teachings of the great religions. In spite of the fact that Christianity was still strictly banned at the time, he boldly argued that guards should be encouraged to accept the "Western teaching" that "all men are brothers" and strive to emulate the example of self-sacrifice set by Jesus Christ, who "allowed himself to be crucified for the crimes of people all over the world." Second, Yamada emphasized the idea that in the West the main purpose of the jails was to educate prisoners. It was thus essential that teachers should be appointed. He suggested that unemployed warriors might be used for this task, or else commoners who were well versed in the teachings of Shingaku. Third, Yamada argued that, as in the prisons of the West, all aspects of inmates' lives should be carefully regulated. The jails themselves should be kept immaculately clean and inmates kept busy with work. Times for sleeping, rising, and prayers also needed to be strictly enforced, and most important of all, inmates were to be prohibited from talking to each other, especially about any form of criminal activity. Anyone who broke this rule was to be removed from the company of the other prisoners and punished severely. Finally, in the longest article of his proposal, Yamada argued that those who had been sentenced to long-term imprisonment should not be housed in the same jail as those still awaiting trial. Instead they should be sent to a special jail that would concentrate particularly on "education and reform" *(kyōka)* over a period of several years. Teachers at this jail would be given responsibility for assessing the progress of inmates, and eventually decide when to release them. Former inmates would be paid for the work they had performed in jail, but their activities would continue to be monitored closely for another two years after their release. During this period, Yamada noted, some prisoners would inevitably fall back into their former ways and have to be sent back to the jail, but those who demonstrated a genuine change of heart could be allowed to return to their villages, or else be given new plots of land to farm elsewhere.

Overall, Yamada's proposal is a remarkable document. Like Yoshida, Hashimoto, and Kusaka, he was clearly influenced by the idealized vision of the American prison presented in the *Haiguo tuzhi*, but writing a decade or so later, he had also begun to think much more carefully about how a jail based on education and reform might actually operate. Particularly striking was his call for the creation of a specialist institution that would confine people who had been formally sentenced to imprisonment as a punishment separately from those who were simply being held as a matter of administrative convenience. As Yamada himself noted, punishments such as long-term imprisonment had always been viewed unfavorably by the authorities in Tokugawa Japan, but the idea of an institution specifically designed for convicts now began to open up the possibility of a penal system in which imprisonment would play a far more substantial role than ever before. In this sense, Yamada's proposal represented the first real hint of a revolution that would sweep away the old regime of capital and corporal punishments.

As noted in the previous chapter, some would argue that late Tokugawa institutions such as the Stockade for Laborers had already marked a step in the direction of a modern, Western prison, but if this was the case, it is worth noting that no one in Bakumatsu or even early Meiji Japan seems to have made the connection. Yamada perhaps came the closest when he noted that the same principles of reform he had recommended for adoption in the jails might also be applied fruitfully in institutions like the workhouse he had helped to establish in Matsuyama. Clearly, though, he did not see the workhouse as a Japanese version of the prisons he had read about in the West. On the contrary, what made the idea of the Western prison appealing was the fact that it seemed so dramatically different from anything that then existed in Japan.

To some extent, no doubt, the interest that people such as Yamada showed in the Western prison was also fueled by an awareness of the rising tide of social disorder and unrest in the Bakumatsu period. In his stimulating essay on the "birth of the prison" in Japan, Yasumaru Yoshio has

emphasized the significance of the emergence of powerful gangs of gamblers and outlaws in the lead up to the Restoration.[43] As we have seen, such
gangs had existed on a small scale from much earlier in the Tokugawa
period, but Yasumaru's description suggests that these new organizations
were unprecedented in terms of both their size and sophistication. In 1849,
for example, he notes that the Kantō Regulatory Patrol needed an army of
over one thousand warriors, backed up by some five hundred peasant laborers, to rout a single heavily armed gang that had been operating from the
northern Kantō plain under the leadership of a man named Seiriki.[44] The
best-known Bakumatsu gang leader of all, however, was Kunisada Chūji
(1810–50). Eventually captured and crucified by the Bakufu, his story lives
on in popular folklore in large part because of his reputation for generously
distributing alms to the needy and poor.[45] Regardless of whether this Robin
Hood–like reputation is deserved, it is clear that through a combination of
wealth and violence men like Kunisada came to wield considerable power
in some regions of the country. In this regard, Yasumaru has drawn parallels
with Eric Hobsbawm's analysis of the origins of the Sicilian Mafia, and
argues that the rise of gangs was symptomatic of the power vacuum left in
many areas by the breakdown of older structures of authority.[46] We have
seen in earlier chapters that so long as they were willing to cooperate,
organizations of outlaws and gamblers could, in fact, be quite useful to
warrior officials in many situations, but there were limits, and by the middle of the nineteenth century those limits were being put under considerable strain.

Disorder was not limited to the countryside either. For most of the
1860s, Edo was plagued by increasing unrest. The situation was particularly grave after 1862 when the Bakufu decided to relax the "alternate
attendance" requirements that had forced the daimyo to maintain a substantial presence in the shogunal capital for more than two centuries. As
the daimyo retreated, so too did much of the wealth that had been concentrated in the city, and large numbers of people were soon forced to find
new ways to make ends meet. Some tried to turn the climate of political
crisis to their own advantage. A Bakufu decree from 1863 noted, for example, that bands of ruffians had begun calling on wealthy townsfolk and
forcing them to hand over money as proof of their support for the campaign to "expel the barbarians."[47] Finally, of course, there was the wave
of millenarian uprisings and carnivalesque dancing that spread across the
middle of the country in the period leading up to the final collapse of the
Bakufu and outbreak of the Restoration war. These developments undoubtedly helped to create an atmosphere in which those in, or aspiring
to, authority were especially receptive to new strategies for bringing about
a "restoration" of order.

Again, though, we must be cautious about explaining the early interest in Western ideas and institutions solely in terms of their presumed effectiveness in overcoming the problems and contradictions of the old social order. Given the way in which the Western prison was presented in texts like the *Haiguo tuzhi*, it seems likely that it would have attracted at least some attention almost regardless of the prevailing social conditions. This institution, afterall, promised to transform criminals and other troublemakers into honest, reliable members of society without the use of violence and without costing anything to run. Moreover, if the glowing descriptions of the American prison proved to be a kind of carrot for those interested in penal reform, in the years following the signing of the first "unequal treaties" with the West, it would also become increasingly clear that there was a significant stick—the institution of "extraterritoriality."

Anachronistic Space, Extraterritoriality, and the Politics of Civilization

As the opening pages of Foucault's *Discipline and Punish* remind us so powerfully, for Europeans in the late eighteenth and nineteenth centuries (and ever since), the dramatic shift away from public punishments directed at the body to a penal system based on incarceration and reform of the criminal soul quickly became a key marker of the temporal boundaries of the modern world.[48] As the ideas of the Enlightenment thinkers spread, public executions, mutilation, and torture, which had previously been accepted as essential tools for the maintenance of proper social and moral order, came instead to be seen as relics of a different, less civilized age.[49]

What Foucault and other scholars of the rise of the prison in the West do not note, however, is that Europe's so-called Age of Improvement was also its great Age of Empire, and that the two were intimately connected. Key in this regard was the rise of what Anne McClintock has called the notion of "anachronistic space"—the understanding that as European empires expanded across the globe, their masters uncovered a living panorama of earlier "stages" of human history.[50] As the great English parliamentarian Edmund Burke (1729–97) explained to a friend in 1777, "We need no longer go to History to trace [Human nature] in all its stages and periods. . . . now the Great Map of Mankind is unrolld [sic] at once; and there is no state or Gradation of barbarism and no mode of refinement which we have not at the same instant under our view."[51] It goes without saying that Europe was thought to stand alone at the center of this "Great Map." As McClintock puts it, the physical journey back from the outer reaches of empire came to be seen as "rehearsing the evolutionary logic of historical progress, forward and upward to the apogee of the Enlightenment in the

European metropolis."[52] There were many different markers of the boundaries between advanced, metropolitan Europe and the "anachronistic space" found in the rest of the world, but given the fact that harsh physical punishments had become such an important symbol of the barbarism of Europe's own past, it is not surprising that they constituted one of them. Such punishments, it should be emphasized, were not understood simply as signs of backwardness in matters of criminal justice. One of the central arguments developed by the Enlightenment thinkers was that brutal punishments were detrimental to the *general* health of a society because they inured people to the sight of violence and suffering and thus deadened their humanity. It followed from this that a society in which harsh punishments remained commonplace must also be a society inhabited by brutes and savages. In this sense, punishment came to be seen as a good indicator of a society's *overall* level of civilization.[53]

Japan's association with harsh punishments and strict laws had been firmly established in the European imagination long before Perry's expedition to "open" the country. In their earliest reports home, the Westerners who traveled to the "Far East" in the sixteenth and seventeenth centuries had described the "severe justice" practiced by warrior lords at the end of the Warring States period.[54] In *A True Description of the Mighty Kingdoms of Japan and Siam*, published in English translation in 1663, Francis Caron and Joost Shorten listed "their punishments" as "rosting, burning, crucifying both waies, drawing with four Bulls, and boyling in Oyl and Water."[55] Caron and Shorten noted also that those who committed serious crimes in Japan were usually punished "in person and posterity," with close relatives accompanying them to the grave. Other early accounts described how even the pettiest of thefts was punishable with death, and few failed to mention the decidedly un-Christian practice of "legal suicide" by "ripping up the belly."[56]

The most important factor of all in establishing Japan's reputation for pagan brutality at this time was undoubtedly the ruthless persecution of Iberian missionaries and their native converts to Christianity, which had begun under Hideyoshi and come to a bloody climax in the 1640s under the third Tokugawa shogun, Iemitsu.[57] The dramatic nature of the persecution conducted at this time was, of course, part of a deliberate strategy, intended by Japan's new warrior rulers to send a clear message to all foreigners not to interfere in Japanese affairs. Yet, even after the so-called closing of the country, a steady trickle of reports from Europeans stationed at the Dutch trading post in Nagasaki continued to provide confirmation of the severity of Japanese justice. The accounts provided by travelers such as Engelbert Kaempfer (whose description of the execution ground at Suzugamori was introduced in chapter 1) inspired Montesquieu in *The Spirit of the Laws* to point specifically to Tokugawa Japan as an example of the dangers of relying too heavily on harsh punishments: "Souls that are everywhere startled and made more atrocious can be guided only by a greater ferocity," he summed up. "This is the origin and spirit of the Japanese laws."[58]

In spite of Japan's reputation for brutality, prior to the late eighteenth century there were obvious limits to the contrast that could be drawn between punishments in the West and those practiced in other parts of the world. Again, as anyone who has read Foucault's account of the 1757 execution of Damiens the regicide is aware, Europe's absolute monarchs were just as capable of devising horrifying methods of execution as the fiercest of Japanese warlords, and in general it is fair to say that penal practices in early modern Europe and Japan differed from each other not so much in kind, as in degree.[59] Montesquieu would certainly have agreed with this assessment. Ultimately, the case of Tokugawa Japan was of interest to him precisely because it provided evidence of how harmful the principles of punishment that were then in use in his own society (terror, vengeance, etc.) could be if left unchecked.

As the reform movement in the West began to gain momentum, and Enlightenment ideas pushed questions of punishment to the center of public discourse, descriptions of Japanese penal practices began to take on new significance. Instead of simply marking Japan as a pagan land where Christians were unwelcome, the accounts of beheadings, crucifixions, and torture that continued to circulate in travel writings in the early nineteenth century now served to confirm Japan's status as an Oriental country, positioned firmly behind the nations of the West on the "Great Map" of human progress.[60] This was more than just an issue of image; as the Western empires expanded in East Asia, it was also to have grave practical ramifications. For one thing, whereas in the past stories of harsh punishments had served (as they were intended to do) as a warning to foreigners to stay away from Japanese shores, they could now be construed as a reason to approach. The "civilized" nations, after all, had an obligation to protect their own subjects and citizens from the brutality of "Oriental" justice.

Following the U.S. takeover of California in 1848 and the growth of interest in transpacific travel and trade, American newspapers in particular began to publish sensationalized accounts of the "gross barbarity" with which foreign sailors and adventurers who landed in Japan were treated, and the "cruel" conditions they endured in Japanese jails. As the New York Courier and Enquirer concluded in 1849 after a group of shipwrecked American whalers had been safely (!) returned from Japan by a sloop of war named the Preble, the stories of these "unhappy mariners" demonstrated "the necessity of making some arrangement with [the Japanese government] involving the better usage of those who are cast upon their shores."[61] Not surprisingly then, when Perry received his commission from President Millard Fillmore two years later, the publicly stated goal of his mission to

Japan was not just to secure the opening of ports so that provisions and supplies could be obtained but also to win assurances from the shogun's government that any Americans found on Japanese shores would be treated in a manner appropriate for citizens of a civilized nation.[62] In this sense, the issue of punishment, jails, and the general specter of Oriental barbarism was, from the very outset, to play a central role in shaping Japan's encounter with the Western imperial powers.

Once formal contact had been established it was not long before the Japanese authorities were also forced to accept plans for the establishment of permanent foreign settlements, and in this context the issue of how to protect Western subjects from the horrors of native justice became all the more pressing. In other parts of the globe a solution to this problem might have come in the form of outright conquest and the establishment of formal colonial rule, but in the "Far East," where it proved expedient for the agents of empire to work with or around existing regimes, an alternative solution was found in the redeployment and reformulation of the archaic custom of extraterritoriality.[63]

In its original form, extraterritoriality had its roots in the Levant, where rulers of the Ottoman Empire, believing it inappropriate and impractical to require Christian traders to uphold Muslim laws, had allowed them to live according to those of their own religion.[64] In the nineteenth century, this privilege, which had once been granted willingly to facilitate trade, was now extracted with the direct use or threat of force and enshrined in formal treaties. In East Asia, extraterritoriality in its modernized form was first obtained for Western subjects in China in the wake of Britain's victory in the first Opium War, but it was also a central feature of the first commercial treaties imposed on Japan in the late 1850s.[65] For Captain F. Brinkley, longtime correspondent for the London *Times* and a leading figure in Japan's expatriate community from his arrival there in 1867, the reasons for this were obvious:

> It has always been regarded as axiomatic that the subjects or citizens of Western countries, when they travel or reside in Oriental territories, should be exempted from the penalties and processes of the latter's criminal laws. In other words, there is reserved to a Christian the privilege, when within the territories of a pagan State, of being tried for penal offenses by Christian judges. . . . This system was, of course, pursued in Japan's case.[66]

Beyond these matters of "principle," extraterritoriality meant in practice that Westerners accused of committing crimes or violating contracts in Japan would be judged in consular courts presided over by other members of the local foreign community. Initially the Tokugawa authorities may have seen little reason to object to these arrangements. The notion of "using barbarians to control barbarians" (*i-i zhi-i* in Chinese) was well established in East Asian statecraft, and under the system of consular courts Westerners could be expected to deal with their own lawbreakers, thereby saving the Japanese authorities unnecessary trouble.[67]

It was not long, however, before the Japanese began to realize that in reality extraterritoriality was more likely to provide European traders and adventurers with de facto immunity from prosecution than to serve as an expedient measure for controlling them. Consider the well-known case of an Englishman named Moss who, in 1860, embarked on a duck-hunting expedition in the vicinity of the shogun's castle in Edo.[68] A Bakufu regulation specifically prohibited the use of firearms in the area on penalty of death, and, as Moss was returning home, Japanese officials approached and tried to stop his servant who was carrying a sack full of poached ducks. Moss responded by opening fire, seriously wounding one of the officials before he was finally overpowered and arrested. He was initially taken to the local jail, but in accordance with the principles of extraterritoriality, he was soon handed over to British officials for trial. The case was heard by a British consul together with two "assessors" from the expatriate British community. The consul found Moss guilty of malicious shooting and recommended that he be fined and deported from Japan, but the assessors, who considered even this too heavy a punishment for one of their countrymen, insisted that he be found not guilty. As a result of the deadlock the case was referred to the British minister, Sir Rutherford Alcock, who, fearing the possibility of reprisals against the foreign community, not only confirmed the consul's punishment but added to it a term of three months' imprisonment. Moss was sent to Hong Kong to serve this sentence, but on appeal to the colonial Supreme Court there it was found that Alcock had overstepped his authority in ordering both a fine and imprisonment (he was allowed to order one or the other). As a result, Moss was not only released but also awarded damages for wrongful imprisonment. His fine of one thousand dollars had by this point already been paid by sympathetic members of the foreign community in Yokohama.

That Alcock attempted to have Moss's punishment stiffened suggests that not all of those who were tried in consular courts were able to escape punishment so easily. Yet, even in cases where a punishment was handed down, Japanese officials were often frustrated by the leniency of sentencing.[69] In 1868, for example, an American sailor named Paul Masco was put on trial in consular court after stabbing a samurai named Aoki Tsutomu in the back during a drunken fit, causing his death several weeks later.[70] Masco was found guilty of assault with a deadly weapon but not of murder because the court found no evidence that the act had been premeditated. He was sentenced to deportation from Japan and imprisonment for just one year. According to Tokugawa practice the infliction of a mortal injury would ordinarily have been punished with death by decapitation, and in the eyes of the Japanese authorities the fact that the man killed was of warrior status only added to the seriousness of the crime. Apart from lodging a formal protest stating that Masco's sentence "was far too lenient for the aforementioned crime," there was, however, little the Japanese officials could do.[71] In an early submission to the Meiji government, which is also revealing of the way that the protection of women quickly became a theme in male discourses of nationalist resistance, the influential bureaucrat Inoue Kowashi (1843–95) summed up the accumulated sense of official frustration and powerlessness by noting that "in our current situation when a foreigner rapes one of our women, we are not even able to arrest him for the crime."[72]

Western leaders, for their part, were not entirely oblivious to the inadequacies of the system of extraterritoriality and the resentment that it caused in Japan. As is well known, the years immediately following the signing of the first commercial treaties in 1858 had seen a series of attacks on foreigners by radical "men of spirit" determined to "expel the barbarians" from sacred Japanese soil.[73] Prior to 1862 these attacks were aimed mainly at individuals, but in July of that year the British legation in Edo was targeted, and in 1863 radicals in Chōshū Domain convinced the leadership there to open fire on foreign ships attempting to pass through the Straits of Shimonoseki. A year later, as the Western powers were preparing to launch a combined retaliatory attack on Chōshū, a resolution was tabled in the British House of Lords arguing that in the interests of maintaining friendly relations with Japan, Britain should offer to revise the existing treaty. The mover of the resolution, Earl Grey, who had been secretary at war in the lead up to the Opium War, was no doubt well aware of the problems that the issue of extraterritoriality had caused in China, and he insisted that

> if we wish to remain on good terms with Japan it is in the first place indispensable greatly to restrict the operation of what is called the "extraterritoriality" clause. . . . If . . . it should be thought necessary to adhere to the principle of "extraterritoriality" at all, and I am by no means sure that we ought . . . , it ought to be confined within the narrowest limits possible, and the privilege should be enjoyed within a very restricted space set apart in the different open ports for the residence of foreigners and for carrying on their trade.[74]

While Grey's views are suggestive of the extent to which British leaders were aware of the resentment that extraterritoriality had helped generate in Japan, the rebuttal of his speech by the then foreign minister, Lord John Russell, is more revealing of prevailing attitudes. Russell began by appealing to the idea that extraterritoriality had always been a central feature of "our intercourse with Eastern nations":

> What is the history of our intercourse with China and with Turkey? Have we not entered into arrangements with China of this very character? Would we be

justified, then, in adopting an entirely new plan in regard to Japan, saying that the Japanese should be allowed to prevail in the case of any British subject who might be accused of committing an offense against them?

This invocation of extraterritoriality as a tried and true method for dealing with Oriental nations was, however, just the beginning. It was only when he reminded his audience of the terrible barbarities of Japanese justice that Russell's argument reached its rhetorical climax:

> Your Lordships must bear in mind that Japanese laws are most sanguinary. What should we say if a young English merchant had been brought before the Japanese tribunals, subjected to torture, put to death, being disemboweled, and, in short, suffering the horrid torture which the code of the country inflicts? And what should be said if we were to admit the application of the Japanese law to British offenders, that all the relations of the criminal should be put to death for his offense? Is it desirable, under those circumstances, that we should abandon a plan which has now been acted upon for three centuries, in accordance with which, when we enter Oriental nations, we carry with us our own tribunals and our own notions of justice?[75]

This description of Tokugawa justice was, of course, little more than a caricature, but it hardly mattered.[76] Russell's impeccable credentials on domestic penal reform (he had been home secretary in the 1830s and 1840s) meant he was ideally positioned to decry "sanguinary" justice wherever it was practiced, and by simply reminding his fellow lords of the images of Japanese punishment that had long circulated in the West he was easily able to ensure the defeat of Grey's resolution.[77] It would be decades before the possibility of revising the extraterritoriality provisions was seriously considered again.

Ironically, in the years that followed, it was Western insistence that radical samurai who attacked foreigners should be severely punished that did the most to ensure a steady flow of evidence in support of the view that Japanese justice was, indeed, "most sanguinary." The Namamugi incident of 1862, in which an English merchant named Richardson was attacked and killed by warriors from Satsuma Domain, was an important development in this regard. Coming just a month after the attack on the British legation, the incident prompted Russell, in his capacity as foreign minister, to demand sizable indemnities from both Satsuma and the Bakufu on threat "of reprisal or blockade, or both."[78] The Bakufu soon gave in to the British demands, but in early 1863, after Satsuma refused to follow suit, a squadron of seven gunboats was dispatched to the domainal capital of Kagoshima. When it became clear that Satsuma was still unwilling to negotiate, the gunboats were ordered to open fire, destroying large sections of the city, including the domain's model industrial establishment, the Shūseikan, within a few hours. The conflict was not completely one-sided. Satsuma forces succeeded in inflicting some damage of their own on the British warships, which eventually withdrew to make repairs. In spite of this small "victory," however, it was not long before Satsuma officials agreed to pay the indemnity that had been demanded of them and to execute Richardson's murderers if they were ever caught.

The British assault on Kagoshima served as a warning to warrior officials all over the country that attacks on foreigners could easily become a pretext for Western military action, and in the years that followed every effort was made to ensure that anyone who launched such an attack was brought to justice in the presence of representatives of the Western powers. As a result, detailed eyewitness accounts of Japanese executions now began being reported back to audiences in the West with increasing frequency. In 1864, for example, just a few months after the debate over treaty revision in the House of Lords, two British soldiers were killed in Kamakura by a loyalist named Shimazu Seiji. Shimazu and his two accomplices were quickly arrested by the Bakufu, and arrangements were made for their executions to be held in Yokohama so that members of the foreign community there would be able to attend. Over the next several months descriptions of the way these men met their deaths were featured in newspapers such as the *Illustrated London News*, which carried not just written reports but also full-page illustrations.[79] In the case of Shimazu Seiji these illustrations depicted his execution and the parade through the streets of Yokohama the previous day—a scene that for its Victorian audience would surely have been suggestive of the processions to execution at Tyburn that had by this time come to symbolize all that was wrong with the old "bloody code" and that can only have helped to confirm Japan's place in "anachronistic space."[80]

Political historians of the Bakumatsu period have often pointed to 1864, the year in which Shimazu died, as a turning point.[81] By the end of that year many of the most radical "men of spirit" had been killed in failed attempts to foment rebellion, and those who managed to survive were forced to rethink their strategies for facilitating change. Increasingly, the main locus of political activity shifted back to the great domains, in particular, to Satsuma and Chōshū, which eventually began working with each other to overthrow the Tokugawa regime. Joined by three other large domains from the southwestern part of the country, they launched their campaign to take control of the country in the name of the emperor at the very end of 1867. Within a matter of weeks they had routed Bakufu forces in the battle of Toba-Fushimi and secured control of Kyoto, but almost immediately after this a series of attacks on foreigners by warriors fired up by the rhetoric of the loyalist movement presented the leaders of what would soon become the Meiji government with their first foreign relations crisis.

Figure 9. The execution of Shimazu Seiji as portrayed in the *Illustrated London News*, March 16, 1865. Note that the onlookers are mostly Westerners. Author's private collection.

The first incident began on the outskirts of the recently opened treaty port of Kobe, where a group of foreigners made the mistake of cutting across the path of a company of loyalist warriors from Okayama Domain who had been sent to guard the southwestern approach to Kyoto for the fledgling government. Provoked by what they took to be an open display of disrespect, the warriors opened fire on the foreigners and seriously injured several of them. When news of this attack reached representatives of the Western powers, who had already been put on edge by the outbreak of what appeared to be civil war, they immediately decided to take action to secure their own interests. Within a day the combined forces of Britain, France, and the United States had taken military control of the foreign settlement at Kobe and seized all Japanese ships in the harbor.[82]

The position of the anti-Bakufu coalition at this time was hardly secure. The battle of Toba-Fushimi had been an important first step to taking control of the country, but Edo had yet to surrender to the new imperial army, and it was still far from clear whether domains in other parts of the country would chose to fight for the Tokugawa cause. Given this situation, the leaders of the would-be imperial government could hardly risk adding the Western powers to their list of enemies. When prompted by Britain's Sir Harry Parkes, they quickly agreed to send the high-ranking courtier Higashikuze Michitomi to meet with foreign representatives to try and diffuse tensions. It was in this context that the Western powers received their first formal notification of the "Restoration of Imperial Rule" (*ōsei fukko*). At the same time, Higashikuze assured representatives of the foreign powers that the emperor intended to honor all existing treaties and would guarantee the safety of all foreign subjects in Japan. The Western representatives, for their part, responded to these assurances with two demands: they required a formal apology for the attack at Kobe and insisted that the officer who had issued the order to open fire be severely punished.[83] Within a matter of weeks officials in Okayama had been forced to hand over the man in question, who was subsequently ordered to disembowel himself in the presence of the foreign representatives. This was the first time that foreigners had ever been invited to witness the act of "harakiri."[84]

The dramatic death of the officer from Okayama was meant to bring the incident at Kobe to a close, but just a few days later there was a second attack on foreigners by samurai aligned with the new government. This time warriors from Tosa Domain opened fire on a party of French sailors from the gunboat *Dupleix* who had come ashore at the port of Sakai, on the opposite side of Osaka Bay from Kobe. Eleven sailors were killed in the attack, and the French representative to Japan, Léon Roches, who was already sympathetic to the Tokugawa, responded with outrage when he learned what had happened.[85] In addition to an indemnity of some fifteen thousand dollars and several lesser demands, he insisted that *all* of those involved in the attack be put to death.[86] Less than a week later the captain of the *Dupleix* and other French representatives were invited to the temple of Myōkokuji to watch twenty of the Tosa warriors commit harakiri. After witnessing the deaths of eleven of these men (one for each of the French sailors killed) the captain of the *Dupleix*, whether as an act of mercy or simply because he could stomach no more, requested that the executions stop.[87] The sentences of the remaining nine warriors were then commuted to exile.

As diplomatic historian Ishii Takashi has noted, the willingness of the Meiji leaders to deal swiftly and severely with those responsible for the attacks at Kobe and Sakai was a key factor in their success in winning early recognition from the Western powers as a legitimate government.[88] The command performances of harakiri, that most "typically Japanese" of rituals, were quickly accepted by their Western audiences as proof of Higashikuze's earlier claim that loyalists in the new regime did not intend to implement their old calls to "expel the barbarians."

At the same time, descriptions of these events, which were soon circulating in the West, only served to further reinforce the "sanguinary" image of Japan's punishment system. As *Harper's Magazine* made clear in an article published in 1869, in the immediate aftermath of the Meiji Restoration Westerners were more convinced than ever that "the savage barbarity which characterized the punishments of the Middle Ages is still a feature of punishment in Japan."[89] This belief, in turn, provided all the justification the Western powers needed to maintain the system of extraterritoriality.

As we have already seen, extraterritoriality represented a serious compromise of Japanese sovereignty, and in the years following the Meiji Restoration it would continue to be resented for this reason alone. By way of conclusion, however, it is important to note that extraterritoriality and the fear that citizens of Western countries might be exposed to Oriental justice helped imbue the "unequal treaties" as a whole with an air of moral legitimacy that they would not otherwise have had. The main purpose of the treaties had always been to ensure that Western commercial interests enjoyed favorable conditions for conducting trade. Extraterritoriality certainly contributed to this by ensuring that contractual disputes between foreigners and Japanese were tried under foreign law and in consular courts, but, even more important, the treaties also gave the Western powers the right to set customs rates and tariffs on imports and exports at levels that suited them. In addition, the "most favored nation" clause inserted in the commercial treaties meant that any concessions granted to one of the treaty powers automatically became the right of all. Taken in isolation, these sections of the treaties could only be explained in terms of the West's determination to use every possible advantage to maximize profits and power. Because they were linked to the question of punishment, however, the treaties as a whole could be presented as something more than that. The West's real concern, it would be argued, was not commercial or political gain, but to uphold the standards of modern "civilization" in a thoroughly alien environment.

In an important sense then, the West's imposition of extraterritoriality might well be seen as an early example of what would today be called "the imperialism of human rights." By using this term I do not mean to imply that issues of human rights are unimportant or that they have only ever been pursued for cynical reasons. Nor do I wish to suggest that Tokugawa punishments were, in fact, gentle and humane. Clearly this was not the case. Yet, as we have seen, the Western powers themselves were not above demanding the use of harsh punishments when it suited their interests. More to the point perhaps, it is clear that in the case of the "unequal treaties" imposed on Japan in the mid-nineteenth century, the evidence of harsh punishments and the image of backwardness that went with it served to justify a range of semicolonial institutional arrangements that were, in fact, unrelated to questions of criminal justice.

For the most part, of course, what were advantages for the West were disadvantages for Japan, and under the Meiji government "treaty revision" was quickly taken up as the central goal of Japanese foreign policy. At first the Meiji leaders seem to have been hopeful that this would be relatively easy to achieve, but they soon began to realize that the Western powers— and, in particular, Great Britain—would only agree to change the existing arrangements if and when Japan could prove its civilization worthy of equal treatment. Punishments and the judicial system were crucial in this regard. Extraterritoriality would never be abolished while the specter of white men being crucified or forced to disembowel themselves could still be raised. And, so long as extraterritoriality remained in place, it would be difficult to revise other aspects of the treaties. As a result, penal reform and criminal justice in the early Meiji period were never matters of domestic concern alone. From the outset they were intimately linked to Japan's struggle to escape from "anachronistic space" and the inferior status it was assigned within the imperialist world order of the late nineteenth century. This, in turn, would soon help to ensure that the early fascination with utopian tales of the Western prison would begin to be translated into something more concrete.

CHAPTER 6

Restoration and Reform:
The Birth of the Prison in Japan

IT DID NOT TAKE the Meiji leaders long to begin dismantling the system of punishments they inherited from the Tokugawa. Within a month of announcing the "Restoration of Imperial Rule" they had already ordered the compilation of a new set of provisional penal regulations *(kari keiritsu)* for use in areas under their direct control, and in December 1868, just weeks after the last significant pockets of military resistance to their authority had finally been crushed, Iwakura Tomomi (1825–83), the court noble who had come to play a central role in the new regime, petitioned the throne with a call for extensive penal reforms.[1] The resulting decree, issued to officials all over the country, declared that, "among the hundreds of reforms to be implemented in conjunction with the Restoration of Imperial Rule, the penal laws are a matter of life and death for the multitudes and are thus in urgent need of correction."[2] It then announced that although the military struggles of the previous year had prevented the government from finalizing a new set of penal laws, some changes were to go into effect immediately. Crucifixion was to be strictly limited to cases of regicide and parricide, and burning alive was to be completely abolished. All forms of banishment were to be replaced with "penal servitude" *(tokei)*, and as soon as proper facilities had been built, criminals sentenced to exile were to be sent to the northern island of Ezochi (later renamed Hokkaido). In addition, the decree ordered that under the new regime no theft of less than one hundred *ryō* (as opposed to the traditional ten *ryō* outlined in the One Hundred Articles) was to be punished with death, and finally, that capital sentences issued anywhere in the country would henceforth require the explicit approval of the imperial court.

The speed with which these dramatic changes were introduced is all the more remarkable when compared with the old regime's reluctance to tamper with any aspect of the penal laws. During the Bunkyū Reforms of 1862, arguably the most important attempt to restructure the Bakufu in the years leading up to its collapse, members of the shogun's senior council had pledged themselves to "reform every aspect of the old laws, *with the exception of the penal laws.*"[3] This was not so much an expression of priorities as an indication of the way that Bakufu leaders continued to see the existing system of punishments as one of the fundamental cornerstones of warrior governance. Five years later, a series of reform attempts and policy shifts had done little to strengthen the Bakufu's position, and in the final months of 1867 Japan's last shogun, Tokugawa Yoshinobu, tried to outmaneuver his opponents by resigning his post and proposing to the emperor that a council of great lords be convened in Kyoto to consider the future of the country. At this point, Yoshinobu added penal law to the list of matters the council might discuss, but he also urged the emperor to authorize formally the continued use of existing laws and punishments. Still the preeminent political figure in the country at the time, the former shogun soon received the reply he wanted: although the imperial court now reserved the right to determine all matters relating to the government of the realm, it was the emperor's intention that the "great and good laws" *(migoto ryōhō)* established by Yoshinobu's "Tokugawa forebears" should remain in place "without change."[4] Right up until the final days of the Tokugawa period, in other words, significant changes to the old system of criminal justice seemed only a distant possibility. How then are we to explain the urgency with which penal reform was pursued by the new regime?

Even at this early point the Meiji leaders' concern with the unequal treaties was undoubtedly an important factor. The Bakufu's inability to stand up to the Western intruders had, after all, been at the heart of loyalist anger and frustration with Tokugawa rule, and although supporters of the imperial cause had gradually come to realize that radical attempts to "expel the barbarian" were pointless, they had become increasingly interested in the possibility of negotiating new treaties that would allow Japan to "stand unashamed before all nations and all ages to come."[5] In 1868 the Meiji leaders had clearly not yet reached a full understanding of the changes that treaty revision would entail, but given the central place of extraterritoriality in the existing treaties there can be little doubt that they recognized the need for some form of penal and judicial reforms.

While the question of treaty revision would become increasingly important in the years that followed, domestic considerations also were crucial to the initial burst of reforms. At a time when the appeal of the emperor had yet to be established in the minds of large sections of the population, alleviation of harsh punishments provided the Meiji leaders with a simple way to establish his credentials as a benevolent ruler and to mark the end of what Iwakura's petition had specifically referred to as "the age of warrior rule." In this regard, it is worth recalling that throughout the Tokugawa period medieval chronicles such as the *Hōgen monogatari* had helped sustain the belief that, before the rise of the warrior clans in the twelfth century, the imperial court had successfully governed the country for more than three centuries without once resorting to the death penalty. By taking immediate action to end some of the harshest Tokugawa punishments then, leaders of the new regime may well have seen themselves as giving concrete expression to the ancient traditions of imperial rule they had pledged to "restore." Beyond this, the changes ordered by the new government also had important ramifications for the overall structure of the Japanese polity. As we saw in chapter 3, the right to order executions independently—and, in particular, crucifixions and burnings alive—had long marked the exalted status of the daimyo within the Tokugawa system. By abolishing burning alive, severely restricting the use of crucifixion, and insisting that *all* sentences of death be approved directly by the emperor, the new government now withdrew this long-standing prerogative of the daimyo and signaled its intention to pursue the centralization of judicial authority. This aspect of the new policies did not go completely uncontested. Soon after receiving the December order, the daimyo of Tosa, one of the domains that had been centrally involved in the Restoration, petitioned the government for a number of concessions, including the right to continue using the punishment of burning alive and ordering executions without consultation. The request was bluntly rejected. Burning alive was to be abolished "without fail," and all death sentences were to be approved directly by the emperor because, it was explained, "the lives of the people are of the greatest concern [to him]."[6]

Viewed within a broader historical framework, the reforms of the first year of Meiji can also be seen as the culmination of well over a century of domestic debate and criticism of the old system of punishments. As noted in chapter 4, from early in the eighteenth century a series of influential thinkers had criticized crucifixion and burning alive as overly harsh, and several had also called for a restriction of the use of the death penalty for theft. Most obvious of all, perhaps, the Meiji government's quick decision to replace banishment with the traditional Chinese punishment of penal servitude was clearly influenced by the arguments in favor of such a change first articulated by Ogyū Sorai in the 1720s. When it received an inquiry from Ina Domain concerning the reasons for this reform, the government replied that "the primary intent behind the abolition of banishment and its replacement with penal servitude was to ensure that there would be no one in the realm without a registered abode."[7] The penal system, in other words, would no longer be allowed to contribute to the spread of rootlessness—precisely the problem that had been at the heart of Sorai's critique.[8]

In retrospect, of course, the early moves to tighten controls over the population and to alleviate harsh Tokugawa punishments can be easily slotted into the general narrative of Meiji modernization. Yet, once again, we must be careful not to overemphasize the smoothness of the Tokugawa—Meiji transition, or the manner in which a new social order began to take root. The early years of the new era were in many ways a time of competing visions, experimentation, and false starts. In this regard it is important to note that the decision to replace banishment with penal servitude was understood at the time as one part of a broader shift toward the use of Chinese dynastic codes as the new government's primary model for legal reform. This, in fact, was the single most important legacy of Tokugawa thought for the early development of Meiji law. As the writings of Haku- seki, Sorai, and Shundai all make clear, interest in Chinese legal traditions had grown dramatically in the early eighteenth century, in large part be- cause of the direct encouragement and sponsorship provided by Yoshimune in the context of his own efforts to formalize and codify existing warrior laws.[9] In the end, Chinese influence on Bakufu law had remained small, but in two or three daimyo domains there were significant experiments with codification along Chinese lines. By far the most prominent example was that of Kumamoto, which, in 1754, instituted a domainal penal code modeled directly on that of the Ming dynasty.[10] As a result of this, the domain's reputation as a center for Chinese legal scholarship spread rap- idly, and it was no coincidence that in the first months of 1868, when the Meiji leaders established an Office of Criminal Law to begin the work of compiling a provisional code, they looked primarily to officials from Kumamoto to staff it.[11]

In addition to the simple fact that there was already an established body of experts for the new government to draw upon, the early interest in Chi- nese legal models makes sense for a number of other reasons. In general terms, of course, it reflects the enormous prestige that continental civiliza- tion and scholarship continued to command in Japan in the early Meiji years, but at the same time it also fitted neatly with the idea of "restoring" the classical traditions of imperial rule. Japan's ancient Ritsuryō system had, after all, borrowed heavily from the laws and institutions of China's Tang dynasty (618–907), and it is clear that in the first years of the new era the Meiji leaders looked to this system for inspiration in much the same way that their counterparts in the French and American Revolutions had looked to ancient Greece and Rome. By the middle of 1869 the new gov- ernment's administrative structures had been completely reorganized along the lines of the ancient system of "eight ministries." This included a fully fledged "Ministry of Punishments" (gyōbusho), which now subsumed the earlier Office of Criminal Law and took over the work of preparing a Chinese-style code for the Meiji regime.[12] At the same time, the govern- ment also pressed ahead with more piecemeal reforms to the penal system. In mid-1869 the old practices of parading condemned criminals through the streets, pillorying, and "pulling the saw" were all abolished, and by early 1870 tattooing was also added to the list of defunct punishments.[13] As this suggests, the criminal "body-as-sign" was rapidly retreating from Japan's political landscape, and with the completion of the Meiji govern- ment's first national criminal code, the Shinritsu kōryō (Outline of the New Code), in early 1871, the process took another important step forward.

Intended to serve only as an interim code until a more refined set of laws could be completed, the *Shinritsu kōryō* not only confirmed all of the earlier penal reforms, it also marked a formal end to crucifixion, perhaps the single most important symbol of the old penal regime.[14]

By this time, with the domestic situation seemingly under control, the Meiji leaders were able to begin devoting more of their attention to the question of the unequal treaties. Already in 1869 Iwakura had submitted an official statement to the throne complaining that, "the current situation, in which the troops of foreign countries are stationed in our ports and resident Westerners are dealt with by officials from their own countries, even when they have broken our laws, constitutes a grave insult to our imperial nation."[15] Two years later he had begun preparing to lead a diplomatic mission, which would include many of the most powerful members of the new regime, on an extended tour of the United States and Europe. Often remembered today as a highly successful "study tour," the Iwakura mission's main objective was to convince the Western powers to reopen treaty negotiations. And it was in conjunction with this goal that the Ministry of Foreign Affairs distributed copies of the *Shinritsu kōryō* to representatives of the treaty powers in early 1871.[16] It was hoped that providing concrete evidence that significant penal reforms had already been undertaken by the new government would help to convince the foreign powers to give up their claims to extraterritoriality.

As Iwakura and his companions quickly discovered on their arrival in the United States, however, it would take a great deal more than this initial display of reformist zeal to persuade Western governments to abandon the privileges and protections that their gunboats had secured for them. The new Chinese-style penal code certainly did nothing to help the Japanese leaders' cause. The Western world's own brief fascination with Confucian models of government had ended with the eighteenth century, and by this time China had been recast as the epitome of "Oriental despotism." Indeed, as noted in chapter 5, it was precisely in order to protect British subjects from *Chinese* laws that the institution of extraterritoriality had been introduced to East Asia in the first place. Had the Western representatives cared to look for it, of course, specific proof of the inadequacy of the *Shinritsu kōryō* itself could have been found in clauses allowing for the continuation of various Tokugawa practices such as judicial torture, legalized suicide, and so on. Even if the new code had met the highest possible standards on paper, moreover, there would still have been the question of how it was to be applied and of the conditions in which foreign suspects and convicts would have to live while in Japanese custody. If the goal of treaty revision was ever to be achieved, in other words, it would not be enough simply to introduce new laws and abolish old punishments. Attitudes, practices, and institutions would also have to be remade. Some of the most important early contributions in this regard came not from powerful officials but from a low-ranking warrior from Okayama Domain named Ohara Shigechika (1834–1902).

OHARA SHIGECHIKA AND THE COLONIAL ORIGINS OF
THE MODERN JAPANESE PRISON

As an active member of the loyalist movement, Ohara had gained considerable firsthand experience of life in Tokugawa era jails in the lead up to the Restoration.[17] In 1864, at the height of the loyalist terror campaign, he was arrested and left to languish in an Okayama jail for some two years for his role in the assassination of a Bakufu spy.[18] Soon after his release he was back in jail again, this time as a result of his involvement with loyalists in Kyoto.[19] Fortunately for Ohara, the collapse of the Bakufu allowed him to escape more serious punishment, and after the Restoration his active support for the loyalist cause quickly became a valuable asset. Early in 1868 he was chosen to serve as a domainal representative (kōshi) in the Meiji administration and before the end of that year he had secured an appointment in the Office of Criminal Law.

Unable to forget his own experiences in what he later called the "hellish world" (jigoku sekai) of Tokugawa era jails, he decided to use this new position to inspect some of the jails under the new government's control. At the end of 1869 he submitted a personal report to the minister of punishments highlighting the abuses of the rōnanushi system and the unbearable filth that characterized the institutions he had seen. Although there had already been significant changes to the laws of the Bakufu in general, he noted, nothing had been done to reform the jails; in order to rectify this situation he proposed that a separate Office for Jails be created within the Ministry of Punishments.[20] The proposal was approved, and at the beginning of 1870 Ohara was appointed acting head of the new office, with direct responsibility for both the old Kodenmachō Jailhouse and the Ishikawajima Stockade, which, in keeping with the government's plan to replace banishment with penal servitude had recently been designated an official "place of servitude" (tojo).[21] By coincidence, 1870 was also the year in which the brilliant artist Kawanabe Kyōsai (1831–89) was arrested by the authorities for mocking the Meiji leaders in one of his paintings. His depiction of the central guardhouse (ōbanya) where suspects in Tokyo (as the old city of Edo was now officially known) were sent to await interrogation provides us with a clear picture of the conditions in which prisoners lived at this time.[22] Ohara, for his part, immediately took steps to try and ease the suffering of inmates by improving sanitation, providing better care for the sick, and, at Kodenmachō in particular, limiting the role of inmate-officials

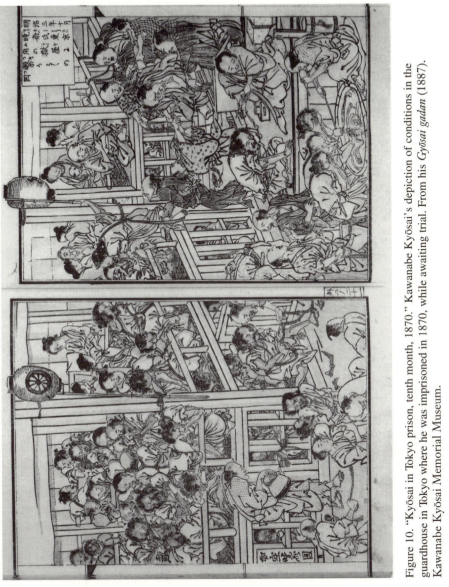

Figure 10. "Kyōsai in Tokyo prison, tenth month, 1870." Kawanabe Kyōsai's depiction of conditions in the guardhouse in Tokyo where he was imprisoned in 1870, while awaiting trial. From his *Gyōsai gadan* (1887). Kawanabe Kyōsai Memorial Museum.

in the day-to-day running of the jail.[23] As a result of these changes, the number of inmates who died of diseases in jail in Tokyo fell dramatically, from 1,176 in 1870 to just 144 in 1871.[24]

As important as these initial efforts were for inmates at the time, Ohara was convinced that in the long run proper reforms would only be possible after gaining a better understanding of Western prisons. In this he was undoubtedly influenced by the Bakumatsu activists and thinkers discussed in chapter 5. Being from Okayama, Ohara almost certainly knew of the work of Yamada Hōkoku from neighboring Matsuyama Domain, but when speaking in public, it was the influence of Yoshida Shōin and Hashimoto Sanai, both remembered as martyrs of the Restoration, that he emphasized.[25] Shōin's admiration for American prisons may also have been an important asset for Ohara at the end of 1870 when he met with Kido Taka-yoshi (1833–77), one of the most powerful men in the new government, to discuss the need to learn more about Western penal systems. Kido had himself been a student of Shōin's in Chōshū, and soon after their meeting Ohara won official approval for his plan to lead one of the Meiji era's first official study missions abroad.[26] Unlike later Meiji missions, however, Ohara's destination was not the United States or Europe but the British colonies of Hong Kong and Singapore.[27]

Although budgetary constraints may have been a factor in Ohara's decision to examine prisons in nearby Asia rather than the more distant centers of the Western world, his official submission to the government suggests that he was genuinely convinced that British colonial prisons would provide the best possible model for study. The brief but glowing description of the Hong Kong prison that had just been published by Shibusawa Eiichi in his account of the Bakufu's 1867 mission to Europe may well have contributed to his enthusiasm.[28] Yet, what Ohara himself argued to the government was that,

> It will be best for us to build our nation's jails (gokusei) on the basis of a system in which people, like ourselves, from countries in which life is sustained through the consumption of rice are held together with people from meat-eating countries. This will enable us in the future to reach a point where we can confine foreigners [in our jails] and thereby achieve our national policy objectives (kokuze).[29]

In other words, if treaty revision and the abolition of extraterritoriality were ever to be achieved, the Japanese would have to be ready to imprison "meat-eating" Westerners alongside "rice-eating" Asians, and in this regard the British prisons in Hong Kong and Singapore, where Chinese and Indian prisoners were confined in the same facilities as Europeans, would provide an ideal point of reference.

Ohara's thinking on these matters was almost certainly influenced by members of the British legation in Japan. During his first year at the Office

for Jails he claimed to have made every effort to consult with "knowledge-
able persons" about Western prisons, and by late 1870 the editors of the
Yokohama-based *Japan Weekly Mail* (a leading expatriate newspaper) had
already run an article strongly endorsing his decision to inspect the prison
at Hong Kong. Their reasoning, however, varied somewhat from his own:

> We understand that the Japanese government intend sending an officer to Hong-
> kong to inspect the jail. The Hongkong jail is very extensive, being capable of
> containing eight or nine hundred prisoners, and it seldom has less than four
> hundred occupants. The system on which it is conducted is much eulogized by
> those who have studied the matter. The superintendent seems in a striking man-
> ner to have solved the difficulty of adapting European notions of order and hu-
> manity in prison discipline to the essential requirements of such establishments
> in the East. There can be no doubt that the Japanese commissioners will be much
> struck by such an example of the European treatment of criminals. It remains to
> be seen whether the Japanese will think themselves justified in adopting a similar
> mode of treatment in the case of their own prisons.[30]

Whereas Ohara's primary concern was with the technical problem of how
to establish institutions that would be suitable for incarcerating people
from different cultures, the *Japan Weekly Mail* stressed instead "the difficulty of adapting European notions of order and humanity" to conditions
in "the East." The orderly, humane prison is, in other words, understood
to be a unique product of Western culture, and although the Japanese commissioners would inevitably be impressed by the "European treatment of
criminals," it was doubtful that their own Oriental traditions would allow
them to emulate what they observed. Of course, even in the face of such
doubts British officials were always keen to play teacher to "backward natives," a role that served both to confirm their own sense of cultural superiority and to justify their presence in East Asia. They also had a strong
interest in helping the Meiji regime find ways to enforce social order, and
in planning his trip Ohara was offered "every possible assistance" by the
British minister, Sir Harry Parkes, and his vice minister, F. O. Adams. It
was, no doubt, at their suggestion that the Singapore prison, long held up
by the British as a model of colonial penal administration, was added to his
itinerary.[31] But their greatest contribution to the success of the mission was
the appointment of a consular official named John Carey Hall to serve as
Ohara's guide and interpreter. Hall was not only fluent in Japanese, but
also well acquainted with Japanese legal traditions, having been assigned
the task of making a detailed study of Bakufu laws when he first took up
his post in Japan in 1867.[32]

   After half a year of preparation, Ohara and Hall departed Yokohama at
the end of July 1871, accompanied by two other officials from the Ministry
of Punishments.[33] This was still a full four months before the departure of

the famous Iwakura mission, and because Ohara's was the first group sent abroad to investigate a Western criminal justice system, he was instructed to take detailed notes on everything he saw. During their travels, Ohara and the other officials met with police magistrates and chief justices, toured the local courthouses, and were tutored by Hall on English criminal procedure. What they learned about the English judicial system was eventually published in a separate report, full of praise for the "fair and merciful" nature of English trials.[34] Yet the mission's main purpose was to study the colonial prisons, and this was indeed where most of their energies were concentrated, as Hall's official account of their activities makes clear.

In Hong Kong, Ohara and his companions spent the first ten days of their eighteen-day visit at the famous Victoria Jail, where they "inspected every part of the building and enquired minutely into every detail of its management." According to Hall, the overall impression the prison left on the three commissioners was "profound":

> The separate cells, the careful sanitary arrangements as to ventilation, sewerage etcetera, the classification of the prisoners, their orderly prosecution of their various tasks, the perfect discipline, the machine-like regularity with which every movement was carried out, and the scrupulous cleanliness that reigned everywhere struck them with a sense of admiration which they did not attempt to conceal. The difference, they said, between this and the best of Japanese prisons was as that between a Daimio's [sic] palace and a peasant's hovel.[35]

In Singapore too, the commissioners spent a full week visiting "every department of the prison," and although Hall's account suggests that the prison system there was generally inferior to that of Hong Kong, they were nonetheless able to gain a number of important insights during their stay. From its very founding under Sir Stamford Raffles, much of the basic infrastructure of the colony had been built and maintained using the labor of prisoners transported from British India, and according to Hall, the colonial engineer, Major J.F.A. McNair, imparted a range of "useful information regarding the employment of convicts on public works."[36] Even more important, McNair introduced Ohara and his colleagues to the work of the great British utilitarian Jeremy Bentham (1748–1832) and his famous plans for a "panopticon"—a structure in which inmates would constantly feel as though they were under observation from a central watchtower, and in which the idea of surveillance would serve as a tool for promoting reform.[37] In the end, the panopticon was never built in precisely the way that Bentham had envisioned, but, as McNair explained, the basic idea had a profound impact on the subsequent development of prison design, and it now also inspired Ohara to coin a new term to describe the kind of institution he hoped to see built in Japan. The Western prisons he had inspected and heard descriptions of were, after all, nothing like a Tokugawa jailhouse *(rōya)*, in which prisoners were held together in communal rooms, ruled over by semiautonomous inmate-officials. Nor were they simple cages *(ori)*, or structures for confining prisoners *(gokusha)*. Instead, as Bentham's plans made clear, they were places in which the ability to watch inmates (and make them feel watched) was key. He thus took the Chinese characters for surveillance *(kan)* and jail *(goku)* and combined them to create the word, *kangoku*—surveillance jail—which, to this day, remains the term used to describe a modern prison building in Japanese.[38]

After arriving back in Japan at the beginning of October 1871, Ohara immediately began work on a document outlining how a modern prison should ideally operate. The resulting "Prison Rules" (literally "Rules for Surveillance Jails") were eventually completed in 1872, but even before this his firsthand observations of Western penal practices began to have a significant impact on the direction of reforms. A proposal submitted to the Ministry of Punishment at the end of 1871 calling for the abolition of flogging, for example, was almost certainly his work. It began by noting that light beatings were ineffective because they caused only temporary embarrassment for the criminal, while heavier beatings were undesirable because they tended to cause permanent injury. Either way the outcome was not good, and for this reason, it noted, "the Western nations have, for the most part replaced [flogging] with hard labor."[39] There were many advantages to putting criminals to work: not only would it teach them how to make an honest living in the outside world; it also helped to strengthen their bodies and encouraged them to "reject . . . their previous evil ways, thereby opening up a path to discipline and repentance [*chōkai kaigo*]."[40] Hard labor, in other words, simultaneously helped to promote reform at the practical, physical, and moral levels. Given this, it only made sense that Japan too should quickly follow the example of the Western nations and replace flogging with short periods of "imprisonment with hard labor" *(chōeki)*. As a general rule ten blows with the stick could be replaced with ten days of hard labor, twenty blows with twenty days, and so on. In addition, the proposal also suggested that the government consider introducing "hard labor for life" *(shūshin kuyaku)* as a punishment for serious crimes that were not considered deserving of death. This too was almost certainly a product of Ohara's observations of British colonial prisons, where "lifers" were generally treated as a separate category of prisoner.

In any case, by the middle of 1872 both the replacement of flogging with short periods of hard labor and the introduction of life imprisonment with hard labor had been approved. As a result, the laws of the Meiji government now made provision for sentences of penal servitude stretching from ten days to life. This was particularly significant given the fact that in late 1870 the three existing classes of exile had been replaced with penal servitude for terms of five, seven, or ten years, all to be served in Hokkaido.[41] These

two developments together meant that the range of punishments available
to officials was increasingly limited to variations on the two basic alternatives of hard labor or death—and the death penalty too was in the process
of being dramatically reformed. In this, once again, Ohara was to play an
important role.

Reform of the death penalty at this time did not simply entail the abolition of older forms of execution. From the very first months of the new
era members of the Office of Criminal Law had discussed the possibility
of introducing the Chinese punishment of "strangulation" *(kōshu)* as a less
severe grade of capital punishment than decapitation, and in 1871, with
the completion of the *Shinritsu kōryō*, it officially became part of the Meiji
penal system.[42] Of course, the introduction of this new punishment soon
gave rise to the practical problem of how to administer it. In anticipation
of this, the authors of the *Shinritsu kōryō* had included a diagram and instructions for the construction of a special garroting device, consisting of
a single wooden post, with a hole at neck level through which a rope could
be passed to form a noose. Once the noose had been positioned around
the condemned person's neck, it was to be tightened and secured at the
back of the post, so that when the platform on which he was standing was
removed, he would choke to death. According to an account left by the
carpenter who built the first of these devices, a well-known magician
named Iso Mataemon was asked by the government to conduct an initial
"trial run" before it was put into official use. As soon as he had lost consciousness, his assistants removed the rope from around his neck and revived him—whereupon he assured the officials present that "not even the
strongest of people will be able to survive [this device]."[43] Given Iso's own
survival, the value of this guarantee was, of course, questionable, and sure
enough in the first year of its use there were at least three reports of prisoners in different parts of the country returning to life after being "executed"
on the device. There were also reports that even when the device worked,
prisoners suffered "unspeakable" pain and took an unacceptably long time
to die.[44] In response to these problems, Ohara decided to use the drawings
he had made of the British gallows in Hong Kong and Singapore to build
a model for possible use in Japan. In early 1873, after several months of
experimentation to confirm their efficiency, the new gallows were officially
adopted and the British punishment of hanging became a standard part of
the Japanese penal repertoire.[45]

A further boost for the cause of penal and legal reform came in the
middle of 1872 with the appointment of Etō Shimpei (1834–74) as head of
the newly renamed Ministry of Justice.[46] Etō was a warrior from Saga Domain who had played a key role in the Restoration movement, and in the
early years of the new era he quickly became one of the government's most
enthusiastic proponents of a Western model for legal reform. From as early

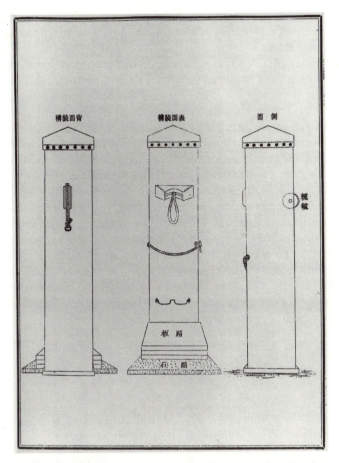

Figure 11. Diagram of the garroting device introduced under the *Shinritsu kōryō* of 1871 for executions by the new method of strangulation. It was replaced in 1873 by British-style gallows, designed by Ohara Shigechika. *Hōki bunrui taizen* (1889), 54:142.

as 1870 he had proposed the reorganization of the central administration into separate executive, legislative, and judicial branches and also helped initiate experiments with the compilation of a French-style civil code. As justice minister, one of his primary goals was to assert the ministry's exclusive authority over judicial matters, and in conjunction with this he ordered the creation of a national system of lawcourts that would be fully independent of regional administrative officials. In this Etō met with considerable opposition, in particular from the Ministry of Finance, which refused to provide him with the funds he needed to properly implement his plans. He nevertheless pushed ahead as best he could and also continued to encourage various other reforms.

In the latter part of 1872, for example, Etō proposed that the practice of allowing sons to exact revenge on their father's murderers be abolished. At the time there was still considerable support for the notion that "revenge killings" were an admirable expression of filial piety and martial spirit, but Etō insisted that to allow individuals to take justice into their own hands in this way served only to undermine the authority of the state, and in early 1873 the practice was finally banned.[47] It was also under Etō that the practice of maintaining special jail rooms for prisoners of high status was abolished. In the future, the old "upper rooms" were to be used instead to keep pretrial suspects separate from convicts, whose sentences had already been determined. This was the first time that such a distinction had been drawn.[48] Yet, as far as the administration of penal institutions is concerned, by far the most important development during Etō's term as justice minister was the official promulgation in 1872 of Ohara's "Prison Rules with Charts" *(Kangoku soku narabi ni zushiki)*—a document that also has relevance for our understanding of the larger vision of social order that was beginning to emerge in the early Meiji years.[49]

Panoptic Visions: Ohara's Prison Rules and the New Social Imaginary

The revolutionary tone of the 1872 "Prison Rules" is clear from the very first paragraph. "What is a prison?" it begins by asking.

> It is a means to hold criminals in custody in order to discipline them.
>
> The purpose of a prison is to show people love and benevolence, not to do them violence. Its purpose is to discipline people, not to cause them pain.
>
> Punishments are applied because there is no other choice. Their purpose is to expel evil in the interests of the nation.[50]

The emphasis placed here on discipline *(chōkai)* and the idea that the prison is a tool for promoting "the interests of the nation" are striking, but it is also important to note the strong sense of hope and idealism that these opening lines were intended to convey. As Naoyuki Umemori has pointed out, the modern prison described in Ohara's 1872 "Prison Rules" was a kind of utopian space[51]—with strong echoes of the idealized American prisons that Shōin, Sanai, and others had dreamed of in the 1850s. This is clear also from Ohara's description of what would constitute an appropriate setting for a prison. All prisons, he stipulated, should be built in a peaceful,

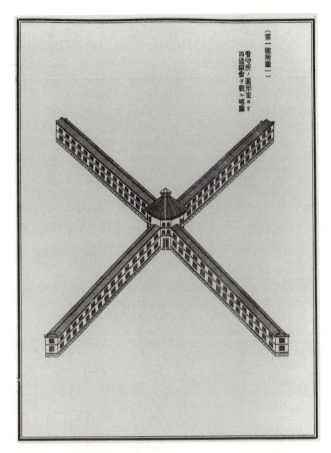

Figure 12. Illustration of a Western-style prison in Ohara Shi-gechika's 1872 "Prison Rules with Charts." *Hōki bunrui taizen* (1889), vol. 57:79.

elevated location, with plenty of fresh air and spacious grounds full of beautiful flowers and trees, the cultivation of which would help inmates attain "a joyful state of mind." Meanwhile, inside the prison, complete and perfect order was to reign. Prison buildings, Ohara noted, should all be built of stone or brick, and the bars should be made of iron. The basic design (depicted in the accompanying charts) was to be that of a cross: four main wings were to extend out from a central watch tower, and in keeping with the principles of Bentham's panopticon, the interior was to be kept clear of "all barriers and obstacles" so that inspection of the entire prison could be achieved in "a single glance" *(ichimoku dōshi)*. The task of surveillance was also to be facilitated by the careful distribution of bodies across space. Ideally, each individual prisoner was to be housed in his own separate cell. If this was not possible, Ohara's "Rules" allowed that up to five prisoners might share a cell, but in such cases a minimum of three square meters of space was to be allowed for each individual. According to the theories of the English, Ohara explained, any less space than this would harm the inmates' health and encourage the spread of disease.

Under Ohara's "Rules" there were some categories of prisoner who were to be held separately from the rest. In keeping with Etō's earlier reform, a strict division was to be maintained at all times between convicts and pre-trial suspects. Female prisoners were to be housed in special women's prisons (jokan), and sick inmates were to be removed to prison hospitals (byō-kan). In stark contrast to the old Kodenmachō Jailhouse, however, Ohara's plans left no room for the division of people into self-policing units insulated from outside supervision.

In this regard, the "Rules" closely reflected broader changes that were beginning to sweep Japanese society. Literary scholar Maeda Ai has, for example, pointed to the parallels that can be drawn between the panopticism of Ohara's "Prison Rules" and the principles that were to guide the remaking of urban space in Meiji era Tokyo.[52] In the years after the Restoration the old gates and barriers (kido) that had been used to partition off and delimit the hundreds of small block associations and communities within Edo were steadily torn down, and plans were laid for the creation of broad Parisian-style boulevards that would cut clear swathes of vision through the city. One key reason for these changes was the need to facilitate the flow of traffic and commerce, but, as with Ohara's "Prison Rules," the creation of open spaces (parks and boulevards) and the clearing away of dark, overcrowded corners (slums) would also come to be justified in terms of the new imperatives of public health and hygiene: air must circulate and light must be allowed in. As in the new prisons, moreover, wood was ideally to give way to brick in all new construction primarily to reduce the risk of fire, but also to convey a sense of civic grandeur and permanence. In conjunction with all of this, the state's ability to watch and monitor the city and its residents was dramatically enhanced by the formation of a professional metropolitan police force, a process that had begun just under a year before the completion of the new "Prison Rules" with the recruitment of over three thousand new constables (rasotsu) drawn directly from the warrior ranks of domains loyal to the new regime.[53]

At an even broader level, Ohara's emphasis on the need to clear away barriers and obstacles that might impede a sweeping, central gaze can also be linked to the Meiji government's efforts to restructure and streamline the Japanese polity as a whole. The abolition in 1871 of the semiautonomous domains and the creation of a new unitary state was clearly a crucial development in this regard. Of greatest direct relevance for Ohara's vision of space in the new prisons, however, was the dismantling of the formal structures of the old status system and the emergence of a new understanding of the people as subjects under the direct, unifying authority of the emperor. The year 1869 was an important turning point in this regard. This was when all townsfolk and peasants had officially been designated "commoners" (*heimin*) and granted the right to take surnames, a privilege formerly reserved for warriors. The warriors had also been recast as "gentry" (*shizoku*) or, in the case of the great lords, as "nobles" (*kazoku*). As noted in chapter 2, in 1871 the government formally abolished the old outcast status designations and announced that outcasts too were now to be treated as commoners. And, in that same year the Meiji leaders ended the old prohibition of marriage across status lines and decreed that members of the gentry should no longer feel obliged to wear their hair in a particular style or carry swords. As the nonbinding nature of this decree suggests, the curtailment of the privileges of former warriors was a much more delicate task for the new government than the ending of the special status of the outcasts had been. Even so, when the government promulgated its new Conscription Act in 1873, the future direction of things was already clear: warriors were no longer to be born—they were to be made. And, as the duty to fight began being dispersed across the entire male population, the basic justification for warrior privilege also disappeared.

The commitment to human malleability and mutability that underlay the introduction of conscription was, of course, also central to the vision of the modern prison, and just as the transformation of peasants into soldiers was understood to depend on regimentation and drill, so too did Ohara's "Rules" lay out a strict daily timetable for all convicts to follow.[54] Every morning they were to rise at six o'clock, clean their cells and latrines, eat breakfast, and be ready to commence work by seven. Lunch was to be taken between eleven and one, except in the summer, when an extra hour was allowed for the midday break. Work would then resume until five o'clock, after which prisoners would bathe, eat dinner, and be locked in their cells by six. At one level, the emphasis placed here on regular, timed sessions of labor clearly anticipated the work regime of the modern factories that would eventually begin to spread across Japan (although the workday then would rarely be as short as that envisaged by Ohara!).[55] In the sense that the primary focus of the prison was not the production of *things* but the improvement of *people*, a comparison can also be made with the national system of schools (*gakusei*) that the government had announced its intention to create in 1872, only a few months before the completion of the "Prison Rules."[56] Just as students in the new schools would gradually progress through a series of grades, so too did Ohara's "Rules" provide for a succession of five separate classes of labor through which all convicts would have to pass. Beginning in class five, they would be fitted with heavy chains and made to perform the dullest forms of physical labor (hauling and smashing rocks, clearing land, etc.). Over time they would be promoted to higher classes of labor. Their chains would be lightened, they would be given an opportunity to develop skills, and eventually allowed to teach other inmates. Once they reached class one, they would also start being paid nominal wages, to be collected upon "graduation."

Like schoolchildren, factory workers, and newly conscripted soldiers, the daily activities of prisoners were also to be carefully policed by their superiors. In order to ensure that inmates were properly accounted for at all times, Ohara's "Rules" called for four daily inspections: before breakfast, at the beginning and end of lunch break, and in the evening before locking the cell doors. At these inspections each guard was to have the prisoners in his charge line up in a straight line. Officers would then check numbers and mark a roll. Each guard was to be assigned no more than ten prisoners, and one officer was to supervise five guards. Collectively they were to be responsible for monitoring every detail of the inmates' lives. The "Rules" outlined what kind of food should be served, what kind of reading materials should be permitted, and even the temperature of the prisoners' bath water at different times of the year. They also stipulated that each inmate was to be issued a uniform, clearly marked with an identifying number. Cleanliness and hygiene were to be emphasized at all times, and prisoners were to strengthen their bodies through regular exercise performed in special exercise yards (*undōjo*) attached to the prison.

For those who breached regulations, the "Rules" provided for various forms of physical punishment, including leg irons, the ball and chain, confinement in dark isolation cells, and up to thirty lashes with a whip. At the same time, Ohara looked forward to a time when the collection of statistics would provide a more subtle tool for the management of people and populations. Whenever a new inmate was admitted, officials were to begin by listing his name, sex, place of origin, and crime in a register. They were then to measure the prisoner's height and weight and note any distinguishing features. If the prisoner was a repeat offender, this too was to be recorded, and if he had committed a serious offense, a careful sketch was to be made of his face to aid in his apprehension if he ever escaped. In addition, the "Rules" stipulated that at the end of every year each prison in the country was to produce and submit to the Ministry of Justice a table detailing the total number of inmates imprisoned over the course of the year, the number of inmate deaths, the number of officials employed, total expenditure, and so on. All of this would allow the government to keep watch on prison guards and officials, just as they kept watch on the prisoners.

Overall, Ohara's vision for the future Japanese prison could hardly have differed more dramatically from the chaotic realities of imprisonment in Tokyo depicted by Kyōsai in 1870 or from the status-based compartmentalization of the old Kodenmachō Jailhouse. But not all aspects of the "Rules" marked a complete break with the past. Of particular interest in this regard are the provisions Ohara made for the establishment of special "reformatories" (chōjikan), separate from ordinary convict prisons. To some extent, no doubt, the idea for these reformatories was influenced by the colonial houses of correction that Ohara had observed in Hong Kong and Singapore, but there is also good reason to suspect a link with the old Stockade for Laborers. According to the "Rules," the reformatories would be used to confine and provide job training for several different groups of people. First there were criminals under the age of twenty who had completed terms in an ordinary prison but who were considered likely to get into more trouble if released. They were to be joined by juvenile delinquents whose parents asked that they be incarcerated, small-time criminals deemed worthy of special treatment, and finally "poor, unregistered persons not easily returned to their place of origin" after completing prison terms. Ohara's reformatories, in other words, were to confine and train much the same kind of people who would have been sent to the old stockade under the Tokugawa.

While it is thus possible to find some evidence of continuity with certain aspects of Tokugawa practice, it would nevertheless be a mistake to overemphasize this aspect of the "Prison Rules." Overall, Ohara envisaged nothing less than the total abolition of the old Tokugawa jails and their replacement with a fundamentally different kind of institution—one that not only reflected the macrolevel restructuring of Japanese society at this time but also exemplified the new microlevel strategies of order and organization and the new culture of time and space that would increasingly come to shape and regulate individual lives. In all of these ways, Ohara's "Rules" are emblematic of the beginning of Japan's transformation into what Foucault would term a "disciplinary society."

At the same time, however, it is also true that the mere existence of a blueprint for the future can itself hardly be taken as a guarantee of implementation. When the new "Prison Rules" were first circulated to officials in 1872, they were prefaced with a statement explaining that it was not yet possible for the government to build new prisons in all parts of the country. Work on the construction of the first such institution would soon begin in Tokyo, but in all other areas officials would be expected to adhere only to those sections of the "Rules" relating to labor and the general treatment of inmates.[57] As it turned out, even this cautious approach to the implementation of the new "Rules" proved difficult to sustain. At the beginning of 1873, Etō was informed that the Justice Ministry's budget for the year would be less than half of what he had originally requested, and soon afterward regional authorities were ordered to suspend all attempts to implement the new "Prison Rules" until proper investigations had been made into the costs they were likely to entail.[58] As an interim solution to the acute shortage of prison facilities, the government also granted the regional authorities permission to resume the use of flogging to deal with petty crime.[59]

In spite of these setbacks the new "Prison Rules" were not abandoned. They remained on the books as national law, and before long the Ministry of Justice issued further instructions to regional authorities explaining that although they were no longer *required* to implement the "Prison Rules," they were still *encouraged* to do so wherever it was "convenient."[60] The promulgation of a second Chinese-style criminal code, the *Kaitei ritsurei* (Revised Code), in the middle of 1873 also helped to restore some of the momentum that had been lost in the preceding months. One important change under this new code, which again reflected the steady shift away from a society based on formal status divisions, was a dramatic curtailment of "special punishments" *(junkei)* for former warriors. In earlier Meiji codes these had included various forms of house arrest, assignment to guard duty in Hokkaido (in place of exile), and also that great marker of Japanese "Otherness," legally enforced "suicide" by disembowelment. Under the *Kaitei ritsurei* all of these measures were replaced by the single punishment of "confinement" *(kinko)* for periods ranging from ten days to life.[61] Initially, confinement could be served at home, making it little more than a continuation of the older penalty of house arrest, but in mid-1874 it was replaced with "confinement in prison" *(kingoku).*[62] Thus, while warriors and nobles continued to receive special consideration, the kinds of punishments to which they could be sentenced became increasingly similar to those of commoners.

The *Kaitei ritsurei* also confirmed the government's commitment to the abolition of flogging and banishment, which were both replaced with the one standard punishment of "imprisonment with hard labor" *(chōeki).*[63] In practice, flogging continued to be used in some areas until the end of the 1870s, but, even so, the prominent place given to imprisonment in the *Kaitei ritsurei* increased pressure on officials everywhere to open or expand facilities for incarcerating criminals. In the first half of 1874 alone new institutions for imprisonment with hard labor *(chōekijō)* were established in the city of Osaka and in six prefectures across the country.[64] None of these was particularly impressive in terms of its architecture or internal organization; at least one of them was nothing more than an old domainal granary hurriedly converted to serve a new purpose. In the summer of 1874, however, Ohara was finally given permission to proceed with the construction of Japan's first Western-style prison.

The Birth of the Prison (and the Death of a Leader)

When he completed his "Prison Rules," Ohara had initially hoped to be able to build a new prison in Tokyo on the same grand scale as those he had seen in Hong Kong and Singapore, and in 1872 the Justice Ministry had, in fact, received permission to take over the expansive grounds of the former residence of the daimyo of Kaga Domain in Hongō for this purpose.[65] Following the severe cutbacks imposed by the Ministry of Finance, however, this tract of land was reassigned to the Ministry of Education as the site for a different kind of disciplinary institution, the nation's first imperial university (now Tokyo University).[66] Plans for a Western-style prison were put on hold indefinitely, and soon afterward Ohara was transferred from the Office of Prisons to a teaching post in the Justice Ministry's new law school, the *Meihōryō*. This, however, did not stop him from taking a strong interest in prison affairs, and after the promulgation of the *Kaitei ritsurei* reports of sudden increases in inmate numbers prompted him to conduct a new round of inspections of the Tokyo jails.[67] In spite of the changes he had introduced in 1871 he found that inmates were once again being "piled together like firewood in a stack. Divided into groups of between seventeen . . . and twenty-five people, they were forced together into spaces the size of four tatami mats. As a result of this, a great many were falling ill and dying."[68] The worst affected, moreover, were not those who had actually been convicted of serious crimes but rather pretrial suspects, petty offenders, and parties to civil cases who (following Tokugawa practice) were being held in conjunction with an official investigation.

As noted earlier, under Justice Minister Etō's direction, efforts had begun being made to keep suspects strictly separated from convicted criminals, and Ohara's "Prison Rules" also encouraged efforts to keep hardened criminals away from other inmates. The problem, however, was that there were no proper facilities in which to confine these other groups. The "upper rooms" of the old Kodenmachō Jailhouse had quickly proved insufficient for the purpose, and as an interim solution officials had begun making use of converted stables and other old, abandoned buildings in the grounds of the residences of former Bakufu officials. According to Ohara, these were generally so dark and putrid inside that "even animals and beasts would have been unable to sustain life in them."[69] Eventually he convinced senior officials in the Justice Ministry to accompany him on a tour of these facilities, and afterward they quickly agreed to make funds available for a new Western-style prison building to be used for the temporary detention of criminal suspects and parties to civil suits.

A site was chosen at Kajibashi, close to the headquarters of the newly established metropolitan police department. It was a much smaller area of land than Ohara had been allocated in 1872, and budgetary restraints inevitably meant that the new structure had to be built entirely of wood rather than the stone or brick recommended in the "Prison Rules." Even so, when construction was completed at the end of 1874, Ohara must have been pleased with the result. Narushima Ryūhoku (1837–84), a former Bakufu official and journalist who was held at Kajibashi in 1876 after being arrested for violating the Meiji government's new Press Law, later described the building as follows: "The design follows that of a Western jail and forms a cross shape. There are two stories, divided into a total of eight sections. Each section has ten cells, making for a total of eighty cells. On both the top and bottom stories there is a guard in the middle [of the prison] who keeps watch in all four directions." Overall then, while it may have been small, the new structure clearly adhered to the key principles laid out in the "Prison Rules." This was Japan's first modern prison, and it was not long before the new design was copied in other parts of the country; first in the frontier town of Sapporo in 1875, and soon afterward in important regional centers such as Urawa, Utsunomiya, Kumamoto, and Hiroshima.[70]

If all of this provides yet more evidence of the rapid pace with which penal reform was pursued in the years immediately following the Restoration, it is, of course, also true that in 1874 penal and legal practice continued to be shaped by a range of different influences. Although the *Kaitei ritsurei* was undoubtedly more thorough and sophisticated than any of the earlier Meiji codes, it was still based primarily on Chinese legal models, and in spite of all of the changes that it ushered in, the imprint of older strategies of punishment remained clearly evident in it. There is perhaps no more poignant reminder of this fact than the ironic death of Etō Shimpei, the pioneering advocate of judicial reform.

Soon after his confrontation with the Ministry of Finance, Etō had left the Ministry of Justice to take up a position as councillor (*sangi*), one of the highest posts in the Meiji administration, and for several months after this he played a central role in the affairs of government. Following the return of the Iwakura mission in September 1873, however, strong differences of opinion quickly began to develop between members of the government who had gone on the mission and those who had been left behind. The disagreement between the two groups eventually came to a head over the question of the new regime's unsettled relationship with Yi-dynasty Korea. Just prior to the Iwakura mission's return, leaders of the caretaker government, including Etō, had unanimously agreed that the Restoration hero Saigō Takamori should be sent to Korea as a special envoy of the Meiji government. This decision is often said to have been the first step in an ill-conceived plan to foment war with Korea, and the returned members of the Iwakura mission have generally won praise from historians for using

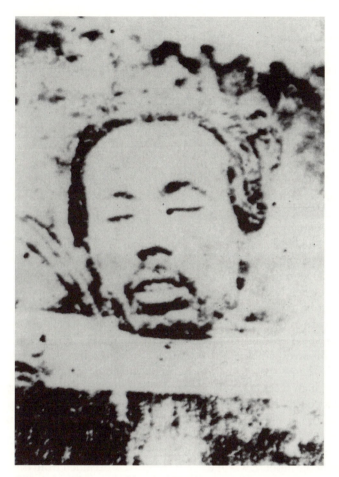

Figure 13. The severed head of Etō Shimpei, former justice
minister. Unknown photographer, 1874.

their power and influence to veto it. Their wisdom in this matter, it is
argued, reflected the new maturity and understanding of international relations they had gained as a result of their recent experiences in the West.
Etō's biographer, Mōri Toshihiko, has, however, questioned this interpretation. According to him, Etō and the other leaders who approved Saigō's
mission had no intention of provoking a conflict with Korea. Instead, he
suggests that members of the Iwakura mission deliberately promoted the
notion that they were irresponsible warmongers in order to discredit and
dislodge a group of leaders who had grown increasingly powerful during
their eighteen-month sojourn abroad.[71] Either way, the outcome of the
conflict is beyond dispute. By the end of 1874 the Meiji leadership had

split, with Etō, Saigō, and many other leading figures from the caretaker administration resigning their positions in protest at the high-handed manner in which their plans had been rejected.

Initially, Etō remained in Tokyo where he, like other former members of the government such as Itagaki Taisuke and Gotō Shōjirō, threw his support behind a public call for the creation of a popularly elected parliament that would serve as a check on the "despotism of those in power" (*yūshi sensei*). Whereas Itagaki and Gotō would go on to become leaders of a new kind of political opposition movement, however, Etō's attention was increasingly focused on events unfolding in his native domain of Saga, where thousands of disgruntled samurai had formed themselves into activist bands to protest the policies of the central government and its refusal to "chastise Korea." Eventually he decided to return to Saga to try and calm the situation there, but soon after his arrival hostilities broke out between the local samurai groups and troops sent by the central government. Caught in the middle of the conflict, he sided with the Saga forces and quickly found himself a prisoner of the same leaders whom, just a few months earlier, he had engaged in heated debates over the future direction of the nation. In spite of the fact that they had only recently returned from their travels in the "enlightened" West, these leaders were only too happy to fall back on established methods for dealing with Etō. Within just two days of his arrest a judge who had been handpicked by Ōkubo Toshimichi (1830–78), now the most powerful man in the government, found him guilty of high treason. In light of his "failure to fear the authority of the imperial court," the judge ordered that Etō be stripped of all status privileges and punished with public display of his severed head—a measure still provided for under the *Kaitei ritsurei*.[72] The sentence was carried out immediately, just as it would have been under the old regime, but the influence of the modern world was not completely excluded from the process. After the execution, a photograph of Etō's severed head was taken to serve as a permanent record of his death and to ensure that the message of this penal sign was disseminated well beyond the borders of Saga.

CHAPTER 7

Punishment and Prisons in the Era of Enlightenment

IF THE EXECUTION of Etō Shimpei in 1874 provides us with a valuable reminder of the persistence of older strategies of punishment and power in the years immediately following the Restoration, the two decades that followed his death were to see the completion of Japan's penal revolution. This, of course, is not to imply that all change suddenly stopped in 1895. Japan's current penal code was not issued until 1907. Its current prisons law followed in 1908, and, as in other wealthy, capitalist nations, its penal system ever since has been characterized by a continual series of experiments and debates, scandals and improvements, investigations and reforms.[1] Yet by 1895 the key pieces were all in place: a Western-style penal code, a system of independent lawcourts, a national network of prisons to which the overwhelming majority of those found guilty of crimes were now being sent, and, finally, a group of academic and bureaucratic experts who would monitor, study, and scrutinize the system and keep Japan abreast of the latest international trends and developments.

All of this was clearly part of the much broader transformation of Japanese society that took place in the first half of the Meiji period. As our analysis of Ohara Shigechika's ambitious 1872 "Prison Rules" has shown, plans for the creation of a modern prison system were, from the outset, connected to a new vision of the social order overall, as well as to new techniques of disciplinary power that were to spread rapidly throughout society in the years that followed. In place of self-regulating status groups, people's lives would now increasingly be shaped by their progress through a series of institutions designed to mold them into modern subject-citizens. The powerful military leader and bureaucrat, Yamagata Aritomo (1838–1922), laid this out clearly when universal elementary education and male conscription were first being planned in the early 1870s: "Men will enter elementary schools at six, advance to high schools at thirteen, finish schooling at nineteen, and then enter the army . . . , and there will be no men who are not soldiers and no people without learning."[2] Women's lives too were to be shaped by the new disciplinary institutions. In 1875 the first Women's Normal School was established at Ochanomizu in Tokyo to train women to serve as teachers in the new primary school system, and when Western style hospitals began to proliferate in the wake of the Medical

Order of 1874, they were recruited to work as nurses. Later, in the 1880s, when textile factories began to be established, it was young women who were recruited to form the first generation of Japan's industrial labor force.[3]

The prison, of course, would be for those who somehow fell through the disciplinary cracks and continued to resist, defy, and destroy. At least in theory, even they would now be reformed and remade, and in this sense the prison (like the asylum) can be seen as having completed the new order, by closing off one of the few avenues of escape from the normalizing effects of regimentation and drill.[4] Yet, as important as it is to note these general connections, patterns, and schemas, we must be careful not to lose sight of the fact that the penal reforms of the late 1870s and 1880s were ultimately driven by their own specific dynamic. At the heart of this dynamic was the Meiji regime's publicly stated goal of securing revision of the unequal treaties, and by the middle of the 1870s it was clear that, if this were ever to be achieved, Japan would have to do more than just implement sweeping reforms; it would also have to reconceptualize its own position in the world. As a result, a full decade before Fukuzawa Yukichi's infamous call for Japan to "leave Asia" and "turn our backs on the bad company we have kept [there]," bureaucrats and officials had already begun to shift their attention away from the Chinese and colonial Asian models that had guided their initial efforts at penal reform and instead look directly to the metropolitan centers of the Western world. While the general framework of reform was increasingly shaped by a small group of Western or Western-educated experts, the decision to commit scarce resources to the creation of a modern penal system was simultaneously driven by a different set of motivations. Specifically, the Meiji leaders began to realize that the modern prison was not just an idealistic dream, or an institutional hurdle standing in the way of a larger goal, but also something that could serve their immediate interests and needs. In this sense it provides a powerful example of how ambiguous the impact of the changes ushered in during Japan's era of "civilization and enlightenment" were, and how the ideology of "progress," initially imposed from without, was to become an important asset for the Meiji regime in its own domestic struggles. It shows, in other words, that the process of "nation building" in Meiji Japan cannot be understood simply in terms of opposition and resistance to Western imperialism, and that the forces of empire and nation were, in fact, deeply interconnected and intertwined.

Enlightenment and Law: Toward a Modern Penal Code

As is well known, the push to master Western-style "civilization" in the early Meiji period was spearheaded by a small group of intellectuals known as the "Meirokusha" or "Meiji Six Society." Named after the year it was founded (Meiji 6 = 1873), the group met regularly to discuss and debate key issues of the day, and from 1874 it also began to publish its famous "journal of enlightenment," the *Meiroku zasshi*.[5] Western legal practices were a key concern of many members of the group, but the single most outspoken advocate of reform of the criminal justice and penal systems was Tsuda Mamichi (1829–1903). In the last years of the Tokugawa period, Tsuda had begun studying Dutch under Mitsukuri Genpo (1799–1863), one of the scholars responsible for translating Dutch legal texts for Mizuno Tadakuni in the 1840s. Then, in 1862 he was sent to Holland for three years by the Bakufu to learn more about conditions in the West.[6] While abroad he compiled an extensive set of notes on contemporary Dutch legal practices, and soon after the Restoration he was recruited to serve in the new government's Office of Criminal Law. Within a matter of months his vocal calls for radical Westernization had earned him a transfer to a regional post in Shizuoka, but such setbacks did not silence him.[7] After the launch of the *Meiroku zasshi*, he wrote a series of articles critiquing various aspects of the early Meiji judicial system and calling for urgent reforms.

Tsuda's first articles appeared in the summer of 1874 and took up the question of judicial torture: "No evil in the world is more wretched, and no injury in history more poisonous than torture," he wrote. Not only was it unjust and improper, he also pointed out that its use was now one of the key markers of the backwardness of the non-European races. The fact that under the influence of European imperialism some members of the "Mongol and black races" had already taken steps to abolish torture and implement other progressive reforms proved that race itself was no barrier to change. What was needed was "knowledge, civilization, and enlightenment," and if the Japanese people did not wish to be judged incapable of these things, it was essential that they too abandon the practice of torture immediately. Failure to do so, Tsuda emphasized, would also have important practical consequences: "If we do not abolish torture, we cannot eventually ride forth side by side with the various countries of Europe and America. If we do not abolish torture, we cannot conclude equal treaties with them. If we do not abolish torture, we cannot place under our laws the European and Americans settled in our country."[8] This closing reference to the issue of the treaties helped ensure that Tsuda's articles had an immediate impact on the government, and soon afterward the Justice Ministry ordered officials to limit the use of torture wherever possible and to lodge a special report for all cases in which its use had been deemed unavoidable.[9]

Perhaps encouraged by such signs of change, Tsuda went on to make an even more radical proposal in the August 1875 issue of the *Meiroku zasshi*, calling for nothing less than the abolition of all forms of death penalty. Citing passages from the Chinese classics in tandem with the example of Beccaria in Europe, he argued that the aim of punishment should be to reform and correct criminals, not to match one act of violence with another. It was for this reason, he suggested, that the government had taken its laudable decision to prohibit "revenge killings" two years earlier. Given this, surely it made sense for the government now to take the next step and abolish capital punishment entirely, for in the end, he argued, the only punishments that served both to protect other members of society from further harm and achieve the goal of reform, were imprisonment and penal servitude.[10]

Tsuda's views stimulated considerable debate, and over the course of the 1870s others within the educated elite began to make similar calls for reform. Ultimately, though, the single most important stimulus to change at this time came from the French legal scholar Gustave Emile Boissonade de Fontarabie (1825–1907), who had been recruited to serve as a permanent adviser to the government during Etō Shimpei's term as justice minister.[11] Boissonade began teaching students at the government's new law school (*Meihōryō*) soon after his arrival in Japan in 1874, but one of his most famous contributions to judicial reform came the following year when (so the story goes) he came across a man being tortured by officials within the grounds of the Ministry of Justice. Shocked by what he had seen, he wrote to Ōki Takatō (1832–99), Etō's successor, calling for the immediate suspension of all such practices.[12] A month later he followed this letter up with a longer "Mémoire sur l'abolition de la torture," which concluded by stating bluntly that Japan would never convince the Western powers to consider ending extraterritoriality until all forms of torture had been completely eradicated.[13] This point, of course, was precisely the same one that Tsuda Mamichi had articulated in the *Meiroku zasshi* a year earlier. But, as Tezuka Yutaka has noted, such were the racial politics of "civilization and enlightenment" in the 1870s that the views expressed by a European expert inevitably carried greater weight than those of a Japanese, and within just two months of receiving Boissonade's "Mémoire" the Ministry of Justice proposed the total abolition of torture to the newly created Senate (*Genrōin*).[14] The Senate, for its part, was initially reluctant to approve the proposal, arguing that to remove such an important instrument of authority would inevitably lead to an increase in violent crime. By the middle of the following year, however, a series of compromise reforms had been approved. These effectively ended the old requirement that a formal confession of guilt be obtained before judgment was passed in criminal cases, so that although the *threat* of torture remained, the motivation actually to use it was gone.[15]

In the years that followed pressure to proceed with the formal abolition of torture continued to come from various quarters, including the flourishing English-language press in the treaty ports of Yokohama and Kobe. In 1877, for example, when rumors circulated that the government was planning to grant special permission for the use of torture in the trials of rebel soldiers captured during Saigō Takamori's failed Satsuma Rebellion, the *Japan Gazette* and the *Japan Herald* immediately seized upon them as proof that the earlier reforms had not been genuine and that Japan was still a long way from instituting the changes necessary to justify ending extraterritoriality.[16] This, in turn, was reported back to the vernacular press, forcing the government to respond with a statement denying that the use of torture had ever been sanctioned. In fact, special approval for the use of torture had indeed been sought by the officials sent to Kyushu to try the rebels, but once the Meiji leaders realized the foreign press had received word of the plan, they immediately issued instructions prohibiting its use.[17]

The issue of torture was raised again in 1878, when Japanese papers reported that the influential American scholar David Dudley Field had given a speech at the International Law Association in Frankfurt in which he had pointed specifically to the continued use of torture and barbarous punishments in Japan and China as justification for the maintenance of extraterritoriality.[18] These reports appeared at about the same time that new efforts to achieve treaty revision were being made by Foreign Minister Terajima Munenori (1832–93), and although he was to have some success in negotiations with the United States on the issue of tariff autonomy, with regard to extraterritoriality the Western powers made it clear that there was no possibility of change. All of this undoubtedly contributed to the Senate's decision finally to approve the formal abolition of torture in 1879.

It would be a mistake, however, to conclude that foreign pressure alone had been enough to determine the timing of this reform. An official memorandum from Justice Minister Ōki argued that, although the issue of torture had been an ongoing source of embarrassment in negotiations with the Western powers, the government's decision to wait had been wise: to have abandoned the threat of judicial torture at an earlier stage, he wrote, when there was no police force in place and the procedures for conducting trials on the basis of evidence had not yet been properly understood, would inevitably have meant unleashing a flood of violent crime and treason.[19] It was, in other words, only after the Japanese state had fully embraced the idea of creating a body of professional judges and police, whose full-time task would be to watch, investigate, and intervene in society to maintain order, that it could afford to abandon the last vestiges of the old regime of punishments and its economies of fear. In this regard it makes sense that 1879, the year in which the government finally decided it was ready to end the use of judicial torture, was also the year in which the public display of severed heads, the last of the old Tokugawa punishments, was abolished.[20]

These changes were important in themselves, but they also paved the way for the promulgation in 1880 of Japan's first Western-style penal code. Drafted by Boissonade and based loosely on the Napoleonic Code, the new penal code marked a dramatic break from both Tokugawa tradition and the Chinese-inspired codes of the early Meiji period. With regard to punishments, it made provision for only one form of death penalty—hanging—and apart from fines, all of the other penalties it sanctioned were variations on imprisonment: servitude *(tokei)*, exile *(rukei)*, imprisonment with hard labor *(chōeki)*, imprisonment without labor *(kingoku)*, and short-term imprisonment *(kinko)*.[21] The key differences between these five categories were, first, the place where the prison term was to be served (servitude and exile were to be served on an island, removed from the Japanese mainland); second, whether the prisoner would be forced to work (those sentenced to exile and imprisonment without labor were exempted); and, finally, the length of the term (exile and servitude ranged from twelve years to life, imprisonment with and without labor both ranged from six to eleven years, and short-term imprisonment from eleven days to five years). In this way, the new penal code marked the completion of Japan's formal transition from a system in which there were a wide range of different penalties, most of which involved an act of overt physical violence inflicted on the body of the criminal, to one in which imprisonment was the primary mode of punishment.

Not just the official punishments marked a break with the past. The new penal code, together with the new code of criminal procedures that accompanied it, offered the strongest evidence yet of the Meiji government's determination to bring all aspects of its approach to the administration of justice in line with the expectations of the Western powers. Not surprisingly, soon after its promulgation a new round of efforts to secure revision of the treaties was launched. Yet, although Foreign Minister Inoue Kaoru (1835–1915) could now point to the existence of a Western-style penal code and to the government's plans to prepare new civil and commercial codes under the supervision of Western experts, the great powers still refused to consider allowing the Japanese full judicial autonomy. In her popular 1880 book, *Unbeaten Tracks in Japan*, the intrepid Victorian travel writer Isabella Bird summed up official sentiment as follows:

> Legal reform is one of the most important questions which the Government has to face, and the promulgation of a code, however admirable, is only the first step. It not only involves the reconstruction of the Courts, the abolition of the present system of procedure, and the creation of a new judicature, but a revolution in Japanese traditional notions of justice, and in the customs which are interwoven with centuries of national life. In the present primary stage of reform, the administration of justice fails to command the confidence of foreigners, and foreign governments are naturally unwilling to surrender the extra-territorial rights acquired by treaty.[22]

Clearly then, just as Ohara Shigechika had predicted, it would take more than the promulgation of a Western-style law code alone to convince the powers to agree to end extraterritoriality. Actual practices and procedures would also be scrutinized, and in this regard prisons, whose central position in the penal system was confirmed under the new code, were of particular importance.

PRISONS, REFORM, AND REBELLION

In the early months of 1876 responsibility for prison affairs was transferred from the Ministry of Justice to the new Home Ministry, and by the end of that year the old Kodenmachō Jailhouse, which had stood in the same place for well over two centuries, was torn down to make way for a small park.[23] This offered further evidence of the passing of the old order, and to some extent it can also be seen as a logical continuation of the reforms that Ohara had initiated in the early 1870s.[24] Yet, as with the issue of judicial torture, early Japanese calls for prison reform were ultimately bolstered and amplified in the minds of the Meiji leaders by the criticisms and observations made by Westerners. Particularly important in this regard was an American missionary named John Cutting Berry (1847–1936).

In 1873 Berry, a medical doctor by training, was asked to help treat an outbreak of beriberi in the Kobe Jailhouse.[25] Observing the unhygienic and overcrowded conditions there, he wrote to the prefectural governor, Kanda Takahira (1830–98) proposing extensive reforms. Encouraged by Kanda's positive response, and no doubt also sensing an opportunity to proselytize, Berry decided to write to Foreign Minister Terajima and to the U.S. minister in Japan asking permission to visit prisons in different parts of the country. His aim, as conveyed to the ambassador, was to help

> relieve Japan of the suspicion with which Foreign Powers must ever regard the genuineness of its desire for social reform, if such reform does not extend to its prison life, and overcome one serious objection in the minds of some of the Representatives of Foreign Powers to allowing subjects to be placed wholly under Japanese jurisdiction.[26]

At first the Foreign Ministry was reluctant to allow Berry to proceed with his inspections for fear that they would only lead to more negative publicity for the Japanese government. Eventually, however, Berry was able to arrange a meeting with Ōkubo Toshimichi, the powerful home minister, and after promising not to make his findings public, he was granted permission to visit the four largest jails in the Kansai region.[27] On the basis of what he saw there and what he had been able to learn of the latest ideas about prison management in the West, Berry then prepared a lengthy and detailed report, proposing such things as the introduction of a system for classifying prisoners, the provision of halfway houses to help prisoners reestablish themselves after their release, the establishment of proper training facilities for guards, and the appointment of prison chaplains. The report was translated into Japanese in the middle of 1876 and presented to Ōkubo, who ordered that copies be printed and distributed to government officials in every part of the country.[28]

According to Ohara Shigechika, Berry's report convinced many who had previously scoffed at the mention of prison reform to take the issue and its connection to the unequal treaties seriously.[29] Over the next few years an independent Prisons Bureau was established within the Home Ministry, a mission was dispatched to investigate prison conditions in Europe, and in 1878 the first of a series of reports on the progress that had been made to improve prison conditions in Japan was submitted to the Third International Prisons Conference in Stockholm.[30] Underlying all of this was, of course, the Meiji government's concern to demonstrate to the great powers that Japan was indeed capable of achieving "civilization" along modern, Western lines. Yet, as historians of political repression such as Richard H. Mitchell have noted, it was also from around this time that the Meiji leadership began to realize that modern prisons could be an extremely useful tool for achieving their domestic goals in the face of growing popular opposition and hostility.[31]

The first wave of serious, organized opposition to the Meiji government's reforms came in the form of armed uprisings by groups of former samurai, who resented being stripped of the privileges that had been their birthright under the old status system. The 1874 Saga Rebellion, which cost Etō Shimpei his life, was an important harbinger of things to come, but it was not until 1876, when the government moved to ban former samurai from wearing their swords in public and end the payment of their hereditary stipends, that discontent peaked. In October of that year, three samurai rebellions broke out almost simultaneously in Kumamoto, Akitsuki, and Hagi. These were put down with relative ease, but just a few months later, in February 1877, a much larger rebellion broke out in Satsuma under the leadership of Saigō Takamori, one of the best-known heroes of the Restoration movement. The government's army of conscripts prevented the uprising from spreading beyond the southern corner of Kyushu, but even so, it took them a full six months to defeat the rebel forces. By the end of the year a total of around forty-three thousand persons had been tried for their involvement and twenty-seven hundred were sentenced to some form of imprisonment.[32]

This sudden and sizable influx of rebel prisoners presented the government with a serious problem, for what prisons there were across the country at this time had already been pushed to their limits by the systematic abolition of alternative punishments earlier in the 1870s. Toward the end of 1877 the Home Ministry proposed to the government that rather than attempting to expand the various local jailhouses that had survived from

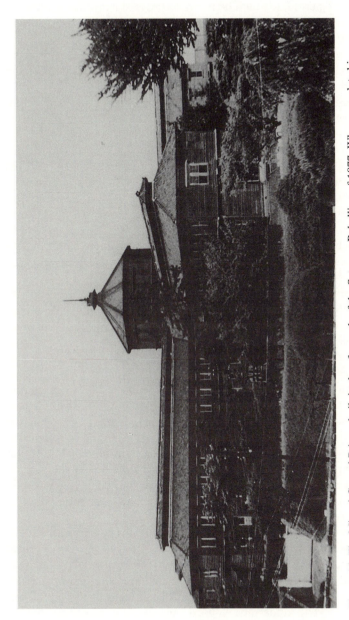

Figure 14. The Miyagi Central Prison, built in the aftermath of the Satsuma Rebellion of 1877. When completed in 1879, it was the largest building in the Tōhoku region, with room for over one thousand prisoners. Photograph courtesy of Shigematsu Kazuyoshi.

the Tokugawa period, it would be better to proceed with the construction of an entirely new prison at Miyagi, near Sendai, in northeastern Honshu, far removed from the rebel's base in southern Kyushu.[33]

Within ten days of submitting its proposal for the Miyagi prison the Home Ministry was granted permission to proceed, and allocated 160,000 yen from the emergency budget for subduing the Satsuma rebels. By this time, three hundred officers from Saigō's vanquished army had already been sent to Sendai and were being housed in the old domainal jailhouse there. They were now put to work building the new structure under the supervision of Onoda Motohiro (1848–1919), a police official who had also served as an officer with the government forces during the rebellion.[34] The new prison was modeled on an institution in Leuven, Belgium and, in terms of its overall form, followed a standard design for modern penitentiaries, with six two-story cell blocks radiating out from a central observation tower. Unlike the Western prisons on which it was based, the Miyagi Prison was built entirely of wood, but when it was completed in the middle of 1879 it was the single largest building of any kind in the Tōhoku region, with room for more than one thousand prisoners.[35]

In spite of the unprecedented scale on which the Miyagi Prison had been built, the Home Ministry soon realized that it was still not large enough to hold all of the rebels, let alone relieve the overcrowded conditions in the older jails scattered around the country. In the middle of 1878, therefore, it came up with a plan to divide the country into a total of five prison zones, each of which would be served by its own massive "central prison" (*shūchikan*), to be modeled after the French Maisons Centralé. These central prisons, which the Home Ministry initially planned to open at Miyagi, Tokyo, Aichi, Osaka, and Fukuoka, would hold prisoners serving longer sentences for more serious crimes, so that local-level authorities would be responsible only for those awaiting trial or serving relatively light sentences.[36] At first, this plan was rejected as overly ambitious, but by the end of the year the pressing need for facilities in which to imprison the rebels convinced the government to approve the construction of a second large-scale prison on the outskirts of Tokyo.

It was no coincidence that Kosuge, the site for this new prison, was also the place where the government had earlier encouraged a group of private entrepreneurs to establish Japan's first modern brickworks. The aim of this venture had been to ensure a local supply of red bricks, which were essential to the government's plan to transform large areas of the capital into showpieces of Meiji modernity. As fiscal considerations forced the government to scale back its plans for tearing down the old wooden buildings of Edo and replacing them with Western-style streets of brick and mortar, however, the privately run brickworks began to fall into financial difficulty.[37] It was in this context that the Home Ministry came up with its plan to transform the entire operation into the nation's first prison-factory. Not only would this help to relieve the overcrowded conditions in Tokyo's prisons and jails, where inmate populations had nearly doubled as a result of legal reforms and the Satsuma Rebellion, it would also help bring down the price of bricks and thus, it was hoped, encourage private citizens to begin building with them.[38] The proposal was quickly approved and Watanabe Koreaki (1845–1900), a police official who had served as a judge during the Saga Rebellion and chief of the government's police force in Kagoshima during the Satsuma Rebellion, was appointed to oversee construction.[39] Under him, those members of Saigō's rebel army who had not already been sent to Miyagi were put to work with other prisoners from the capital, firing the bricks that would be used to build the famous Western-style buildings in Tokyo's Ginza district, as well as the prison cells in which they themselves would eventually be confined. The construction at Kosuge was to take another five years to complete, but by the middle of 1879 it was officially designated as the nation's second central prison after Miyagi.[40]

As already noted, in the immediate aftermath of the Satsuma Rebellion, the Home Ministry had planned to build a total of five central prisons, with four on the main island of Honshu and one at Fukuoka in Kyushu. Toward the end of 1879, however, Itō Hirobumi (1841–1909), who had succeeded Ōkubo as home minister the previous year, foreshadowed an important change in policy in a letter to Prime Minister Sanjō Sanetomi. Itō began by noting that of the five classes of imprisonment provided for under the new penal code that was to be made public the following year, servitude and banishment were both to be served on islands.[41] This was fully in keeping with the contemporary French practices on which Boissonade had modeled Japan's new code, but, as Itō pointed out, it gave rise to the practical problem of which islands should be used.[42] Throughout the Tokugawa period, he noted, there had been problems with the practice of exiling criminals to islands, and when the Meiji government had experimented with sending convicts from Tokyo to the nearby islands of Hachijōjima, Niijima, and Miyakejima earlier in the period, the results had been disastrous for the local people.[43] The problem was compounded by the fact that the number of convicts to be transported was large. Drawing on statistics collected for 1875 and 1876, Itō estimated that about two thousand persons were likely to be sentenced to servitude or exile each year. With the minimum sentences for both punishments set at twelve years, it required only a simple calculation to determine that, at present rates, the government would have to be prepared to incarcerate a total of some twenty-four thousand people in island prisons in twelve years' time. None of the small islands southwest of Tokyo that had historically been used for the punishment of exile would be suitable for the long-term confinement of such

large numbers of prisoners. Not only would it be difficult to build the
necessary prisons and staff them with guards; there would also be insufficient land available for putting prisoners to work. According to Itō, however, there was one possible solution:

> It is my belief that criminals should be transported to Hokkaido. Hokkaido's
> climate and natural features are not like the other islands [of Japan], but there
> are hundreds of miles of land there and in that vast territory criminals could be
> put to work clearing land or working in mines. On days when it is extremely cold
> and everything is frozen over they could be given suitable indoor work. Then,
> when banished prisoners and those sentenced to servitude are released according
> to the rules that apply to them, they could work cultivating the land or in some
> form of industry, and it can be expected that they would eventually have children
> and increase the population [of Hokkaido].[44]

Itō's proposal to transport prisoners sentenced to servitude or exile to Hokkaido was approved by the Council of State (*dajōkan*) early in 1880, and
soon afterward a Home Ministry official named Tsukigata Kiyoshi (1845–
94) was sent to set up the new prison. Tsukigata had no prior experience
in prison affairs, but, like both Onoda Motohiro at Miyagi and Watanabe
Koreaki at Kosuge, he had served as an officer with the government forces
during the Satsuma Rebellion.[45]

Working with the help of an Ainu guide, Tsukigata eventually settled on
a site in an area called Kabato on the Ishikari River, forty kilometers up-
stream from the frontier capital of Sapporo.[46] By early 1881 prisoners had
begun arriving from the main island, and once the winter snow had melted
construction got underway. The plan, initially, was to build a truly enormous prison, capable of holding a total of eleven thousand prisoners, but
budgetary considerations forced the Home Ministry to settle for a considerably smaller institution, with an official capacity of seventeen hundred.[47]
As Itō's replacement as home minister, Matsukata Masayoshi (1835–1924),
explained in a submission to Prime Minister Sanjō, this was far from
enough to meet the government's needs. There were, he noted, more than
four thousand prisoners serving life sentences at this time, and with the
Miyagi and Kosuge prisons already stretched to their limits, they would all
have to be sent to Hokkaido. In order to make this possible, Matsukata
proposed using the funds that were to have been used to build more central
prisons on the main island to establish a second Hokkaido prison.[48] Thus,
within a month of the opening of the Kabato Prison in September 1881,
work began at a new site to the east of Sapporo, in an area called Sorachi.
Watanabe Koreaki was transferred from Kosuge to set up and run the new
prison, and with its completion in the middle of 1882 the question of how
to cope with the sudden increase of prisoners that came in the wake of the
Satsuma Rebellion was finally resolved.[49] At the same time, Hokkaido, at

Japan's geographical periphery, came to occupy a central place in the nation's penal imagination.

As Itō's original proposal makes clear, the decision to begin transporting prisoners to Hokkaido can be explained in narrowly legal terms, as a response to Boissonade's 1880 penal code and its stipulation that punishments of servitude and exile be served on islands. Yet this development was not without pre-Meiji roots. From the 1780s concern about the encroachment of tsarist Russia on Japan's northern frontier had led scholars and Bakufu officials alike to consider a number of plans for the possible colonization of Ezo (as Hokkaido was then known).[50] The best-known of these plans called for the relocation of a large community of outcasts, under the authority of Danzaemon, to settle and develop Ezo, but in the early 1790s, Honda Toshiaki, whose criticism of the inefficiency of Tokugawa punishments was discussed in chapter 4, developed an alternative proposal.[51] In a submission to Matsudaira Sadanobu, he argued that rather than wasting the productive potential of criminals by executing or banishing them, they should instead be pardoned and sent to Ezo, where they could be of real service to the nation *(kokueki ni nari)* working to clear land.[52] Honda's proposal was not taken up, but later, in the early 1860s, after the Bakufu had agreed to open the port of Hakodate to ships from Russia and the other Western powers, it did establish two small stockades in Ezo, which were used to confine petty criminals and unregistereds.[53] Moreover, as noted in chapter 6, within months of the Restoration, the new Meiji government had also announced its intention to begin sending all criminals sentenced to exile to Ezo.

Clearly then, the Meiji policy of sending prisoners to Hokkaido was not without significant Tokugawa period precedents. Yet, it is important that we also acknowledge the profoundly modern nature of this undertaking. Although it may have dreamed of the possibility, in reality the Bakufu could never have launched a policy that involved transporting thousands of convicts to its northern frontier, housing them in new prisons, and then putting them to work. Apart from the expense, it simply did not have at its disposal the kinds of architectural and disciplinary technologies needed to confine and control such large numbers of people over extended periods of time. Even at its peak, the Edo Stockade for Laborers had held no more than five hundred or six hundred inmates, and they were confined for significantly shorter periods of time than those in the new prisons. The Ezo stockades built in the 1860s were smaller still, holding a maximum of only forty or fifty inmates. Yet, even if the fiscal and practical difficulties of confining much larger numbers of people could have been overcome, the Bakufu would still have been constrained by its doctrine of benevolence and the principles of the status system. It was, after all, one thing to confine a few hundred marginal people on an island in Edo Bay and put them to work for a few years, but quite another to incarcerate several thousand prisoners, many of whom were former samurai, and ship them off to the wilds of Hokkaido for minimum terms of twelve years. The Meiji government was able to accomplish this only because the constraints that had bound and limited the old regime had now been cast aside. To begin with, the introduction of a new taxation system meant that the Meiji state was not as fiscally fragile as the Bakufu had been, while the introduction of the new theories and techniques of discipline and surveillance that had been developing in the West since the onset of the Industrial Revolution made it physically possible to institutionalize and control larger bodies of people than ever before. Most important of all, the emphasis now placed on the cruelty of older forms of punishment and practices such as judicial torture meant that even as the construction of massive new prisons helped the government enforce acceptance of its own domestic political agenda, it could, at the same time, also point to them as evidence of its commitment to the cause of progress—"civilization and enlightenment."

Given the existence of this neat ideological cloak, it should come as no surprise that the number of people confined in Japanese prisons increased dramatically from the middle of the 1870s. In 1876, the year before the outbreak of the Satsuma Rebellion, there were just under thirteen thousand convicts in the fledgling prison system. By 1879, when the central prisons at Miyagi and Kosuge were opened, this number had doubled, and by 1882, when the second Hokkaido prison was completed at Sorachi, it had increased to thirty-three thousand persons.[54] Even more dramatic increases were to follow.

In the first half of the 1880s, the wave of samurai rebellions that had earlier swept the southwestern part of the country gave way to new kinds of resistance to the Meiji regime in the form of the Movement for Freedom and Popular Rights (*jiyū minken undō*). Although this movement had its origins in the early 1870s when Itagaki Taisuke and Gotō Shōjirō of Tosa Domain left the central government and began experimenting with the formation of Western-style political parties, by the end of the decade local popular rights societies had proliferated all over the country, with village elites at their core. From late 1881 a confluence of key events began to push the movement into its most active and volatile phase. The government's announcement that it would open a national parliament within ten years and its ouster of Ōkuma Shigenobu from the ranks of the ruling oligarchy led to the formation of two new national opposition parties, Ōkuma's Constitutional Progressive Party (*rikken kaishintō*) and Itagaki's Liberal Party (*jiyūtō*). Over the next few years the Liberal Party in particular became a focus for popular discontent, which grew dramatically as a result of the deflationary economic policy launched by Matsukata Masayoshi, now finance minister, in the fall of 1881. The infamous "Matsukata deflation" plunged the country into a severe depression that lasted for more than four years. Farmers were particularly hard hit, and this helped fuel a series of violent rural protests, uprisings, and clashes that began with the Fukushima Incident of 1882 and reached a peak in 1884 with a succession of incidents, most famously at Kabasan, Nagoya, and Chichibu.[55] These incidents presented the Meiji oligarchs with a serious and sustained challenge from below, but as Fukushima's infamous Governor Mishima was quick to grasp, they also provided the government with an opportunity to crackdown on the opposition movement just as it was beginning to gather momentum.[56]

Nowhere is the full extent of this crackdown more clearly reflected than in the prison population statistics for this period. Between December 31, 1882, and December 31, 1885, the number of convicts in Japanese prisons increased from 33,000 to 63,000. The total prison population, including those being held for investigation or awaiting trial, rose from 44,000 to almost 79,000.[57] (Amazingly enough, the 1999 figure was 46,000 people in prison, out of a national population four times larger than it was in the 1880s.) Most revealing of all, however, are statistics for the number of convicts admitted to the prison system annually in the early 1880s. In 1882 there were a total of 84,000 new admissions. One year later, this figure had risen to 144,000, and by 1885 it stood at 167,000.[58] Of course, the political crackdowns were not the only factor contributing to this dramatic increase in the rate of incarceration. The Matsukata deflation contributed to an increase in various kinds of illegal activity, and enforcement of the 1880 penal code may also have helped to push prisoner numbers up.[59] Nevertheless, by allowing the government to remove and silence many thousands of participants in the Popular Rights Movement, as well as others whose hardships would have made them sympathetic to it, the veritable "great confinement," which took place between 1876 and 1885 and more particularly between 1881 and 1885, clearly helped the Meiji oligarchs maintain control over the country. At the end of 1884, the Liberal Party was disbanded, and from 1885 Japan's prisoner population leveled off for a time, before it slowly began to climb again in the 1890s. Yet, it was not only the political aims of the Meiji oligarchs that were served by the burgeoning prison system: the capacity to incarcerate large numbers of people also opened up the possibility of new forms of economic exploitation, and it did not take the Meiji leaders long to realize that prison *labor* too could be an extremely useful tool for building a new society.

"This Too Is for the State": Prison Labor, Colonization, and Capital

One early indicator of the emphasis that would be placed on putting prisoners to work in the Meiji period was the new role found for the Ishikawa-jima Stockade for Laborers in the latter part of the 1870s. Although the

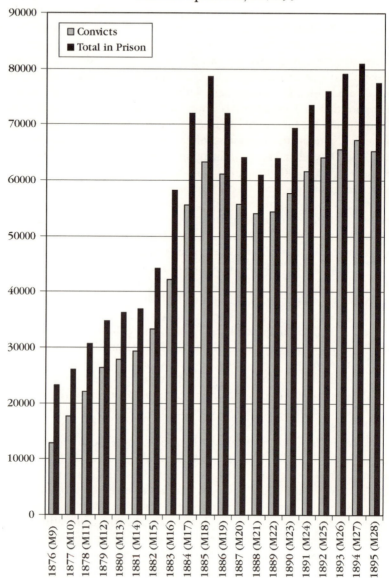

Figure 15. Prison population, 1876–1895 (Meiji 9–28). Numbers are for the prison population on December 31 of each year. *Nihon teikoku tōkei nenkan*, vols. 8 (1989), 13 (1894), 16 (1899).

old stockade had been used to confine some of those found guilty of crime under the Tokugawa, its role in the punishment system had always been supplementary and marginal when compared with the Kodenmachō Jailhouse. Yet, while the old jailhouse was torn down almost without notice in 1876, the Ishikawajima Stockade with its facilities and tradition of putting inmates to work was kept and transformed into one of Tokyo's most important new prisons.

As with the central prisons discussed previously, the major turning point for the Stockade for Laborers came in 1877, the year of the Satsuma Rebellion. Although it had continued to operate under a succession of new names during the first decade of the new era, it was now chosen as the destination for more than three hundred defeated rebels and placed under the direct control of the Home Ministry's Police Bureau.[60] By 1878 control of the two other existing prison facilities in the capital, at Ichigaya and Kajibashi, had shifted to the "main branch" at Ishikawajima, and although some of the old Edo period buildings still remained, by 1879 the grounds of the stockade had been dramatically expanded and transformed. The extent of the changes can be judged by comparing two plans of the Ishikawajima grounds, one from 1871 and the other from 1879.

The first thing to notice from these plans is the expansion of the Ishikawajima grounds over the course of the 1870s. Whereas in 1871 they had covered only a small area on the edge of the island, by the end of the decade they had come to cover almost all of it, and included several large new buildings. Together with the new Y-shaped cell block and the Western-style prison office, the most striking addition to the facilities on Ishikawajima were the neat rows of buildings in the new "factory area." Over the coming years, these were to see the introduction of various new kinds of labor. Oil extraction, the mainstay of the old stockade was already being phased out, and the operation of printing presses soon took its place as the job to which inmates at Ishikawajima were most commonly assigned. At a time when Japan still had no manufacturing sector to speak of, various other kinds of industrial work were also introduced at the Ishikawajima Prison. From 1879, for example, prisoners at Ishikawajima began making fire alarms and extinguishers, which were distributed to government offices all over the country. Western-style leather tanning and shoe manufacturing were introduced at around the same time under the supervision of a German technician.[61] In addition, prisoners were put to work outside the prison grounds on various projects around the city. In 1880, for example, prisoners from Ishikawajima were sent to lay a new railroad between Ueno and Takazaki, and in 1883, when the capital experienced a particularly severe winter, prisoners were dispatched to clear the snow from railroad tracks around the city.[62]

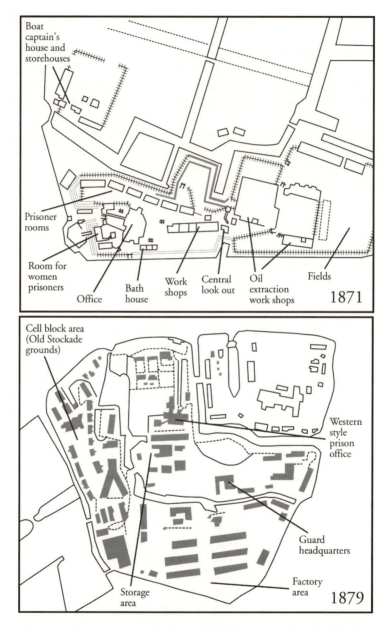

Figure 16. Plans from 1871 and 1879 showing the transformation of the grounds of the old Stockade for Laborers into the Ishikawajima Prison. Adapted with permission from Shigematsu Kazuyoshi, "Ninsoku yoseba to Ishikawajima kangoku," pp. 345, 356.

It was no coincidence that many of the tasks the prisoners at Ishikawajima were made to perform in the 1870s and 1880s were connected with key symbols of Meiji modernity: printing presses, shoes, and railroads. After all, while "free" workers could not always be convinced to shift quickly from older forms of industry to newer (often unpleasant) ones, prison labor could be commanded at will. This was true everywhere, of course, not just at Ishikawajima. We have already noted that the Tokyo Central Prison was established at Kosuge specifically so that its inmates could be put to work firing bricks in the furnaces there, but similar stories can be told for other prisons in the capital. In 1881, for example, a full two years before the launch of the famous Osaka Spinning Company and its factories full of women workers, the female prisoners incarcerated at Ishikawajima had all been transferred to the Kajibashi Prison, where they were put to work making textiles in a special "factory for women prisoners" (*kangoku jo kōjō*).[63]

Away from the capital, in areas where new facilities could not be established as quickly, authorities were more likely to put prisoners to work on projects in the outside world. Yanagida Kunio (1875–1962), the famous folklorist, wrote that as a child growing up in Hyōgo Prefecture in the early 1880s it was common to see columns of prisoners dressed in their distinctive red uniforms being marched through the streets. They were put to work building roads, and later, when they had earned the trust of their guards, they were also sent to private homes to perform various menial tasks. Yanagida remembered groups of two or three prisoners coming to his home to mend and repaper the sliding doors and screens.[64] When traveling in Yamagata Prefecture in the late 1870s, Isabella Bird witnessed a similar kind of prison labor. She wrote that the roads there were "being improved by convicts in dull red kimonos printed with Chinese characters," and that they also "worked for wages in the employment of contractors and farmers."[65] All of this suggests that for a time the sight of prisoners being put to work was commonplace in Meiji Japan. Yet, from the beginning of the 1880s, the most dramatic examples of the exploitation of prison labor were in places well removed from public view— underground and at the peripheries of the new Japanese empire.

In his initial proposal to transport convicts to Hokkaido, Itō had argued that once there, prisoners could be usefully employed in two lines of work—clearing land for agriculture and mining—and it was indeed these tasks that the first wave of prisoners sent to Hokkaido were made to perform. Hokkaido's first central prison at Kabato began primarily as an agricultural prison, and as soon as it was completed prisoners were put to work clearing the dense, bear-infested forests in surrounding areas.[66] Mining was not possible at Kabato, because there were no significant mineral deposits nearby, but when Hokkaido's second central prison was being planned, the site at Sorachi was chosen precisely because of its proximity to a known coal deposit.[67] Japanese leaders had, in fact, fantasized about the possibility of finding rich deposits of precious metals in Ezo from the early eighteenth century.[68] When proper surveys were finally conducted in the early Meiji period the results were, on the whole, disappointing, but in 1873 an American engineer did locate significant coal reserves at a place called Horonai.[69] The Hokkaido Colonization Office was keen to start mining these reserves, and at the end of the decade it received a large grant from the central government to do so. Experienced miners were initially brought in from the main island, but as the mine's operations expanded, it suffered from severe labor shortages.[70] As a result, when the Home Ministry announced that it intended to build a second central prison in Hokkaido, officials at the Colonization Office urged that a site near the mine be chosen.[71] The Sorachi Prison was completed in 1882, and from 1883 to 1894 between eight hundred and twelve hundred prisoners were sent to work in the Horonai mine each year. Some "free" miners continued to be hired, but prisoners, who could be employed at a quarter of the cost of ordinary labor, soon accounted for well over 80 percent of the work force.[72]

There must have been considerable enthusiasm for the Sorachi Prison in the government, for less than a month after its completion officials at the home and industry ministries submitted a joint proposal for the construction of another central prison in the vicinity of an even larger coal deposit. The location this time was at the other end of the Japanese archipelago at Miike in Kyushu. According to the proposal, the mine at Miike had continued to expand since it first came under government ownership in 1873, but labor shortages were now preventing it from growing to its full potential. Attempts had been made to use prisoners from surrounding prefectures to help make up these shortages, but it had always proved difficult to gather enough of them. The proposal concluded by noting that the construction of a central prison with a capacity of around one thousand prisoners would overcome this problem and help to ensure the smooth development of the Miike mine.[73] Construction of the new prison began almost immediately, and by 1883 the government was ready to send the first of thousands of prisoners to work in the mines. Three years later Miike's coal output surpassed that of the Mitsubishi company's Takashima mines, making it the biggest producer in Japan. In 1886 it accounted for more than 20 percent of the coal produced nationally, and although its share of the national total declined gradually after this, prison labor helped it maintain its position as the largest coal mine in the country well into the twentieth century.[74]

In 1886 a third major mining project involving the use of prison labor was launched near Shibecha in eastern Hokkaido. The mine extracted sulfur, which was essential for the production of gunpowder and matches, and for the vulcanization of rubber. The existence of a huge sulfur mountain at a place called Atosanupuri had, in fact, been known to the officials of Matsumae Domain from the late Tokugawa period, but it was only with the opening of the Kushiro Central Prison at Shibecha that it began to be exploited. Unlike the Miike and Horonai mines, the operation at Atosanupuri was from the outset privately owned. Its original owner was a Hakodate-based entrepreneur who needed only a few hundred prisoners to work the mine, but in 1887 ownership passed to the founder of the newly emerging Yasuda conglomerate, Yasuda Zenjirō (1838–1921), and a dramatic expansion took place. By the end of 1887 output had trebled, and by the end of 1888 it had more than trebled again.[75] The number of prisoners working in the mine increased to around five hundred, with still more working on related projects: a railway link was built between the mine and the prison, as were river, road, and telephone links with the port of Kushiro, some fifty kilometers away.[76]

Yasuda's was not the only private concern in the mining industry to benefit directly from the use of prison labor. From 1876 the Mitsui Trading Company (Mitsui bussan), which had particularly close ties to key members of the Meiji regime, was given the right to sell all coal produced at Miike, and in 1889 the government decided to go one step further and sell off the mine itself to Mitsui. Under the agreement reached at this time, the government also agreed to continue supplying prison labor from the Miike Central Prison for the mine, which was to play a significant role in the early expansion of the Mitsui empire. As Masuda Takashi (1848–1938), Mitsui's first modern president, later explained,

> The profits generated through the sale of coal from Miike were not so great, but what was more important was the growth that it allowed. It was through the export of coal from Miike that our trading company began to expand overseas. Miike was also the mainstay of our mining company. In broad terms, it is fair to say that Mitsui's overall expansion was based on Miike. Certainly, if there had been no trading company, and no mining company, but only a bank, then Mitsui would not have grown to what it is today.[77]

Domestic demand for coal was to grow dramatically in the wake of the Sino-Japanese and Russo-Japanese wars, but earlier in the period cheap prison labor at Miike helped Mitsui compete with and undercut the price of British coal all over East Asia. This, in turn, allowed it to open its first trading company offices in Shanghai, Singapore, Hong Kong, and, before long, all along the coast of southern China. By the end of the Meiji period, moreover, the Horonai coal mine in Hokkaido was also to come under Mitsui control. Like Miike, Horonai and the railways that serviced it were sold off by the government in 1889 to the newly formed Hokkaido Coal and Rail Company (Hokkaidō tankō tetsudō kaisha). Initially, the company's main investors were the emperor and other members of the Meiji aristocracy, but as operations expanded its management was handed over to the Mitsui conglomerate. Needless to say, Sorachi Central Prison, which by 1890 held over three thousand prisoners, continued to supply labor for the mine.[78]

Of course, the fact that the Meiji government was increasingly willing to deploy its army of prisoner-workers in order to promote the growth of private industry and business did not mean that it stopped using them directly itself to develop basic infrastructure. Particularly in Hokkaido, where a new phase of colonization was launched in 1886 under the governorship of Iwamura Michitoshi, prison labor was to play a crucial role in this regard. In the middle of the 1880s colonization of the northern island had slowed to a crawl, in large part because of the abolition of the Hokkaido Colonization Office in 1882 and its replacement with three separate prefectural governments. Iwamura's appointment marked the end of this cumbersome arrangement, and with administration of the entire island restored to a single office he was expected to jump-start the colonization process. One of his main goals was to build a system of roads into the interior, and in order to facilitate this, his office was given direct control of the three Hokkaido central prisons.[79]

Prisoners from Kabato started work on the first of the new roads within three months of Iwamura's arrival in Hokkaido, and they were soon joined by prisoners from Sorachi and Kushiro.[80] Initially they worked in the vicinity of the prisons so that they could be returned to them at night, but later, as the roads stretched further afield, temporary work camps and branch prisons were established in strategic locations across the island. Some of these branch prisons were eventually to become permanent facilities, including one at Abashiri, which continues to hold a special place in the Japanese popular imagination not unlike that of Alcatraz in the United States.[81] Abashiri, in fact, marks the end point of the main highway built by prisoners in the Meiji period. It was completed in 1891, and traverses Hokkaido from east to west, passing through some of the most difficult and densely forested parts of the island.

By 1894, when the use of prison labor on outside projects began being phased out, a total of some seven hundred kilometers of new road in Hokkaido had been built by prisoners.[82] As expected, the completion of these roads opened the interior to settlement, both by private individuals and the famous *tondenhei* soldier-settlers, who were recruited from the ranks of the former samurai to double as farmers and guards on the northern frontier.[83] Prisoners in Hokkaido also helped pave the way for these "pioneers" by building close to fifteen hundred outposts for the *tondenhei* and clearing large tracts of land for farming. They dredged long stretches of river in order to make the interior accessible by boat, and all over Hokkaido they were responsible for the construction of bridges, electricity lines, flood prevention walls, local government offices, and schools.[84]

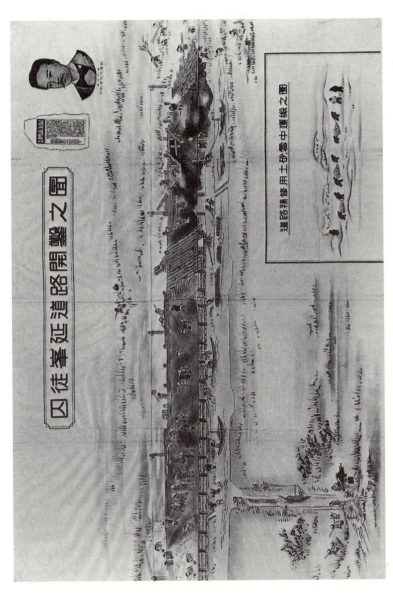

Figure 17. Convicts from Kabato Central Prison building a road in Hokkaido. The inset shows conditions in the harsh winter months. The figure looking down paternalistically from the top right-hand corner of the image is Tsukigata Kiyoshi, first warden of the prison. Tsukigata Kabato Museum.

There can be no doubt that prison labor played a crucial role in the colonization of Hokkaido and, more generally, in the early development of Japanese capitalism. Yet all of this came at a terrible human cost. Between 1884 and 1894 close to 44,000 people died in Japanese prisons.[85] Mortality rates were particularly high during the government's crackdown on the Popular Rights Movement. In 1885 alone more than 5,500 people, or 7 percent of the total inmate population, died, and in 1886 this figure rose to almost 12 percent (9,007 dead).[86] These were years in which much of Japan was swept by epidemics of cholera and dysentery, but the government's own statistics show that only a relatively small percentage of the prison deaths resulted from epidemic disease. Far more important were factors such as malnutrition, exhaustion, and "accidents" while working.

Some sense of the conditions under which prisoners were forced to work can be gained from the following description of the Horonai mine, written by a professor from Tokyo Imperial University in 1893:

> The drinking water is filthy. It is putrid and not fit for consumption. As a result, the prisoners [in the mine] contract illnesses of the digestive system, chronic stomach disorders, and diarrhea. . . . There is no distinction between the latrines and the eating areas. In the places where the prisoners move around they breathe in dust and air contaminated with gases from the mine and coal dust. Many prisoners thus contract lung diseases. It is possible to gauge the amount of coal dust flying around in the air just by observing the color of the prisoner's clothes. After just one day the red prison uniforms turn brown. After a month they are completely black.[87]

Not surprisingly, Tanaka Osamu has calculated that when prisoners from the Sorachi Prison did eventually stop being sent to work in the Horonai coal mine the death rate, which had previously averaged about 4 percent a year, immediately dropped to around 1.7 percent.[88] Things were similarly bad at the Kushiro Prison. In June 1887, soon after Yasuda Zenjirō had taken control of the sulfur mines, about half of the three hundred prisoners then working there were taken ill with dropsy, a condition caused by malnutrition. Forty-two died immediately, and by the end of the year this figure had risen to eighty-three, just over 10 percent of the total inmate population.[89] Mines are, of course, always dangerous places to work, but conditions for prisoners were also bad elsewhere. In Hokkaido the highest death rates of all were for prisoners working on the highway across the island. In 1889 prisoners from Sorachi had begun working their way toward the east coast, but in 1891, in order to speed the project along, a group from the Kushiro Prison was sent to Abashiri to start building from the other direction. For six months they worked in shifts, day and night, until the road link was completed. In the process, 186 of the 1,015 prisoners sent to work on the road died, and a firm foundation for the new Abashiri Prison's enduring infamy was laid.[90]

To some extent, the harsh conditions under which prisoners worked can be explained simply in terms of what was economically expedient. Perhaps the most callous contemporary assessment of the economic advantages of using prisoners for physically demanding and dangerous work was provided by Itō Hirobumi's Harvard-educated adviser, Kaneko Kentarō (1853–1942), after he visited Hokkaido in 1885:

> When there are large numbers of serious criminals as there are today, government expenditure on prisons increases uselessly, and so if we put prisoners to work on necessary projects and they weaken and die because they cannot cope, then . . . , when we are told of the difficulties of paying prison costs, the reduction in numbers should be thought of as a helpful measure.[91]

Economics was not the only factor driving the harsh treatment of prisoners in the 1880s, however. In contrast to the 1870s, when Ohara Shigechika had idealized the modern prison and its capacity to "heal" criminals, a much greater emphasis had now come to be placed on the punitive aspects of incarceration. Rather than seeing this trend in terms of the resurgence of "native traditions," it is important to note that it was, in fact, largely the result of the more realistic understanding of contemporary Western penal systems that Japanese officials had gained.

Onoda Motohiro, the police official who had earlier been sent to supervise construction of Miyagi Central Prison, played a key role in this development. Before the Miyagi prison was completed, Onoda had been sent on a study mission to Europe with his mentor Kawaji Toshiyoshi (1834–79), the main architect of Japan's modern police force. His orders were to make detailed studies of European prison systems, and in 1880 he returned to Japan with an extensive report on what he had observed. The report, later published in book form, argued that there were essentially two approaches to prison administration in Europe that emphasized either discipline (*chōkai shugi*) or guidance and education (*yūdō shugi, kyōkai shugi*).[92] Onoda was a strong proponent of the former approach. "Both psychologically and physically," he argued, "the point of confining prisoners is to inflict pain, and an unbearable feeling of weariness, so that not only those who are inmates in prison but also other good citizens have a sense of how fearful it is to be a prisoner."[93] Onoda reserved especially high praise for the prison system of England, where he claimed "the strictest discipline [*gensei no kiritsu*] is used to deal with prisoners" and "the primary aim is to inflict pain and suffering." Prisons there, he added approvingly, were known by all to be "a living hell in this world."[94]

Onoda's views were to have a significant impact on government policy in the 1880s. The "Revised Prison Rules" of 1881, which Onoda was assigned to help Ohara Shigechika prepare, provide an early indication of the shift in thinking.[95] In contrast to Ohara's original 1872 "Prison Rules," which took a fundamentally utopian view of the modern prison and emphasized the need to treat prisoners with benevolence and love, the "Revised Prison Rules" outlined a much bleaker, more practical approach to the minutiae of prison administration.[96] Even more dramatic than this was the impact of Onoda's ideas on a set of secret instructions issued to prison officials by Yamagata Aritomo as home minister in 1885. Just a few months earlier, Yamagata had given a public address to prison wardens from all over the country stressing the need to educate prisoners and treat them with understanding.[97] Now, however, in language clearly inspired by Onoda, he admonished the same officials to remember that "the fundamental idea behind the prison is to inflict discipline, suffering, and unbearably hard labor, so that prisoners learn to be fearful of jails and reject the evil temptation to commit more crimes."[98] He also warned officials not to put the creation of profits before the primary goal of discipline. According to his new instructions, in other words, any economic benefits derived from the exploitation of prison labor were to remain secondary to the main goal of inflicting unforgettable pain and suffering.

The prisoners that these policies aimed to crush did not accept their fates passively. For one prisoner at Kabato Central Prison, protest came in the form of an ironic sentence scratched into the side of brick he was about to fire in a kiln. Next to his name and a thumbnail sketch of himself, he wrote, "So hot! This too is for the state."[99] The political activist and writer Baba Tatsui (1850–88) sought revenge for his wrongful imprisonment at the hands of the Meiji state by publishing a damning exposé of Japanese prison conditions in an American newspaper, where it was bound to cause the government embarrassment.[100] Others found more immediate ways of expressing their anger and despair. In the period between 1877 and 1885 well in excess of a thousand inmates a year responded to the misery inflicted on them in Meiji prisons by simply breaking out, and despite the best efforts of officials like Onoda, it was not until 1898 that this figure fell below a hundred a year.[101] Riots, arson, and attacks on guards were also common.[102]

For most of the 1880s the government's main response to such acts of rebellion and resistance by prisoners was simply to apply more force. This was particularly true at the central prisons, where most political prisoners and serious offenders were sent. In 1883 the Home Ministry responded to endemic rioting and unrest at Tokyo Central Prison by permanently stationing a regiment of military police there.[103] This was also considered for the Kabato and Sorachi prisons in 1884, but it was decided instead to issue pistols to all guards there, in addition to the sabers that were standard for prison personnel at the time.[104] Pistols were also issued to guards at the

Kushiro Prison when it opened the following year, and from that time on, escapees in Hokkaido were shot on sight.[105] Of course, guards did not necessarily need guns in order to kill inmates. According to Dan Takuma (1858–1932), president of the Mitsui mining company, guards quelled a riot at Miike in 1883 by skewering prisoners to death using bamboo spears.[106] In general, Miike had one of the worst reputations for trouble and unrest, but because prisoners there worked underground, there was little chance of escape, and for most of the 1880s the Home Ministry considered it sufficient to station an armed guard at the entrance to the mine. In 1889, however, when the Mitsui company wanted reassurance about the labor force at its new mine, the government ordered that a regiment of military police be stationed there too.[107]

While there is thus no denying the brutality of the early Meiji prison system, it is also true that from the end of the 1880s a combination of new developments meant that many of the crudest, most obvious forms of abuse began being curbed. At one level, this can be seen as the start of the kind of unending cycle of reforms typical of modern penal systems. But at the same time the process was given a particular inflection because of Japan's ambivalent place within the global system of empire, and the government's need to impress the Western powers with the nation's attainment of "civilization."

CHRISTIANS, TREATIES, PENOLOGISTS, AND REFORM (AGAIN)

One important consequence of the Meiji government's extensive use of the new prison system to crack down on critics and political opponents was a growing awareness of and interest in prison conditions among journalists and writers. As Maeda Ai, Umemori Naoyuki, and Hirota Masaki have all pointed out, from the beginning of the 1880s, prison diaries and memoirs became an important literary genre for Meiji intellectuals, and prison issues were increasingly taken up and debated in the newspapers.[108] At the same time, the growing influence of Christianity among Meiji elites in the 1880s helped to inspire a small but dedicated group to begin working in the new prisons to improve conditions for inmates. Particularly important were the efforts of Hara Taneaki (1853–1942).

Hara's connection to criminal justice stretched back to his childhood in the late Tokugawa period. Born into a family of Bakufu retainers, at age twelve he had begun training to succeed his father as an officer of the Edo town governors.[109] After just a few years, however, the Restoration put an abrupt end to his apprenticeship. Finding himself unemployed, he decided to equip himself for the new era by studying English, and his subsequent contact with American missionaries soon led him to convert to Christianity. By the early 1880s he had found a new career for himself selling woodblock prints in the Jimbocho district of Tokyo, but the real turning point in his life came in 1883, when he made the mistake of commissioning a print that criticized the government's crackdown on the Popular Rights Movement in Fukushima the previous year. For this he was sentenced to three months in prison and sent to Ishikawajima. Conditions there were terrible: Hara claimed to have woken up one morning in the prison morgue, having been taken for dead in the night. Shocked by experiences such as this, he was moved to write a report to the Home Ministry on his release from prison calling for urgent reforms. On the basis of this report, he found himself appointed prison chaplain at a new prison in Kobe the following year.

Over the next several years Hara became closely involved with a group of Protestant missionaries associated with Dōshisha College in Kyoto, including John C. Berry, who further encouraged him in his work in the prisons.[110] Hara's most important contributions, however, came after he left the Kansai region. In 1888 he was asked to accompany a group of convicts being transferred from Kobe to Kushiro Central Prison in Hokkaido. Hara had already heard terrible stories about conditions in Hokkaido prisons, and upon his arrival he decided to inspect the sulfur mine at Atosanupuri, where most of the prisoners from Kushiro were then working for the Yasuda conglomerate. Horrified by what he saw, he immediately called upon the warden, Ōinoue Terusaki (1848–1912), to bring an end to the use of prison labor there.

Ōinoue was so impressed by Hara's plea that he not only took steps to end the prison's contract to supply labor for Yasuda, he also convinced him to move to Hokkaido and become the Kushiro prison's first chaplain.[111] In the years that followed, Hara and Ōinoue, who also converted to Christianity, succeeded in filling all of the prison chaplaincies at Hokkaido prisons with members of the Dōshisha group. In this they were, of course, motivated in large part by a desire to find areas of public life in which to establish a base of Christian influence, but this did not stop them from working to make genuine improvements in prison conditions by, among other things, establishing halfway houses and introducing recreational sports as an alternative to constant labor. In 1891 Ōinoue was appointed head of all three Hokkaido central prisons, and in this position he was able to oppose successfully a government plan to expand the use of prison labor at the Horonai mine.[112] Increasingly, however, Ōinoue's position on prison labor, and the influence of the Christian group in Hokkaido prisons generally, became a source of resentment among other prison officials, and at the height of the jingoistic fever that spread during the Sino-Japanese War of 1894–95, he was accused of disloyalty to the emperor and forced to resign.[113] When his replacement appointed a Buddhist (Shinshū) priest as prison chaplain at Kabato, all of the Christian chaplains, including Hara, resigned in protest. After returning to Honshu, Hara continued to promote the development of halfway houses for prisoners, and in 1898 one of his former Protestant colleagues from Hokkaido, Tomeoka Kōsuke (1864–1934), was appointed chaplain at the new Sugamo Prison in Tokyo. Tomeoka's appointment, however, immediately met with strong opposition from leaders of the Shinshū sect, who were able to turn it into a major political issue by appealing to the idea that Christian teachings were incompatible with the "national essence" (kokutai). After eight months of furor, and the collapse of a government over the issue, Tomeoka was eventually forced out of his position. In the years that followed, he was to become an important figure in efforts to establish reformatories for juvenile delinquents and various other social welfare projects, but his resignation nevertheless marked the end of significant Christian involvement in the prison system.[114]

Although the role of the Christian chaplains in Hokkaido was important, they were by no means the only ones to take an interest in prison conditions in the second half of the 1880s. One clear indication of this was the uproar caused in 1887 over the introduction of a new kind of prison labor to prisons in Kobe, Osaka, and Okayama. The idea behind the "punishment rock" (zaiseki), as it was known, was simply to exhaust prisoners by making them carry an unbearably heavy rock around the prison grounds for days on end.[115] This was, of course, fully in keeping with Yamagata's instructions to put prisoners to work in order to inflict on them pain and suffering, but within months of its introduction it had been taken up in the local newspapers. Before long opposition was voiced in the Osaka Municipal Assembly, and eventually a petition for its abolition was lodged with the central government by the Osaka Bar Association.[116] Although opponents of the punishment rock gave various reasons why it should be abolished, what they emphasized more than anything else was that its continued use would make Japan a laughing-stock among civilized nations and hinder its attempts to achieve treaty revision.[117]

The irony of this was that the inspiration for the punishment rock had in fact been the treadmills and cranks that were in widespread use in British prisons at this time. These devices were described enthusiastically by one British magistrate as "the most tiresome, distressing, exemplary punishment that has ever been contrived by human ingenuity," and it was after seeing them in action on a trip to England that the then governor of Hyōgo first came up with the idea of finding something similar for use in Japan.[118] By this time however, the government was well aware that what was acceptable in the civilized countries of the West and what would be judged so in

Japan were not necessarily one and the same. In July 1887 yet another round of treaty negotiations had broken down over the issue of extraterritoriality and the criminal code, and it was patently clear that if Japan was ever to achieve its goal, it could not afford to give the powers any reason at all to question the civilized nature of its criminal justice system.[119] Not surprisingly, then, the punishment rock was abolished at the end of 1887, and from around the same time the government began stepping up its efforts to put a more progressive face on its prison system.

The wave of prison reforms that began in the late 1880s has often been explained by historians in terms of the rise of German influence on the Japanese legal and justice systems, but they can also be thought of in terms of a growing interest in the idea of "social science." The main architect of the reforms was Kiyoura Keigo (1850–1942), a key member of Yamagata Aritomo's powerful political clique who would later serve as justice minister and eventually, in the Taisho period, as prime minister. In 1886 Yamagata appointed him head of the Home Ministry's Police and Prisons Bureau with instructions to make whatever reforms necessary to convince the Western powers to agree to treaty revision. Kiyoura believed that what was most needed was "the infusion of civilized principles of science" (*bunmei-teki gakuri no chūnyū*) into both the police and prison systems.[120] To facilitate this, he asked the prominent legal scholar, Hozumi Nobushige (1855–1926) of Tokyo Imperial University, to recommend two students who might be retained and trained by the Home Ministry to serve as academic advisers. For prison affairs, Hozumi recommended Ogawa Shigejirō (1863–1924), a recent graduate of the Tokyo Senmon Gakkō (forerunner of Waseda University) who had just submitted a thesis on European penal systems. By the end of the year, he had been appointed as Japan's first professional penologist.[121] Ogawa soon began publishing translations of the latest Western penological theories, and over the next decade he would become an important figure both domestically and as a representative of Japan overseas.

Another important step toward encouraging the dissemination and discussion of ideas about prison management and reform came in 1888 with the establishment of a professional association called the *Dai Nippon kangoku kyōkai* (Prisons Society of Great Japan). The first edition of the new society's monthly journal explained the importance of its mission, noting that, although much had been accomplished since the Restoration, there were still many in Japan who did not understand that in the West a nation's level of civilization was judged according to the conditions in its prisons.[122] In addition to listings of relevant government announcements, the journal consisted of articles by prominent officials and translations of European writings on penology. Early issues showed a strong French influence, and perhaps partly in order to counter this, Ogawa, who favored German penology, helped launch a rival publication, the *Keisatsu kangoku gakkai zasshi* (Police Prisons Association Journal) the following year.

The remarkable appearance of this second professional journal in 1889 coincided with two other noteworthy events that furthered the development of Japanese penology and its role in the prison system. First, Ogawa was given the task of compiling a new (third) set of national "Prison Rules." In keeping with the emphasis that he and Kiyoura placed on the application of scientific principles, the new rules laid out an elaborate system for the classification and collection of information about individual prisoners, who were now to be treated as subjects for study. Additional changes were made to bring the prison system in line with the most "advanced" Western practices. Persons detained while awaiting trial were now to be designated "criminal case defendants" (*keiji hikokunin*) and guaranteed more lenient treatment than other prisoners; doctors were to make regular checks on the health of prisoners punished with reduced rations or solitary confinement; juvenile delinquents were to be sent to privately run reformatories instead of regular prisons; and the practice of detaining in special facilities (*betsubō ryūchi*) separate from the main prison buildings convicts who had completed their official terms but could not find a guarantor was abolished.[123] The Tokugawa practice of admitting juvenile delinquents to penal institutions at the request of their parents was also abolished, as was the Meiji practice of appointing "messengers" (*denkokusha*) and "foremen" (*yūkōsha*) from among the prisoners, which was seen as a remnant of the old *rōnanushi* system.

The second notable development of 1889 was the arrival in Japan of Kurt von Seebach (1845–1891), a leading disciple of the famous German penologist Karl Krohne. Von Seebach had been warden of Berlin's Moabit Prison when he was recruited as an official adviser to the Japanese government by Home Minister Yamagata on a trip to Europe the previous year.[124] In addition to making inspections of prisons across the country, his duties in Japan included giving regular lectures on penology at the new National Training Center for Prison Officers (*Kokuritsu kangokukan renshūjo*), which was established by the Home Ministry at the beginning of 1890.[125] Yamagata and his underlings clearly had high hopes for von Seebach and they were, no doubt, greatly distressed when he died the following year from a disease contracted while inspecting prisons in Hokkaido. This, after all, was hardly the kind of incident likely to inspire confidence in the Japanese prison system overseas.

In spite (or perhaps because) of his early death, von Seebach's ideas are generally credited with having laid the foundations for the future development of the Japanese prison system. As a former officer in the Prussian army, he stressed above all else the importance of maintaining strict discipline, but also emphasized that pain should be inflicted on prisoners only in order to encourage reform and never as an end in itself. In keeping with the principles already laid out by Ogawa in his "Prison Rules," he also maintained that the only way to promote reform was to study each prisoner carefully as an individual and then tailor his treatment accordingly. To facilitate this, prisons were to be kept relatively small (housing no more than five hundred inmates), and wherever possible, prisoners were to be confined in their own individual cells. He also argued strongly in favor of the construction of new, state-of-the-art prisons as the only way to achieve real reform and thus bring prisoner numbers down.[126]

Even before von Seebach's arrival in Japan the Home Ministry had recognized the need to begin building prisons that would be judged of a high-enough standard to allow for the eventual incarceration of westerners. In 1888 the original Tokyo Central Prison at Kosuge had been knocked down and a new facility, based on the half-radial design of the New Jersey State Prison in Trenton and the Pentonville Penitentiary in London, erected in its place.[127] It was within this large new structure, made entirely of red bricks fired in the prison kilns, that von Seebach's National Training Center for Prison Officers was established in 1890, and in 1893 plans and photographs of it were even sent to the United States to be part of the Japanese display at the World's Fair in Chicago.[128] Yet, while the government was able to use the Kosuge prison to advertise its enlightened credentials in this way, there was much about its design that failed to satisfy experts like von Seebach and Ogawa. There were, moreover, still many prisons in Japan that the government would have preferred to keep out of Western view altogether. The old Ishikawajima Prison, which sat prominently in the middle of Tokyo Bay, was a prime example. It had by this time fallen into a state of serious disrepair, and in 1891 the Home Ministry decided that rather than rebuild on the Ishikawajima site, it would replace it with a new, truly world class prison at Sugamo on the outskirts of the capital.[129]

The task of designing the new Sugamo Prison fell to Tsumaki Yorinaka (1859–1916), an American-trained architect, who had just returned from three years of further study in Germany. In the years that followed, Tsumaki would design a series of monumental buildings for the Meiji state, including the Tokyo City Hall in 1894, the Tokyo Court House in 1896, the Tokyo Chamber of Commerce in 1899, and the Yokohama Specie Bank in 1904.[130] Yet none of these buildings was more impressive than the Sugamo Prison. In all, it would take four years to build, and when it was finished, it was one of the three largest buildings in the country, rivaled only by the Bank of Japan and the National Armory.[131] The perimeter of the prison, which was over 1.6 kilometers long, was bounded by a massive

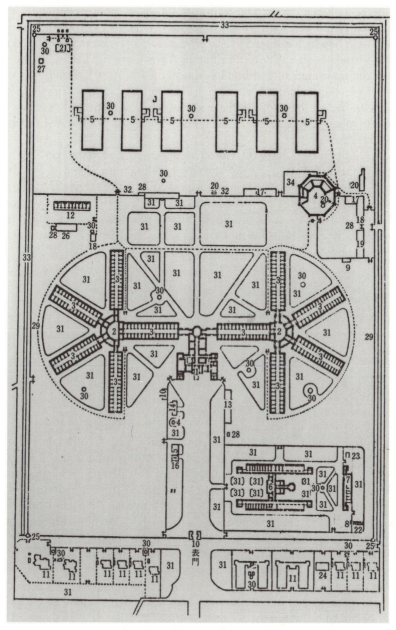

Figure 18. The architectural plans of the "international prison" built at Sugamo. Courtesy of Shigematsu Kazuyoshi.

5-meter-high brick wall. The main gate was over 4 meters tall and made of wood reinforced with iron. Inside there were two tall watch towers, from each of which radiated five large cell blocks. These were designed to hold a total of some twenty-four hundred prisoners.[132] This was far more than the maximum of five hundred prescribed by von Seebach, and the need to accommodate so many also made it impossible to provide individual cells. Yet, in the end, the sheer size of the new institution was key to its true role as a monument to Meiji Japan's attainment of modernity and civilization.

In October 1895, when Meiji officials gathered to open the Sugamo Prison, they celebrated not just the new building but the arrival of a new era. A year earlier, Foreign Minister Mutsu Munemitsu (1844–97), himself a "graduate" of the Meiji prison system (having spent over six years in Miyagi Central Prison following the Satsuma Rebellion), announced the successful negotiation of a new treaty with Great Britain.[133] Extraterritoriality and consular jurisdiction, it was agreed, would end on July 17, 1899. After that time, Westerners accused of crimes in Japan would be tried by Japanese judges in Japanese courts and, if found guilty, would serve out their sentences in Japanese prisons. Of course, over the next four years further efforts would have to be made to ensure that the prisons were properly prepared for the arrival of the first Westerners (as late as April 1899, concern was expressed in the British Parliament about the suitability for British subjects of the food and accommodations provided in Japanese prisons).[134] Nevertheless, in 1895 the hardest battles seemed to have been won.

In addtition to the new "international prison" at Sugamo, Japan could now fairly claim to have outgrown its need for Western advisers and to have produced its own world-class penologist. Ogawa's textbook study of penology, *Kangokugaku*, had been published in the same year the revised treaties were signed, and he was absent from the opening of Sugamo only because he had been sent to represent Japan at the Fifth International Prisons Conference in Paris.[135] There he would emphasize the great progress that Japan had made in introducing German-style discipline to its prisons and eradicating the abuses of the older French-style approach. As evidence of this he could point to the government's decision in 1894 to begin phasing out the use of prison labor on outside projects in Hokkaido. By this time, of course, the process of colonization was well under way, and as ever growing numbers of free settlers arrived, the problems caused by escapees had begun to outweigh the usefulness of the chain gangs. This helped to pave the way for the triumph of a purer form of discipline in the prisons, but it was also true that Japan, in general, was on the verge of becoming a new kind of nation. In this regard it is significant that the opening of the Sugamo Prison had coincided with Japan's resounding victory over China

Figure 19. The monumental brick gate of the completed Sugamo Prison. Courtesy of Shigematsu Kazuyoshi.

in its first modern war. During that conflict, the disciplinary techniques that both countries had imported from the West were tested on the battle-fields and in munitions factories, and in the end it was Japan's superior mastery of them that had set it apart from the now decidedly "Oriental" Chinese. The next step would be to refine and improve the application of such techniques, but by 1895 "modernity" and "civilization" appeared within close reach, and discipline had been firmly established as the key.

Punishment, Empire, and History in the Making of Modern Japan

> *In the department of jurisprudence vast progress has been made. I doubt whether any nation on earth can show a more revolting list of horrible methods of torture and punishment in the past with so great amelioration in so short a time. Their cruel and bloody codes were mostly borrowed from China.*
>
> William Elliot Griffis, *The Mikado's Empire* (1890)[1]
>
> *While there will be little difficulty with the semi-civilized and savage aborigines, only the severest measures will subdue the Chinese, and much allowance must be made if the Japanese have to inflict punishment which, in these days, and amongst civilized people, would be termed barbarous*
>
> W. A. Pickering, *Pioneering in Formosa* (1898)[2]

WHEN FIRST CONFRONTED with descriptions of the Tokugawa Bakufu's arsenal of brutal punishments, it is difficult to imagine that the Meiji period transition to a penal system based on the modern prison could have constituted anything other than a clear-cut example of human progress. One of the aims of this book, however, has been to challenge and complicate such straightforwardly Whiggish interpretations of the results of Japan's encounter with Western modernity.

There is, of course, no denying the bloody nature of Tokugawa punishments, and it is certainly not my intention to advocate a return to public floggings, burnings at the stake, or judicial torture. Yet, as the first three chapters of this book demonstrate, even at their bloodiest, Tokugawa punishments were never acts of unthinking violence. They formed part of a sophisticated system for maintaining order that was not entirely lacking in restraint or compassion. Indeed, while one of the basic goals of this system was to keep subjects in fear of the shogun and his allies at all levels of society, it also served as a tool for promoting his image as a "benevolent ruler." This was true in cases where his officers chose to exact revenge (or allowed it to be exacted) on those who had caused others real harm by their actions. It was also true when they systematically turned a blind eye to petty violations or publicly forgave groups of prisoners in solemn ceremonies of amnesty conducted at the shogunal tombs.

As noted in chapter 4, from the beginning of the eighteenth century criticisms of the Tokugawa punishment system began to be voiced by scholars such as Ogyū Sorai, Dazai Shundai, and, eventually, Nakai Riken. For the most part, however, these criticisms did not focus on the brutality or cruelty of existing punishments. (For Shundai, in fact, the problem was that they were not brutal enough!) Rather, their main concern was with the system's apparent inability to maintain order, particularly during periods of extreme social distress. Some reforms were forthcoming—most notably the establishment of the Edo Stockade for Laborers—but the basic principles of the system remained unchanged from the late seventeenth century on. Even at the very end of the period, when a handful of scholars and activists became fascinated by what they had begun to learn about prisons in the West, there is little evidence to suggest that they imagined such institutions would serve to replace the existing array of violent public punishments, or that practices such as judicial torture would be abolished. These things only came to be targeted for criticism and reform after the signing of the unequal treaties and Japan's initiation into the West's politics of civilization. At that point, the same practices that had previously marked the shogun's power and position at the apex of status system society quickly came to serve instead as markers of Japan's backwardness and inferiority as a nation within the modern "comity of nations."

It did not take the new Meiji leadership long to realize the implications of this image and to begin taking measures to rectify it. As noted in chapter 6, the most dramatic public punishments (crucifixion and burning alive) were abolished quickly after the Restoration, and Ohara Shigechika's mission to investigate the prison systems of British colonies in Asia (clearly an indicator of Japan's initial position in the imperial world order) was one of the first sent overseas by the new government. There was greater resistance to the abolition of practices such as judicial torture, flogging, and even the gibbeting of severed heads, but they too were soon identified by foreign advisers and "enlightened" Meiji critics alike as being offensive to the sensibilities of the "civilized world" and thus targeted for reform.

Once again it should be emphasized that it is not the aim of this book to trivialize the important reforms that were made in the first decades of the Meiji period. It is certainly true that during the period of "civilization and enlightenment" many genuinely horrible practices did finally come to be seen for what they were. Yet, at the same time, as argued in chapter 7, the emphasis that now came to be placed on the barbarity of older practices also helped to provide an ideological cloak for the introduction of new forms of barbarity. Thus, throughout the 1880s and 1890s the Meiji government could point to its construction of a national network of prisons in which thousands of people died and many more were forced to live and work for years on end in truly miserable conditions as evidence of its genuine commitment to "progress" and modern "civilization." And although the brutality of Tokugawa punishments could be more openly extreme than those of the Meiji period, the introduction of the modern prison and the notion of incarceration for the purpose of reform made it possible to inflict suffering and pain more consistently and on a larger body of people.

It is tempting to assume that the cruelties and excesses of Meiji prisons were a product of their simply not being modern enough or that they represented an especially sinister product of the combination of "Japanese spirit and Western technology" (*wakon yōsai*). For the most part, however, the most disagreeable aspects of the early Meiji prison system can be linked directly to a Western source. The Home Ministry's central prisons were, for example, modeled directly on the French Maisons Centralé, and the practice of transporting convicts to Hokkaido was first developed as a result of provisions laid out in the 1880 Penal Code by Gustave Boissonade, the same "Western expert" who is remembered in Japan today as a hero for his role in bringing an end to the use of torture. Later in the 1880s it was the example of the prison systems of western Europe, and in particular Great Britain, that led Onoda Motohiro to stress the importance of inflicting pain and suffering on prisoners as a deterrent to recidivism. Onoda also argued in favor of expanding the use of prison labor in Hokkaido by pointing specifically to the way in which the British had colonized an entire continent by sending their convicts to Australia.[3] Had he studied in America rather than in Europe, he might just as easily have drawn his inspiration from the "convict leasing system," which was introduced in the southern United States in the wake of the Civil War, and which was to play a vital role in the industrialization and development of the New South well into the twentieth century.[4] Either way, it is clear that the Meiji state's exploitation of prison labor did not put it out of step with the practices of the "civilized" world.

In this regard, it is also worth noting that in stark contrast to the shock and outrage expressed by Westerners at the sight of public executions or torture, the reactions of those who came into contact with Meiji period chain gangs ranged from accepting to approving. Isabella Bird immediately equated the convicts she saw working on the roads in Yamagata Prefecture with British "ticket-of-leave men," while her compatriot A. H. Savage Landor, encountering a group of chained prisoners working near Kushiro in Hokkaido in the early 1890s, commented simply that "the Government wisely makes use of these convicts in opening roads and other public works" and that "a great part of the Japanese population of Yezo [Hokkaido] is composed of exiles and ex-convicts."[5]

Ironically, unlike other parts of the "civilized world," the Meiji government's need to compensate for the fact that Japan was not a white nation and to impress the Western powers meant that by the mid-1890s, when treaty revision was approved, many of the crudest abuses of the new prison system had begun to be curbed. The government was able to accentuate this general trend at the beginning of 1897 when, in an act of amnesty strongly reminiscent of the Tokugawa period, it chose to release a total of almost ten thousand prisoners nationwide, and drastically reduce the sentences of many thousands more, as part of the official state ceremonies to mourn the death of the empress dowager.[6] Yet, at the same time, it is also well known that prisons continued to be used throughout the prewar period to silence political critics and other "undesirable" elements of Japanese society—including followers of the so-called new religions, for example.[7] Moreover, while the use of prison labor on outside projects was phased out at most prisons other than Miike (where it continued into the Shōwa period), the early access that both government and private industry had to thousands of bonded workers was to have a lasting impact on the organization of labor in a number of key industries. Particularly in mining, railway, and road construction, economic historians such as Tanaka Osamu, Hashimoto Tetsuya, and Yamada Moritarō have shown how the "free" workers who were recruited to augment or replace prison labor from the 1890s on often found themselves living in the same kind of dormitories that had originally been built to confine convicts working away from their prisons.[8] Known also as *naya* or *hamba*, these dormitories were commonly referred to as "prison rooms" (*kangokubeya*). Those who lived in them were subject to constant surveillance by guards, not only to keep them working, but also to prevent them from escaping before the expiration of their contracts. Although beyond the scope of this book, it also seems likely that a link can be drawn between the exploitation of prison labor in the Meiji period and the extensive use of Korean forced labor in Hokkaido and elsewhere in the 1930s and 1940s.[9] It may even be possible to link the traditions of Meiji prison labor with the Japanese army's infamous use of prisoners of war to build railways and roads in Southeast Asia during the Pacific War.

Whether or not such historical leaps can be justified, it is certainly worth noting that 1895, the year in which the new Sugamo Prison was completed in Tokyo, was also the year in which Japan defeated Qing dynasty China in its first modern war. As a result of this victory, the Japanese, who had themselves only just convinced the Western powers to revise the treaties imposed on them in the 1850s, were able to extract their own unequal treaty from the Qing in 1896.[10] This was not the first time that the Meiji state had used the tools of "civilized" diplomacy to assert its supremacy over an Asian neighbor. As early as 1876 a Japanese gunboat had been sent to "open" Korea and force it to accept an unequal treaty in what was effectively a reenactment of Perry's arrival in Japan.[11] Yet, whereas Korea was a relatively small, militarily weak country whose relationship to the Tokugawa shogunate had long been (mis)represented in Japan as one of obeisance, China had traditionally stood at the center of the East Asian world order, and Japan had not simply made a flamboyant show of force against it—it had decisively defeated it in war.[12]

The outcome of the first Sino-Japanese War was also important because it gave Japan territorial control of Taiwan, its first overseas colony. Again, it is true that Japanese expansion into neighboring areas can be traced back well before 1895, but unlike the Ryukyus, Hokkaido, or even the Ogasawara Islands, whose incorporation into the Meiji state could be understood in terms of the absorption of territories and peoples who had long been subjected to some form of Japanese control or domination, the case of Taiwan was something quite different.[13] It was a prize of war that had been wrenched away from the Qing empire in a dramatic, European-style act of military conquest, which put Japan in charge of a large (Chinese and aboriginal) population over whom it had never before exercised any form of authority or influence.

In the context of the late nineteenth century, the founding of a formal colonial empire offered yet more evidence of Japan's steady progress toward the attainment of "equality" with the West. After all, what made the Western powers "great" was not simply the superiority of their domestic institutions, or even the "civilized" values they embodied, but rather their ability to project those values (and, of course, their own power) outward, for the "betterment" of all mankind. In this sense, the project of empire was also a final test of Japan's credentials as a modern nation: the Japanese may have shown themselves to be good students of the West, but had they really mastered the principles of modern civilization well enough to take on the task of teaching others? Were they really ready, in other words, to share the "white man's burden"? These were not abstract, philosophical questions. The deeply humiliating experience of the "Triple Intervention" of 1895, in which France, Germany, and Russia had used their combined power and influence to "persuade" the Meiji leaders to give up strategic territories that it claimed from China at the conclusion of the Sino-Japanese War, convinced most Japanese that the Western powers would continue to exploit any signs of weakness or failure to their own advantage. The specific implications of this for Japan's occupation of Taiwan were very clear. As one contributor to the *Kangoku kyōkai zasshi* (Prisons Society Journal) put it in 1896: "The great powers . . . have long drooled over the possibility of adding this island to their territories . . . [and] they will be watching very carefully to see how our empire governs Taiwan."[14] Key to "success" in Taiwan, the writer continued, would be the establishment of a modern penal system; without it "trust in Japanese law" would evaporate, causing "all of our efforts there to come to naught."[15] Yet, what exactly did it mean to create a *colonial* penal system? What, in other words, were the principles of modern "civilization" that Japan was to project outward as part of its drive to attain parity with the West as a "great power" in its own right?

DISCIPLINING NATIVES: JAPANESE PRISONS IN COLONIAL TAIWAN

As the Japanese established their control over Taiwan in 1895–96, they quickly abolished all traces of the old system of justice that had operated under the Qing. Initially, the army issued harsh emergency regulations for punishing a range of basic crimes, but by August 1896 these had been repealed, and the provisions of the Japanese penal code were formally extended to the newly occupied territory.[16] As had been the case in Japan itself, the introduction of the code created an immediate need for facilities in which sentences of incarceration could be carried out, and in order to meet this need, Japanese authorities all over the island soon began converting old local government offices, shrines, and warehouses into makeshift prisons.[17] In Taipei, or Taihoku, as the colonial capital was known to its new rulers, an old Qing army garrison near the south gate of the city wall was earmarked for this purpose.[18] A few months after its opening in early 1896, the population of the garrison prison stood at around 120 inmates, but by the beginning of 1900 it had already increased tenfold to more than 1,200.[19] Similarly dramatic increases were reported all over the island.

One important reason for this increase was the enactment of the infamous Bandit Punishment Ordinance (*hito keibatsu rei*) in 1898 under the fourth governor general, Kodama Gentarō (1852–1906), and his chief of civil administration, Gotō Shimpei (1857–1929). The ordinance, introduced as part of Kodama's campaign to crush the "outlaw" groups that continued to plague Japanese attempts to "pacify" the island, effectively made any open act of resistance to Japanese rule punishable by death, and in the years immediately following its enactment it was employed ruthlessly.[20] In a speech delivered in Tokyo in 1901, the then warden of Taihoku Prison boasted to his colleagues that since 1899 he had personally overseen the executions of almost 300 Taiwanese "bandits."[21] This was, in fact, only a small portion of the total number (2,616) hanged in those three years under the ordinance. Yet it was not just the large number of inmates awaiting execution that helped swell prison populations in Taiwan at this time.[22] The Bandit Punishment Ordinance also included provisions for the punishment of accomplices and associates with what were, by the standards of the day, extremely long prison terms. Between 1898 and 1902, a total of 664 persons were sentenced to life in prison under the ordinance. There were also 479 sentences longer than ten years, and 258 sentences of five years or more handed down in this period.[23]

Far from meeting with condemnation, it should be noted, the ruth-lessness of the Kodama administration's approach at this time was fully supported by Western observers. Consider the passage from the British "expert" on colonial affairs W. A. Pickering, cited in full at the beginning of this conclusion. Written just after the enactment of the Bandit Punishment Ordinance, it specifically claimed that "only the severest measures will sub-due the Chinese" and that "much allowance must be made if the Japanese have to inflict punishment which in these days, and amongst civilized peo-ple, would be deemed barbarous."[24] Such expressions of support, of course, did nothing to solve the practical problems that Kodama's harsh policies had created for the fledgling colonial prison system. Not only had there been a significant increase in the overall size of the inmate population, the proportion of long-term prisoners, who were more likely to create trouble, had skyrocketed. Meanwhile, the prisons themselves were still the same makeshift facilities that had been established in the first years of the Japa-nese conquest. The number of escapes was high, as was the number of inmates who were shot dead in the attempt each year, and riots were be-coming increasingly common.[25] Clearly, something had to be done, and by 1900 the colonial administration had begun to explore various possible solutions.[26]

The administration's first response to the problem of overcrowding and unrest in the prisons in Taiwan was to request permission from Tokyo to begin transferring inmates to facilities in Japan. It proposed that all "serious offenders" from Taiwan (including those convicted under the Bandit Pun-ishment Ordinance) be sent to Miike Central Prison in southern Kyushu, where they could be put to work in the coal mines alongside hardened criminals from other parts of the empire.[27] Not surprisingly, this proposal was quickly rejected by the Home Ministry, which had little interest in permitting an influx of colonial convicts into Japan proper. Prisoners from Taiwan would have to be dealt with in Taiwan. Faced with this reality, the colonial administration soon announced a plan to build three new peniten-tiaries of its own at Taihoku, in the north of the island; Taichū, in the middle; and Tainan, in the south. An architect from the Justice Ministry was dispatched to draw up plans, and after three years of work the prisons were finally completed in 1904.[28]

All three of the new prisons were impressive structures, but Taihoku, in particular, was the jewel in colonial Taiwan's carceral crown. Consider the following description penned by the writer and politician, Takekoshi Yosa-burō (1865–1950), in the English-language edition of his 1905 survey *Japa-nese Rule in Formosa*:

Figure 20. Map of central Taihoku (Taipei) from 1914, showing the massive stone prison built by the Japanese in 1904 in the bottom right hand corner. Author's personal collection.

Many people, even in Tokyo, must be surprised when they find that the Sugamo Prison or the other prisons in Tokyo are such fine, lofty, brick buildings. But in Taihoku the prison is built of stone which is superior even to brick. It cost ¥310,000 to build, and may be said to have been planned on a more extensive scale than any other building in the city. It covers about fifty acres, and has fifteen or twenty acres of land around it. There is accommodation for 1,200 prisoners at one time; the building is well lighted, and all the passages and floors are covered with cement, so that not a spot of bare ground is to be seen anywhere. If anything is dropped, the sound reverberates through the building.[29]

It is, of course, no coincidence that the main point of comparison in this passage is Sugamo and "the other prisons in Tokyo." By exceeding the standards of the very institutions that had helped Japan achieve legal "equality" with the West, the Taihoku Prison seemed to offer concrete proof of the nation's continued "progress" and, at the same time, of its genuine commitment to spreading the benefits of modern civilization to its new colony.

It is worth noting that what made the Taihoku Prison such an impressive building for Takekoshi was not just its scale or even its perfect sterility but also the material from which it was built. At a time when most prisons in Japan were still made of wood or, at very best, brick, the new colonial prison had been built with stone, the same material used in all the great penitentiaries of the West. Yet the meaning of the stone used in the Taihoku Prison went much deeper than Takekoshi's description alone might suggest. In a speech delivered at the Prisons Society in Tokyo soon after the new Taihoku penitentiary was completed, Tejima Heijirō, the head of the colonial government's Department of Legal Affairs, proudly explained to his audience the source of the stone. In Taiwan, he noted, unlike Japan, potentially useful things were often just left lying around. Taihoku, for example, had previously been surrounded on all sides by a massive city wall, but by knocking it down and making use of the stone contained in it, the colonial authorities had been able to build their new prison, "now the most beautiful sight in Taihoku," for a fraction of what it would have cost elsewhere.[30] Needless to say, what Tejima presented as an admirable example of bureaucratic efficiency carried very different implications for the subject population in Taiwan. The old city wall, which had once offered residents protection from outside aggression, had now been transformed into a prison, designed specifically to entrap and punish them. Throughout the colonial period it would serve as a symbol of Japanese authority.

While the symbolic significance of the stone in the Taihoku Prison walls was surely not lost on a colonial official such as Tejima, in his speech to the Prisons Society in Tokyo (as perhaps in his own mind) he chose to emphasize the practical advantages of the new building. The completion of the three new prisons in Taiwan led to a dramatic decrease in the number of escapes across the island and helped improve security, but what excited Tejima most was that inmates could now be put to work in proper prison workshops. Like bureaucrats all over the world, Tejima hoped that the sale of prison-made goods might eventually help offset operating costs. Yet, there was another, more important reason for his enthusiasm. Japanese entrepreneurs in Taiwan, he explained, were desperate to employ skilled "native" workers, and now that workshops had been built, the prisons had begun to serve as "industrial schools" *(kōgyō gakkō)*, providing inmates with "advanced" Japanese training in a range of different trades, from masonry and joinery to needlework and shoe making. As a result, he noted, demand for prison-trained workers in Taiwan was now so high that colonists regularly asked officials to notify them in advance whenever inmates were about to be released.[31] Takekoshi corroborates this aspect of colonial penal policy, noting that, "since the Japanese occupation, such trades as are required to meet Japanese needs are learned principally in the prisons."[32]

In reality, of course, it was not just the new trade skills inmates learned in prison that made them attractive employees for Japanese colonists. Equally important was the fact that they had become used to following orders barked at them by Japanese prison guards and officials. One important factor in this regard was language: after just one decade of colonial rule there were still relatively few Taiwanese who could speak Japanese. As far as the colonial authorities were concerned, however, this was not the real problem. Takekoshi summed up the official Japanese attitude when he noted that "most Formosans [are raised] like wild animals, without being taught to obey." As a result, he argued, "when they are brought to prison they learn for the first time in their lives what discipline and order mean."[33]

At one level, this vision of the colonial prison as a machine for transforming "wild animals" into obedient, productive workers can be seen as evidence in support of the view that colonialism should be seen as essentially *continuous* with the general processes by which all modern societies are formed.[34] Taken at face value, the statements of Takekoshi and Tejima suggest that the new prisons established by the Japanese in Taiwan were intended to serve as a kind of disciplinary vanguard that would jump-start the formation of a reserve army of docile, hardworking proletarians and spread an acceptance of the gray rhythms of modern life, which make possible the "organized power of armies, schools and factories."[35] But while it is important to acknowledge that power in modern colonial settings, as elsewhere in the modern world, was not just repressive but also productive, we must be careful that our awareness of coeval developments and "colonial modernities" does not lead us to obscure the issue of unevenness and *its* production. We must also recognize that to accept the disciplinary claims of a colonial regime uncritically is to run the risk of reinscribing the colonizer's fantasy that he did in fact bring order (rather than just *a new kind of* order) to a previously unordered world, and that before him there had indeed been nothing but chaos—an untamed jungle populated only by "wild animals." More than just narcissism, this fantasy served a strategic purpose, allowing colonial officials to explain (and dismiss) acts of willful resistance and opposition (i.e., conscious decisions not to obey *them*) in terms of general ignorance and unruliness (i.e., an inability to obey *anyone*).

In this regard we should also remember here that prison was not just a place to discipline and punish; it was also a site for the production of knowledge and, in the colonial context, served specifically to produce knowledge of *difference* and, more specifically, *backwardness*. Thus, in the colonial prisons of Taiwan, the queues in which men tied their hair were quickly equated with Chinese filth; the effects of opium addiction were equated with Chinese weakness; and, most important of all, Chinese prisoners were consistently found to be lazier and more troublesome than Japanese prisoners.[36] As one of the early wardens at Taihoku summed up, "the life-styles of lower-class people everywhere are undisciplined, but the people there [in Taiwan] are particularly lacking in discipline *(nao issō fukitirsu).*"[37]

On the one hand, as we have already seen, the discovery of this kind of difference could be used to justify the strict application of disciplinary techniques and practices to colonial subjects, who would thereby learn, in theory at least, to be more like the (always already well-disciplined) Japanese. On the other hand, it could also be used to authorize new forms of *differential* treatment. Understood in this context, it makes sense that in 1904, the very same year in which colonial Taiwan's great new engines of disciplinary power, the penitentiaries, were finally completed, the Japanese authorities also announced the introduction of a special form of punishment that would serve as an alternative to imprisonment for Chinese and Taiwanese men found guilty of minor crimes: flogging.[38]

FLOGGING FORMOSA: EMPIRE AND THE POLITICS OF PUNISHMENT

Flogging had a long history of use in Taiwan under the codes of the Qing empire, but along with other "backward" Qing punishments, it had been abolished by the Japanese soon after their takeover of the island in 1895. One explanation for its revival a decade later is simply that it provided a cheap and easy way to clear out the overcrowded colonial prisons.[39] But this does not really make sense. As the chief procurator for the Taiwan Supreme Court, Odate Koretaka (1854–?), pointed out in a strongly worded memorandum to the governor-general opposing the introduction of flogging, the "success" of Kodama's campaign to eradicate the "bandits" meant that by 1903 the inmate population had already declined significantly from its peak in 1901–2.[40] The problem of overcrowding, in other words, was no longer particularly pressing. With the completion of its three new prisons in 1904, moreover, the colonial regime was better placed than ever before to accommodate (and discipline) the prisoners in its custody. This does not mean that questions of cost were entirely irrelevant to the decision to introduce flogging. But, in the end, flogging provided a means not so much for cheaply reducing the size of the prison population (which, in fact, remained steady in the years after its introduction) as for cheaply increasing the total number of men who could be subjected to some form of punishment by the colonial regime.

In this regard it is crucial to note that the introduction of flogging was timed to coincide with a dramatic expansion in the colonial police force's powers to dispense summary justice—a fact that helped to ensure that flogging very quickly came to occupy a central place in the colonial government's penal repertoire. Of the twenty-five hundred men subjected to flogging in its first year of use under the Japanese, more than 70 percent (eighteen hundred people) were tried summarily by the police rather than by a regular court.[41] After this the use of flogging expanded rapidly, so that for most of the 1910s an average of more than six thousand men were being flogged in the colony each year. Throughout this period the percentage of those sentenced summarily by the police continued to account for about two-thirds of the total number flogged.[42]

The decision to introduce flogging in Taiwan established a precedent that was soon being followed in other parts of Japan's expanding empire. In 1908 colonial authorities in the "Kwantung leased territories" in southern Manchuria began using the punishment, and in Korea too it was "retained" for use during the period of Japan's "Residency General."[43] Eventually, in 1912, two years after Korea was formally "annexed" by Japan, a new "Korean Flogging Ordinance," based closely on the earlier Taiwanese ordinance, was issued as part of a broader program of legal reforms. As both Edward Baker and Chulwoo Lee have noted, the use of flogging in colonial Korea was particularly extensive. According to official statistics, an average of more than thirty thousand people were flogged annually in the first six years of formal Japanese rule. In 1916 this number rose to more than fifty-two thousand and although the colonial authorities stopped publishing statistics after this point, there is reason to believe that it continued to climb in the second half of the 1910s.[44]

Initially, of course, there was no way of knowing that the introduction of flogging in Taiwan would have these broader consequences, but even so it did not go unchallenged. As already noted, the chief procurator of the Taiwan Supreme Court, Odate Koretaka, was quick to make his opposition known to Governor-General Kodama. Not only did the proposal make little practical sense at a time when prison populations were decreasing and order had finally been established on the island, it was also wrong in principle, he argued. The Meiji government had, after all, abolished flogging in Japan some two decades earlier precisely because it had recognized it as a barbaric practice. To reintroduce it now, he insisted, as a punishment reserved specifically for Chinese and Taiwanese men could only be seen as the most flagrant violation of the emperor's stated policy of treating his colonial subjects with "impartiality and equal favor" (*isshi dōjin*).[45] Predictably, these objections had little impact on Kodama, who approved the introduction of flogging regardless, but this was not the end of opposition to the introduction of flogging. When news of it eventually reached Tokyo at the beginning of 1904, the country's leading penologist, Ogawa Shigejirō, immediately took up the attack.

In an article published first in the *Kangoku kyōkai zasshi*, then expanded into a separate pamphlet, and finally reprinted in the prestigious *Hōgaku kyōkai zasshi* (Law Society Journal), Ogawa decried the introduction of flogging in the strongest possible terms.[46] After decades of progressive penal reforms, he argued, this one decision now threatened to undermine the dignity of the entire criminal justice system, which he and others had worked so hard to build. Citing evidence from Roman and Chinese antiquity, as well as various modern authorities, he described in vivid detail how a cane or whip could eat away at a person's skin until it was stripped raw and noted the permanent damage that often resulted. Flogging, he insisted, was a "cruel and unusual punishment" (*inkei*) left over from the "dark ages" (*chūko mōmai no jidai*). This, however, was only part of what was at stake.

Lying at the heart of the decision to revive flogging in Taiwan, Ogawa argued, was the notion that in order to be effective, punishments had to be adjusted to a people's overall "level of civilization" (*mindo*): *backward people would only understand backward punishments*. Yet, he asked, what if Japan's leaders had accepted this proposition at the beginning of the Meiji period? Judging from the state of the Japanese people's "level of civilization" at that time, they would never have been able to implement a program of progressive penal reforms. Instead, the Japanese would have remained in the same "ignominious" (*fumeiyo naru*) situation as their Chinese and Korean neighbors, ruled over by officials who used torture and all manner of barbaric punishments, from flogging to gibbeting of severed heads. In this regard, Ogawa noted, the great lesson of Japan's experience since the Meiji Restoration was that the adoption of civilized punishments was crucial to the task of *elevating* the cultural level of a people. By the same token, to introduce harsh punishments, as the colonial officials in Taiwan now planned to do, could only have a negative impact. This, he noted, had been Montesquieu's basic insight: barbaric punishments encourage barbaric behavior.

Why then had officials in Taiwan chosen to ignore these important lessons from Japan's own recent past? For Ogawa, the answer was obvious. Without even considering the possibility that the colonial authorities' inspiration may have come from East Asian "tradition," he pointed squarely to the example of the Western powers. According to him, it was "the so-called civilized peoples" of the West, "who call themselves civilized Christians," who had first developed and continued to promote the notion that people of "other races" should be treated differently from themselves. For Ogawa, the most egregious example of this "self-serving and arbitrary view of things" was provided by the United States where, at the dawn of the twentieth century, the systematic lynching *(rinchi seido)* of black people still went unchecked, and where, in prisons all over the South, slavery had simply been replaced with a new system for buying and selling black workers known as "convict leasing" *(riizu shisutemu)*.[47] Yet, he continued, as horrific as the American example was, this kind of discrimination and abuse was hardly exclusive to the United States. In subduing the native peoples of South America, Asia, Africa, and Australia, he argued, the imperialist powers of the West had all used slave labor, torture, and other forms of brutality that would never have been tolerated in their home countries. Flogging, he pointed out, was probably the most common of all such forms of colonial brutality. In French and Dutch colonies it was employed extensively as an "extra legal" measure, but there were also examples of it being formally sanctioned in law. The British courts in Singapore and Hong Kong, for example, were known to sentence Chinese colonial subjects to floggings on a regular basis, and the Germans, in their new colonies, had specifically authorized it as a punishment for Africans, in spite of the fact that its use was not permitted under the German imperial penal code.

Clearly, it was precedents such as these that the colonial authorities in Taiwan had chosen to follow in drafting their own flogging ordinance, and in so doing, Ogawa concluded, they had provided a perfect example of the kind of mindless "worship of foreign countries" *(gaikoku sūhai)* for which the Japanese were so often criticized. Rather than weighing the advantages and disadvantages independently, they had simply decided to copy Western practices. As a result, he argued, they had not only succeeded in reviving a truly barbaric form of punishment; they had also allowed the hypocrisy of Western racism to infiltrate and taint the Japanese legal system, effectively creating a separate class of people (colonial subjects) who were not considered worthy of equal treatment before the law.

There is good reason to believe that Ogawa was correct in his views about the importance of Western "models" for colonial Taiwan's flogging ordinance. Tsurumi Yūsuke's 1937 biography of Gotō Shimpei states that the original inspiration for introducing corporal punishment to the colony came directly from Lord Cromer, Britain's consul general in Egypt. In a conversation with an associate of Gotō's, who subsequently relayed the information to him, Cromer reportedly advised the Japanese that when governing territories where the "level of civilization" was low, it was essential to use summary justice and floggings, both of which had been employed in such places since "time immemorial."[48] Tay-Sheng Wang has also noted that under Gotō's direction the colonial authorities in Taiwan had begun systematically studying the justice systems of various Western colonies around the world in order to formulate their own program of reforms.[49] Primary responsibility for this project had been given to Tejima Heijirō, the chief of legal affairs, whose comments about the disciplinary potential of the new prisons were noted earlier, and it was under his name that the original proposal to introduce flogging had been submitted.[50]

Interestingly, the fact that the Flogging Ordinance was originally inspired by Western colonial practices did not prevent the authorities in Taiwan from drawing on Japanese "traditions" to help implement it. The official history of the colonial police force tells us that in 1904 two Japanese prison guards with experience of administering floggings in the "homeland" in the first years of the Meiji period were sent all over Taiwan to show personnel at prisons and police stations how to inflict the punishment correctly.[51] Yet, in the end, even the method of flogging that these guards taught offers clear evidence in support of Ogawa's arguments. Under Taiwan's Flogging Ordinance, a cane was to be applied to the buttocks (*shiri*) of the prisoner, which was in keeping with the standard British practice, and not along the backbone, as stipulated under the "traditional" codes of both Tokugawa Japan and Qing China.[52]

Perhaps if there had been widespread acceptance in Japan of the idea of becoming a Western-style colonial power, none of this would have been particularly controversial or troubling. Yet, at the beginning of the twentieth century, when memories of Japan's own struggle to avoid colonization were still relatively fresh, many members of the Meiji elite remained deeply ambivalent about such a prospect. This ambivalence clearly did not prevent Japan's aggressive acquisition of new territory, but it did create an expectation that Japanese rule would somehow be different and better than Western colonialism. As Komagome Takeshi has noted, in 1905, a full decade after the Japanese conquest of Taiwan, a prominent member of the imperial Diet in Tokyo could still complain that it "truly makes my skin crawl" (*jitsu ni zotto suru*) to hear Prime Minister Katsura Tarō openly describe the island as a "colony" (*shokuminchi*).[53] For the most part, Japanese officials were able to avoid this word and the negative connotations it carried, by using the terms "home territories" (*naichi*) and "outer territories" (*gaichi*), which were borrowed from imperial China.[54] Instead of "colonialism," moreover, many liberal-minded members of the Meiji elite had specifically come to understand *their* project of empire as a process of "extending the homeland" (*naichi enchō*) to encompass neighboring peoples, who would thus be able to share all of the advantages of Meiji Japan's successes and progress.[55] Now, however, with his pointed critique of the flogging ordinance, Ogawa had raised the possibility that, regardless of the labels applied to it, Japanese rule in Taiwan might indeed be little different from the exploitative, hypocritical colonialism of the Western powers. From the point of view of the colonial authorities, therefore, his arguments could hardly be left unanswered.

The efforts of colonial officials to discredit Ogawa's critique were given a boost in March 1904 by Hozumi Nobushige, who, as professor of law at Tokyo Imperial University, commanded unrivaled influence in Japanese legal circles at the time. At a public meeting, the proceedings of which were later published in the *Hōgaku kyōkai zasshi*, Hozumi responded to questions about the controversy sparked by Ogawa's articles by arguing that although it was not good to apply different punishments to people on the basis of race or class alone, the use of corporal punishments itself should not be dismissed out of hand. Indeed, for certain types of offender—in particular, for recidivists and juvenile delinquents—he argued that flogging could offer a superior alternative to short-term imprisonment.[56] While stopping somewhat short of a full endorsement of the new Taiwan flogging ordinance, his comments clearly helped to undermine the position laid out by Ogawa, who was himself one of Hozumi's former students. In the months that followed, moreover, Hozumi's initial response was skillfully taken up and elaborated upon by the then chief justice of the Taiwan Supreme Court, Suzuki Sōgen (1863–1927).

Suzuki had been handpicked to defend the use of flogging by Gotō Shimpei, and in a long essay published in both the *Hōgaku kyōkai zasshi* and the *Kangoku kyōkai zasshi* in the summer of 1904, he set out to turn the tables on Ogawa by effectively repositioning *him* as the one whose ideas had been unduly influenced by the West.[57] Ogawa's problem, Suzuki argued, was that during his long years of study in Europe, he had succumbed to the irrational "fervor" of the Christian penal reformers. His record as Japan's most vocal opponent of the death penalty had already marked him as a sentimental idealist, and now with his critique of Taiwan's flogging ordinance he had provided the public with yet more evidence of his inability to think rationally about questions of penal reform.

The decision to introduce flogging in Taiwan, Suzuki insisted, was not a discriminatory measure but simply a practical one, based on a realistic assessment of the limitations of imprisonment as a form of punishment. Taking his cue directly from Hozumi, he emphasized the idea that for many kinds of offender prison was little more than a "school for crime" (*hanzai gakkō*). Why continue to spend large sums of money incarcerating such persons? Flogging was cheaper, and it caused real pain and humiliation without disrupting the offender's family life, which, for Suzuki, was "the source of all virtue." Of course, as with any form of punishment there was always the possibility of abuse, but so long as it was properly regulated, he insisted, the likelihood of flogging causing a person permanent physical damage was small. It was in light of these basic facts, Suzuki argued, that a number of Western nations, including Germany and Denmark, had recently begun to consider the possibility of reviving the use of flogging, not only in their overseas colonies, as Ogawa had claimed, but also in their "home" territories.

According to Suzuki, the growing interest in flogging worldwide offered clear evidence of its general desirability as an alternative to imprisonment. Yet, he also insisted that for Ogawa to suggest on the basis of this broader trend that officials in Taiwan were somehow guilty of mindless imitation of the West was simply preposterous. If anything constituted an example of unthinking "worship of the West," he argued, it was surely the decision of the early Meiji leaders to abolish flogging in the first place. This was, after all, a punishment that had been used with good effect in Japan and other parts of East Asia for centuries, and it was only with the sudden influx of radical French ideas in the early Meiji years that it had been swept away without proper debate or reflection. Understood in this context, Suzuki suggested, the decision to revive flogging in Taiwan, like the earlier struggles to stop the enactment of a liberal, French-inspired civil code in the 1890s, offered proof that Japanese scholars and officials had now finally gained the maturity to begin thinking for themselves again.

In one sense, there was a strong element of symmetry in the arguments presented by Ogawa and Suzuki. Writing as they did in the wake of Japan's success in throwing off the shackles of the unequal treaties, both men firmly rejected and sought to undermine the notion of a stable hierarchy of progress that separated an "advanced" West from a "backward" Japan. They also both sought to assert the value of different aspects of Japanese "tradition." For Ogawa, the principles of the Enlightenment provided a set of universal values that could be used both to critique the barbarity of the West's racist policies and to bolster what he called the great East Asian tradition of "benevolent government" (*jinsei*). Above all else, he suggested, it was this tradition of benevolence that should guide Japan's penal policies, both at home and in its colonies. On the other hand, Suzuki argued that, at least as far as flogging was concerned, Japanese "traditions" had already been sufficiently advanced *before* the arrival of the West. Early Meiji officials had been blinded to this reality because of their unthinking faith in the superiority of all things Western, but the recent growth of interest in corporal punishments in the European nations implied that, in some respects, it was *they* who were now finally catching up to Japan. In a more fundamental sense, perhaps, Suzuki's rebuttal of Ogawa also provides an excellent example of the way in which the Orientalist structures of knowledge that served to excuse the hypocrisy of Western imperial domination could be taken up and redeployed in postcolonial discourses to quash or marginalize more liberal tendencies. In spite of Ogawa's lengthy and rigorous critique of Western racism and colonial policy, Suzuki was ultimately able to dismiss him as having taken an overly "Westernized" position on flogging, precisely because to be liberal was itself seen to be Western, even when it ran counter to actual Western practices.

At another level, Suzuki's arguments also gained much of their power from the fact that they did have some basis in truth. Efforts to improve the modern prison system may have been ongoing in Japan, but by the beginning of the twentieth century the utopian fantasies of the early Meiji period had long since given way to a more realistic understanding of the limitations and problems created by mass incarceration. Yet, if flogging really was a *universally* desirable alternative to the prison, as Suzuki argued, why was it that officials in Taiwan had decided to apply it *selectively* to colonial subjects, and not to Japanese from the "home territories" or, for that matter, to westerners in Taiwan? Ultimately, *this* was the fundamental problem that Ogawa had identified at the heart of the flogging ordinance, and it was not something that Suzuki could easily ignore. Even Hozumi Nobushige, in his initial public defense of the measure, had been forced to concede that it was not good practice to apply different punishments to different groups of people solely on the basis of their class or race. Rather than try to defend the selective application of flogging at the level of principle, therefore, Suzuki instead slyly explained it away as a purely jurisdictional matter. As much as the colonial officials would have liked to apply the new flogging ordinance to all residents of Taiwan equally, he suggested, they simply did not have the necessary authority over Japanese or westerners in the colony to do so. Eventually, perhaps, the Diet in Tokyo would decide to emulate the innovative policies developed in Taiwan and reintroduce flogging as a punishment under the imperial penal code. Until that time, however, the authorities in Taiwan had no choice but to limit the application of their new policy to the colonial subjects who were under their direct control.

In reality, of course, there was never any danger that flogging would be resurrected in Japan's "home territories," and Suzuki, of all people, must have been aware that his claims about the colonial government's lack of jurisdiction over Japanese subjects in Taiwan had no substance. As Odate pointed out when the idea of reviving flogging was first proposed, the real question for colonial officials had been how they could possibly *avoid* applying the punishment to Japanese and westerners in Taiwan.[58] At one level, none of this mattered very much. For Suzuki and his superiors, the main aim was to silence Ogawa and other critics of the flogging ordinance—and in this they succeeded. There was no further debate of the issue for well over a decade, and as a result, the way was cleared for the use of flogging not only in Taiwan but throughout the expanding colonial empire. Yet, the fact that Suzuki had felt it necessary to build this kind of public defense against Ogawa's charges of "Western-style" racism is also deeply revealing of the ideological awkwardness at the heart of Japan's imperial project. Japanese officials implemented racist policies, and yet they were not entirely comfortable defending them in openly racist terms for fear of exposing the illegitimacy of their activities. Somehow the strategic fiction of universal principles and impartial treatment had to be maintained.

As noted earlier, Meiji Japan's own history of semicolonial domination by the Western powers and the widespread skepticism about the nature of Western imperialism to which this history had given rise, were undoubtedly important factors here. Yet, to some extent, this kind of contradiction can also be seen as one of the defining characteristics of modern colonialism in general. As Dipesh Chakrabarty and Uday Singh Mehta have both reminded us, for British liberals, the question of how a "free" country that proclaimed self-rule to be the highest form of government could simultaneously defend its policies of despotism in South Asia and other parts of the globe was a profound source of awkwardness and contradiction from the late eighteenth century on.[59] Ultimately, this awkwardness shaped the dynamics of political change under colonial regimes, by creating an opportunity for colonized peoples to use the colonizer's own stated principles to criticize and push for change. In this regard, although Suzuki's arguments effectively suppressed domestic criticism from Japanese "experts" like Ogawa, we should not be surprised to learn that in the years that followed colonial subjects continued to point to the selective use of flogging as clear evidence of the fundamentally discriminatory nature of Japanese rule. Even for a figure such as Lin Xiantang, who saw cooperation with the Japanese as the only way to improve the lot of ordinary people in Taiwan, flogging, together with measures such as the "Bandit Punishment Ordinance," stood out as a critical issue, while for Korean nationalists in the 1910s it was to become one of the most obvious symbols of Japanese colonial brutality and hypocrisy.[60]

It was, of course, precisely as a way of covering the gap between high-minded principles and discriminatory realities that the logic of historicism was so useful for colonial regimes. *Eventually* the colonizers had every intention of treating their colonial subjects as equals, but as yet they were simply not ready. *Their histories*, the argument went, had not yet lifted them to a sufficiently high level. As we have seen, this was exactly the kind of thinking that Ogawa insisted lay behind the introduction of flogging in Taiwan in the first place, and in spite of Suzuki's tactical denial, it was not long before the idea of "levels of civilization" reemerged as the dominant theme in public discussions of the measure.[61] Takekoshi's *Japanese Rule in Formosa* was first published just a year after the debate between Ogawa and Suzuki, but in it he could already state unashamedly that the main reason for the introduction of flogging was simply that "Formosans and Chinese have such low ideas of living and so little sense of shame that they do not mind in the least being sent to prison for a time."[62] It was largely in order to give credence to this notion that Takekoshi had included the glowing description of the new Taihoku Prison cited earlier. "From a humanitarian standpoint," he emphasized, "no fault can be found with the prisons in Formosa," but "when I considered that a Formosan could live comfortably with his wife and family on 2 1/2 d. a day, enjoying an occasional pipe of opium as well, I understood how it was that they did not particularly object to being confined in such a grand building which seemed almost as perfect as it could be."[63] This is how Takekoshi's British translator rendered his arguments into English, but in the original Japanese version the point is even clearer: "It was when I saw this almost perfect prison building [at Taihoku] that I understood for the first time why flogging had been introduced."[64]

The architectural and humanitarian "perfection" of the Taihoku Prison offered proof of just how advanced and progressive the Japanese were. And yet, in the colonial context, this was also a weakness: for the lowly Formosans, Japanese prisons were simply *too* civilized. This did not mean that the colonial prisons should be abandoned (ironically, they were still deemed suitable for more serious offenders, who could be held and disciplined over an extended period of time), but they would have to be supplemented with a form of punishment that "the natives" (*dojin*) could more readily understand.[65] As Baker and Lee have noted, the same arguments were used to justify the expanded use of flogging in Korea: not only was flogging an "old Korean custom," which had been respectfully "preserved" after the annexation, it was also a punishment well suited to the uneducated, backward people of the peninsula.[66] Indeed, officials argued, the level of civilization in Korea was so low that "in comparison with Taiwan, the need for flogging is even more acute (*issō setsujitsu naru*)."[67]

As Ogawa had so astutely observed in his critique of the flogging ordinance, for the Japanese, the fundamental problem with such arguments was that it was not so long ago that they had been viewed by the Western powers in the same way they viewed the people they now ruled over. They too had been cast as backward Orientals, whose past had produced a low "level of civilization"—and yet, in a very short period of time, they had shown themselves capable of understanding and adopting the "advanced" practices of modern civilization wholesale. Why then should this not also be true of Japan's Asian colonies? In the end, it was because Suzuki was unable to answer this question that he had been forced to argue for the *universal* value of flogging and to fall back on the strategic lie of jurisdictional limitations. In the years that followed, however, the emergence of new ideas about history began to fill in some of the ideological gaps created by the practice of empire and to obscure the problem that Ogawa's critique had posed.

EMPIRE'S ACCOMPLICE

Already in the years leading up to treaty revision, influential Western observers such as W. E. Griffis, the best-selling author of *The Mikado's Empire*, had begun to explain away various unfortunate aspects of the Tokugawa past, including its "cruel and bloody codes," by blaming them on the pernicious, alien influence of the Chinese.[68] This is, of course, deeply ironic given that for most of the Tokugawa period Chinese legal scholarship had been viewed as the main alternative to indigenous traditions of warrior law and that the initial "civilizing" reforms of the early Meiji years were pursued within the framework of a Chinese-inspired criminal code. Importantly, though, for a Western audience, Griffis's argument had the distinct advantage of explaining Japan's "success" without invalidating the Orientalist world view that continued to legitimize the activities of Western imperialists in Asia. It was not that Orientalist assumptions were fundamentally mistaken (*Chinese* justice really was cruel and barbaric) but simply that the Japanese were a special case, and now, having thrown off the oppressive weight of Chinese influence (i.e., having "left Asia"), the essentially progressive spirit of their nation was finally being revealed to all.

Within Japan such views meshed well with elements of the nativist scholarship of the late Tokugawa period, which had bemoaned the polluting effects of Chinese culture on all aspects of life, and Griffis's understanding may itself have been shaped by an awareness of this current in Japanese thought. Yet Japan was not just a passive repository of ideas for Western Orientalists. As Stefan Tanaka has shown, by the early years of the twentieth century Japanese scholars had themselves begun to engage actively in the production of their own forms of Orientalist knowledge—drawing in large part on Tokugawa period traditions of Chinese scholarship to stake their own claim as the "real" experts on the East.[69] On the one hand, Tanaka notes, pioneers of the emerging field of *tōyōshi* or "Oriental history," were driven by a strong desire to redeem some aspects of the East Asian heritage that was such an important source of Japanese distinctiveness vis-à-vis the West. Yet, on the other hand, they felt compelled to find ways to distinguish Japan's past from that of its neighbors—to create, in other words, an explanation for the fundamental divide between stagnant, Oriental Other and dynamic, modern Self.

This problem was also crucial for scholars working in the newly emerging field of Japanese "national history" (*kokushi*). As Thomas Keirstead has shown, one of the reasons why the study of the "medieval" period has long held a privileged place within the Japanese historical profession is that in the early years of the twentieth century it was identified as the era in which the nation broke with its Oriental roots and, with the rise of feudalism, began to tread a path that was at once "uniquely Japanese" *and* remarkably similar to that of modern Europe.[70] Whereas the preceding ancient period was characterized in terms of the importation of Chinese political models on the one hand, and the (feminine) cultural achievements of the Heian court on the other, the newly defined "middle ages" was seen as a period of masculine vitality, in which the emergence of a virile warrior class sparked the same kind of indigenous institutional progress that European scholars had already claimed as characteristic of their own pasts.[71]

Given the central importance that issues of law had played in Japan's encounter with Western modernity, it should come as no surprise that this was also one of the first areas in which evidence of early indigenous "progress" was identified. Keirstead points to an essay published in 1906 by the great pioneer of Japanese legal history Nakada Kaoru (1877–1967) in which he argued that, although there was nothing in Japan's past that could compare with Roman law, the legal tradition developed by the warrior lords of medieval Japan was remarkably similar to another key strand of European legal heritage, namely, Germanic law: "It never ceases to amaze me how closely Japan's [medieval] legal system and legal principles . . . resemble those of the Franks," he wrote.[72] As Keirstead points out, the discovery of such "surprising" parallels with European history served to imbue Japan's premodern heritage with a new sense of value. Specifically, what scholars such as Nakada implied was that Japan's "success" in developing its own modern institutions was not simply a matter of clever imitation or borrowing from the West.[73] As Asakawa Kan'ichi, another pioneer in the study of medieval Japan, summed up in 1903, "the dawning of the national sense in 1868 was made possible by the training the people had received during the seven centuries of feudalism."[74]

This discovery in the first decade of the twentieth century of the deep historical roots of Japan's "success" in becoming a powerful modern nation and the concomitant distinction drawn between "national" and "Oriental" history clearly had significant implications for Japan's colonial empire. Whereas in 1904 Ogawa had been able to assert that Japan's situation on the eve of the Meiji Restoration had been essentially similar to that of its Asian neighbors, there was now a growing body of "scientific" proof that they were, in fact, separated by centuries, rather than just a few decades, of divergent development. Of course, it would be a mistake to adopt an overly instrumentalist view of the emergence of this new strand of knowledge—as if scholars of the medieval period had deliberately set out to find materials that would bolster the cause of empire.[75] At the same time, however, if we accept the basic proposition that the writing of history is inevitably informed by perceptions of the present, then it makes sense that the growing feelings of national pride and confidence that the Japanese public learned to embrace in the late Meiji period should also have affected its understanding of the past. And, if the modern science of history had proved that the key to the distinctive strengths of the Western nations lay deep in *their* own pasts, then why should the same not also have been true for modern Japan?

Empire itself was, of course, one of the main sources of the growing sense of national confidence. As the case of flogging shows so clearly, the possession of formal colonies not only served to move Japan into the exclusive European club of "imperial powers," it also created an arena in which its position as an "advanced" nation could be institutionalized vis-à-vis subject populations—whose "backwardness" was then attested to by Japanese "visitors" like Takekoshi, as well as officials and a growing body of "specialist" scholars. In this sense, the discourse of empire and the discourse of national history formed a neat logical circle, with one providing evidence of national superiority, and the other a powerful, logical explanation for that superiority, which in turn helped to legitimize the discriminatory structures that reinforced and reproduced it .[76]

It was not just those who embraced an openly superior attitude toward other Asians who ended up contributing to the formation of Japan's imperial world view. Even Ogawa, who had explicitly rejected the idea that discriminatory measures could be justified in terms of differing "levels of civilization," played his part. Ogawa, after all, never expressed opposition to the project of imperialism itself but only to the way in which it was being conducted in Taiwan under the Kodama administration. He argued that rather than emulate the hypocritical Western model of empire, Japan should remain focused on the "true" goal of facilitating the spread of progress and civilization in other parts of Asia. For Ogawa, in other words, Japan's achievements may not have given it the right to oppress, but they had certainly created an opportunity, and perhaps even an obligation, to lead. It makes sense then that in the years following the debate over flogging in Taiwan, Ogawa himself was to become deeply involved in teaching other Asians how to establish and run a "civilized" penal system.

In 1908 Ogawa accepted a post as the Qing dynasty's first foreign adviser on penal affairs, and for the next two years he lectured extensively on prison administration and criminal law at Beijing Law School. This allowed him to exert considerable influence over the development of Chinese ideas about prisons and penology.[77] His massive study of the subject remained the standard point of reference for Chinese scholars and officials up until the Communist Revolution, and his explanation of Western approaches to prison design provided the primary inspiration for the construction of China's first "model penitentiaries," including the famous Beijing Number One Prison. At the same time, his work in China also helped to establish him as an authority on developments there, and after his term as adviser to the Qing expired in 1910, he traveled to Washington, D.C., to attend the Eighth International Prisons Congress, where he was able to report to his Western colleagues on what he had achieved there, as well as what remained to be done. To label such activities as "imperialist" in and of themselves would, no doubt, be unfair. Yet, just as the presence of Western advisers in Japan in the early Meiji period had offered proof of the positive role that the Western powers were playing in East Asia, Ogawa's activities in China clearly lent credibility to Japanese claims to be a civilizing influence in the region and bolstered Japan's credentials as the leading nation of Asia. In this sense, his work in China remained deeply *complicit* with the logic of empire.

If the knowledge that Japanese experts (both within the formal empire and without) were teaching other Asians how to become "modern" served to reassure the Japanese of their achievements, it was on the battlefield that the ultimate proof of those achievements came. By 1905 the Japanese had followed up their decisive victory over the decaying Qing empire by demonstrating their ability to take on and defeat one of the "great powers" of Europe. For anticolonial thinkers in many parts of the world, including the great African American sociologist W.E.B. Du Bois (1868–1963), Japan's victory over tsarist Russia was crucial because it presented such a defiant challenge to the smugly complacent logic of white supremacy. The "color line" had been breached, Du Bois wrote, and the Japanese now beckoned to the rest of the nonwhite world to follow them across it.[78] As the case of Ogawa makes clear, the dream of the Japanese leading the nonwhite peoples of the world forward into a new era of equality was hardly unknown in late Meiji Japan. Eventually, moreover, this apparently liberal position would be incorporated more fully and directly into Japanese imperial ideology in the form of concepts like the Greater East Asian Co-Prosperity Sphere, which were supposed to distinguish Japanese expansionism from that of the Western empires. Yet, for most Japanese at the time, the fundamental lesson of the Russo-Japanese War was not that nonwhites could defeat whites but rather that they, *the Japanese*, had been able to do so. For them, in other words, Japan's achievement was not about "the color line." It was about the *nation* and its proper place in the world.

RACE, NATION, AND HISTORY'S QUIET TRIUMPH

As Du Bois might well have predicted, however, the problem of the color line turned out to be one that the logic of nation could not so easily transcend. In the early decades of the twentieth century, Westerners continued to express admiration for Japan's achievements, but at the same time they found it difficult to abandon the idea that modern civilization was a uniquely European (i.e., white, Christian) phenomenon. Success on the battlefield brought new power and accolades for the "remarkable" Japanese, but it also fueled fears of the "Yellow Peril," and throughout the Western world skepticism about the extent to which a people who were "so different" could really have understood the principles of civilized society was never fully dispelled. Ironically, in some cases, the very same discriminatory practices that the Japanese had learned from the Western colonial powers, and which their own sense of equality with the West served to justify, provided a trigger for such skepticism—often to the advantage of colonial populations.

In 1919, for example, as news of Japan's brutal suppression of the March First Independence Movement in Korea captured headlines around the globe, Korean nationalists and their allies found that *they* could now use flogging as a weapon with which to fight back and exact their own form of punishment in the court of world opinion. In *The Case for Korea*, a book indicting the horrors of Japanese rule, the Korean exile Henry Chung included an entire chapter on flogging ("The Official 'Paddle'"), which drew extensively on missionary reports that circulated in the United States in the aftermath of March First. One such report, originally published in the *New York Times* in July 1919, noted that under Japanese colonial law, Korean men could be punished with

> ninety blows of the bamboo rod ... that this is no light matter you may well imagine. . . . A large number of cases now coming to the private [i.e., missionary] hospitals are of men who have been thus beaten until they are nearly done for. All this in a land which boasts before the world of its thoroughly acquired modern civilization, an associate of the great allied nations of the world.[79]

The Canadian missionary Frank W. Schofield was even more forthright in his condemnation. After describing in graphic detail the way floggings were conducted by the colonial police, he concluded: "The truth is this; the militaristic Japanese are still uncivilized and barbarous at heart, and so one constantly sees his real brutal, naked self appearing."[80] Fifteen years after the attainment of treaty revision, the Japanese thus found themselves once again haunted by the specter of "Oriental barbarism," now resurrected in the context of an anticolonial struggle.

Specific practices and policies could always be reformed, of course, and in the aftermath of the March First Movement the use of flogging was abolished in both Korea and Taiwan, as part of the well-documented shift from a general policy of military to (less openly harsh) "cultural" rule in the colonies.[81] While acknowledging that "the infliction of pain on a person was ... at variance with modern ideas regarding punishment," the official explanation for the change also stressed the fact that flogging had become "more and more unsuitable" for use in the colonies because of "the remarkable awakening and progress" that had been achieved by the subject populations under Japanese rule.[82] (Presumably, in the Kwantung territories, where flogging was retained as a punishment for Chinese men right up until the end of World War II, the Japanese authorities were never so successful.)[83] Even as the Japanese began to turn to more subtle forms of control and increasingly sophisticated forms of imperial ideology, however, the racially informed skepticism of Western critics persisted and, as the twentieth century wore on, became a growing source of distress for members of the Japanese elite.

In their search for answers, some became convinced that the problem was not of the present (after all, what more could they do to show that they were a civilized people?) but rather of the past. Westerners simply did not understand the true nature of Japanese history. Takekoshi Yosaburō, for example, who had been so convinced that Japan's colonial policies in Taiwan would help it win the respect of the other "great powers," pointed to comments made by a French scientist named Gustave Lebon in the mid-1920s as typical. Engaging the then Japanese ambassador to France in conversation, Lebon had reportedly likened Japan's trajectory as a nation to that of a meteor, "which one night flashes across the sky to the wonderment of mankind below" and then "passes out of sight as suddenly." Having risen so quickly, he argued, the nation's demise must inevitably follow because "it was against the law of evolution . . . that anything should develop [with such] prodigal energy as Japan had done in 50 short years and yet remain in existence." [84] Over the course of the 1930s Takekoshi's determination to set the record straight and correct such basic "misunderstandings" of Japan's past led him to publish two major historical works of his own in English. The first of these was a detailed analysis of the premodern roots of Japan's modern economic development (a topic that has remained a "Japanese studies" perennial ever since), while the second was a shorter, more polemical work outlining Japan's proper place in world history.[85] In both cases, his primary concern was to show that "Japan has become a world power as a result, not of achievements of half a century or so, but of the developments made along the same path of progress as has been followed by the peoples of the oldest history in Europe."[86]

The drive to document Japan's journey along "the same path of progress" that the Europeans had trodden was not just about convincing skeptical foreigners of the depth of the nation's credentials as a modern power. More important, it served to bolster the confidence of the Japanese people in their own position as "world leaders." And, in the 1930s and 1940s, as the rise of "imperial fascism" and a new phase of aggressive expansion on the continent brought the country to the brink of total war, the cravings for such reassurance only grew.[87] It is in this context that we should understand the rediscovery of the Stockade for Laborers by Japanese legal historians in the early Shōwa period. It was in 1943, at the height of the Pacific War, that the Stockade for Laborers was first explicitly described as an indigenous protoprison and held up as concrete evidence that Japan had been moving in the direction of a "modern" penal system well before the arrival of Perry.[88] In other words, even in relation to punishment, which had at the time served as a marker of Japanese backwardness vis-à-vis the West, it now turned out that the gap in "levels of civilization" had never been as great as previously believed. The echoes of wartime ideology are clear enough: the example of the stockade offered yet more proof that Japan had always been an *essentially* advanced nation, destined by history to lead the world forward into a bold, new era.

Wartime theories about the origins of the Japanese penal system might reasonably have been expected to disappear in the postwar period like the bans on jazz and permed hair, or the replacement of English baseball terminology with "native" Japanese words. But this was not the case. As noted in the introduction, within the larger context of the Cold War, the general notion that Japan's premodern past held the secret to its "successful" development after 1868 was enthusiastically taken up by many Western scholars who sought to identify the keys to "modernization"—and who drew extensively on prewar Japanese scholarship in order to do so. In Japan itself, the new generation of historians who emerged in the immediate postwar decades was generally much less willing to take a rosy view of the nation and its past and, instead, put considerable effort into searching for clues as to "what went wrong." Yet, even so, the idea that the Stockade for Laborers was an embryonic version of the modern prison has been a remarkably persistent one. In 1974, as Japan stood on the verge of an era of unprecedented economic prosperity and resurgent global power, a group of leading Japanese legal historians came together to produce a landmark collection of essays on the stockade that identified it, once again, as the "starting point for our nation's modern system of punishment by deprivation of liberty" (*waga kuni kindai-teki jiyū kei no kigen*).[89] Admittedly, some contributors to the volume (most notably Hiramatsu Yoshirō) offered more nuanced explanations of the stockade's place in history, arguing that it should, in fact, be seen as a kind of early "public security measure" rather than as a direct forerunner of the modern prison. Yet, the dominant interpretation was still strong enough in the 1980s to find its way into many high school textbooks, and it was only in the 1990s, with Tsukada Takashi's path-breaking research, that an attempt was made to break fully with the older interpretations and develop an understanding of the stockade within its own specific social and historical context.[90]

There are various ways to explain the dogged persistence of the idea of the Stockade for Laborers as a protoprison. For one thing, it is an idea that fits neatly with the dominant structures and biases of established historical knowledge, satisfying the historian's desire to pinpoint origins, while also confirming the primacy of "the nation" as a natural framework within which to search for them. Thus, it is not difficult to see how once introduced, it has quickly slipped into the annals of "historical common sense." At another level, the idea of "indigenous sources" can also be understood as a problem of language. After all, as part of their efforts to achieve "civilization and enlightenment," reformers and bureaucrats in the Meiji period had to invent a whole new vocabulary with which to describe the institutions and practices being imported wholesale from the West. Ohara Shigechika's coining of the word for prison is just one example among hundreds: within the realm of crime and punishment alone, the words for judge, court, defendant, police, and so on were all Meiji neologisms. Early Meiji scholars and bureaucrats were well aware that these new terms and the things they represented would not make immediate sense to people, and that they would have to be learned over time. Eventually, however, they came to seem natural and normal, and, as they did, it was instead the older language of justice and power from the Tokugawa period that came to seem alien and difficult. At this point, it became the task of legal historians to explain the meanings of the older language, but in order to do this, they had to "translate" it into what had become "modern Japanese."

This need to explain the language of the past is, in the end, the best evidence we have of the profound rupture that occurred during Japan's transition to modernity, yet, ironically, the act of translation also serves to make the past seem deceptively familiar by couching it in terms of the present. Thus, the answer to the question "What was the Stockade for Laborers?" all too easily becomes, "It was something like a modern prison." This is not just an issue for professional historians. In postwar Japan (as elsewhere) popular culture has played a crucial role in promoting an easy sense of seamless continuity with the past. Many of the most popular television programs in Japan today portray Tokugawa period officials such as Ōoka Echizen-no-kami or Hasegawa Heizō as idealized, kimono-clad equivalents of modern-day police detectives, investigating crimes and dispensing a familiar brand of justice to easily identifiable bad guys. The official punishments announced (but never enacted) at the end of each formulaic episode help to generate a sense of titillating "authenticity" (*uchi kubi gokumon* [literally, decapitation followed by display of the severed head] is a phrase familiar to any schoolchild in Japan today), but they are hardly intended to convey an awareness of the unsettling strangeness of the past.

It goes without saying that interpretations of history, especially when presented as entertainment, will always be influenced by the present. Yet an understanding of the Tokugawa past that sees it as essentially the same as Japanese society today serves not only to obscure all memory of the "original sins" that made possible the growth of both state and capital in the early Meiji period but also to disguise the integral role that imperialism, first Western and later Japanese, played in the making of modern Japan. In this regard, if we are to recover any sense of the true nature and consequences of the social revolution of the early Meiji period, it is imperative that we continue to search for and struggle with those aspects of the premodern past that are not easily translated or explained in terms of the present. More is at stake in all of this, however, than simply the recovery of true, or at least truer, understandings of the past. More fundamentally, it is about realizing the possibility that human beings and the societies they form need not, and should not, remain the captives of history.

Notes

1. An original copy of the *Tokugawa bakufu keiji zufu* can also be found in the Criminal Museum at Meiji University. For a scholarly reprint, see Iyoku Hideaki, "Fujita Shintarō hen ga 'Tokugawa bakufu keiji zufu' (fukkoku to kaisetsu)," *Meiji daigaku hakubutsukan hōkoku* 4 (March 1999): 49–104. Commercial reprints are also common, although they are often incomplete.

2. On the place of the "poison women" in Meiji popular culture, see Christine Marran, "'Poison Woman' Takahashi Oden and the Spectacle of Female Deviance in Early Meiji," *U.S.-Japan Women's Journal, English Supplement* 9 (1995): 93–110. See also Hirota Masaki, "Bunmei kaika no jendaa: 'Takahashi Oden' monogatari o megutte," *Edo no shisō* 6 (May 1997): 79–95.

3. The literature on the history of punishment in the West is now vast, but on the early American republic, see, for example, Louis P. Masur, *Rites of Execution: Capital Punishment and the Transformation of American Culture, 1776–1865* (Oxford: Oxford University Press, 1989); David J. Rothman, *The Discovery of the Asylum: Social Order and Disorder in the New Republic*, 2nd ed. (Boston: Little Brown, 1990); and Michael Meranze, *Laboratories of Virtue: Punishment, Revolution and Authority in Philadelphia, 1760–1835* (Chapel Hill: University of North Carolina Press, 1996).

4. The best-known study of the "penal revolution" in France and the West more generally is, of course, Michel Foucault's masterpiece *Discipline and Punish: The Birth of the Prison*, trans. Alan Sheridan (London: Peregrine Books, 1979). For a less ambitious, more empirically focused overview of penal reform in France, see Gordon Wright, *Between the Guillotine and Liberty: Two Centuries of the Crime Problem in France* (New York: Oxford University Press, 1983).

5. The classic study of penal reform in England is Leon Radzinowicz, *A History of English Criminal Law and Its Administration from 1750* (London: Stevens, 1948), vol. 1. For a more recent overview, see J. A. Sharpe, *Judicial Punishment in England* (London: Faber and Faber, 1990). On John Howard and the rise of the prison, see Michael Ignatieff, *A Just Measure of Pain: The Penitentiary in the Industrial Revolution, 1750–1850* (London: Macmillan, 1978), and Randall McGowen, "A Powerful Sympathy: Terror, the Prison, and Humanitarian Reform in Early Nineteenth-Century Britain," *Journal of British Studies* 25.3 (July 1986): 312–34.

6. For a critique of the Eurocentric notion that Japan was "closed" to the world during the Tokugawa period, see Ronald P. Toby, *State and Diplomacy in the Early Modern Japan: Asia in the Development of the Tokugawa Bakufu* (Stanford: Stanford University Press, 1984).

7. There is now a burgeoning literature on the history of punishment and the prison in the non-Western world. Important works include Michael R. Dutton, *Policing and Punishment in China: From Patriarchy to "the People"* (Cambridge: Cambridge University Press, 1992); Frank Dikötter, *Crime, Punishment and the Prison in*

Modern China (New York: Columbia University Press, 2002); Ricardo D. Salvatore and Carlos Aguirre, *The Birth of the Penitentiary in Latin America* (Austin: University of Texas Press, 1996); David Arnold, "The Colonial Prison: Power, Knowledge and Penology in Nineteenth Century India," *Subaltern Studies* 8 (1994): 43–77; Satadru Sen, *Disciplining Punishment: Colonialism and Convict Society in the Andaman Islands* (New Delhi: Oxford University Press, 2000); Darius Rejali, *Torture and Modernity: Self, Society and State in Modern Iran* (Boulder, Colo.: Westview Press, 1994); Peter Zinoman, *The Colonial Bastille: A History of Imprisonment in Vietnam, 1862–1940* (Berkeley: University of California Press, 2001).

8. Robert N. Bellah, *Tokugawa Religion: The Values of Pre-Industrial Japan* (Glencoe, Ill.: Free Press, 1957).

9. Thomas C. Smith, "Premodern Economic Growth: Japan and the West," in his *Native Sources of Japanese Industrialization, 1750–1920* (Berkeley: University of California Press, 1988), pp. 15–49.

10. Ronald P. Dore, *Education in Tokugawa Japan* (Berkeley: University of California Press, 1965). John W. Hall, *Tanuma Okitsugu (1719–1788): Forerunner of Modern Japan* (Cambridge, Mass.: Harvard University Press, 1955).

11. Takashi Fujitani makes a similar point in his brilliant essay, "*Minshūshi* as Critique of Orientalist Knowledges," *positions* 6.2 (fall 1998): 308–11.

12. It was, of course, this basic idea that Europe has a monopoly on real history that first gave rise to the institutional habit of dividing scholars of the premodern West, who were appointed to "history departments," from historians of premodern societies in other parts of the world, who were placed in departments based on "civilizations" or "area studies."

13. T. Fujitani, "*Go for Broke*, the Movie: Japanese American Soldiers in U.S. National, Military and Racial Discourses," in *Perilous Memories: The Asia-Pacific War(s)*, ed. T. Fujitani, Geoffrey M. White, and Lisa Yoneyama (Durham: Duke University Press, 2001), pp. 251–55. See also Fujitani, "*Minshūshi* as Critique," p. 310.

14. On this point, see also Harry [H. D.] Harootunian, *Overcome by Modernity: History, Culture and Community in Interwar Japan* (Princeton: Princeton University Press, 2000), pp. xiii–xiv.

15. For an explicit statement of this view, see, for example, Ronald Dore's 1984 introduction to the second edition of *Education in Tokugawa Japan*, which begins by comparing Japan's development in the decades following the Meiji Restoration with that of Tanzania since independence, with no mention at all of the history of Western colonialism and imperialism in Africa.

16. Dipesh Chakrabarty, *Provincializing Europe: Postcolonial Thought and Historical Difference* (Princeton: Princeton University Press, 2000), p. 8. See also Uday Singh Mehta, *Liberalism and Empire: A Study in Nineteenth-Century British Liberal Thought* (Chicago: University of Chicago Press, 1999), pp. 77–114.

17. Chakrabarty, *Provincializing Europe*, p. 8.

18. As Chakrabarty points out, the same historicist logic has also been used by ruling elites within so-called developing countries to justify their own failures, corruption, and, in many cases, authoritarian styles. Chakrabarty, *Provincializing Europe*, p. 9.

19. Testuo Najita and J. Victor Koschmann, *Conflict in Modern Japanese History: The Neglected Tradition* (Princeton: Princeton University Press, 1982). Among the works on peasant protest produced in the wake of the Vietnam War were Herbert Bix, *Peasant Protest in Japan, 1590–1884* (New Haven: Yale University Press, 1986); Anne Walthall, *Social Protest and Popular Culture in Eighteenth-Century Japan* (Tuscon: University of Arizona Press, 1986); Stephen Vlastos, *Peasant Protests and Uprisings in Tokugawa Japan* (Berkeley: University of California Press, 1986); and William W. Kelly, *Deference and Defiance in Nineteenth-Century Japan* (Princeton: Princeton University Press, 1985).

20. Of course, not all work on Tokugawa Japan falls neatly into a single subfield or category, but there can be no doubt that intellectual history and economic history have been particularly active areas of scholarship in recent decades. A useful overview of key works in intellectual history can be found in Samuel Hideo Yamashita, "Reading the New Tokugawa Intellectual Histories," *Journal of Japanese Studies* 22.1 (winter 1996): 1–48. Three sophisticated examples of recent work in economic and social history are David L. Howell, *Capitalism from Within: Economy, Society and the State in a Japanese Fishery* (Berkeley: University of California Press, 1995); Kären Wigen, *The Making of a Japanese Periphery, 1750–1920* (Berkeley: University of California Press, 1995); and Luke S. Roberts, *Mercantilism in a Japanese Domain: The Merchant Origins of Economic Nationalism in Eighteenth-Century Tosa* (Cambridge: Cambridge University Press, 1998).

21. The development of the field of legal history in Japan in the early twentieth century is discussed in more detail in the conclusion.

22. The origins of this interpretation of the Stockade for Laborers can be traced back to Miura Shūkō's pioneering *Hōseishi no kenkyū* (Tokyo: Iwanami shoten, 1919), but it was in 1943 that it received its first explicit articulation in Tsuji Keisuke's introduction to the *NKGS*, a collection of documents that remains a basic resource for the history of punishment in Japan. The significance of the timing of this statement is considered in the conclusion. In the postwar era the idea of the stockade as a kind of protoprison has been taken up in a series of studies by scholars such as Tokyo University professor Ishii Ryōsuke, most notably in the collection of essays that appeared as Ninsoku yoseba kenshōkai, ed., *Ninsoku yoseba shi* (Tokyo: Sōbunsha, 1974).

23. On the "crime wave," see Joanna Innes and John Styles, "The Crime Wave: Recent Writing on Crime and Criminal Justice in Eighteenth Century England," *Journal of British Studies* 25.4 (October 1986): 480–35.

CHAPTER ONE: SIGNS OF ORDER

1. The alleviation trope is central to most histories of Tokugawa punishment, but for one of the most influential and sophisticated examples, see Ishii Ryōsuke, *Edo no keibatsu* (Tokyo: Chūō kōronsha, 1964). Ishii's argument about the shift from "general deterrence" *(ippan-teki yobō)* to "special deterrence" *(tokubetsu yobō)* is particularly relevant. See pp. 10–18. For a general overview in English of the history of capital punishment in Japan from ancient times to the present, see Petra Schmidt, *Capital Punishment in Japan* (Leiden: Brill, 2002), especially pp. 9–34.

2. On the use of these punishments during the Warring States era, see Hosokawa Junjirō et al., eds., *Koji ruien hōritsu no bu* (Tokyo: Jingu shichō, 1902–), 1:744–45, 749, 753–56. Quartering and boiling alive were also used by the shogunate in its campaign to suppress Christianity. On this see 2:231, 257–58, and Michael Cooper, trans. and ed., *They Came to Japan: An Anthology of European Reports on Japan, 1543–1640* (Berkeley: University of California Press, 1965), pp. 385–98.

3. For an example of a real beheading with a saw in the Warring States period, see Yamashina Tokitsugu, *Tokitsugu kyō ki* (Tokyo: Kokusho kankōkai, 1914–15), 1:493. The last real beheading with a saw in Edo took place during the reign of the third shogun, Iemitsu (1623–51); see Sakuma Osahiro, "Keizai yōsetsu" [1893], in *Edo jidai hanzai keibatsu jireishū*, ed. Hara Taneaki and Osatake Takeki (Tokyo: Kashiwa shobō, 1982), pp. 125–26.

4. Tsukada Takashi, *Mibunsei shakai to shimin shakai* (Tokyo: Kashiwa shobō, 1992), pp. 34–36. See also Katsumata Shizuo, "Mimi o kiri, hana o sogu," in *Chūsei no tsumi to batsu*, ed. Amino Yoshihiko et al. (Tokyo: Tokyo daigaku shuppankai, 1983), p. 38.

5. For a discussion of the early expansion of Bakufu powers, see Harold Bolitho, *Treasures among Men: The Fudai daimyo in Tokugawa Japan* (New Haven: Yale University Press, 1974), pp. 7–19.

6. For the order to enforce the "laws of Edo" *(Edo no hatto)*, see the "Buke shohatto" [1635], in *Kampō shūsei*, pp. 6–8. On the inspectors, see "Junkeishi jōrei" [1667], in *TKKZ* 3:328.

7. "Jibun shioki rei" [1697], in *TKKK* 1:315–16.

8. *KKSK*, pp. 453, 840–42, 1077–78.

9. On the *Osadamegaki*, see Dan Fenno Henderson, "Introduction to the Kujikata Osadamegaki (1742)," in *Hō to keibatsu no rekishiteki kōsatsu*, ed. Hiramatsu Yoshirō hakase tsuitō ronbun shū hensan iinkai (Nagoya: Nagoya Daigaku shuppankai, 1987), pp. 490–544.

10. Ibid., p. 529.

11. "Keibatsu daihiroku" [ca. 1819], National Archive of Japan. For a printed version, see Iyoku Hideaki, ed., *Hōsei shiryō kenkyū 1* (Tokyo: Gannandō, 1994), pp. 349–75.

12. Sakuma, "Keizai yōsetsu," p. 118.

13. For early European descriptions of Japanese punishments, see Cooper, *They Came to Japan*, pp. 151–68. For a Tokugawa period assertion that crucifixion was introduced with Christianity, see Dazai Shundai, "Keizairoku" [1729], *NKT* 9:617.

14. The twelfth-century collection of stories, *Konjaku monogatari shū*, contains numerous references to people being "strung up" *(haritsuke, hattsuke, hatamono)*. In Yomada Yoshio et al., eds. *Konjaku Monogatori shū: Nihon koten bungaku taikei* (Tokyo: Iwanami shoten, 1959–63), see, for example, tales 13:38 (3:247–49), 16:26 (3:477–78), 29:3 (5:138–42), and 29:10 (5:156).

15. Hiramatsu Yoshirō, "Bakumatsu ki ni okeru hanzai to keibatsu no jittai," *Kokka gakkai zasshi* 71.3 (1957): 92–95; *KKSK*, pp. 1058, 1063–64. In 1787, the one other year for which statistics are available, there were fifty-six executions, including three crucifixions and two burnings at the stake in Edo. According to one Tokugawa official, it was not unheard of for six or seven people to be burned alive in a single year. *Kyūjishimonroku*, p. 102.

16. Clive Emsley, *Crime and Society in England 1750–1900*, 2nd ed. (London: Longman, 1996), pp. 256–57. The Bloody Code was the name used to describe the unreformed criminal stautes of England, under which, in the eighteenth century, an extraordinarily broad range of crimes had been made punishable with death.

17. On executions in early modern Europe, see, for example, Sharpe, *Judicial Punishment*, pp. 31–36; Ignatieff, *Just Measure*, ch. 2; D. Hay, "Property, Authority and the Criminal Law," in *Albion's Fatal Tree: Crime and Society in Eighteenth-Century England*, ed. Hay et al. (London: Peregrine, 1977), pp. 17–64; Peter Linebaugh, *The London Hanged: Crime and Civil Society in the Eighteenth Century* (London: Penguin, 1991); and R. van Dülmen, *Theatre of Horror: Crime and Punishment in Early Modern Germany* (Cambridge: Polity Press, 1990).

18. For my own initial attempt to understand Tokugawa punishments as "popular theater," see D. V. Botsman, "Punishment and Power in the Tokugawa Period," *East Asian History* 3 (June 1992): 1–32.

19. For an early example, from 1622, see Tokyo Daigaku shiryō hensanjo, ed., *Dai Nihon shiryō (Dai Jūni-hen)* (Tokyo: Tokyo Daigaku shuppankai, 1906), 44:143–44. See also *Kampō shūsei*, p. 58.

20. Ignatieff, *Just Measure*, pp. 21–22. See also Peter Linebaugh, "The Tyburn Riot against the Surgeons," in Hay et al., *Albion's Fatal Tree*, pp. 65–117.

21. *Dai Nihon shiryō* 44:143–44. The risk that a public execution might spark disorder was naturally greater in a large urban center such as Edo or London where onlookers could count on a degree of anonymity. For this reason, the Bakufu was less wary about conducting executions before crowds in rural areas.

22. This practice was not followed in all cases. The One Hundred Articles stipulated that a prisoner's dead body was to be pickled in this way if his crime had been murder of a master or parent, transgression of a barrier, or treason.

23. Hiramatsu, "Bakumatsu ki," pp. 340–43.

24. Sakuma, "Keizai yōsetsu," p. 110.

25. For detailed descriptions, see *NKGS* 1:661–62, 667–72. Although "trial cutting" was overseen by Bakufu officials, the task of testing the swords on the bodies of executed criminals was delegated to a specialist swordsman named Yamada Asaemon in the late seventeenth century. For the remainder of the Tokugawa period both the name and responsibilities of the first Asaemon were passed on to successive generations of his descendants, who were also able to develop a profitable side trade in the sale of human body parts for medical purposes. Understandably enough, the Yamada family and its trade have long been a staple of popular history in Japan. For one recent example, see Ujiie Mikito, *Ō Edo shitai Kō: Hito kiri Asaemon no jidai* (Tokyo: Heibonsha, 1999).

26. On the medieval origins of this practice, see Katsumata Shizuo, "Shigai tekitai," in Amino et al., *Chūsei no tsumi to batsu*, p. 57.

27. Mishima Masayuki, ed., *Gofunai bikō* [1846] (Tokyo: Yūzankaku, 1963), 1:260, 266–67.

28. *TSKS* 3:177.

29. *TSKS* 3:178; Yasuda Seiichi, ed., *Ōi chō shi* (Tokyo: Ōi chō shi hensan kankōkai, 1923), p. 106; Shinagawa-machi yakuba, ed., *Shinagawa chōshi* (Tokyo: Shinagawa machi yakuba, 1932), 2:105–7.

30. *TSKS* 3:162.

31. *TSKS* 3:174.

32. Katsumata Shizuo, "Ie o yaku," in Amino et al., *Chūsei no tsumi to*, pp. 21–4. I am grateful to Anne Walthall for raising the issue of *kegare*.

33. It was not only in Edo that the execution grounds were located on the outskirts of town. In his observations of conditions in Japan at the end of the seventeenth century, Engelbert Kaempfer noted that execution grounds were "always located outside . . . cities and villages." Engelbert Kaempfer, *Kaempfer's Japan: Tokugawa Culture Observed*, trans. and annotated by Beatrice M. Bodart-Bailey (Honolulu: University of Hawai'i Press, 1999), p. 258. On medieval Kyoto's main execution at Awadaguchi, one of the main entrances into the city, see Shigematsu Kazuyoshi, *Nihon keibatsu shiseki kō* (Tokyo: Seibundō, 1985), p. 149.

34. On the great highways of the period, see Constantine Nomikos Vaporis, *Breaking Barriers: Travel and the State in Early Modern Japan* (Cambridge, Mass.: Council on East Asian Studies, Harvard University, 1994). It should be noted that when the shogun and other important personages used the Nikkō-kaidō for official purposes, they took a detour in Senjū that allowed them to avoid the execution grounds. When there was no way for them to do this, as in the case of travel along the Tōkaidō, for example, the corpses on display at the execution ground were cleaned away especially. This, of course, is further evidence that there was concern about pollution. For an illustration of the Nikkō-kaidō route and detour, see Kodama Kōta, ed., *Nikkō dōchū bunken nobe ezu* (Tokyo: Tokyo bijutsu, 1988), leaf 1. On cleaning up the execution grounds, see Sakuma, "Keizai yōsetsu," p. 104.

35. On these embassies, see Toby, *State and Diplomacy*.

36. Kaempfer, *Kaempfer's Japan*, p. 348. The presence of dogs and crows feasting on human remains is a recurring theme in descriptions of Edo's execution grounds. On this, see Ujiie, *Ō Edo shitai kō*, p. 11; Tanaka Satoshi, *Chizu kara kieta Tōkyō isan* (Tokyo: Shōdensha, 1999), p. 212; Yasuda, *Ōi chō shi*, p. 102; and Katsu Kokichi, *Musui's Story*, trans. Teruko Craig (Tuscon: University of Arizona Press, 1995), p. 41. As Tsukamoto Manabu has noted, the image of dogs happily devouring human remains contributed directly to their unpopularity in Edo. See his *Shōrui o meguru seiji* (Tokyo: Heibonsha, 1983), ch. 3.

37. Matsura Seizan, *Kasshiyawa zokuhen* [1832] (Tokyo: Kokusho kankōkai, 1911), 3:269–70.

38. Matsura Seizan, *Kasshiyawa* [1821] (Tokyo: Heibonsha, 1977), 2:47. Cf. Tanaka, *Chizu kara kieta Tōkyō isan*, p. 213.

39. Matsura Seizan, *Kasshiyawa zokuhen*, 3:141.

40. On popular representations of one famous Edo-period gang, see Gary P. Leupp, "The Five Men of Naniwa: Gang Violence and Popular Culture in Genroku Osaka," in *Osaka: The Merchants' Capital of Early Modern Japan*, ed. James L. McClain and Wakita Osamu (Ithaca: Cornell University Press, 1999), esp. pp. 141–55.

41. The full title of the play, first performed in 1823, was *Ukiyozaka hyaku no inazuma*. For an English synopsis, see Samuel L. Leiter, ed., *Kabuki Encyclopedia* (Westport, Conn.: Greenwood Press, 1979), pp. 382–83.

42. For the route used in 1796, see *NKGS* 1:678–79. Cf. Kodama Kōta, ed., *Fukugen Edo jōhō chizu* (Tokyo: Asahi shimbunsha, 1994).

43. "Keibatsu daihiroku"; *NKGS* 1:676.

44. *NKGS* 1:686.

45. Ronald Toby and Kuroda Hideo, eds., *Asahi hyakka rekishi o yominaosu 17: Gyōretsu to misemono* (Tokyo: Asahi shimbunsha, 1994). On the particular significance of the foreign embassies, see Toby, *State and Diplomacy*, pp. 35, 64–76, 203–9.

46. *KKSK*, p. 1058.

47. Sakuma, "Keizai yōsetsu," p. 126.

48. *NKGS* 1:739. For evidence that "pulling the saw" was still practiced in Edo as late as 1851, see "Tempō kirei" [ca. 1852], Shizuoka Prefectural Library. It was also used in other areas of the country well into the nineteenth century. In Tottori Domain, for example, there were twelve cases recorded between 1801 and 1848. *KKSK*, p. 211.

49. Hiramatsu, "Bakumatsu ki," p. 103; *KKSK*, p. 1060.

50. "Keibatsu daihiroku"; Sakuma, "Keizai yōsetsu," pp. 71–79; *NKGS* 1:581–600.

51. *NKGS* 1:581–600. Hiramatsu's figures suggest that roughly half of the persons flogged in Edo between 1862 and 1864 were also punished with tattooing. In some cases tattooing was used as a punishment in its own right.

52. It was also under Yoshimune that the practice of cutting the neck of those sentenced to beheading with a saw and smearing blood on the bamboo saws was reintroduced. According to Ishii Ryōsuke, over the first century of Tokugawa rule, the punishment had been stripped of all of its former horror. This was clearly an attempt to restore an element of that. Ishii, *Edo no keibatsu*, p. 59.

53. "Keibatsu daihiroku"; *KKSK*, p. 919.

54. *NKGS* 1:612.

55. *NKGS* 1:605–9. After tattooing, the prisoner was usually held at one of the hospices (*tame*; see chapter 3), not in the jailhouse itself.

56. For examples of people who tried to burn, cut, or cover up their tattoos with more elaborate designs, see Hiramatsu, "Bakumatsu ki," pp. 103–4. The case of Tetsu, a thirty-five-year-old woman who tried to burn off a tattoo using moxa because she was scared that the man she had just married would see it is particularly poignant. The tradition of elaborate tattoos is, of course, kept alive in Japan today by Yakuza gang members. For a richly suggestive, if not entirely reliable, account of tattooing in Japan, see Donald Richie, *The Japanese Tattoo* (New York: Weatherhill, 1980).

57. *NKGS* 1:646–48.

58. House arrest (*oshikome*) was usually for a period of between ten and one hundred days. There were also several special forms of house arrest that were specifically applied to the members of particular status groups. These are considered in chapter 3.

59. See article 70 of the One Hundred Articles. In the early seventeenth century burning at the stake was also used to execute Christians. *NKGS* 1:711–12.

60. According to Mitamura Engyo, the problem was exacerbated by thieves who quickly learned that the confusion caused by fires in a densely populated area created ideal conditions for them to work their trade. See Mitamura Engyo, *Engyo Edo bunkō 6: Edo no shiranami*, ed. Asakura Haruhiko (Tokyo: Chūō kōromsha, 1997), pp. 152–53. Cf. Mary Elizabeth Berry, *The Culture of Civil War in Kyoto* (Berkeley: University of California Press, 1994), p. 101. On the fire-fighting system in Edo,

see William W. Kelly, "Incendiary Actions: Fires and Firefighting in the Shogun's Capital and the People's City," in *Edo and Paris: Urban Life and the State in the Early Modern Era*, ed. J. McClain, J. Merriman, and Ugawa Kaoru (Ithaca: Cornell University Press, 1994), pp. 310–31.

61. On the development and significance of the term *kōgi*, see Fukaya Katsumi, "Kōgi to mibunsei," in *Taikei Nihon kokka-shi: Kinsei*, ed. Hora Hidesaburō et al. (Tokyo: Tokyo Daigaku shuppankai, 1975), p. 165. In English, see Mary Elizabeth Berry, *Hideyoshi* (Cambridge, Mass.: Council on East Asian Studies, Harvard University, 1982), pp. 157–58.

62. It did not matter whether the original motive for murder was theft or not. The very act of stealing from a corpse was considered serious enough to warrant the standard death penalty. See, for example, *Reiruishū* 2:280 (#670).

63. Hiramatsu Yoshirō, *Edo no tsumi to batsu* (Tokyo: Heibonsha, 1988), p. 96.

64. For a general discussion of adultery, see Ujiie Mikito, *Fugi mittsū: Kinjirareta koi no Edo* (Tokyo: Kodansha, 1996). In English, see Amy Stanley, "Adultery and Punishment in Tokugawa Japan" (senior thesis, Harvard University, 1999).

65. The phrase used to describe rape in the One Hundred Articles (art. 48) is typically euphemistic but still clear enough in meaning: Literally, "forced impropriety without the consent of the woman" *(onna no kokoro-e kore nashi ni oshite fugi)*. For adultery the word *mittsū* (literally, "secret relations") is used. For pre-Tokugawa period precedents, see Hitomi Tonomura, "Sexual Violence against Women: Legal and Extralegal Treatment in Premodern Warrior Societies" in *Women and Class in Japanese History*, ed. Hitomi Tonomura, Anne Walthall, and Wakita Haruko (Ann Arbor: University of Michigan Center for Japanese Studies, 1999), pp. 135–52.

66. For a general discussion of this practice, see D. E. Mills, "Kataki-uchi: The Practice of Blood-Revenge in Pre-Modern Japan," *Modern Asian Studies* 10.4 (1976): 525–42.

67. For examples of people rewarded in this way, see ibid., p. 528; David L. Howell, "Private Violence and Public Virtue in Late Tokugawa Japan" (paper presented at the Princeton University Conference on Premodern Japanese History, Princeton, 1995).

68. Mills, "Kataki-uchi," p. 531. Although the overall numbers did not change much, Mills notes that the proportion of revenge killings carried out by commoners (as opposed to samurai) increased over time.

69. Arai Hakuseki, "Oritaku shiba no ki" [1716], translated by Kate Wildman Nakai in Dan Fenno Henderson, "Chinese Legal Studies in Early Eighteenth Century Japan: Scholars and Sources," *Journal of Japanese Studies* 30 (November 1970): 30–31. Commenting on the general importance of Chinese legal studies at this time, Henderson argues that the early eighteenth century deserves "recognition as a third reception of foreign law in Japan—or more accurately a mini-reception midway between Japan's two major foreign law borrowings" of T'ang codes in the eighth century and Western ones in the late nineteenth (p. 22).

70. Herman Ooms stresses the eclectic nature of Tokugawa political ideology in his *Tokugawa Ideology: Early Constructs, 1570–1680* (Princeton: Princeton University Press, 1985). On hierarchy, see esp. pp. 91, 157–58. In a more recent discussion of the "Tokugawa juridical field," Ooms has stressed the importance of the "fundamental hierarchizing 'imaginary'" of the era for an understanding of the articles of

the *Osadamegaki*. See his *Tokugawa Village Practice: Class, Status, Power, Law* (Berkeley: University of California Press, 1996), p. 327. My argument here is similar to his, although as discussed in chapter 3, I do not agree with his overall characterization of the Tokugawa status system.

71. Sir James Ansty, *General Charge to All Grand Juries* [1725], cited in J. M. Beattie, *Crime and the Courts in England, 1660–1800* (Oxford: Clarendon Press, 1986), p. 79, n. 10.

72. In spite of the pervasiveness of ideas about the importance of social hierarchy, E. H. Norman's classic work, *Andō Shōeki and the Anatomy of Japanese Feudalism* (Washington, D.C.: University Publications of America, 1979), serves as a reminder that there were some remarkable individuals who were able to transcend it.

73. On Ōshio and his rebellion, see Tetsuo Najita, "Ōshio Heihachirō (1793–1837)," in *Personality in Japanese History*, ed. Albert M. Craig and Donald H. Shively (Berkeley: University of California Press, 1970), pp. 155–79.

74. Asao Naohiro et al., ed., *Nihon-shi Jiten* (Tokyo: Kadokawa shoten, 1996), p. 147.

75. Anne Walthall, trans. and ed., *Peasant Uprisings in Japan: A Critical Anthology of Peasant Histories* (Chicago: University of Chicago Press, 1991), esp. pp. 28–31 and ch. 1. In his comprehensive study of peasant uprisings, James White has noted that, although there was an increase in popular protests and uprisings in the latter half of the Tokugawa period, the Bakufu tended to punish participants less often and less severely than in the past. From this he concludes that the regime had "lost its grip, its teeth, and its resolve." Yet, given the fact that protests in the latter part of the period were increasingly directed against local village and merchant elites, rather than at warrior officials, an alternative explanation might be that the warrior state had less direct incentive to get involved. This would be in keeping with the general principles of status system society, discussed below in chapter 3, and would also help to explain the anxieties of a merchant-scholar such as Nakai Riken in the late eighteenth century (chapter 4). See James W. White, *Ikki: Social Conflict and Political Protest in Early Modern Japan* (Ithaca: Cornell University Press, 1995), esp. p. 284.

76. Yamamoto Hirofumi, "Edo no tōnin to keibatsu kannen," in Mitamura Engyo, *Engyo Edo bunkō 6: Edo no shiranami*, pp. 402–4. The collections of cases that make up the *Oshioki Reiruishū* even include special sections devoted to crimes involving "theft from an official building, or of official property." I am indebted to Yamamoto's essay for leading me to the two cases discussed here.

77. *Reiruishū* 2:271–72 (#598).

78. *Reiruishū* 2:270–71 (#597).

79. On the distribution of the *Osadamegaki* and other key legal texts, see *KKSK*, pp. 546–50. Hiramatsu argues that careful control of the official copies of legal texts helped the Bakufu enforce a uniform set of standards for punishments in different parts of the country. On this, see pp. 554–55.

80. Takahashi Satoshi, *Edo no soshō* (Tokyo: Iwanami shinsho, 1996), p. 76. One excellent example of this kind of copy book has been preserved in the Mōri ke monjō collection at the Yamaguchi Prefectural Archive. Titled "Zaikasatsu gaki" [n.d.], it lists the contents of signs detailing the crimes of some seventy criminals executed between 1825 and 1846. Each entry is glossed with *furigana* to make it

easier to read. I am grateful to Miyazaki Katsumi for his assistance in finding this important document.

81. *KKSK*, p. 553.

82. Takahashi, *Edo no soshō*, pp. 72–78.

83. On the legal inns, see ibid., pp. 57–71; *KKSK*, pp. 717–18.

84. Takahashi, *Edo no shosō*, p. 77.

85. The Bakufu distinguished between two categories of legal cases. The first *(deiri suji)* included cases in which one party brought a complaint against another and the Bakufu served as adjudicator. The second *(ginmi suji)* included cases in which a party was interrogated by the Bakufu, usually for some criminal act. The courtyards of white sand (it was actually more like gravel) were used in both kinds of case but the procedures described here are for the second category of "interrogative" cases. For more details on this division and the procedures used in the first category of cases, see Dan Fenno Henderson, *Conciliation and Japanese Law: Tokugawa and Modern*, vol. 1 (Seattle: University of Washington, 1965). For a detailed description of the "courtyards of white sands," see *KKSK*, pp. 735–36.

86. *KKSK*, pp. 689–93.

87. *KKSK*, pp. 694–96.

88. The term *bugyō* is often translated as "magistrate," but "governor" is used here to reflect the fact that there was no separation of administrative and judicial responsibilities in the Edo period. The other common translation, "commissioner," sounds too modern.

89. *Kyūjishimonroku*, p. 190; *KKSK*, p. 752.

90. *KKSK*, p. 762.

91. *KKSK*, p. 768.

92. *Reiruishū* 6:55 (#588); *KKSK*, p. 863.

93. *KKSK*, p. 896. For the rare cases in which parties refused to place their stamp on the official documents, see pp. 905–7.

94. *KKSK*, p. 775.

95. Article 83 of the One Hundred Articles. The crimes for which formal torture could be applied were murder, arson, robbery, breach of a checkpoint, and conspiracy. In practice, Hiramatsu argues that the standards of proof needed to authorize torture were often not high.

96. A much wider range of tortures was used in the early Tokugawa period. These included branding with a hot iron *(hizeme)*, riding the "wooden horse" *(kiba)*, various kinds of water torture *(mizuzeme; mizurō)*, and torture with human feces *(kusozeme)*. See Sakuma Osahiro, "Gōmon jikki" [1893], in Hara and Osatake, *Edo jidai hanzai keibatsu jireishū*, pp. 221–22. The discussion of the four standard techniques of torture used in the latter period is based on Sakuma's "Gōmon jikki" and the "Keibatsu daihiroku."

97. This method of torture may well have been borrowed from China. It is remarkably similar to the technique described in Philip Kuhn, *Soulstealers: The Chinese Sorcery Scare of 1768* (Cambridge, Mass.: Harvard University Press, 1990), pp. 14–17.

98. Sakuma, "Gōmon jikki," p. 242.

99. Ibid., pp. 250–58.

100. *KKSK*, pp. 829–30.

101. Sakuma, "Gōmon jikki," p. 252.

102. *KKSK*, pp. 797, 838.

103. *KKSK*, p. 829.

104. *Kyūjishimonroku*, pp. 101–2.

105. Mary Elizabeth Berry, "Public Life in Authoritarian Japan," *Daedalus* 127.3 (summer 1998): 138. This statement does, of course, give rise to questions about whether there has ever been a society that was not, at least to some degree, "authoritarian."

CHAPTER TWO: BLOODY BENEVOLENCE

1. On "benevolence" and "compassion" in Tokugawa ideology, see Ooms, *Tokugawa Ideology*, pp. 56, 66–69, 89–92; Fukaya Katsumi, *Hyakusho naritachi* (Tokyo: Hanawa shobō, 1993), pp. 15–26; Irwin Scheiner, "Benevolent Lords and Honorable Peasants: Rebellion and Peasant Consciousness in Tokugawa Japan," in *Japanese Thought in the Tokugawa Period 1600–1868: Methods and Metaphors*, ed. Tetsuo Najita and Irwin Scheiner (Chicago: University of Chicago Press, 1978), p. 46; White, *Ikki*, p. 36.

2. Ooms, *Tokugawa Ideology*, pp. 66–69.

3. Hosokawa, *Koji ruien hōritsu no bu*, 1:257–58.

4. *KKSK*, pp. 593–94. In theory the principle of an "eye for an eye" was supposed to be upheld even in cases where the killer had been acting in self-defense or was not fully conscious of his actions *(ranshin)*. In practice, however, Hiramatsu suggests that in such cases the relatives of the deceased person were more or less coerced into showing their own "benevolence" by issuing "requests for leniency."

5. For one such example, see *Minami Denmachō nanushi Takano-ke nikki gonjo no hikae* [1700–1712], (Tokyo: Tokyo-to, 1995), pp. 104–5, 116.

6. For a recent study that examines the reasons for the popularity of these figures, see Fujita Satoru, *Tōyama Kinshirō no jidai* (Tokyo: Azekura shobō, 1992). On Ōoka, see Tsuji Tatsuya, *Ōoka Echizen no kami* (Tokyo: Chūō kōronsha, 1964). In general, the legends associated with these men can be linked to a much older Chinese "crime mystery" tradition. For Ihara Saikaku's contribution to the genre, see *Tales of Japanese Justice*, trans. T. M. Kondo and A. H. Marks (Honolulu: University of Hawai'i Press, 1980).

7. Yoshimura Shigenori, ed., *Hōgen monogatari shinshaku* (Tokyo: Daidōkan shoten, 1940), p. 198. Cf. William R. Wilson, trans., *Hōgen monogatari: Tale of the Disorder in Hōgen* (Tokyo: Sophia University Press, ca. 1971), pp. 68–69. On the abandonment of capital punishment in the three centuries prior to the Hōgen Rebellion, see also Schmidt, *Capital Punishment*, pp. 10–12.

8. Suzuki Shōsan, "Roankyō" [ca. 1630], in *Suzuki Shōsan dōnin zenshū*, ed. Suzuki Tesshin (Tokyo: Sankibo busshorin, 1962), p. 169. The English translation cited here is from Royall Tyler, trans., *Selected Writings of Suzuki Shōsan* (Ithaca: Cornell University China-Japan Program, 1977), pp. 112–13. Also cited in Ooms, *Tokugawa Ideology*, p. 141.

9. For a detailed analysis of the scroll, see Mabuchi Miho, "Maruyama Ōkyo hitsu 'Nanfuku zukan' ni tsuite," *Bijutsushi* 47.1 (October 1997): 65–81.

10. Cited in Beatrice Bodart-Bailey, "The Laws of Compassion," *Monumenta Nipponica* 40.2 (summer 1985): 183–84. See also Tsukamoto Manabu, *Shōrui o meguru seiji*.

11. Arai Hakuseki, "Oritaku shiba no ki" [1716], translated in Kate Wildman Nakai, *Shogunal Politics: Arai Hakuseki and the Premises of Tokugawa Rule* (Cambridge, Mass.: Council on East Asian Studies, Harvard University, 1988), p. 138. On Hakuseki's response to Tsunayoshi's policies in general, see pp. 133–39.

12. Ibid., p. 138.

13. Arai Hakuseki, "Tokushi yoron" [1712], translated in Nakai, *Shogunal Politics*, p. 138. Cf. Joyce Ackroyd, trans., *Lessons from History: The Tokushi Yoron by Arai Hakuseki* (St. Lucia: University of Queensland Press, 1982), p. 300. Ackroyd's translation incorrectly implies that Hakuseki called for an end to *all* capital punishment.

14. In extreme cases a child who had committed an act of arson might be executed by decapitation, but even this was not as severe as the adult punishment of burning at the stake. *TKKK* 5:72.

15. *TKKK* 5:73–74. Because the rule applied only to first-time offenders, it was not entirely unheard of for children to be flogged.

16. *KKSK*, p. 973; "Rōgoku hiroku" [ca. 1800] in *Edo no keibatsu fūzoku shi*, ed. Ono Takeo (Tokyo: Tenbōsha, 1998), p. 463. For a statement of the basic principle that women were not to be given special treatment or consideration in the determination of punishments, see *Reiruishū* 1:197–98 (#207).

17. *KKSK*, pp. 974–75.

18. *KKSK*, pp. 976–78; *Reiruishū*, 1:298–301 (#208, #209).

19. Sakuma, "Ginmi no kuden" [ca. 1890], in Hara and Osatake, *Edo jidai hanzai keibatsu jireishū*, pp. 263–64.

20. Yoshida Shōin, "Kaikoroku" [1854], in *Yoshida Shōin zenshū*, ed. Yamaguchi-ken kyōikukai (Tokyo: Iwanami shoten, 1935), 7:399.

21. Hiramatsu, *Edo no tsumi to batsu*, pp. 86–87.

22. Vaporis, *Breaking Barriers*, pp. 175–79. For another example of official flexibility in enforcing regulations concerning the checkpoints, see the judgment given in *Reiruishū* 1:326 (#225), concerning a man named Senhachi who broke through a checkpoint with a woman companion. The judgment states that although the punishment for this crime would ordinarily have been crucifixion, Senhachi was to have his sentence reduced by one grade because he voluntarily returned to the jailhouse after being released when a fire broke out there. Generally, a punishment one grade less severe than crucifixion would have meant *gokumon* or, at the very least, death, but in yet another benevolent stretch of legal reasoning the judgment explained that because crucifixion is a form of death sentence, Senhachi's punishment would in fact be one degree less than death, that is, exile to an island.

23. White, *Ikki*, p. 297.

24. The rules for judging who was responsible for an accidental fire and how they should be punished were quite complicated. Some important factors included how much damage was done by the fire and where the shogun was at the time of the fire. See article 69 of the One Hundred Articles.

25. *KKSK*, p. 968. Given that the punishments for accidental fires laid out in the One Hundred Articles generally involved some form of house arrest, the act of fleeing to a temple may not, in fact, have been that advantageous for the individual

in question. Presumably, however, an official pardon helped limit the extent to which other members of the community (headmen, neighbors, etc.) were implicated and punished.

26. On the *enkiri dera*, see Diana E. Wright, "Severing the Karmic Ties That Bind: The Divorce Temple Mantokuji," *Monumenta Nipponica* 52.3 (autumn 1997): 357–80.

27. Abe Yoshio, *Meakashi Kinjirō no shōgai* (Tokyo: Chūkō shinsho, 1981), pp. 16–22.

28. For a valuable study of amnesties in imperial China, see Brian E. McKnight, *The Quality of Mercy: Amnesties and Traditional Chinese Justice* (Honolulu: University of Hawai'i Press, 1981). It should be noted that McKnight falls into the trap of seeing the use of amnesties primarily as evidence of the limited capacities of the traditional state to deal with large numbers of prisoners.

29. Nakai, *Shogunal Politics*, p. 137; Takayanagi Shinzō, "Tokugawa Bakufu no sharitsu ni tsuite (1)," *Hōgaku* 12.9 (1943): 740.

30. Unless otherwise indicated, the information on amnesties is from *KKSK*, pp. 1023–50.

31. Sō Nanshiki, "Kyūbaku jidai taisha iiwatashi no gaikyō," *Keisatsu Kangoku Gakkai Zasshi* 4 (1891): 27–28. Also *NKGS* 1:1060–61. Hiramatsu notes that it was also common for those who were pardoned in this way to receive a small amount of money before they left: five hundred *mon* from the head priest and an additional two hundred *mon* from the governor. See *KKSK*, p. 1047.

32. Philip Brown has characterized the Tokugawa polity generally as a "flamboyant state." See his *Central Authority and Local Autonomy in the Formation of Early Modern Japan* (Stanford: Stanford University Press, 1993), pp. 232–33.

33. Kuroda Toshio, *Rekishigaku no saisei: Chūsei shi o kumi naosu* (Tokyo: Azekura shobō, 1983), pp. 116–22. See also Tsukada Takashi, *Kinsei Nihon mibunsei no kenkyū* (Kōbe: Hyōgo buraku mondai kenkyūjo, 1987), p. 10. In general, my views on the formation and nature of outcast groups in premodern Japan have been largely shaped by Tsukada's work.

34. Some historians have argued that the particular form of Buddhism that entered Japan at this time was heavily influenced by Hindu ideas about purity and pollution. On this, see Okiura Kazumitsu, "Zen Ajia teki shiza kara mibun sabetsu o kangaeru," *Buraku kaihō* 352 (January 1993): 165–66.

35. Nagahara Keiji, "The Medieval Origins of the Eta-Hinin," *Journal of Japanese Studies* 5.2 (summer 1979): 388.

36. Kuroda Hideo, *Kyōkai no chūsei, shōchō no chūsei* (Tokyo: Tokyo Daigaku shuppankai, 1986), pp. 144–54. Cf. Tsukada, *Kinsei Nihon mibunsei*, p. 11.

37. Tsukada, *Kinsei Nihon mibunsei*, p. 11. The gradual specialization of various outcast groups in particular tasks helps explain the existence of a range of different categories of outcast in Edo society.

38. Nagahara, "Medieval Origins," pp. 392–94; Ooms, *Tokugawa Village Practice*, p. 280, n. 73. It should be noted that punishment did not necessarily mean corporal or capital punishment of the kind that became commonplace in the Edo period. Nagahara cites a case from 1352 in which outcasts were sent to destroy the house and warehouse of a moneylender as punishment for some unspecified crime.

39. Nagahara, "Medieval Origins," p. 397.

40. Ooms, *Village Practice*, p. 279; Gerald Groemer, "The Creation of the Edo Outcaste Order," *Journal of Japanese Studies* 27.2 (summer 2001): 269.

41. Ooms, *Village Practice*, p. 280.

42. Yokota Fuyuhiko, "Senshi sareta shokunin shūdan," in *Nihon no shakai shi 6: Shakai-teki sho shūdan*, ed. Asao Naohiro et al. (Tokyo: Iwanami shoten, 1988), p. 313.

43. Ibid., pp. 307–16.

44. Ibid., pp. 312, 314.

45. Ibid., p. 315.

46. To be fair, Yokota does note the significance of outcast involvement in the administration of punishments but only as a secondary factor. Groemer makes a similar point but sees outcast involvement in punishments in the Tokugawa period more as an extension of older practices. See Groemer, "Edo Outcaste Order," p. 287.

47. It is not clear when the Tokugawa authorities first began assigning the outcasts responsibility for tasks related to punishment. Until quite recently historians in Japan had seen the 1660s and 1670s as a key turning point (e.g., Watanabe Hiroshi, "Eta," in *Kokushi daijiten*, ed. Kokushi daijiten henshū iinkai [Tokyo: Yoshikawa kōbunkan, 1985], 2:279), but Tsukada has shown conclusively that this understanding is based on a misreading of a key document. He suggests that outcasts probably carried out some punishment-related tasks for the warrior authorities from the very beginning of the Tokugawa period and perhaps even earlier. Tsukada, *Kinsei Nihon mibunsei*, pp. 56–57.

48. For the procedures for particular punishments, see "Keibatsu daihiroku."

49. It was, in fact, customary for condemned prisoners to pay the outcasts responsible for this task a small fee to ensure that their heads would be properly washed of blood after execution. See Ishii, *Edo no keibatsu*, p. 37.

50. On the three-way relationship between outcast workers, condemned persons, and onlookers at the execution grounds, see Tsukada, *Mibunsei shakai*, pp. 55–58. Cf. Tsukada Takashi, "Shokei to sarashi no ba," in Toby and Kuroda, *Gyōretsu to misemono*, pp. 54–55. The one form of public punishment that did not involve outcast workers was flogging, perhaps because floggings were not considered a particularly harsh form of punishment, or because they did not usually involve the spilling of blood. Tattooing, which involved the use of needles and hence some contact with blood, was conducted exclusively by outcast workers.

51. In this regard, it is also worth noting that over the course of the seventeenth century warriors began to distance themselves from various brutal practices of their predecessors, including "testing swords" on live outcast victims who had committed no offense other than to be in the wrong place at the wrong time. On this, see Ujiie, *Ō Edo shitai kō*, pp. 72–77.

52. The tendency to focus on the role of the state is one of the basic problems with Herman Ooms's attempt to explain the situation of Edo period outcasts in terms of the notion of "state racism." Although state policies clearly contributed to the problem, it is too simplistic to suggest that they were solely responsible for the discrimination faced by the outcasts. Similarly, to reduce the historically specific patterns of discrimination faced by the outcasts to the modern issue of "racism"

only serves to confuse and obscure an already complex issue. See Ooms, *Village Practice*, pp. 243–304.

53. Tsukada, *Kinsei Nihon mibunsei*, esp. p. 25.

54. Ibid., pp. 24–26. The example Tsukada discusses at some length here involved two groups of *eta* who, in 1823, became embroiled in a dispute over which of them had the right to perform guard duties at the main jailhouse in Oshi Domain.

55. For an example of the kind of power struggle in which successive generations of Danzaemon were involved, see Groemer, "Edo Outcaste Order," pp. 276–80.

56. Cited in Tsukada, *Kinsei Nihon mibunsei*, p. 24.

57. Tsukada, *Mibunsei shakai*, pp. 55–58. Ooms also makes reference to this section of Tsukada's work but has missed the main point of the argument, which is to show that the situation of the outcasts cannot be understood simply in terms of officially sanctioned discrimination. See Ooms, *Village Practice*, p. 251.

58. Cited in Tsukada, *Mibunsei shakai*, p. 57.

59. Ibid.

60. The existence of a link between the outcasts' right to carry spears *(naga dōgu)* in public and their involvement in punishment-related duties was formally articulated by the Danzaemon family in its official genealogy ("Danzaemon yuishogaki"), compiled in the 1720s to help legitimate and secure the position of the outcasts. For the relevant section of the genealogy, see Tsukada, *Kinsei Nihon mibunsei*, pp. 56–57.

61. Ōsaka-fu, "Shimin byōdō ni kansuru yukoku" (9/15/1871), cited in Suzuki Ryō, "Nihon kindai shi kenkyū ni okeru buraku mondai no ichi," *Rekishi hyōron* 368 (1980): 6.

62. Suzuki, "Buraku mondai no ichi," pp. 7–9. Suzuki notes that the "liberation" of outcasts in Kyoto from their "official duties" as executioners and guards also meant an immediate and substantial loss of income. The notice informing the outcasts of Amabe-mura that their services were no longer required by the Kyoto municipal government also stated that their regular annual payment of three hundred ryō had been canceled. The outcasts' exclusive rights to collect the carcasses of dead animals (and thus monopolize leather production) had already been canceled nationally several months earlier.

63. Ibid., pp. 9–15.

CHAPTER THREE: THE POWER OF STATUS

1. For one recent example in English, see Ooms, *Village Practice*, pp. 243–304.

2. On the introduction of the "four estates" model to Japan from China and its relationship to the realities of status in the Tokugawa period, see Asao Naohiro, "Kinsei no mibun to sono henyō," in *Nihon no kinsei 7: Mibun to kakushiki*, ed. Asao Naohiro (Tokyo: Chūō kōronsha, 1992), pp. 14–34.

3. Ooms, *Village Practice*, pp. 125–34, 341–42.

4. Ibid., p. 327.

5. John W. Hall, "Rule by Status in Tokugawa Japan," *Journal of Japanese Studies* 1.1 (autumn 1974): 39–49.

6. Asao, "Kinsei no mibun," pp. 22–35. See also Hitomi Tonomura, *Community and Commerce in Late Medieval Japan: The Corporate Villages of Tokuchin-ho* (Stanford: Stanford University Press, 1992).

7. As an administrative unit the *chō* usually flanked both sides of a city street, and as such they do not coincide neatly with any English term. "Block association" is used here as an imperfect approximation. For a detailed analysis of the evolution of the *chō* over the course of the period, see Yoshida Nobuyuki, "Chōnin to chō," in *Kōza Nihon Rekishi 5: Kinsei 1*, ed. Rekishigaku kenkyūkai (Tokyo: Tokyo Daigaku shuppankai, 1985), pp. 151–88.

8. As John Haley notes, under the Tokugawa regime, the village "In effect . . . had the security of the administrative state along with the freedom of the outlaw." See his *Authority without Power: Law and the Japanese Paradox* (Oxford: Oxford University Press, 1991), p. 62.

9. Prior to the move to Kodenmachō in the 1610s the main Edo jailhouse had been located on the outer side of Tokiwabashi, one of the main bridges linking the area of the city where the townsfolk lived with Edo castle. *NKGS* 1:122–23.

10. The use of wooden bars on all four sides of the building was first developed in 1683. *NKGS* 1:149.

11. "Rōgoku hiroku" [ca. 1800], in Ono, *Edo no keibatsu fūzoku shi*, p. 416. Registered and unregistered commoners first began being separated into different jail rooms in 1755. Ishii, *Edo no keibatsu*, p. 120.

12. "Rōyashiki nenreki" [1725], in *TSKS* 3:139. Cf. *NKGS* 1:122.

13. "Rōya shiki, Asakusa tame, yōjōsho, Shinagawa tame hisho" [n.d.], manuscript, Hōsei shiryōshitsu, Tokyo University. Another freestanding building containing two extra upper rooms was added in 1865—a fact that probably reflects the Bakufu's struggle to control warrior opposition in the final years of the period.

14. On conditions in the different jail rooms, see *NKGS* 1:155, 340–41.

15. *NKGS* 1:149. Even when the overall inmate population shrank, the number of inmates in individual jail rooms was kept high because of the practice of alternating between use of the eastern and western wings of the jailhouse each month. This was done to combat the accumulation of filth and stench and was only abandoned in the hottest months of the summer when it made more sense to spread the inmates out as thinly as possible. *NKGS* 1:217.

16. *NKGS* 1:36.

17. The figure of the *rōnanushi* has remained alive in the popular imagination thanks in large part to a Kabuki play written by Kawatake Mokuami (1816–93) in the early Meiji period. Mokuami set the final scenes of the play inside the old jailhouse, using descriptions from former guards and inmates to recreate for the public this previously hidden world. Imaoka Kentarō, "Meiji jūnen dai no Mokuami—'Shisenryō koban ume no ha' o chūshin ni," *Edo bungaku* 21 (1999): 100–107. For the play itself, see Kawatake Mokuami, "Shisenryō koban ume no ha," in *Meisaku kabuki zenshū*, ed. Toita Yasuji et al. (Tokyo: Tōkyō sōgensha, 1970), 12:65–124.

18. For the official "welcoming" ceremony, see "Rōgoku hiroku," pp. 435–36. On the tortures described here, see "Minami senyōshū" [1800], in Hosokawa, *Koji ruien hōritsu no bu*, 3:250–52.

19. "Rōgoku hiroku," pp. 454–55.

20. Yoshida Shōin, "Edo gokki" [1855], ed. Yamaguchi-ken Kyōikukai (Tokyo: Iwanami shoten, 1939), in *Yoshida Shōin zenshū*, 2:293. As a warrior, Shōin himself was imprisoned in one of the upper rooms at Kodenmachō, but his companion, Kaneko Jūnosuke, was placed in the lesser jail until Shōin bribed a guard to move him. Yasumaru Yoshio, " 'Kangoku' no tanjō," in *Bakumatsu Meiji-ki no kokumin kokka keisei to bunka henyō*, ed. Nishikawa Nagao and Matsumiya Hideharu (Tokyo: Shinyōsha, 1995), p. 286. Cf. Yasumaru Yoshio, ed., *Kangoku no tanjō: Asahi hyakka rekishi o yominaosu 22* (Tokyo: Asahi shinbunsha, 1995), pp. 14–15.

21. Ishii, *Edo no keibatsu*, pp. 156–60.

22. Minami Kazuo, "Takano Chōei no datsugoku," *Nihon rekishi* 244 (September 1968): 128–30; Yasumaru, " 'Kangoku' no tanjō," p. 287; Tsurumi Shunsuke, *Takano Chōei* (Tokyo: Asahi shimbunsha, 1985), p. 205. On the policy of releasing prisoners when fire threatened the jailhouse, see *NKGS* 1:303–4.

23. For the official "rules of the jailhouse," see *TKKK* 1:54. It should also be noted that the *rōnanushi* was also granted a range of formal privileges including extra rations of food and the right to a regular haircut. *NKGS* 1:340.

24. *NKGS* 1:78–82, 202–6.

25. J. Leavell, "The Policing of Society," in *Japan in Transition*, ed. Hilary Conroy, Sandra T. W. Davis, and Wayne Patterson (Rutherford: Fairleigh Dickinson University Press, 1984), p. 23.

26. Takano Chōei, "Wasuregatami" [ca. 1840], in *Nihon no shisō taikei*, ed. Satō Shōsuke et al. (Tokyo: Iwanami shoten, 1971), 55:177–78.

27. See "Rōya shiki, Asakusa tame, yōjōsho, Shingawa tame hisho," for the original version of this list. Cf. "Minami senyōshū," p. 257; Ishii, *Edo no keibatsu*, pp. 121–22; *NKGS* 1:202–3.

28. *NKGS* 1:203, n. 1 (3).

29. *NKGS* 1:225–27.

30. On warrior ranks, see Kasaya Kazuhiko, "Bushi no mibun to kakushiki," in Asao Naohiro, *Mibun to Kakushiki*, pp. 179–224. For a vivid description of the importance of rank in determining the seating order of the daimyo in their audiences with the shogun, see Reinier H. Hesselink, *Prisoners from Nambu: Reality and Make-Believe in Seventeenth Century Japanese Diplomacy* (Honolulu: University of Hawai'i Press, 2002), pp. 18–19.

31. J. McClain and J. M. Merriman, "Edo and Paris: Cities and Power," in McClain, Merriman, and Ugawa, *Edo and Paris*, pp. 20–21.

32. Andrew Fraser, "Town-Ward Administration in Eighteenth-Century Edo," *Papers in Far Eastern History* 27 (March 1984): 131–32.

33. Kikuchi Isao, *Kikin no shakaishi* (Tokyo: Azekura shobō, 1994), pp. 137–141.

34. There are even some examples of communities whose "village rules" listed death as the official punishment for thieves. See Kikuchi, *Kikin no shakaishi*, pp. 135–36; Mizumoto Kunihiko, "Kōgi no saiban to shūdan no okite," in *Saiban to kihan: Nihon no shakaishi 6* (Tokyo: Iwanami shoten, 1987), p. 294; Ochiai Nobutaka, "Kinsei sonraku ni okeru kaji, nusumi no kenshōken to shinpan no kinō," *Rekishi hyōron* 442 (1987): 67–74. For a discussion of a village lynching in English, see Ooms, *Village Practice*, chs. 1 and 4. For a village-level cover-up gone wrong, see Takahashi, *Edo no soshō*, which reminds us that village authorities could also help to shelter people from the full wrath of shogunal law. Cf. Hall, "Rule by Status,"

p. 44. It should also be noted that lynchings were not limited to country areas. In Osaka, mobs attacked and killed child pickpockets known as *chibo* often enough for the authorities there to issue a formal ban on the practice in 1800. See Ōsaka-shi, ed., *Ōsaka-shi shi* (Osaka: Osaka-shi, 1965), 2:215.

35. Mizumoto, "Kōgi no saiban," pp. 285–86.

36. *KKSK*, pp. 460–61. On the intendants generally, see Ishikawa Junkichi, *Edo jidai daikan seido no kenkyū* (Tokyo: Yoshikawa kōbunkan, 1963).

37. On the complexities of policing the different jurisdictions into which the capital was divided, see Katō Takashi, "Governing Edo," in McClain, Merriman, and Ugawa, *Edo and Paris*, pp. 49–53.

38. For the sake of both brevity and clarity I have chosen to omit a full discussion of the complex system of jurisdictions and judicial responsibilities held by different Bakufu officials. For a useful overview, primarily in the context of "civil" disputes, see Henderson, *Conciliation and Japanese Law*, 1:63–97. For Hiramatsu's definitive account, see *KKSK* (pp. 458–59).

39. In areas distant from Edo there were a few officials, such as the governors for Nagasaki and Sado, who had the independent power to authorize punishments up to the level of "heavy banishment." In the Kansai region and areas further west, matters were further complicated by the presence of the castellans in Osaka and Kyoto (*Ōsaka jōdai; Kyōto shoshidai*), who (in theory at least) had the power to approve all punishments and were only required to send inquiries to the senior councillors in cases that involved high-ranking warriors. The reality, however, was somewhat more complex. See *KKSK*, pp. 518–19.

40. *KKSK*, pp. 562, 567.

41. *KKSK*, p. 988. Cf. Eiko Ikegami, *The Taming of the Samurai: Honorific Individualism and the Making of Modern Japan* (Cambridge, Mass.: Harvard University Press, 1995), pp. 253–54.

42. *Kyūjishimonroku*, p. 82. For more details on seating, see *KKSK*, pp. 736–38; Henderson, *Conciliation and Japanese Law*, 1:145–46; Ooms, *Village Practice*, p. 335.

43. *NKGS* 1:750. For an interesting discussion of the evolution of *seppuku* over several centuries and its larger meaning for Japanese society, see Ikegami, *The Taming of the Samurai*, pp. 255–59.

44. Perhaps because of the volatile political situation, at the very end of the period there are some examples of warriors in Edo being beheaded within the grounds of the jailhouse. *NKGS* 1:756, n. 4.

45. *NKGS* 1:746.

46. *TKKK* 3:420; *KKSK*, pp. 571–73.

47. Sakuma, "Gōmon jikki," pp. 232–34.

48. *KKSK*, pp. 1008–9.

49. Cited in *KKSK*, p. 1008. For the full text of this decision, see *Reiruishū* 7:83–85 (#45). For cases in which the principle that any theft by a warrior was punishable with death was upheld, see also *Reiruishū* 3:485–86 (#1507), 6:287–91 (#836), 6:293–94 (#839), 9:348–52 (#1027).

50. For a helpful discussion of the different ranks of servants and low-level retainers in warrior households, see Gary P. Leupp, *Servants, Shophands and Laborers in the Cities of Tokugawa Japan* (Princeton: Princeton University Press, 1992), pp. 41–47.

51. Cited in *KKSK*, p. 1009. For the full decision, see *Reiruishū* 6:501–4 (#1047).

52. *KKSK*, p. 1009. *Tempō shūsei* 2:766 (#6330); Hosokawa, *Koji ruien hōritsu no bu*, 3:37–39.

53. Commoners could also be sentenced to banishment for gambling-related offenses, but not merely for gambling. Cf. Article 55 of the One Hundred Articles.

54. *KKSK*, p. 1009. For another example of foot soldiers and lackeys being punished less severely than higher-ranking warriors but more severely than commoners, see *Reiruishū* 7:230–33 (#109).

55. *NKGS* 1:9. As Hitomi Tonomura has noted, this was a practice that had been used to humiliate and shame women in Japan from well before the Tokugawa period. See her "Sexual Violence against Women: Legal and Extralegal Treatment in Premodern Warrior Societies," in Tonomura, Walthall, and Wakita, *Women and Class in Japanese History*, p. 146.

56. Mega Atsuko, *Hankachō no naka no onna tachi* (Tokyo: Heibonsha, 1995), p. 10.

57. Ibid., pp. 132, 166–67. Hiramatsu notes that the principle that any theft by a warrior was punishable with death extended also to warrior women. See *KKSK*, p. 1009, n. 6.

58. For an overview of Bakufu policies on prostitution, see Sone Hiromi, "Prostitution and Public Authority in Early Modern Japan," in Tonomura, Walthall, and Wakita, *Women and Class in Japanese History*, pp. 169–85. On male prostitutes and their regulation, see Gregory M. Pflugfelder, *Cartographies of Desire: Male-Male Sexuality in Japanese Discourse, 1600–1950* (Berkeley: University of California Press, 1999), pp. 116–24.

59. Tsukada, *Mibunsei shakai*, pp. 128–32.

60. Ibid., p. 132. Like the *rōnanushi*, the brothel keepers of Yoshiwara were notorious for inflicting unofficial ("private") punishments on the prostitutes who worked for them. See Miyatake Gaikotsu, *Shikei ruisan* [1922] in *Miyatake Gaikotsu chosakushū*, ed. Tanizawa Eiichi and Yoshino Takao (Tokyo: Kawade shobo shinsho, 1985), 4:557. Cf. Sone, "Prostitution and Public Authority," p. 178.

61. Although enslavement was generally considered a special punishment for women, there are also cases from early in the period of young boys who were enslaved with their mothers. See Tsukada, *Mibunsei shakai*, p. 39.

62. Ishii, *Edo no keibatsu*, pp. 87–88.

63. Tsukada, *Mibunsei shakai*, p. 39.

64. *KKSK*, p. 1011. See esp. note 1. For a moving account of the life of a woman from Tosa Domain who lived with her siblings under house arrest for some forty years in the seventeenth century because of her father's political downfall, see Tomie Ōhara, *A Woman Called En*, trans. Kazuko Furuhata and Janet Smith (London: Routledge and Kegan Paul, 1986). I am grateful to Anne Walthall for this reference.

65. *KKSK*, pp. 1010–11.

66. *KKSK*, pp. 1016–17.

67. *KKSK*, pp. 1017–18, 1021. An exception to this rule was made for lords with high positions in the Bakufu, so as to ensure that the operations of government were not disrupted by the misbehavior of low-ranking warriors.

68. Douglas Hay makes a similar argument for eighteenth-century England, noting that by hanging a rogue aristocrat from time to time the ruling classes were able to maintain popular faith in the idea of "equality before the law." See his "Property, Authority and the Criminal Law," pp. 33–34.

69. "Passing" was most common for outcasts who sought to live among commoners, but there were also cases of commoners taking up residence among outcasts. On this, see Hatanaka Toshiyuki, "Mibun o koeru toki," in *Mibunteki Shūen*, ed. Tsukada Takashi, Yoshida Nobuyuki, and Wakita Osamu (Tokyo: Buraku mondai kenkyūjo, 1994), pp. 282–324.

70. See, for example, Howell, "Private Violence and Public Virtue in Late Tokugawa Japan."

71. On peasants being promoted to warrior status, see, for example, Yabuta Yutaka, "'Hei' to 'nō' no aida," *Rekishi hyōron* 593 (September 1999): 2–15. See also J. Leavell, "The Development of the Modern Japanese Police System" (Ph.D. dissertation, Duke University, 1975), pp. 13–14. For an example of a peasant family that was able to buy its way to warrior status, see Takahashi, *Edo no shosō*, pp. 100–101.

72. For Ogyū Sorai's views on the advantages of hired retainers, see Minami Kazuo, *Edo no shakai kōzō* (Tokyo: Hanawa shobō, 1969), pp. 175–76.

73. On the *hitoyado*, see Matsumoto Ryōta, "Hitoyado," in *Iwanami kōza Nihon tsūshi 15*, ed. Asao Naohiro et al. (Tokyo: Iwanami shoten, 1995), pp. 315–32.

74. Records of the Yasuzō case are in *Reiruishū* 6:287–91 (#836). On Asahina, see Hayashi Jussai et al., eds., *Kansei chōshū shokafu* [1812] (Tokyo: Zoku gunshōruijyū kanseikai, 1964), 9:63.

75. Yoshida Nobuyuki, *Kinsei toshi shakai no mibun kōzō* (Tokyo: Tokyo daigaku shuppankyoku, 1998), pp. 249–51. Cf. Leupp, *Servants, Shophands and Laborers*, p. 147.

76. Tsukada, *Kinsei Nihon mibunsei*, pp. 239–42. Tsukada's research suggests that in 1849 there were over four thousand *hinin* under the authority of Kuruma Zenshichi and Matsuemon. The other two chiefs in Edo were Zensaburō of Honjō Fukagawa and Kyūbei of Yoyogi. Cf. Takayanagi Kaneyoshi, *Hinin no seikatsu* (Tokyo: Oyamakaku, 1981), pp. 34–35.

77. Takayanagi, *Hinin no seikatsu*, pp. 68–80.

78. Tsukada, *Kinsei Nihon mibunsei*, pp. 248–51; *NKGS* 1:65. In general, prisoners of warrior status were not handled by *hinin* workers: townsfolk were instead recruited to escort them to the governors' offices, and so on.

79. Chōbei was not responsible for recruiting *hinin* workers to assist with official punishments or torture but only with the more mundane tasks noted here. Responsibility for organizing outcast workers to perform official punishments lay with Danzaemon, the *eta* headman, and Kuruma Zenshichi, the most powerful of the four *hinin* chiefs in Edo. Chōbei was first given jobs to perform at the jailhouse in 1722 and was allocated land next to the jailhouse moat the following year for his hut. Tsukada, *Kinsei Nihon mibunsei*, p. 250.

80. "Rōgoku hiroku," pp. 437–38. According to the "Rōgoku hiroku," there were also cases in which *hinin* women were asked to serve as temporary *rōnanushi*. Cf. *NKGS* 1:82, 186–87.

81. Tsukada, *Kinsei Nihon mibunsei*, p. 244; Hosokawa, *Koji ruien hōritsu no bu*, 3:328–29; *TKKK* 1:20–21, 4:165–66.

82. Matusdaira Sadanobu claimed that more than one thousand people died in the hospices each year. See his *Uge no hitogoto* [1816], in *Uge no hitogoto, Shūgyōroku* (Tokyo: Iwanami shoten, 1969), p. 119.

83. Tsukada Takashi, "Edo Asakusa shinchō," in *Nihon toshi nyūmon 2: Chō*, ed. Takahashi Yasuo and Yoshida Nobuyuki (Tokyo: Tokyo Daigaku shuppankai, 1990), pp. 170–71. Also Tsukada, *Mibunsei shakai*, pp. 139–207.

84. *KKSK*, pp. 371–73, 1074–75; Sakuma Osahiro, *Edo machi bugyō jiseki mondō* [ca. 1890] (Tokyo: Jimbutsu Ōraisha, 1967), p. 160.

85. *KKSK*, p. 370. Cf. article 103 of the One Hundred Articles.

86. Katō Yasuaki, *Nihon mōnin shakaishi kenkyū* (Tokyo: Miraisha, 1974), p. 224.

87. Ibid.; *KKSK*, pp. 391–401; Tsukada, *Mibunsei shakai*, pp. 41–42.

88. *KKSK*, p. 394; Tsukada, *Mibunsei shakai*, p. 41. This form of execution was also practiced as a form of "community justice" in some villages early in the period.

89. Katō, *Nihon mōnin*, p. 224. Sakuma, *Edo machi bugyō*, pp. 160–61; *KKSK*, pp. 394–95.

90. In addition, cases that involved residents of Edo and one of the warrior lords' fiefs were handled through the governors of the town of Edo. *KKSK*, pp. 65–77. The Osaka town governors and other Kansai-based officials were sometimes also involved in adjudicating multijurisdictional cases in the western part of the country.

91. *KKSK*, pp. 299–302.

92. *KKSK*, pp. 247–48.

93. The key document is the "Jibun shioki rei" of 1697, which can be found in *TKKK* 1:315–16.

94. *KKSK*, p. 198.

95. *KKSK*, p. 197.

96. *KKSK*, pp. 203–5. Komoro was a *fudai* domain of fifteen thousand *koku*.

97. *KKSK*, p. 204.

98. *KKSK*, pp. 210–11.

99. *KKSK*, pp. 211–12.

100. Drawing on the ideas of Mizubayashi Takeshi, Mark Ravina has suggested that the Tokugawa polity be understood as a "compound state" *(fukugō kokka)*, made up of multiple pockets and layers of authority. See his *Land and Lordship in Early Modern Japan* (Stanford: Stanford University Press, 1999), pp. 37–38. While I am generally in agreement with the substance of Ravina's argument, I believe that the concept of status—something that would have had immediate meaning for anyone living in the period—can help us to capture more accurately the nature of the Tokugawa state, while also providing a link to much broader patterns of social organization.

CHAPTER FOUR: DISCOURSE, DYNAMISM, AND DISORDER

1. For a general introduction to Sorai's thought, see Tetsuo Najita, *Tokugawa Political Writings* (Cambridge: Cambridge University Press, 1998), pp. xii–liv; Samuel Hideo Yamashita, "Nature and Artifice in the Writings of Ogyū Sorai (1666–1728)," in *Confucianism and Tokugawa Culture*, ed. Peter Nosco (Princeton: Princeton University Press, 1984), pp. 138–65; Samuel Hideo Yamashita, *Master Sorai's*

Responsals (Honolulu: University of Hawai'i Press, 1994); Olof G. Lidin, *The Life of Ogyū Sorai: A Tokugawa Confucian Philosopher* (Lund: Studentlitteratur, 1973).

2. Ogyū Sorai, *Seidan*, in *NKT* 9:7. This translation is adapted from Ogyū Sorai, *Discourse on Government (Seidan)*, trans. Olof G. Lidin (Wiesbaden: Harrasowitz Verlag, 1999), p. 71. Cf. J. R. McEwan, ed., *The Political Writings of Ogyū Sorai* (Cambridge: Cambridge University Press, 1962), p. 124.

3. Minami, *Edo no shakai kōzō*, pp. 35–36.

4. On the evolution of the office of inspector for arson and theft and its place in the Bakufu chain of command, see *KKSK*, pp. 427–28, 516. For Sorai's view on their inability to cope with a city the size of Edo, see *Seidan*, in *NKT* 9:7; *Discourse*, p. 73.

5. Sorai, *Seidan*, in *NKT* 9:108–9; *Discourse*, p. 215.

6. Sorai, *Seidan*, in *NKT* 9:19–20; *Discourse*, pp. 91–92.

7. Sorai, *Seidan*, in *NKT* 9:9; *Discourse*, p. 75.

8. Sorai, *Seidan*, in *NKT* 9:22; *Discourse*, p. 95.

9. Sorai, *Seidan*, in *NKT* 9:40; *Discourse*, pp. 124–25.

10. Sorai, *Seidan*, in *NKT* 9:18; *Discourse*, p. 89.

11. For Sorai's discussion of punishments, see *Seidan*, in *NKT* 9:174–80. For an English translation, see McEwan, *Political Writings*, pp. 110–17. Cf. *Discourse*, pp. 295–303. On Sorai's reputation as a scholar of Chinese law, see Henderson, "Chinese Legal Studies in Early Eighteenth Century Japan," pp. 21–56.

12. On the deliberate use of criminals to set fires and disrupt neighboring territories by warlords in the sixteenth century, see Mitamura, *Edo no shiranami*, pp. 58–72.

13. Sorai, *Seidan*, in *NKT* 9:177; *Discourse*, p. 300.

14. On the punishment of "penal servitude" as practiced in China under the Ming (1368–1644) and Qing (1644–1912) dynasties particularly, see Derk Bodde and Clarence Morris, *Law in Imperial China: Exemplified by 190 Ch'ing Dynasty Cases* (Cambridge, Mass.: Harvard University Press, 1967), pp. 81–83. For an overview of the "five punishments," see pp. 76–77.

15. Sorai, *Seidan*, in *NKT* 9:177–78; *Discourse*, p. 301.

16. For an example of a domain that experimented with "penal servitude," see note 57.

17. For an overview of Shundai's thought and the place of his *Keizairoku* in it, see Tetsuo Najita, "Political Economism in the Thought of Dazai Shundai (1680–1747)," *Journal of Asian Studies* 31.4 (August 1972): 821–39.

18. Dazai Shundai, *Keizairoku*, in *NKT* 9:621–22.

19. The relevant passage from Mencius can be found in James Legge, trans., *The Works of Mencius* (reprint, New York: Dover Publications, 1970), p. 136 (bk. 1, ch. 1, pt. 1, ch. 6). On Shundai's hostility to Mencius, see Najita, "Political Economism," p. 825.

20. Shundai, *Keizairoku*, in *NKT* 9:606–7.

21. Ibid., 9:608–9.

22. Ibid., 9:622. Perhaps because of his own squeamishness, the one form of bodily mutilation Shundai did not advocate was castration.

23. Bitō Masahide has noted that whereas Sorai's thought shows a basic faith in the ability of all human beings to contribute to the greater good, Shundai was more

pessimistic about human nature and placed greater emphasis on the need to impose strict outside controls on people's behavior. In this sense his proposals for penal reform were clearly in character. Bitō Masahide, "Dazai Shundai no hito to shisō," in *Nihon shisō taikei 34: Sorai gakuha*, ed. Rai Tsutomu (Tokyo: Iwanami shoten, 1972), pp. 509–12. See also Najita, "Political Economism," esp. p. 826.

24. Shundai, *Keizairoku*, in *NKT* 9:608–9.

25. For Shundai's proposal that criminals sentenced to punishments of mutilation should afterward be given work to perform in the place where the crime was committed, see *Keizairoku*, in *NKT* 9:622.

26. Miura, *Hōseishi no kenkyū*, pp. 997–98.

27. As noted in chapter 1, the severing of noses, ears, and fingers had gradually fallen out of use over the course of the seventeenth century. Perhaps because of Arai Hakuseki's influence they were officially abolished in 1709 at the beginning of Ienobu's term as shogun. Hosokawa, *Koji ruien hōritsu no bu*, 2:462–63. It should also be noted that in some of the larger domains, most notably Mito, amputation of the nose and ears continued to be used as a punishment throughout the Edo period.

28. Tetsuo Najita, *Visions of Virtue in Tokugawa Japan: The Kaitokudō Merchant Academy of Osaka* (Chicago: University of Chicago Press, 1987), pp. 16, 150, 187. I am, in general, greatly indebted to Najita's important work on the Kaitokudō scholars. For additional biographical information on Riken and Chikuzan, see also Kobori Kazumasa, Yamanaka Hiroyuki, et al., *Sōsho Nihon no shisōka 24: Nakai Chikuzan, Nakai Riken* (Tokyo: Meitoku shuppansha, 1980), pp. 179–278. For a recent evaluation of Riken's thought, see Nomura Maki, "'Tsūjin' kara no yuutopia—'Kashō kokuō' Nakai Riken no shisō," *Kokka gakkai zasshi* 107.7–8 (1994): 188–236.

29. For a summary of some of Riken's most important policy proposals, see Najita, *Visions of Virtue*, p. 214.

30. The following is a summary of Nakai Riken, *Jukkei bōgi*, in *NKT* 23:707–16. I am also grateful to Dr. John Morris for helping me obtain a copy of a "hanpon" version of the text from the Kano bunko at Tōhoku University. The title of the essay is taken from a passage in "The Canon of Shun" in *The Book of Historical Documents*, in which the sage-king, Shun, takes steps to ease the severity of existing punishments. See Morohashi Tetsuji, *Dai kanwa jiten* (Tokyo: Taishūkan shōten, 1989–90), 10583/10.

31. This was not as common in the Kansai region, where the task of arresting criminals was one of the basic responsibilities given to the *hinin* outcast group. Tsukada, *Mibunsei shakai*, pp. 46, 52–54; *KKSK*, p. 1079. On the "thief takers" of London, see J. A. Sharpe, *Crime in Early Modern England, 1550–1750* (London: Longman, 1984), pp. 111–12; Emsley, *Crime and Society*, p. 223.

32. Tsukada, *Mibunsei shakai*, pp. 42–52.

33. Abe, *Meakashi Kinjirō*, pp. 6–7. Cf. *KKSK*, p. 648. Needless to say, it was not acceptable for a lord to send warrior retainers into another jurisdiction in search of a criminal suspect. For a case in which a group of domainal officials were punished for just such a transgression, see *KKSK*, pp. 233–38.

34. Tsukada, *Mibunsei shakai*, pp. 51–52.

35. *KKSK*, pp. 628–29.

36. This was the response in the first Bakufu decree concerning vagrancy in Edo, issued in 1680. See *Kampō shūsei*, p. 1138 (#2391).

37. *TKKZ* 5:461 (#3409).

38. Minami Kazuo suggests that there were about 5,400 persons under the permanent authority of the *hinin* headmen in Edo by 1722. Minami, *Edo no shakai kōzō*, p. 69.

39. Sorai, *Seidan*, in *NKT* 9:30.

40. Ibid. Sorai's understanding that *hinin* were associated with incidents of arson at this time is supported by a record from 1723 which states that "In conjunction with numerous cases of arson, suspicious persons were rounded up, and when they were questioned, most turned out to be *hinin*." See Kinsei shiryō kenkyūkai, ed., *Shōhō jiroku* (Tokyo: Nihon gakujitsu shinkōkai, 1966), 2:277 (#1942). Lidin's translation of this passage (*Discourse*, p. 110) is quite different from mine.

41. Minami, *Edo no shakai kōzō*, p. 73.

42. Ibid., p. 72.

43. Hiramatsu Yoshirō, "Ninsoku yoseba no seiritsu 2," *Nagoya Daigaku Hōsei Ronshū* 34 (1966): 103.

44. Minami, *Edo no shakai kōzō*, p. 75.

45. Ibid., pp. 75–76.

46. On the way that economic change, official policy, and environmental degradation contributed to the increased hardships of peasants in the eighteenth century, see Walthall, *Social Protest*, pp. 8–9; Herman Ooms, *Charismatic Bureaucrat: A Political Biography of Matsudaira Sadanobu* (Chicago: University of Chicago Press, 1975), pp. 6–7; Conrad Totman, *Early Modern Japan* (Berkeley: University of California Press, 1993), pp. 242–43.

47. On proto-industrialization, see T. C. Smith, *Native Sources*; Howell, *Capitalism from Within*; Wigen, *Making of a Japanese Periphery*; Edward E. Pratt, *Japan's Protoindustrial Elite: The Economic Foundations of the Gōnō* (Cambridge, Mass.: Harvard University Asia Center, 1999). On moneylending, see Ronald Toby, "Both a Borrower and a Lender Be: From Village Moneylender to Rural Banker in the Tempō Era," *Monumenta Nipponica* 46.4 (winter 1991): 483–512.

48. T. C. Smith, "Premodern Economic Growth: Japan and the West," pp. 15–49. For the example of Osaka, see also William Hauser, *Economic Institutional Change in Tokugawa Japan: Osaka and the Kinai Cotton Trade* (Cambridge: Cambridge University Press, 1974).

49. *Temmei shūsei*, pp. 908–9 (#3063).

50. Hiramatsu Yoshirō, "Ninsoku yoseba no Seiritsu to hensen," in *Ninsoku yoseba shi*, ed. Ninsoku yoseba kenshōkai (Tokyo: Sōbunsha, 1974), p. 96. See also Leupp, *Servants, Shophands and Laborers*, p. 169.

51. The full text of the message is reproduced in *Edo Kaishi* 2.8 (1890): 47.

52. Minami, *Edo no shakai kōzō*, pp. 81–82. Hiramatsu, "Seiritsu to hensen," p. 98.

53. For Sadanobu's life, see Ooms, *Charismatic Bureaucrat*. On the significance of the transition from Tanuma to Sadanobu for the political history of the Tokugawa period, see Conrad Totman, *Politics in the Tokugawa Bakufu, 1600–1843* (Berkeley: University of California Press, 1988), pp. 183, 222–23.

54. On Chikuzan's audience with Sadanobu, see Najita, *Visions of Virtue*, pp. 171, 177. For more detail, see Kobori, Yamanaka, et al., *Sōsho Nihon no shisōka 24*, pp. 98–101.

55. Chikuzan's title does not translate easily and so I have chosen simply to romanize it here. Literally, *Sōbō kigen* means something like, "Honest Words from the Grassy Fields," which in turn reflects Chikuzan's position as someone outside the official structures of government, that is, out in the fields. See Morohashi, *Dai kanwa jiten* 30945/243. On Riken's attempt to avoid contact with Sadanobu, see Najita, *Visions of Virtue*, p. 210; Kobori, Yamanaka, et al., *Sōsho Nihon no shisōka 24*, p. 225.

56. Nakai Chikuzan, *Sōbō kigen*, in *NKT* 23:512–14. The idea of the long-term jail is recommended again later as a possible response to juvenile delinquency (p. 535).

57. Bodde and Morris, *Law in Imperial China*, pp. 81–82. There was some change in the practice of "penal servitude" after 1725 when, under the Qing, "convicts stopped being sent to outside provinces and, instead, were thereafter kept within the province of their conviction, there being put to work in government postal stations or . . . in local government yamens." It is, however, unlikely that Japanese scholars, who were mainly influenced by the Ming codes, were aware of this change. As a result of the influence of the Ming codes, Kumamoto Domain introduced "penal servitude" as a substitute for banishment in the 1750s. It is not known whether this was more than an innovation in name alone, but, in any case, the practice of "penal servitude" was certainly well known among scholars in Japan in the second half of the eighteenth century. *NKGS* 1:768.

58. On the background to Sadanobu's famous 1790 "prohibition of heterodoxy," see Robert L. Backus, "The Kansei Prohibition of Heterodoxy and Its Effects on Education," *Harvard Journal of Asiatic Studies* 39.1 (June 1979): 55–106.

59. Hiramatsu, "Ninsoku yoseba no seiritsu 2," p. 112. The timing is particularly significant given the fact that earlier in the same year Sadanobu had rejected a suggestion from the Deliberative Council that he reconsider the 1723 proposal to create a new kind of hospice in the capital.

60. Hiramatsu, "Ninsoku yoseba no seiritsu 2," pp. 117–29. See also his "Ninsoku yoseba no seiritsu 1," *Nagoya Daigaku Hōsei Ronshū* 33 (1965): 20–23, 27–29. In rendering *ninsoku yoseba* as the Stockade for Laborers I follow the example set by the anonymous translator of one of Hiramatsu's survey essays, "History of Penal Institutions: Japan," *Law in Japan* 6 (1973): 1–48. It should be noted that Leupp's translation of the prefix *Kayakugata*, which referred specifically to the inspector of arson and theft, as "temporary extra worker" is incorrect. Leupp, *Servants, Shophands and Laborers*, p. 170. On Heizō, see also Takigawa Masajirō, *Hasegawa Heizō— sono shōgai to ninsoku yoseba* (Tokyo: Asahi shimbunsha, 1975).

61. On Heizō's concern to avoid the problems of the foster home, see Hiramatsu, "Ninsoku yoseba no seiritsu 1," pp. 28–29.

62. "Yoseba kiritsu" [ca. 1791], cited in Hiramatsu, "Ninsoku yoseba no seiritsu 2," p. 124.

63. Interestingly, although Riken did not suggest that wages be paid to inmates in the long-term jail, Chikuzan did. See his *Sōbō kigen*, pp. 313–14. For examples

of inmates being given assistance getting settled after being released from the Stockade for Laborers, see Hiramatsu, "Seiritsu to hensen," p. 110. For Matsudaira Sadanobu's own glowing evaluation of the stockade, see his autobiography *Uge no hitogoto*, pp. 118–19. On the 1829 fire at the stockade offices, see *TKKK* 1:32, and Takashio Hiroshi and Kanzaki Naomi, "Kyōsei kyōkai zō 'Yoseba ninsoku kyūki tome,'" *Kokugakuin Daigaku Nihon bunka kenkyū jo kiyō* 76 (September 1995): 149.

64. Matsudaira, *Uge no hitogoto*, p. 119.

65. Tsukada, *Mibunsei shakai*, pp. 77–78; *Tempō shūsei*, 2:757 (#6318).

66. *Tempō shūsei*, 2:763 (#6322).

67. Tsukada, *Mibunsei shakai*, pp. 74, 88.

68. *NKT* 1:848. Cf. Tsukada, *Mibunsei shakai*, p. 73.

69. In addition to unregistereds, provisions were also made for disobedient servants in warrior households and, according to Matsudaira Sadanobu, delinquent children to be sent to the stockade. See *TKKK* 2:441, and Matsudaira, *Uge no hitogoto*, p. 118.

70. Uezaki Kuhachirō, *Sensaku zasshu*, in *NKT* 20:533.

71. Bix, *Peasant Protest*, p. 111. Walthall puts the number of dead even higher at two million out of a total population of around twenty-six million. *Social Protest*, p. xi.

72. For an official statement of this view see, for example, H. Borton, *Peasant Uprisings in Japan of the Tokugawa Period* (New York: Paragon Book Reprints, 1968), p. 135.

73. Honda Toshiaki, *Keisei Hissaku*, in *NKT* 20:20–21. Translated in Tsunoda Ryūsaku, Wm. Theodore de Bary, and Donald Keene, eds., *Sources of Japanese Tradition* (New York: Columbia University Press, 1964), 2:51.

74. Hiramatsu, "Seiritsu to hensen," pp. 112–14.

75. As Walthall notes, "the 1780s saw over twice as many riots as any previous ten-year period and, in 1787, more city riots than in any other single year for the entire history of the Tokugawa period, including the crises of 1866–67." *Social Protest*, p. 120.

76. E. P. Thompson, "The Moral Economy of the English Crowd in the Eighteenth Century," reprinted in his *Customs in Common* (London: Penguin, 1993), pp. 185–258. For a more detailed description of crowd actions and motivations in Tokugawa period smashings, see Walthall, *Social Protest*, pp. 120–49.

77. On the rumors that triggered the 1783 smashing, see Miyamoto Mataji, *Ōsaka* (Tokyo: Shibundō, 1957), pp. 181–82; Ōsakafu shi henshū senmon iinkai, ed., *Ōsaka-fu shi* (Osaka: Osakafu, 1987) 6:266–67.

78. On the relationship between the Kaitokudō and the house of Masuya, see Najita, *Visions of Virtue*, pp. 226, 248–49.

79. Takayama Hikokurō, "Kyōto nikki" [1783], cited in Kobori, Yamanaka, et al., *Sōsho Nihon no shisōka 24*, p. 220.

80. Ibid., pp. 220–21.

81. Ōsaka-fu shi henshū senmon iinkai, *Ōsaka-fu shi*, 6:284.

82. Takeuchi Makoto, "Tenmei no Edo uchi kowashi no jittai," *Tokugawa rinsei shi kenkyū jo kenkyū kiyō* (1970): 286.

83. On the participants in the 1787 smashing, see ibid., pp. 291–95. Cf. Takeuchi Makoto, "Uchikowashi," in *Edo gaku jiten*, ed. Nishiyama Matsunosuke (Tokyo:

Kōbundō, 1984), p. 584; Walthall, *Social Protest*, pp. 142–46; Ooms, *Charismatic Bureaucrat*, p. 75.

84. Takeuchi Makoto, "Kansei kaikaku," in *Iwanami kōza Nihon rekishi 12: Kinsei 4*, ed. Naoki Kōjirō and Asao Naohiro (Tokyo: Iwanami shoten, 1976), pp. 5–9. See also Ooms, *Charismatic Bureaucrat*, pp. 75–76.

85. Cited in Takeuchi, "Kansei kaikaku," p. 9.

86. As Ooms notes, this was not the first time that Sadanobu found himself appointed to an important position as a result of popular unrest. In 1783 he was appointed daimyo of Shirakawa Domain after riots had broken out there. See Ooms, *Charismatic Bureaucrat*, pp. 50–55.

87. On the Edo Town Office, see Yoshida Nobuyuki, *Kinsei kyodai toshi no shakai kōzō* (Tokyo: Tokyo Daigaku shuppankai, 1991), chs. 1–3. Also Ooms, *Charismatic Bureaucrat*, pp. 100–101; Leupp, *Servants, Shophands and Laborers*, p. 159.

88. Hiramatsu, "Seiritsu to hensen," pp. 115–16.

89. *KKSK*, pp. 523–24, 1076–77.

90. Ishii, *Edo no keibatsu*, p. 80.

91. Hiramatsu, "Seiritsu to hensen," pp. 115–16.

92. While the origins of this view of the stockade's development can be traced back to Miura's 1919 *Hōsei shi no kenkyū* (p. 1016), it was elaborated upon in the immediate postwar period by Maruyama Tadatsuna in his detailed, four-part essay "Kayakugata ninsoku yoseba ni tsuite,"*Hōsei shigaku* 7 (1955): 1–19; 8 (1956): 23–49; 9 (1957): 1–36; 10 (1958): 44–80. Although he was in disagreement with some details of the "accepted view," Ishii Ryōsuke also saw the admission of banished criminals as marking the stockade's transformation into a specialized penal institution. See his "Nihon keibatsu shi jō ni okeru ninsoku yoseba no ichi," in Ninsoku, *Ninsoku yoseba shi*, p. 47. Cf. Tsukada, *Mibunsei shakai*, pp. 66–72.

93. Hiramatsu, "Seiritsu to hensen," p. 117.

94. *Tempō shūsei* 2:879 (#6590), cited in Tsukada, *Mibunsei shakai*, pp. 86–87.

95. Tsukada, *Mibunsei shakai*, p. 88; Minami, *Edo no shakai kōzō*, p. 119.

96. Tsukada, *Mibunsei shakai*, pp. 84–85; Hiramatsu, "Seiritsu to hensen," p. 117.

97. On Ōshio's life and thought, see Najita, "Ōshio Heihachirō," pp. 155–79. Also Najita, *Visions of Virtue*, pp. 293–300.

98. For statements of this view by leading scholars, see Ishii, *Edo no keibatsu*, pp. 196–97; Minami, *Edo no shakai kōzō*, p. 133; and Shigematsu Kazuyoshi, "Ninsoku yoseba to Ishikawajima kangoku," in *Ninsoku yoseba shi*, pp. 315–16. Even Hiramatsu, who explicitly rejects the notion that the Stockade for Laborers was evolving into a modern prison, suggests that it took on an increasingly punitive character as a result of a growing criminal element in the inmate population and the introduction of oil extraction. See his "Seiritsu to hensen," pp. 118–19. For the first truly clearheaded evaluation of the stockade's development, free of the teleological assumptions implicit in much of the work done by legal historians, see Tsukada, *Mibunsei shakai*, pp. 67–72.

99. See text of the discussion of the subject in the Deliberative Council cited in Tsukada, *Mibunsei shakai*, p. 84.

100. Shigematsu, "Ninsoku yoseba to," pp. 315–16. Shigematsu notes that the sight of inmates from the stockade selling oil soon became a common part of Edo

life. Later inmates were also put to work, manufacturing cheap paper for sale in the city.

101. Tsukada, *Mibunsei shakai*, pp. 84, 88.

102. On the Tempō period generally, see Harold Bolitho, "The Tempō Crisis," in *The Emergence of Meiji Japan*, ed. Marius B. Jansen (Cambridge: Cambridge University Press, 1995), pp. 1–52. See also Fujita Satoru, *Tempō no kaikaku* (Tokyo: Yoshikawa kōbunkan, 1999).

103. Tsukada, *Mibunsei shakai*, pp. 90–91.

104. Ibid., pp. 88–89.

105. Ibid., p. 98. Cf. *NKGS* 1:868–70. The report submitted by the governor of the stockade at this time also notes that about one-third of the six hundred inmates was employed at oil extraction and one-third at other jobs, but the remaining two hundred inmates were completely idle.

106. Tsukada, *Mibunsei shakai*, p. 89.

107. *TKKZ* 5:464–65 (#3414).

108. On the construction of the Stockade for Outcasts, see Minami, *Edo no shakai kōzō*, pp. 138–41. For Danzaemon's reports, see "Mushuku karikomi ikken" [1839], (Kyū Bakufu hikitsugi sho, National Diet Library).

109. Leupp, *Servants, Shophands and Laborers*, p. 175. Even in the case of western Europe it is not clear that the workhouses and houses of correction that were built in large numbers from the sixteenth century actually played a significant role in conditioning the idle poor "to the harsh regimen of wage labor necessary to nascent capitalism" (Leupp, p. 167). For a study that takes a more nuanced view of these institutions, see Joanna Innes, "Prisons for the Poor: English Bridewells, 1555–1800," in *Labour, Law and Crime in Historical Perspective*, ed. D. Hay and F. Snyder (London: Blackwell, 1987), pp. 42–122. For an attempt to develop a non-Marxian framework for explaining their rise, see also Pieter Spierenburg, *The Prison Experience: Disciplinary Institutions and Their Inmates in Early Modern Europe* (New Brunswick: Rutgers University Press, 1991).

110. Bellah, *Tokugawa Religion*. For a detailed empirical examination of the role of Shingaku preachers at the Stockade for Laborers, see Takenaka Yasuichi, "Ninsoku yoseba to shingaku," in *Ninsoku yoseba shi*, pp. 197–232. For a stimulating essay that examines the role of Shingaku at the stockade from a Foucaultian perspective, arguing that it can be seen as an ultimately abortive attempt to encourage the emergence of a new form of disciplined subjectivity, see Umemori Naoyuki, "Shingaku to iu tekunorogii," *Waseda seiji keizai gaku zasshi* 328 (1996): 228–60. Although Umemori is too careful to fall into the trap, there is a real danger that in applying Foucault's ideas mechanistically to Tokugawa Japan we simply end up reinforcing the familiar narrative of convergence that takes European social development as the "norm" toward which Japan was steadily moving. See also his discussion of the stockade in "Modernization through Colonial Mediations: The Establishment of the Police and Prison System in Meiji Japan" (Ph.D. dissertation, University of Chicago, 2002), pp. 170–210.

111. Tsukada, *Mibunsei shakai*, p. 95.

112. "Tempō senyō ruishū," cited in Minami, *Edo no shakai kōzō*, p. 103.

113. Hiramatsu, "Seiritsu to hensen," pp. 122–23; Miura, *Hōsei shi no kenkyū*, p. 1016.

114. I have found references to a total of five domains that attempted to replace banishment with confinement in an institution of "penal servitude" before the 1840s, and another three (Matsuyama, Shinjō, Tsuchiura) that constructed stockade-like institutions soon after Mizuno's order. Eventually, in 1867, Nagaoka Domain was also to construct a stockade of its own. For more detail on these institutions, see *MKK*, pp. 291–318; Kanzaki Naomi, "Tsuchiura han tokei sho kō," *Kokugakuin Daigaku Nihon bunka kenkyū shohō* 32.3 (September 1995): 3–6.

115. Tsukada, *Mibunsei shakai*, pp. 93–94. For an analysis of admissions to the Stockade for Laborers between 1862 and 1865, see Hiramatsu, "Bakumatsu ki," pp. 347, 351–54.

116. Minami, *Edo no shakai kōzō*, p. 151.

CHAPTER FIVE: PUNISHMENT AND THE POLITICS OF
CIVILIZATION IN BAKUMATSU JAPAN

1. H. D. Harootunian, *Things Seen and Unseen: Discourse and Ideology in Tokugawa Nativism* (Chicago: University of Chicago Press, 1988), p. 403.

2. For a survey of late Tokugawa thought, see H. D. Harootunian, "Late Tokugawa Culture and Thought," in Jansen, *The Emergence of Meiji Japan*, pp. 53–143. On the impact of nativist ideas on ordinary people in the Ina Valley, see Anne Walthall, *The Weak Body of a Useless Woman: Matsuo Taseko and the Meiji Restoration* (Chicago: University of Chicago Press, 1998).

3. The most obvious expression of the late Tokugawa concern with national strength in a narrow sense came in the form of the so-called national defense literature spawned by writers such as Hayashi Shihei (1738–93), but for other examples of concern with the broader question of building national strength and prosperity, see Najita, *Visions of Virtue*, esp. pp. 170–81, and Luke Roberts's important work on the emergence of *kokueki* thought, *Mercantilism in a Japanese Domain*.

4. Makihara Norio, *Kyakubun to kokumin no aida: Kindai minshū no seiji ishiki* (Tokyo: Yoshikawa kōbunkan, 1998), pp. 7–8.

5. For the role of the imperial gaze in the creation of modern Japanese political subjectivity, see T. Fujitani, *Splendid Monarchy: Power and Pageantry in Modern Japan* (Berkeley: University of California Press, 1996), pp. 24–25, 52–55, 81.

6. On the importance of the "problem of population" for the modern art of government, see Michel Foucault's classic essay "Governmentality" in *The Foucault Effect: Studies in Governmentality*, ed. Graham Burchell, Colin Gordon, and Peter Miller (Chicago: University of Chicago Press, 1991), pp. 87–104. In the same volume, see also Pasquale Pasquino, "Theatrum Politicum: The Genealogy of Capital—Police and the State of Prosperity," pp. 105–18.

7. Donald Keene, *The Japanese Discovery of Europe, 1720–1830*, rev. ed. (Stanford: Stanford University Press, 1969), pp. 16–30. Keene provides a complete translation of Sugita's account of the dissection at Kotsukappara on p. 22. It is worth noting that the dramatic advances made in anatomical science in Europe in the eighteenth century were also largely the product of experiments done with the cadavers of executed criminals. See Linebaugh, "The Tyburn Riot," p. 69.

8. Najita, *Visions of Virtue*, p. 217.

9. Cesare Beccaria, *On Crimes and Punishments and Other Writings*, ed. Richard Bellamy (Cambridge: Cambridge University Press, 1995), p. 63. Cf. Charles de Secondat Montesquieu, *The Spirit of the Laws*, ed. Anne Cohler, Basia Miller, and Harold Stone (Cambridge: Cambridge University Press, 1995), pp. 72–95.

10. Beccaria, *On Crimes and Punishments*, p. 67.

11. On Beccaria's impact in Europe generally, see Franco Venturi, *Utopia and Reform in the Enlightenment* (Cambridge: Cambridge University Press, 1971), pp. 100–116; and Wright, *Guillotine and Liberty*, pp. 3–23. For his impact in England particularly, see Radzinowicz, *A History*, 1:277–85.

12. Ignatieff, *Just Measure*, p. 47.

13. Ibid., p. 53. On the Amsterdam Rasp House, see J. T. Sellin, *Pioneering in Penology: The Amsterdam House of Correction in the Sixteenth and Seventeenth Centuries* (Philadelphia: University of Pennsylvania Press, 1944), and Spierenburg, *The Prison Experience*. Although they are usually characterized as houses of correction, intended to instill the "habits of industry" in a wide range of idle bodies, Spierenburg argues that by the end of the seventeenth century the Amsterdam Rasp House had already taken on the characteristics of a "criminal prison." Either way, it remained relatively small with just over one hundred inmates for most of the eighteenth century. For the classic Frankfurt school interpretation of the emergence of houses of correction across Europe, see Georg Rusche and Otto Kirchheimer, *Punishment and Social Structure* (New York: Columbia University Press, 1939), pp. 24–52.

14. Ignatieff, *Just Measure*, p. 47; Emsley, *Crime and Society*, p. 264.

15. Emsley, *Crime and Society*, p. 265. The end of transportation to the American colonies as a result of the outbreak of the Revolutionary War was another important factor that contributed to the initial interest in the penitentiary idea in Britain.

16. Simon Schama, *The Embarrassment of Riches: An Interpretation of Dutch Culture in the Golden Age* (Berkeley: University of California Press, 1988), pp. 19–21. Cf. Sellin, *Pioneering*, p. 68.

17. Shiba Kōkan, "Oranda tsūhaku" [1805], in *Shiba Kōkan zenshū*, ed. Asakura Haruhiko et al. (Tokyo: Yasaka shobō, 1992), 3:166.

18. F. B. Verwayen, "Tokugawa Translations of Dutch Legal Texts," *Monumenta Nipponica* 53.3 (fall 1998): 336–39.

19. On Lin Zexu, Wei Yuan, and the *Haiguo tuzhi*, see Suzanne Wilson Barnett, "Protestant Expansion and Chinese Views of the West," *Modern Asian Studies* 6.2 (1972): 129–49, and "Wei Yan and the Westerners: Notes on the Sources of the *Hai-kuo t'u chih*," *Ching-shih wen-t'i* 2.4 (November 1970): 1–20. For Wei Yuan more generally, see Jane Kate Leonard, *Wei Yuan and China's Rediscovery of the Maritime World* (Cambridge, Mass.: Council on East Asian Studies, Harvard University, 1984). For Chinese efforts to learn more about the rest of the world in the wake of the Opium War, see Fred W. Drake, *China Charts the World: Hsu Chi-yü and His Geography of 1848* (Cambridge, Mass.: East Asian Research Center, Harvard University, 1975). I am grateful to Pär Cassell for bringing these works to my attention. See also Umemori, "Colonial Mediations," pp. 141–59.

20. Masuda Wataru, *Japan and China: Mutual Representations in the Modern Era*, trans. Joshua A. Fogel (Richmond, Surrey: Curzon Press, 2000), p. 24. See also Ōba Osamu, *Edo jidai no Nicchū hiwa* (Tokyo: Tōhō shoten, 1980), pp. 245–46.

21. Barnett, "Protestant Expansion," p. 140.

22. Ibid., p. 138. According to Barnett, a history of the United States written in Chinese by Bridgman was the main source for the American chapters of the *Haiguo tuzhi*. See "Wei Yüan and the Westerners," p. 10.

23. For the original Chinese passage, see Wei Yuan, *Haiguo tuzhi* [1847], ed. Li Julan (Zhengzhou: Zhongzhou guji chubanshe, 1999), pp. 391–95. For a Japanese version, see the five-volume set of hampon in the rare books collection at the Harvard-Yenching Library titled *Tsūzoku kaikoku zushi Amerika shū no bu* (Osaka: Akitaya Taemon, 1855), 2:16–24. The writings of Kusaka Genzui suggest that the description of American prisons must also have appeared in translations of Wei's chapters published as *Amerika sōki*, but there were exceptions. They do not appear, for example, in the three-volume *Amerika sōki* from 1854 held at the National Archive of Japan.

24. Masur, *Rites of Execution;* David J. Rothman, "Perfecting the Prison: United States, 1789–1865," in *The Oxford History of the Prison*, ed. Norval Morris and David J. Rothman (New York: Oxford University Press, 1995), pp. 111–29.

25. Rothman, "Perfecting the Prison," p. 115. See also Meranze, *Laboratories of Virtue*.

26. Rothman, "Perfecting the Prison," p. 117.

27. On Tocqueville's report, coauthored with Gustave de Beaumont, and its impact in France, see Wright, *Guillotine and Liberty*, pp. 63–65.

28. Ignatieff, *Just Measure*, p. 197.

29. Transportation to Australia began to decline in the 1830s. It was formally abolished as a judicial sentence in 1857, although small numbers of convicts continued to be sent to Western Australia for another decade after this. Emsley, *Crime and Society*, pp. 271–72. See also, A.G.L. Shaw, *Convicts and Colonies* (Melbourne: Melbourne University Press, 1966), pp. 335–60. Ironically, the French began experimenting with transportation (to New Caledonia and Guiana) at about the same time that the English were phasing it out. See Wright, *Guillotine and Liberty*, pp. 92–95.

30. Rothman, "Perfecting the Prison," p. 121.

31. Cited in ibid., p. 124.

32. Norman Johnston, Kenneth Finkel and Jeffrey A. Cohen, *Eastern State Penitentiary: Crucible of Good Intentions* (Philadelphia: Philadelphia Museum of Art, 1994), p. 67.

33. On the background to Yoshida's attempt to stow away on board one of Perry's ships, see H. D. Harootunian, *Toward Restoration: The Growth of Political Consciousness in Tokugawa Japan* (Berkeley: University of California Press, 1970), pp. 202–3.

34. Osatake Takeki, *Meiji bunka sōsetsu* (Tokyo: Gakugeisha, 1934), p. 124.

35. Yoshida Shōin, "Fukudōsaku" [1855], in Yamaguchi-ken kyōikukai, *Yoshida Shōin zenshū*, 2:301. The full text of the essay, summarized later, appears on pp. 301–8.

36. Ibid., p. 301. The word *zensho* or *yokishomotsu* (literally, "good book[s]") in the *Haiguo tuzhi* undoubtedly referred to the Christian Bible, but the term was deliberately vague, and there is no reason to think that Yoshida made the connection.

37. The term *fukudō* was a reference to the efforts of a fifth-century Chinese emperor, reputed to have turned the jails into "halls of blessing" by forcing criminals to see the error of their ways. In addition to Yoshida's own text, see Morohashi, *Dai kan wa jiten*, 24768/94.

38. Osatake, *Meiji bunka*, p. 124.

39. In support of his idea, Yoshida also argued that exile to an island was, in general, an inappropriate punishment for warriors. From what he had heard, warriors who were sent to islands ended up living as the "slaves of peasants" *(hyakusho no dorei)*, an unacceptable fate for a "proud and dignified warrior" *(dōdōtaru shijin)* (p. 304).

40. Kusaka Genzui, "Shisai takuroku" [1859], in *Sabetsu no shosō*, ed. Hirota Masaki (Tokyo: Iwanami shoten, 1991), pp. 431–33. The contents of Kusaka's essay are summarized later.

41. On Yamada Hōkoku's life, see *MKK* 2:301–2.

42. Yamada Hōkoku, "Gokusei kaikaku ikensho" [1864], in *Yamada Hōkoku zenshū*, ed. Yamada Jun (Okayama: Yamada Hōkoku zenshū kangyōkai, 1951), 2:1503. Cf. *MKK* 2:304–5.

43. Yasumaru " 'Kangoku' no tanjō," pp. 288–91.

44. Ibid., p. 291. Cf. Abe Akira, *Edo no autorō* (Tokyo: Kōdansha sensho mechie, 1999), pp. 21–34.

45. On Kunisada Chūji, see, in addition to Yasumaru, Tamura Eitarō, *Ikki, kumosuke, bakuto* (Tokyo: Mikawa shobō, 1935); Takahashi Satoshi, *Kunisada Chūji no jidai: Yomi kaki to kenjutsu* (Tokyo: Heibonsha, 1991); and Abe Akira, *Edo no autorō*, pp. 10–20.

46. Yasumaru, *Kangoku no tanjō*, p. 28. Cf. E. J. Hobsbawm, *Primitive Rebels* (Manchester: Manchester University Press, 1959).

47. Ishii Ryōsuke and Harafuji Hiroshi, eds., *Bakumatsu ofuregaki shūsei* (Tokyo: Iwanami shoten, 1992), 5:539–40 (#5030). On disorder in the city generally, see also 5:538–39 (#5028).

48. Needless to say, I use "Europe" and "Europeans" loosely here, more to indicate a position within the imperial world order of the nineteenth century than to point to a specific geographical region or ethnicity.

49. For a study of the impact of these ideas in Britain, see McGowen, "A Powerful Sympathy." It should be noted that these views were not universally accepted. As McGowen makes clear, there was considerable resistance to penal reform in Britain until at least the 1850s.

50. Anne McClintock, *Imperial Leather: Race, Gender and Sexuality in the Colonial Contest* (New York: Routledge, 1995), pp. 36–42.

51. Cited in ibid., p. 36. See also P. J. Marshall and Glyndwr Williams, *The Great Map of Mankind: British Perceptions of the World in the Age of Enlightenment* (London: J. M. Dent & Sons, 1982), p. 93. I am grateful to Robert Travers for this reference.

52. McClintock, *Imperial Leather*, p. 36.

53. For the use of these ideas by reformers in early nineteenth-century England, see Randall McGowen, "Civilizing Punishment: The End of the Public Execution in England," *Journal of British Studies* 33 (July 1994): 263.

54. For relevant selections from European reports on Japan in the sixteenth and seventeenth centuries, see Cooper, *They Came to Japan*, pp. 151–64.

55. Francis Caron and Joost Schorten, *A True Description of the Mighty Kingdoms of Japan and Siam*, trans. Roger Manley (London: Samuel Brown and John de l'Eclufe, 1663), p. 57.

56. See, for example, Isaac Titsingh, *Illustrations of Japan* (London: R. Ackermann, 1822), pp. 147–48.

57. On the suppression of Christianity, see C. R. Boxer, *The Christian Century in Japan: 1549–1650* (Berkeley: University of California Press, 1951), and George Elison, *Deus Destroyed: The Image of Christianity in Early Modern Japan* (Cambridge, Mass.: Harvard University Press, 1973).

58. Montesquieu, *Spirit of the Laws*, pp. 86–88. Montesquieu's argument was not just that Japanese laws were harsh but that the Japanese people had become so used to brutal punishments that they were no longer intimidated by them. The laws were thus "powerless." In addition to Kaempfer, his other main source on Japan was Constantin de Renneville's *Recueil des voyages qui ont servi à l'etablissement et aux progrès de la Compagnie des Indes* (Amsterdam: Aux dépens d'Estienne Roger, 1702–6).

59. Foucault, *Discipline and Punish*, pp. 3–6. For further examples of the horrors of punishment in early modern Europe, see Radzinowicz, *English Criminal Law*, and van Dülmen, *Theatre of Horror*.

60. See, for example, Titsingh, *Illustrations*, or Philipp Franz von Siebold's account of his first stay in Japan, published in English in 1841 and later reissued as *Manners and Customs of the Japanese in the Nineteenth Century* (Rutland, Vt.: Charles E. Tuttle, 1973). On punishments, see esp. pp. 159–163.

61. "Americans in Japan," reprinted in the *Living Age* 23.284 (October 27, 1849): 148. Not all foreigners who found themselves in Japan at this time complained of their treatment. Ranald MacDonald, who was one of those to be brought home on the *Preble*, claimed to have been met with kindness and to have been extended every hospitality until he was able to be sent back to America. The other sailors rescued by the *Preble* were treated less well, but it was only after repeated attempts to escape from the supervision of Japanese officials that they were put in jail. See William S. Lewis and Naojiro Murakami, eds., *Ranald MacDonald: The Narrative of His Life, 1824–94* (Portland: Oregon Historical Society, 1990).

62. F. L. Hawks, *Narrative of the Expedition of an American Squadron to the China Seas and Japan* (New York, 1857), 1:256–57; W. G. Beasley, ed., *Select Documents on Japanese Foreign Policy, 1853–1868* (London: Oxford University Press, 1955), pp. 99–102.

63. On the different approaches taken to the problem of law in the context of European imperial expansion, see Jörg Fisch, *Cheap Lives and Dear Limbs: The British Transformation of Bengal Criminal Law, 1769–1817* (Wiesbaden: Franz Steiner Verlag, 1983), pp. 1–2.

64. F. C. Jones, *Extraterritoriality in Japan* (New Haven: Yale University Press, 1931), pp. 1–4.

65. For an interesting but ultimately unconvincing article analyzing British legal practices in India in terms of extraterritoriality, see Michael H. Fisher, "Extraterritoriality: The Concept and Its Application in Princely India," *Indo-British Review* 15.2 (1988): 103–22. On the establishment of extraterritoriality in China, see Vi Kyuin Wellington Koo, *The Status of Aliens in China* (New York: Columbia University Press, 1912), pp. 59–166; Hsin-pao Chang, *Commissioner Lin and the Opium*

War (Cambridge, Mass.: Harvard University Press, 1964), pp. 12–3, 138–40. In practice, the British had refused to hand over their subjects for trial by the Chinese from the mid-1780s. It was only after the Opium War, however, that these extraterritorial "rights" were recognized by the Qing. Prior to this it had been an ongoing source of friction. For details of the extraterritoriality provisions in the treaties imposed on Japan, see Jones, *Extraterritoriality*, pp. 27–30.

66. Captain F. Brinkley, *A History of the Japanese People* (New York: Encyclopedia Brittanica, 1915), p. 707. On Brinkley himself, see J. E. Hoare, *Japan's Treaty Ports and Foreign Settlements* (Sandgate: Japan Library, 1994), pp. 156–58.

67. On the principle of "using barbarians to control barbarians" as a possible precedent for extraterritoriality in the context of Qing China, see Joseph Fletcher, "The Heyday of the Qing Order in Mongolia, Sinkiang and Tibet," in *The Cambridge History of China*, ed. Denis Twitchett and John K. Fairbank (Cambridge: Cambridge University Press, 1978), 10:351–408. I am grateful to Ron Toby for this reference.

68. Rutherford Alcock, *The Capital of the Tycoon* (New York: Harper and Bros., 1863), 2:14–16. Cf. Jones, *Extraterritoriality*, pp. 54–57.

69. For a more extensive discussion of Western abuse and manipulation of the system of consular courts, see Inoue Kiyoshi, *Jōyaku kaisei: Meiji no minzoku mondai* (Tokyo: Iwanami shoten, 1955), pp. 33–49.

70. Katō Hideaki, "Bakumatsu Meiji ryōji saiban ni okeru keibatsu," in Hiramatsu, *Hō to keibatsu no rekishiteki kōsatsu*, pp. 171–72.

71. Cited in Katō, "Bakumatsu Meiji ryōji saiban," p. 171. For the full text of the protest, see Gaimusho chōsabu, ed., *Nihon gaikō monjo* (Tokyo: Gaimusho, 1919), 3:571–72.

72. Inoue Kowashi, "Shihōsho kaikaku iken" [1875], in *Inoue Kowashi den shiryō hen*, ed. Inoue Kowashi denki hensan iinkai (Tokyo: Kokugakuin Daigaku toshokan, 1966), 1:54–55.

73. For a full discussion of political developments at this time, see W. G. Beasley, *The Meiji Restoration* (Stanford: Stanford University Press, 1972), pp. 142–241. On the ideological motivations of the "men of spirit," see Harootunian, *Toward Restoration*, esp. chs. 4, 5.

74. *Hansard's Parliamentary Debates* (London: Cornelius Buck, 1864), 3rd ser., vol. 176, p. 585 (House of Lords, July 1, 1864). Cf. Jones, *Extraterritoriality*, p. 72. On the importance of extraterritoriality as an issue in the lead up the Opium War, see Chang, *Commissioner Lin*, p. 214.

75. *Hansard*, vol. 176, pp. 592–93.

76. The caricature was undoubtedly a calculated one. In his speech, Russell specifically cited the writings of George Smith, the bishop of Victoria (Hong Kong), as the main source for his information on Japanese punishments, but Smith's overall impression of Japanese justice was, in fact, quite favorable. He did note the "sanguinary severity of their laws" but also suggested that it was because of them that Japan was "more than usually favored among the countries of Eastern Asia, by its exemption from civil tumults and the general security of life and person." He also made a point of contrasting Japanese officials with Chinese ones, praising them for their honesty and lack of corruption. George Smith, *Ten Weeks in Japan* (London: Longman, Green, Longman and Roberts, 1861), pp. 102–3, 163–64.

77. On Russell's achievements in the home office, see Emsley, *Crime and Society*, pp. 270–73.

78. Cited in Beasley, *Meiji Restoration*, p. 199.

79. *Illustrated London News*, February 25, 1865, pp. 192–93; March 18, 1865, pp. 261–65.

80. On Tyburn, see Linebaugh, *The London Hanged*. The procession to Tyburn was abolished in 1783.

81. The classic statement of 1864's importance as a turning point is Yoshio Sakata and John W. Hall, "The Motivation of Political Leadership in the Meiji Restoration," *Journal of Asian Studies* 16 (1956): 31–50. See also Beasley, *Meiji Restoration*, esp. pp. 214–72. For an alternative periodization, see Conrad Totman, *The Collapse of the Tokugawa Bakufu, 1862–1868* (Honolulu: University of Hawai'i Press, 1980), pp. xxvi–xxxiv.

82. Ishii Takashi, *Zōtei Meiji ishin no kokusaiteki kankyō* (Tokyo: Yoshikawa kōbunkan, 1966), pp. 757–58; Oka Yoshitake, *Reimeiki no Meiji Nihon* (Tokyo: Miraisha, 1964), pp. 7–9.

83. Ishii, *Zōtei Meiji ishin*, p. 762; Oka, *Reimeiki*, pp. 9–15.

84. Ishii Takashi, "Kōbe jiken," in *Kokushi daijiten*, vol. 5, edited by Kokushi daijiten henshi iinkai (Tokyo: Yoshikawa kōbunkan, 1985), p. 515.

85. Ishii, *Zōtei Meiji ishin*, pp. 799–803; Oka, *Reimeiki*, pp. 23–26.

86. Ishii, *Zōtei Meiji ishin*, pp. 803–4.

87. Ibid., pp. 806–8. Ishii suggests that the decision to call an early end to the executions may have had an explicitly political motivation.

88. Ibid., pp. 765–69, 803–9.

89. Abbot Lyman, "Pictures of the Japanese," *Harper's New Monthly Magazine* 39.231 (August 1869): 309.

CHAPTER SIX: RESTORATION AND REFORM

1. "Tasshi setsuroku" [M1/1/17], in *HBT* 54:1. Dates in square brackets are for the old lunar calendar. Dates in the text have been converted to the Gregorian calendar. On the provisional penal regulations of 1868, see *MKK* 1:3–31. For Iwakura's petition, see Kobayashi Yoshinobu, "Meiji ishin to keihō no sentei," *Hōgaku ronsō* 48.5 (1943): 820–21.

2. "Gyōseikan futatsu" [M1/10/30], in *HBT* 54:2.

3. Cited in Kobayashi, "Meiji ishin to keihō," p. 817.

4. Ibid., pp. 817–18; *MKK* 1:4.

5. Cited in Beasley, *Meiji Restoration*, p. 279. See also p. 277 on the 1867 agreement among leading figures in the Restoration movement that treaty revision be adopted as a key goal.

6. Govt. to Yamauchi [M1/12/8], in *HBT* 54:89–90.

7. *HBT* 54:110. Hiramatsu, "History of Penal Institutions: Japan," p. 23.

8. The Meiji government's determination to assert tighter control over the population is also evidenced by its quick introduction of a Chinese-style system of household registration *(koseki)* in 1869. This too was a strategy that Sorai had strongly advocated in *Seidan*.

9. For a survey of the early development of Chinese legal scholarship in the Tokugawa period, see Henderson, "Chinese Legal Studies," pp. 21–56.

10. Maki Kenji, "Higo-han keihō sōsho no seiritsu," *Hōgaku ronsō* 48.5 (1943): 701–47.

11. *MKK* 1:14.

12. *MKK* 1:3–31. For a detailed study of Chinese influence on the early Meiji codes, see Paul Heng-Chao Ch'en, *The Formation of the Early Meiji Legal Order: The Japanese Code of 1871 and Its Chinese Foundation* (Oxford: Oxford University Press, 1981).

13. "Keihōkan shirei" [M2/7/8], in *HBT* 54:117–18.

14. "Jōyu" [M3/12/20], in *HBT* 54:129–94. For a full translation of the *Shinritsu kōryō*, see Ch'en, *Formation*, pp. 83–184. On the penal provisions specifically, see pp. 40–48.

15. Cited in Inoue, *Jōyaku kaisei*, pp. 12–13.

16. "Gaimusho ukagai" [M4/3/27], in *HBT* 54:195.

17. Ohara himself claimed to have been imprisoned on three separate occasions before the Restoration, but I have been able to account for only two of these. Ohara Shigechika, "Hyōgikai no enzetsu," *Dai Nihon kangoku kyōkai zasshi* 14 (June 1889): 43.

18. Ogawa Tarō, "Ohara Shigechika," *Keisei* 8.1 (January 1970): 45.

19. Shigematsu Kazuyoshi, *Mei tengoku byōden* (Tokyo: Nihon gyōseishi kenkyū-kai, 1984), p. 6.

20. Ohara Shigechika, "Moto genrōin gikan Ohara Shigechika kun kōwa 1," *Dai Nihon kangoku kyōkai zasshi* 41 (September 1891): 39–40.

21. For a detailed discussion of the changes that took place at the Stockade for Laborers in this period, see Shigematsu, "Ninsoku yoseba to," pp. 329–44.

22. Shigematsu Kazuyoshi, "Edo ōbanya giga kaidai—Kawanabe Kyōsai junan no haikei to banya no jittai," *Kyōsai* 36 (September 1988): 15–16. On Kyōsai's arrest, see also Timothy Clark, *Demon of Painting: The Art of Kawanabe Kyōsai* (London: British Museum Press, 1993), p. 22. I am grateful to Dr. Clark for bringing Kyōsai's magnificent depiction of the guard house to my attention, and for introducing me to Kawanabe Kusumi, director of the Kawanabe Kyōsai Memorial Museum.

23. Ohara, "Kōwa 1," p. 40; Ohara, "Enzetsu," pp. 43–44; Ohara Shigechika, *Dai Nihon gokusei enkakshi* (Tokyo: Kinkōdō, 1880), p. 47. See also *NKGS* 2:414–16.

24. "Shihōsho jōhyō" [M5/3/1], in *HBT* 57:105.

25. Ohara, "Enzetsu," p. 43. In the same speech he also mentions the former daimyo of Harima Domain, where the treaty port of Kobe was located, as having been an important early reformer.

26. The original travel proposal was submitted in the first month of 1871. Ohara probably gained access to Kido Takayoshi through his immediate superior at the time, Shishido Tamaki (1829–1901), also from Chōshū. Ohara, "Kōwa 1," p. 41; Ohara, "Enzetsu," p. 43.

27. As Umemori Naoyuki has shown in his recent doctoral dissertation, Ohara was not the only official to conduct a study mission to Britain's Asian colonies at this time. In 1872 an official from Kanagawa prefecture named Ishida Eikichi was dispatched to Hong Kong and Shanghai to study the British system of policing. Umemori shows that Ishida's report had a significant impact on the early Meiji

police system and also lays out some stimulating hypotheses concerning the significance of colonial models for the long-term development of both prisons and police in Japan. See his "Colonial Mediations," pp. 55–113. On Ohara's mission, see pp. 115–23.

28. Shibusawa Eiichi, "Journal of a Voyage to the West," in *The Autobiography of Shibusawa Eiichi*, trans. Teruko Craig (Tokyo: University of Tokyo Press, 1994), pp. 154–55. Thanks to Rustin Gates for this reference.

29. Ohara, "Kōwa 1," p. 41.

30. *Japan Weekly Mail*, September 10, 1870, p. 421.

31. The Ohara mission was the third non-British study group to inspect the prison system in Singapore, having been preceded in the 1860s by missions from the Kingdom of Siam and the Dutch East Indies. On this, see J.F.A. Mc Nair and W. D. Bayliss, *Prisoners Their Own Warders: A Record of the Convict Prison at Singapore in the Straits Settlements Established 1825, Discontinued 1873* (Westminster: Archibald Constable, 1899), p. x. For examples of the influence of the Singaporean model *within* the British Empire, see Sen, *Disciplining Punishment*, p. 18; and Clare Anderson, "The Genealogy of the Modern Subject: Indian Convicts in Mauritius, 1814–53," in *Representing Convicts: New Perspectives on Convict Forced Labour Migration*, ed. Ian Duffield and James Bradley (London: Leicester University Press, 1997), p. 172.

32. For Ohara on Hall, see "Moto genrōin gikan Ohara Shigechika kun kōwa 2," *Dai Nihon kangoku kyōkai zasshi* 43 (November 1891): 20. On Hall's employment as a "student interpreter," see the Public Record Office (London) file, F.O. 262/ 208 (Consular correspondence, July—November 1871), f. 61. Hall's translations of the Osadamegaki and other premodern Japanese legal codes were eventually published in the *Transactions of the Asiatic Society of Japan*. They have since been reprinted in a single volume under the title *Japanese Feudal Laws* (Washington, D.C.: University Publications of America, 1979). See also Umemori, "Colonial Mediations," pp. 115–22.

33. A detailed account of the trip can be found in "Mr. Hall's Report" of October 20, 1871, in the Public Record Office file, F.O. 46/142 (Japan correspondence), ff. 204–16.

34. Ohara Shigechika, Amano Mitami, and Kosuke Eishū, *Eikoku Saibansho ryakusetsu: Eikoku shikan Jon Hōru kōyaku* (Tokyo: Keibunbō, 1872). Thanks to Robert Hellyer for locating this document in the Tokyo University library for me.

35. "Mr. Hall's Report," f. 207.

36. Ibid., f. 209. For McNair's own account of the history of Singapore's convict prison, see note 28.

37. Ohara, Amano, and Kosuke, *Eikoku Saibansho ryakusetsu*, p. 2. Ogawa Tarō and Nakao Bunsaku, *Gyōkei kaikakusha tachi no rirekisho* (Tokyo: Kyōsei kyōkai, 1983), p. 16. On the idea of the panopticon, see Foucault's discussion in *Discipline and Punish*, pp. 195–228.

38. Students of Japanese today are more likely to have learned the word *keimusho* (literally, "place for administering punishment"), which began to be used in the 1920s. *Kangoku*, however, continues to be the term used to describe the buildings where convicts are actually imprisoned.

39. "Shihōsho ukagai" [M4/12/26], in *HBT* 54:199. Umemori notes that flogging was used to punish Chinese colonial subjects in Hong Kong when Ohara visited, and suggests that Ohara's proposal can be understood as a critique of this discriminatory practice. Given the wording of the proposal, however, I believe it is better understood as an early attempt to ensure that the Japanese moved closer to the position of the white British rulers and away from that of the Chinese. Umemori, "Colonial Mediations," pp. 124–27.

40. "Shihōsho ukagai" [M4/12/26], in *HBT* 54:199.

41. "Tasshi" [M3/11/17], in *HBT* 54:119–20.

42. According to Ch'en, strangulation was held to be less severe than decapitation in the Chinese legal tradition because it was believed that a person whose body did not remain whole would find it difficult to achieve rebirth in the next world. Ch'en, *Formation*, p. 40. On the inclusion of strangulation in the official list of punishments allowed for under the provisional penal laws of 1868, see *MKK* 1:3–31.

43. Cited in *MKK* 1:292.

44. *MKK* 1:293; Ohara, "Kōwa 2," p. 21.

45. "Fukoku #65" [M6/2/20], in *HBT* 54:204–7.

46. On Etō's life, see Matano Hansuke, *Etō Nanpaku* (Tokyo: Minyūsha, 1914), and Mōri Toshihiko, *Etō Shimpei* (Tokyo: Chūkō shinsho, 1987). On his legal reforms, see Kikuyama Masaaki, *Meiji kokka no keisei to shihō seido* (Toyko: Ochanomizu shōbō, 1993), and Masako Kobayashi Ikeda, "French Legal Advisor in Meiji Japan: Gustave Emile Boissonarde de Fontarabie" (Ph.D. dissertation, University of Hawai'i, 1996).

47. Kikuyama, *Meiji kokka*, pp. 166–68; "Fukoku #37" [M6/2/7], in *HBT* 54:540; Mills, "Kataki-uchi," p. 525.

48. *NKGS* 2:96–97; Hiramatsu, "History of Penal Institutions: Japan," p. 27.

49. The full text of the 1872 "Prison Rules," summarized here, can be found in *HBT* 57:62–105.

50. *HBT* 57:62. For an alternative translation, see Hiramatsu, "History of Penal Institutions: Japan," p. 28.

51. Naoyuki Umemori, "Spatial Configuration and Subject Formation: The Establishment of the Modern Penitentiary System in Meiji Japan," in *New Directions in the Study of Meiji Japan*, ed. Helen Hardacre and Adam Kern (Leiden: Brill, 1997), pp. 743–44. Cf. Maeda Ai, *Toshi kūkan no naka no bungaku* (Tokyo: Chikuma shobō, 1982), p. 176.

52. Maeda, *Toshi kūkan*, pp. 184–90. On the remaking of urban space in Tokyo, see also Fujitani, *Splendid Monarchy*, pp. 66–82, and esp. Fujimori Terunobu, *Meiji no Tōkyō keikaku* (Tokyo: Iwanami shoten, 1982).

53. D. Eleanor Westney, "The Emulation of Western Organizations in Meiji Japan: The Case of the Paris Prefecture of Police and the Keishi-chō," *Journal of Japanese Studies* 8.2 (summer 1982): 310; Obinata Sumio, *Nihon kindai kokka no seiritsu to keisatsu* (Tokyo: Azekura shobō, 1992), p. 33. See also Umemori, "Colonial Mediations," pp. 27–58.

54. On the figure of the soldier in the development of modern strategies of discipline, see Foucault, *Discipline and Punish*, pp. 135–36.

55. On work conditions in the new factories, see E. Patricia Tsurumi, *Factory Girls: Women in the Thread Mills of Meiji Japan* (Princeton: Princeton University Press, 1990).

56. On the establishment of the education system, see S. Yamamura, "Politics and Education in Early Meiji Japan: The Modern Military System and the Formation of the 'Gakusei' " (Ph.D. dissertation, University of California at Berkeley, 1978), pp. 110–14.

57. "Tasshi #378" [M5/11/29], in *HBT* 57:62.

58. Mōri, *Etō*, p. 171; "Tasshi #129" [M6/4/8], in *HBT* 57:107–13.

59. "Shihōsho tasshi #39," in *HBT* 57:107.

60. "Shihōsho tasshi" [M6/4/19], in *HBT* 57:113.

61. The relevant sections of the *Shinritsu kōryō* and the *Kaitei ritsurei* have been reproduced next to each other in Ishii Shirō and Mizubayashi Takeshi, eds., *Hō to chitsujo* (Tokyo: Iwanami shoten, 1992), pp. 148–52.

62. "Fukoku #69" [M6/6/24], in *HBT* 57:116. In practice, many of those sentenced to "confinement in prison" continued to serve their sentences at home because of a lack of suitable prison facilities. It was only in 1878 that the practice of house arrest was fully abolished. See "Naimusho tasshi #34" [M11/4/16], in *HBT* 57:142–43.

63. Ishii and Mizubayashi, *Hō to chitsujo*, p. 143.

64. *NKGS* 2:103.

65. *NKGS* 2:414; *TSKS* 53:130.

66. *TSKS* 54:579, 910. In compensation for the land at Hongō, the Justice Ministry was given another tract of land at Ichigaya, where it did eventually build another prison.

67. Ohara, "Kōwa 2," pp. 21–22. On the general increase in inmate numbers following the promulgation of the *Kaitei ritsurei*, see *NKGS* 2:445–47.

68. Ohara, "Kōwa 2," p. 21.

69. Ibid.

70. Shigematsu Kazuyoshi, *Zukan Nihon no kangokushi* (Tokyo: Oyamakaku shuppan, 1985), pp. 11–12.

71. Mōri, *Etō*, pp. 187–90.

72. Ibid., pp. 209–10.

CHAPTER SEVEN: PUNISHMENT AND PRISONS IN THE ERA OF ENLIGHTENMENT

1. For Foucault's astute observations about how projects to reform the prison have been characteristic of modern penal systems from their very inception, see *Discipline and Punish*, pp. 234–35. For a general history of the prison in Japan up until the 1980s, see Shigematsu, *Zukan*.

2. Cited in Yamamura, "Politics and Education," p. 190.

3. For examples of the importance that came to be placed on educating women, if only to prepare them for their roles as mothers, we need look no further than the arguments made in the early 1870s by "enlightenment" intellectuals such as Mitsukuri Shūhei, Nakamura Masanao, and Fukuzawa Yukichi. See William

Braisted, trans., *Meiroku Zasshi: Journal of the Japanese Enlightenment* (Tokyo: University of Tokyo Press, 1976), pp. 108, 402–4; and Fukuzawa Yukichi, "Kyōto Gakkō no ki," in *Fukuzawa Yukichi on Education*, trans. Eiichi Kiyooka (Tokyo: University of Tokyo Press, 1985), pp. 73–79. On the early training of nurses, see Ōkubo Toshitake, ed., *Nihon ni okeru Berii-ō* (Tokyo: Tokyō hōgokkai, 1930), pp. 20–26, 50–52. On nursing in general, see Kinoshita Yasuko, *Kindai Nihon kangoshi* (Tokyo: Meijikaru fuurendo sha, 1974). On hospitals, see Susan L. Burns, "Contemplating Places: The Hospital as Modern Experience in Meiji Japan," in *New Directions in the Study of Meiji Japan*, ed. Helen Hardacre and Adam Kern (Leiden: Brill, 1997), pp. 702–19. On women factory workers, see Tsurumi, *Factory Girls*.

4. On mental asylums in the early Meiji period, see Susan L. Burns, "Tori tsukareta shintai kara kankin sareta shintai e," *Edo no shisō* 6 (May 1997): 48–62.

5. For an introduction to the Meirokusha and a complete translation of the journal, see Braisted, *Meiroku Zasshi*.

6. On Tsuda in Holland, see Thomas Havens, *Nishi Amane and Modern Japanese Thought* (Princeton: Princeton University Press, 1970), pp. 42–55. Also Verwayen, "Tokugawa Translations," pp. 335–36.

7. Ch'en, *Formation*, p. 12.

8. Translated in Braisted, *Meiroku Zasshi*, p. 96.

9. Tezuka Yutaka, "Meiji shonen no gōmon seido," in *MKK* 3:17–18.

10. Translated in Braisted, *Meiroku Zasshi*, pp. 498–99.

11. For other early Meiji calls for the abolition of the death penalty, see Tezuka Yutaka, "Meiji zenki no shikei haishi ron," in *MKK* 1:305–9. On calls for the abolition of torture, see his "Meiji shonen ni okeru ni, san no gōmon haishi ron," in *MKK* 3:49–87. On Boissonade, see Ōkubo Yasuo, *Nihon kindai hō no chichi— Boasonaado* (Tokyo: Iwanami shinsho, 1977), pp. 32–40. In English, see Kobayashi Ikeda, "French Legal Advisor," pp. 35–43.

12. Tezuka, "Meiji shonen no gōmon seido," p. 19. See also p. 23, n. 15. For the original text of Boissonade's letter, see Gustave Boissonade, *Boasonaado tōmonroku* (Tokyo: Hōsei Daigaku shuppankyoku, 1978), pp. 32–34. Cf. Kobayashi Ikeda, "French Legal Advisor," pp. 166–67.

13. Boissonade, *Boasonaado tōmonroku*, p. 43.

14. Tezuka, "Meiji shonen no gōmon seido," p. 21.

15. Ibid., pp. 24–29.

16. Ibid., pp. 31–32.

17. Ibid., p. 33.

18. Ibid., p. 35. See also p. 37, n. 11.

19. *HBT* 54:377. The modern Japanese police force was created between 1875 and 1881. See Leavell, "Modern Japanese Police System," pp. 72–156; and Umemori, "Colonial Mediations," pp. 27–113.

20. *HBT* 54:319–20.

21. *HBT* 54:394–95.

22. Isabella Bird, *Unbeaten Tracks*, p. 327.

23. *TSKS* 3:161. The park can still be visited today.

24. The Meiji leader's awareness of the need for prison reform was, no doubt, also fostered by their own visits to "model prisons" during their travels abroad on

the Iwakura mission. For one example, see Kume Kunitake, *Tokumei zenken taishi beiō kairan jikki* (Tokyo: Iwanami shoten, 1985), 1:332–33.

25. Ōkubo, *Nihon ni okeru Berii-ō*, pp. 122–23; K. Berry, *Pioneer Doctor*, p. 54.

26. Berry, *Pioneer Doctor*, p. 234.

27. Ibid., pp. 55–56.

28. For the full text of the Berry report, see *NKGS* 2:12–65.

29. Ohara, "Kōwa 2," 23.

30. *NKGS* 2:486, 489. Berry was probably also responsible for the positive view of Meiji penal reforms taken by E. C. Wines in his *State of Prisons and of Child-Saving Institutions in the Civilized World* (Cambridge, Mass.: John Wilson, & Son 1880). For the connection between these two men, see K. Berry, *Pioneer Doctor*, p. 56.

31. Richard H. Mitchell, *Janus-Faced Justice: Political Criminals in Imperial Japan* (Honolulu: University of Hawai'i Press, 1992), pp. 15–23.

32. *NKGS* 2:488.

33. *HBT* 57:213.

34. Ogawa and Nakao, *Gyōkei kaikakusha*, pp. 25–26.

35. Shigematsu, *Zukan*, p. 93.

36. *NKGS* 2: 488.

37. Tokyo-to, *Ginza renga gai no kensetsu* (Tokyo: Tokyo-to, 1955), p. 127.

38. For the text of the Home Ministry's submission, see *NKGS* 2:707–26. It notes that the main Tokyo prison at Ishikawajima, which had previously held no more than 2,000 convicts at any one time, now held some 3,690 as a result of legal reforms and the influx of prisoners after the Satsuma Rebellion.

39. Shigematsu, *Mei tengoku hyōden*, pp. 44–46.

40. *NKGS* 2:488.

41. Shigematsu Kazuyoshi, *Hokkaidō gyōkei shi* (Sapporo: Zufu shuppan, 1970), pp. 120–22.

42. On the importance of transportation for the French penal system at this time, see Wright, *Guillotine and Liberty*, pp. 129–52.

43. On the transportation of criminals to the Izu islands in early Meiji, see *NKGS* 1:633–34.

44. Cited in Shigematsu, *Hokkaidō*, p. 122. Under the new penal code those sentenced to servitude and exile would be allowed to settle on the island to which they had been transported after serving an initial period in prison. Cf. Mitchell, *Janus-Faced Justice*, pp. 17–18.

45. Shigematsu, *Hokkaidō*, p. 131. On Tsukigata, see Shigematsu, *Meitengoku*, pp. 36–43; Kumagai Masakichi, *Kabato kangoku* (Sapporo: Hokkaidō shimbunsha, 1992), pp. 13–27.

46. Tsukigata Kiyoshi, "Hokkai kaiyū ki," (1881, manuscript, Tsukigata Kabato Museum). The place where the Kabato prison was built was called Shibetsuputo by the Ainu, but Tsukigata later decided to rename it after himself. It is still known as Tsukigata village today.

47. Shigematsu, *Hokkaidō*, p. 129. Also *NKGS* 2:742–43.

48. *NKGS* 2:742–43.

49. Shigematsu, *Hokkaidō*, p. 153.

50. Hall, *Tanuma*, pp. 100–105.

51. On the plan to send outcasts to Ezo, see ibid., p. 67; Ooms, *Tokugawa Village Practice*, pp. 296–97.

52. Honda Toshiaki "Ezo tochi kaihatsu gūzon no tairyaku" (1792), cited in Shirayama Tomomasa, "Ezochi yoseba kō," *Hōseishi kenkyū* 13 (1962): 144.

53. Shirayama, "Ezochi yoseba," pp. 156–63.

54. Naikaku tōkei kyoku, *Nihon teikoku tōkei nenkan* (Tokyo: Naikaku tōkei kyoku, 1882–), 8:617–18.

55. Roger W. Bowen, *Rebellion and Democracy in Meiji Japan* (Berkeley: University of California Press, 1980); Stephen Vlastos, "Opposition Movements in Early Meiji, 1868–1885" in *The Cambridge History of Japan*, ed. Marius B. Jansen (Cambridge: Cambridge University Press, 1989), 5: 267–431.

56. Vlastos, "Opposition Movements," pp. 416–26.

57. Naikaku tōkei kyoku, *Nihon teikoku tōkei nenkan*, 8:617–18.

58. Ibid., 8:626.

59. The lines between criminal and political activity at this time were not always clear-cut. On this, see esp. Hasegawa Noboru, *Bakuto to jiyū minken* (Tokyo: Heibonsha Library, 1995). Cf. Yasumaru Yoshio, "Kangoku no tanjō," pp. 305–9. For a list of some of the most prominent political criminals imprisoned at the Sorachi and Kabato Central Prisons at this time, see Mitchell, *Janus-Faced Justice*, p. 19.

60. Shigematsu, "Ninsoku yoseba to," pp. 345, 356. The Stockade for Laborers was first put under the control of the Police Bureau in 1875, but it was not until 1877 that efforts were made to develop it into a full-fledged prison.

61. Ibid., p. 361.

62. Ibid., pp. 362–64.

63. Ibid., p. 357.

64. Yanagida Kunio, *Kokyō nanjūnen* (1959), cited in *Nihon no hyakunen 9: Waki tatsu minron*, ed. Tsurumi Shunsuke (Tokyo: Chikuma shobō, 1967), p. 56.

65. Bird, *Unbeaten Tracks*, p. 267.

66. Shigematsu, *Hokkaidō*, p. 132.

67. Matsukata to Sanjo, in *NKGS* 2:529–30.

68. J. C. Hall, *Tanuma*, p. 102, n. 42.

69. Shigematsu, *Hokkaidō*, p. 151. Thanks to Pia Vogler for providing me with information about Benjamin Smith Lyman, the American engineer.

70. Tanaka Osamu, *Nihon shihon shugi to Hokkaidō* (Sapporo: Hokkaidō Daigaku tosho kankō kai, 1988), pp. 112–13.

71. *NKGS* 2:529–30; Shigematsu, *Hokkaidō*, p. 151.

72. Tanaka, *Nihon shihon shugi to*, pp. 113–14.

73. *NKGS* 2:744–45.

74. Hashimoto Tetsuya, "Miike kōzan to shūjin rōdō," *Shakai keizai shigaku* 32:4 (1967): 46.

75. Tanaka, *Nihon shihon shugi to*, p. 116.

76. Shigematsu, *Hokkaidō*, p. 233.

77. Cited in Hashimoto, "Miike kōzan," pp. 51–52.

78. Tanaka, *Nihon shihon shugi to*, p. 115; Shigematsu, *Hokkaidō*, p. 153.

79. Shigematsu, *Hokkaidō*, pp. 186–87.

80. Ibid., p. 187.

81. Abashiri prison's place in postwar Japanese popular culture was cemented by a series of nineteen films made between 1959 and 1972 under the title *Abashiri bangaichi*. The first of these established the acting career of Takakura Ken, one of the best-known actors of the postwar period. There is still a minimum security prison in Abashiri, but the earlier films also helped turn the town into a tourist destination: The original Meiji era prison has been made into a museum, visited by thousands of tourists each year.

82. Shigematsu, *Hokkaidō*, p. 133.

83. On the growth of immigration to Hokkaido, see Tanaka, *Nihon shihon shugi to*, p. 137.

84. Shigematsu, *Hokkaidō*, p. 133.

85. *NKGS* 2:1036–37. On the human costs of Meiji prison labor, see also Mitchell, *Janus-Faced Justice*, pp. 19–21.

86. Ibid. It was presumably because of the large number of deaths at this time that the Home Ministry decided in February 1886 to inform prison officials that they no longer needed to report them. *HBT* 57:265–66.

87. Cited in Shigematsu, *Zukan*, p. 111.

88. Tanaka, *Nihon shihon shugi to*, pp. 124, 129.

89. Ibid., pp. 126, 128.

90. Shigematsu, *Hokkaidō*, p. 247; Tanaka, *Nihon shihon shugi to*, pp. 126–27; Mitchell, *Janus-Faced Justice*, p. 21. See also Koike Yoshitaka, *Kusaritsuka: Jiyū minken to shūjin rōdō no kiroku* (Tokyo: Gendaishi shuppankai, 1973).

91. Kaneko Kentarō, "Hokkaidō sanken fukumei sho," 1885, official report, Tsukigata Kabato Museum. Cf. Shigematsu, *Zukan*, pp. 99–100; Mitchell, *Janus-Faced Justice*, 19.

92. Onoda Motohiro, *Taisei kangoku mondō roku* (Tokyo: Keishichō, 1889), ch. 2 ("Kangoku no shugi").

93. Ibid., ch. 2, p. 3.

94. Ibid., ch. 6, pp. 72–73. Cf. Onoda Motohiro, "Kangoku jigyō (2)," *Dai Nihon kangoku kyōkai zasshi* 5 (September 1888): 14.

95. Kobayakawa Kingo, *Meiji hōsei shiron kōhō no bu* (Tokyo: Ganshodō, 1943), 2:1175–78. Also Ogawa and Nakao, *Gyōkei kaikakusha*, p. 41.

96. *HBT* 57:162–88. Umemori offers an interesting analysis of the differences between the 1872 "Prison Rules" and the 1881 "Revised Prison Rules," suggesting that they can be understood in terms of an increasingly subjectivist approach to punishment. See Umemori, "Spatial Configuration," pp. 753–54.

97. Hirota Masaki, ed., *Sabetsu no shosō* (Tokyo: Iwanami shoten, 1990), pp. 420–22.

98. *NKGS* 2:568. See also Onoda, *Taisei kangoku*, ch. 2, p. 21, and Tezuka Yutaka, "Meiji nijūnen—zaiseki jiken no ichikōsatsu," in *MKK* 1:132.

99. The brick, which was later excavated from the Kabato Prison's sewerage system, is now on display at the Tsukigata Kabato museum.

100. Tezuka Yutaka, "Baba Tatsui 'Nihon kangoku ron' ni kan suru shin shiryō," in *MKK* 3:159–72. The article, titled "In a Japanese Cage," appeared in the *Evening Star* (Washington, D.C.) in June 1887. Cf. Mitchell, *Janus-Faced Justice*, p. 23.

101. *NKGS* 2:575, 617.

102. *NKGS* 2:445–48. Cf. Hirota, *Sabetsu*, pp. 403–4.

103. *NKGS* 2:587–88.

104. *HBT* 57:253–54.

105. *HBT* 57:265. Shigematsu, *Hokkaidō*, p. 189. The change may explain the drop in escape attempts from 1,269 in 1884 to 786 in 1886. See *NKGS* 2:575.

106. Hashimoto, "Miike kōzan," p. 58.

107. *NKGS* 2:58.

108. Maeda, *Toshi kūkan*, pp. 175–83; Umemori, "Spatial Configuration," pp. 764–65; and Hirota, *Sabetsu*, pp. 406–20.

109. The information in this paragraph is drawn primarily from Hara's own account of his life in Hara Taneaki and Osatake Takeshi, eds., *Edo jidai hanzai keibatsu jireishū* (1930; Tokyo: Kashiwa shobō, 1982), pp. 8–17. See also Mitchell, *Janus-Faced Justice*, p. 21

110. Ōkubo, *Berii-ō*, pp. 146–53.

111. Shigematsu, *Hokkaidō*, pp. 237–38. See also Misu Tatsuo, ed., *Hara Taneaki no Shibecha nikki to sono ashiato* (Kushiro: Kushiro Keimusho, 1998).

112. Shigematsu, *Hokkaidō*, pp. 261–63, 269.

113. For a fuller account of the background to this incident, see ibid., pp. 264–69.

114. Hiramatsu, "History of Penal Institutions: Japan," p. 44. On Tomeoka Kōsuke and social welfare projects in this period, see David Richard Ambaras, "Treasures of the Nation: Juvenile Delinquency, Socialization and Authority in Modern Japan, 1895–1945" (Ph.D. dissertation, Princeton University, 1999).

115. Tezuka, "Zaiseki jiken," pp. 90–106; Mitchell, *Janus-Faced Justice*, p. 21.

116. Tezuka, "Zaiseki jiken," pp. 106–22; *NKGS* 2:578–83.

117. Tezuka, "Zaiseki jiken," p. 110; *NKGS* 2:579–80.

118. Cited in Ignatieff, *Just Measure*, p. 177. For the direct link between the British cranks and treadmills and the Japanese "punishment rock," see Tezuka, "Zaiseki jiken," p. 133.

119. Jones, *Extraterritoriality in Japan*, p. 111.

120. Ogawa and Nakao, *Gyōkei kaikakusha*, pp. 49–50.

121. Ibid., p. 50.

122. Ugawa Seisaburō, "Dai Nihon kangoku kyōkai sōsetsu no shui," *Dai Nihon kangoku kyōkai zasshi* 1.1 (May 1889): 3.

123. *NKGS* 2:601–2.

124. Ibid. See also Hiramatsu Yoshirō, "Keibatsu no rekishi—Nihon," in *Keibatsu no riron to genjitsu*, ed. Shōji Kunio, Hitoshi Ōtsuka, and Hiromatsu Yoshirō (Tokyo: Iwanami shoten, 1972), p. 82.

125. *NKGS* 2:227–28.

126. *NKGS* 2:605–6.

127. Shigematsu, *Zukan*, pp. 72–90.

128. Ibid., pp. 68–69. As Judith Snodgrass has noted, Japan's participation at the Chicago Exposition was designed specifically to project an image of a "civilized" nation, and thereby help secure treaty revision. See her "Japan Faces the West: The Representation of Japan at the Columbian Exposition, Chicago 1893," in *Japanese Science, Technology and Economic Growth Down-Under*, ed. Morris Low and Helen Marriott (Clayton: Monash Asia Institute, 1996), pp. 5–8.

129. Shigematsu, "Ninsoku Yoseba to," pp. 368–70.

130. On Tsumaki Yorinaka, see Muramatsu Teijirō, *Nihon kindai kenchiku gijutsushi* (Tokyo: Shokokusha, 1976), pp. 47–48. For examples of his work, see Inagaki Eizō, *Nihon no kindai kenchiku—sono seiritsu katei* (Tokyo: Kajima shuppansha, 1979), 1:109–11.

131. *NKGS* 2:639.

132. Nihon kōgakkai, ed., *Meiji kōgyō shi Kenchiku hen* (Tokyo: Meiji kōgyōshi hakkō jo, 1930), pp. 245–46.

133. On Mutsu and treaty revision, see Louis G. Perez, *Japan Comes of Age: Mutsu Munemitsu and the Revision of the Unequal Treaties* (London: Associated University Presses, 1999).

134. The state of prisons in Japan was the last issue to be raised in the British Parliament concerning the revised treaties. It was brought up on at least two separate occasions in 1898 and 1899. *Hansard's Parliamentary Debates*, 4th ser. (London: Cornelius Buck, 1898), vol. 62, p. 1139 (House of Commons, July 25, 1898); 70, p. 527 (House of Commons, April 25, 1899).

135. Ogawa and Nakao, *Gyōkei kaikakusha*, p. 133.

CONCLUSION

1. W. E. Griffis, *The Mikado's Empire* (New York: Harper and Bros., 1890), pp. 568–69.

2. W. A. Pickering, *Pioneering in Formosa* (London: Hurst and Blackett, 1898), p. viii.

3. Onoda Motohiro, "Kushiro shūchikan secchi kenpakusho," unpublished report, 1884, Kyōsei toshokan, Tokyo.

4. On the convict leasing system and the use of prison labor in the southern United States, see Alex Lichtenstein, *Twice the Work of Free Labor: The Political Economy of Convict Labor in the New South* (London: Verso, 1996).

5. Bird, *Unbeaten Tracks*, p. 267. A. H. Savage Landor, *Alone with the Hairy Ainu; Or, 3,800 Miles on a Pack Saddle in Yezo and a Cruise to the Kurile Islands* (London: John Murray, 1893), p. 102.

6. Shigematsu, *Hokkaidō*, p. 271; Hiramatsu, "History of Penal Institutions: Japan," p. 42; Mitchell, *Janus-Faced Justice*, p. 22. The "great amnesty" of 1897 had a particularly dramatic impact in Hokkaidō, where a total of 2,495 prisoners were released and allowed to return to the mainland. For a time after this the Abashiri Prison had to be closed because of a lack of inmates.

7. On political repression in the 1920s and 1930s, see Mitchell, *Janus-Faced Justice*, pp. 36–154.

8. Tanaka Osamu, *Nihon shihon shugi to Hokkaidō*, pp. 135–41; Hashimoto Tetsuya, "Miike kōzan to shūjin rōdō," pp. 58–62; Yamada Moritarō, *Nihon shihon shugi bunsek—Nihon shihon shugi ni okeru saiseisan katei haaku* (Tokyo: Iwanami shoten, 1934), pp. 85–89. See also Sumiya Mikio, *Nihon chin rōdō no shiteki kenkyū* (Tokyo: Ochanomizu shobō, 1976), pp. 91–105.

9. On Korean forced labor, see Chōsenjin kyōsei renkō jittai chōsa hōkokusho henshū iinkai, ed., *Hokkaidō to Chōsenjin rōdōsha* (Ebetsu: Sapporo Gakuin Daigaku seikatsu kyōdō kumiai, 1999).

10. Two years later, in 1898, the Japanese imposed another unequal treaty, this time on the kingdom of Siam. See Jones, *Extraterritoriality in Japan*, p. 158.

11. For an even earlier example of Japan's "mimetic imperialism," see Robert Eskildsen, "Of Civilization and Savages: The Mimetic Imperialism of Japan's 1874 Expedition to Taiwan," *American Historical Review* 107.2 (April 2002): 388–424.

12. On diplomatic ties between Tokugawa Japan and Yi dynasty Korea, see Toby, *State and Diplomacy.* On the Sino-Japanese War and its impact on Japanese society, see Stewart Lone, *Japan's First Modern War: Army and Society in the Conflict with China, 1894–95* (New York: St. Martin's Press, 1994).

13. For Japanese expansion into Hokkaido, see Brett L. Walker, *The Conquest of Ainu Lands: Ecology and Culture in Japanese Expansion, 1590–1800* (Berkeley: University of California Press, 2001). On the Ryukyus, see Gregory Smits, *Visions of Ryukyu: Identity and Ideology in Early Modern Thought and Politics* (Honolulu: University of Hawai'i Press, 1999).

14. Fukuzawa Yūtarō, "Taiwan kangoku seido ni tai suru gaiken," *Dai Nihon kangoku kyōkai zasshi* 95 (April 25, 1896): 41.

15. Ibid., p. 42.

16. *TSKE* 2:53–55.

17. Hiyama Yukio, "Taiwan ni okeru kangoku seido no kakuritsu," in *Taiwan Sōtokufu bunsho mokuroku*, ed. Chūkyō Daigaku shakai kagaku kenkyū jo (Tokyo: Yumani shobō, 1993), p. 470. For more details, see Tay-Sheng Wang's impressive study, *Legal Reform in Taiwan under Japanese Colonial Rule, 1895–1945* (Seattle: University of Washington Press, 2000). For a broader perspective, see Edward I-te Chen, "The Attempt to Integrate the Empire: Legal Perspectives," in *The Japanese Colonial Empire, 1895–1945*, ed. Ramon H. Myers and Mark R. Peattie (Princeton: Princeton University Press, 1984), pp. 240–74.

18. Hiyama, "Taiwan ni okeru," pp. 470–74.

19. "Taihoku kangoku cho zaikansha," *Dai Nihon kangoku kyōkai zasshi* 100 (September 15, 1896): 55. Taiwan Sōtokufu Sōtoku kanbō bunsho ka, ed., *Taiwan Sōtokufu tōkei sho* 3 (Taihoku: Sōtoku kandō bunsho ka, 1900), p. 211 (#106).

20. For a translation of the ordinance, see Wang, *Legal Reform*, pp. 196–97.

21. Tsutsui Meirin, "Taiwan kangoku keikyō ni tsuite 1," *Kangoku kyōkai zasshi* 14.8 (August 1901): 31.

22. *TSKE* 2:264–65.

23. Ibid.

24. Pickering, *Pioneering in Formosa*, p. vii.

25. Hiyama, "Taiwan ni okeru," p. 490. Tejima Heijirō, "Taiwan kangoku dan 1," *Kangoku kyōkai zasshi* 18.4 (April 1905): 26.

26. The need for new prisons was also emphasized by the British adviser Montague Kirkwood in his recommendations to the Meiji government on Taiwan in 1898. See section 13 of "Taiwan ni kansuru oboegaki" (March 8, 1898) and section 3 of "Kaakuudo-shi Taiwan ni kansuru oboegaki setsumei hikki" (March 8, 1898), in Gotō Shimpei bunsho, Mizusawa shiritsu Gotōshimpei beinen han, R25 (7–33–2, 7–33–3). Thanks to Adam Clulow for this reference.

27. Tsutsui Meirin, "Taiwan kangoku keikyō ni tsuite 2," *Kangoku kyōkai zasshi* 14.9 (September 1901): 34–37. Cf. Hiyama, "Taiwan ni okeru," p. 507.

28. Tejima Heijirō, "Taiwan kangoku dan 1," p. 28. Smaller "branch prisons" were maintained at Shinchiku, Giran, and Kagi.

29. Yosaburo Takekoshi, *Japanese Rule in Formosa* (London: Longmans, Green, 1907), p. 194. Cf. Takekoshi Yosaburō, *Taiwan tōchi shi* (Tokyo: Hakubunkan, 1905), p. 319. For other glowing accounts of the prisons in Taiwan, see Owen Rutter, *Through Formosa: An Account of Japan's Island Colony* (London: T. F. Unwin, 1923), pp. 202–3; and Poultney Bigelow, *Japan and Her Colonies* (London: Edward Arnold, 1923), pp. 113–15.

30. Tejima, "Taiwan kangoku dan 1," pp. 28–29.

31. Tejima Heijirō, "Taiwan kangoku dan 2," *Kangoku kyōkai zasshi* 18.5 (May 1905): 17–23.

32. Takekoshi, *Japanese Rule*, p. 196.

33. Ibid.

34. On this general idea, see, for example, Bruce Cumings, *Korea's Place in the Sun* (New York: W. W. Norton, 1997), p. 149.

35. Timothy Mitchell, *Colonising Egypt* (Berkeley: University of California Press, 1991), p. xi. Cf. Cumings, *Korea's Place*, p. 149.

36. On queues and laziness, see Tsutsui, "Taiwan kangoku keikyō 2," pp. 25–27. On opium, see Tsutsui, "Taiwan kangoku keikyō 1," p. 32; and "Shūto kin'en no kekka," *Dai Nihon kangoku kyōkai zasshi* 102 (November 1896): 66.

37. Tsutsui, "Taiwan kangoku keikyō 2," p. 27.

38. The relevant law was the Fine and Flogging Ordinance issued on January 12, 1904, and first implemented in May of that year. As the name suggests, it also introduced a new system of fines to be levied exclusively on colonial subjects (*hontōjin* and *Shinkokujin*).

39. Wang, *Legal Reform*, p. 120. The original source of this explanation is Washinosu Atsuya, *Taiwan keisatsu shijūnen shiwa* (Taihoku: Washinosu Atsuya, 1938), pp. 269–73.

40. Odate Koretaka, "Chijōkei fukko sono ta ni kan suru iken," internal memo, July 31, 1903, in Gotō Shimpei bunsho R25 (7–81).

41. *TSKE* 4:908–9.

42. Taiwan Sōtokufu Sōtoku kanbō bunsho ka, *Taiwan Sōtokufu tōkei sho* 20 (1918), p. 290 (#236); *Taiwan Sōtokufu tōkei sho* 25 (1923), p. 252 (#231).

43. On the Kwantung Fine and Flogging Ordinance, see Okamoto Shigeshirō, "Manshūkoku-jin ni chikei o ka suru koto o eru ya," *Hōritsu shimbun* 4003 (July 8, 1936): 2–6. On flogging in colonial Korea, see Mori Tokujirō, "Chikei ni tsuite," in *Chikeiron* (Niida bunko, Tōyō bunka kenkyūjo, Tokyo University, F70/14), pp. 1–35; Edward J. Baker, "The Role of Legal Reforms in the Japanese Annexation and Rule of Korea, 1905–1919" in *Introduction to the Law and Legal System of Korea*, ed. Sang Hyun Song (Seoul: Kyung Mun Sa Publishing, 1983), pp. 201–2; Chulwoo Lee, "Modernity, Legality, and Power in Korea under Japanese Rule," in *Colonial Modernity in Korea*, ed. Gi-Wook Shin and Michael Robinson (Cambridge, Mass.: Harvard University Asia Center, 1999), pp. 31–34.

44. Mori, "Chikei ni tsuite," p. 8; Baker, "Role of Legal Reforms," p. 201.

45. Odate, "Chijōkei fukko."

46. The crux of Ogawa's argument was first published as a short, unattributed "opinion piece" under the title "Taiwan keiritsu no ue ni chijōkei saiyō no gi aru o

kikite shoken o nobu," in *Kangoku kyōkai zasshi* 17.1 (January 1904): 3–15. An expanded version then appeared in Ogawa's name as a sixty-two page pamphlet, "Chikeiron" (Law Faculty Library, Tokyo University, R961–2283-T, n.d.), which was reviewed in the *Kangoku kyōkai zasshi* in February 1904. The pamphlet version was then published in two parts in the *Hōgaku kyōkai zasshi* 22.4 (April 1904): 511–32; 22.5 (May 1904): 697–719. The summary that follows is based primarily on this final version, although due reference has been given to all three.

47. See note 4.

48. Tsurumi Yūsuke, *Gotō Shimpei den* (Tokyo: Gotō Shimpei-haku denki hensankai, 1937), 2:160. Cf. *TSKE* 4:901.

49. Wang, *Legal Reform*, p. 64.

50. With regard to Tejima's original proposal, dated July 25, 1903, see Odate, "Chijōkei fukko."

51. *TSKE* 4:906–7.

52. For the stipulation that the cane be applied to the buttocks, see Article 6 of the Taiwan ordinance.

53. Komagome Takeshi, *Shokuminchi teikoku Nihon no bunka tōgō* (Tokyo: Iwanami shoten, 1996), pp. 33–34.

54. Ibid., p. 34.

55. For the coining of this term by Hara Kei, see Komagome, *Shokuminchi teikoku*, pp. 32–33. See also Mark Peattie, "Japanese Attitudes toward Colonialism, 1895–1945," in Myers and Peattie, *Japanese Colonial Empire*, pp. 101–2.

56. "Hōri enshū kai kiji (Toku ni Taiwan no chikei ni kansuru Hozumi Nobushige hakase no iken)," *Hōgaku kyōkai zasshi* 22.3 (March 1904): 451–54.

57. Suzuki Sōgen, "Ogawa shi no chikeiron o yomu," *Hōgaku kyōkai zasshi* 22.6 (June 1904): 821–36; 22.7 (July 1904): 941–59. The article was republished in *Kangoku kyōkai zasshi* 17.8 (August 1904): 31–34; 17.9 (September 1904): 1–7.

58. Odate, "Chijōkei fukko."

59. Chakrabarty, *Provincializing Europe*, esp. p. 8; Mehta, *Liberalism and Empire*, esp. pp. 28–29.

60. On Lin, see Komagome, *Shokuminchi teikoku*, p. 136. For Korean nationalists, see, for example, Henry Chung, *The Case of Korea* (New York: Fleming H. Revell, 1921).

61. As Tessa Morris-Suzuki has noted, the idea that people on the geographical peripheries belonged to an earlier, less developed stage of history was one that also came to inform Meiji era thinking about the Ainu in the North, and the Ryukyuans in the South. This, no doubt, fed directly into the discourse on Taiwan and other parts of the expanding colonial empire in the twentieth century. See her *Re-Inventing Japan: Time, Space, Nation* (New York: M. E. Sharpe, 1998), pp. 23–34.

62. Takekoshi, *Japanese Rule*, p. 194.

63. Ibid., p. 195.

64. Takekoshi, *Taiwan tōchi shi*, p. 320.

65. In light of Ogawa's arguments, it is instructive to compare Takekoshi's views with those of the then governor of Alabama, Robert Patton, who argued that "the Negro needed different penalties because he simply did 'not regard confinement as punishment.'" Cited in David Oshinsky, *Worse Than Slavery: Parchman Farm and the Ordeal of Jim Crow Justice* (New York: Free Press, 1996), p. 83.

66. Baker, "Role of Legal Reforms," p. 201. Lee, "Modernity, Legality, and Power," p. 33. Although I agree with other parts of Lee's analysis, I do not accept his conclusion that the primary reason for the use of flogging in colonial Korea was "the inability of colonial subjects to adjust themselves to the mundane rhythms of a new kind of economy." To argue that flogging was deployed to make up for something that the Koreans "lacked" (i.e., time discipline) seems to me to come perilously close to replicating the developmentalist logic of the colonial authorities. But even more fundamentally, if the main concern of the Japanese authorities had really been to inure Korean workers to the "mundane rhythms" of capitalist production, then mass incarceration in modern disciplinary institutions would surely have been a more effective response than mass beatings. Lee is far closer to the mark when he notes that flogging served to mark Korean bodies as different, while also keeping the cost of punishment low and terrorizing the colonial population. Alexis Dudden's forthcoming work on law and the manipulation of legal discourse in colonial Korea promises to further enrich our understanding of these issues. See her *Japan's Colonization of Korea: Discourse and Power* (Honolulu: University of Hawai'i Press, forthcoming).

67. Mori, "Chikei ni tsuite," p. 27.

68. Griffis, *Mikado's Empire*, pp. 568–69.

69. Stefan Tanaka, *Japan's Orient: Rendering Pasts into History* (Berkeley: University of California Press, 1993).

70. Thomas Keirstead, "Inventing Medieval Japan: The History and Politics of National Identity," *Medieval History Journal* 1.1 (January–June 1998): 47–71.

71. Ibid., pp. 67–69.

72. Nakada Kaoru, "Ōchō jidai no shōen ni kansuru kenkyū" (1906), cited in ibid., p. 56.

73. Ibid., p. 58. Needless to say, this was not the first time that Japanese scholars had argued for the value of aspects of their premodern heritage. For an overview of early Meiji views of the Tokugawa past, see Carol Gluck, "The Invention of Edo" in *Mirrors of Modernity: Invented Traditions of Modern Japan*, ed. Stephen Vlastos (Berkeley: University of California Press, 1998), pp. 266–67. What was new, however, was that the Japanese past was now understood in direct parallel with the West. That is to say, the value of the past was now being consciously asserted in world historical rather than just national terms.

74. Asakawa Kan'ichi, *Early Institutional Life of Japan* (1903), cited in Keirstead, "Inventing," p. 59.

75. Cf. ibid., p. 62.

76. This, of course, fits with the classic pattern described by Edward Said in his *Orientalism* (New York: Random House, 1978). Unfortunately, as Andre Schmid has recently pointed out, English-language historians of Japan have been slow to explore the connections between the apparatus of colonial empire and the production of knowledge of Asia. See his "Colonialism and the 'Korea Problem' in the Historiography of Modern Japan," *Journal of Asian Studies* 59.4 (November 2000): 962–63. One possible starting point for such an exploration might be the Special Committee for the Investigation of Taiwan's Old Customs (*rinji Taiwan kyūkan chōsa kai*) established by Gotō Shimpei in 1901. The committee, which included Kyoto Imperial University professors Okamatsu Santarō and Oda Yorozu, was re-

sponsible for the production of a series of multivolume studies of law, society, and government, not only in Taiwan, but throughout the Qing empire, and thus contributed significantly to the development of modern "Sinology" in Japan. For a brief discussion, see Huang Zhaotang (Kō Shōdō), *Taiwan sōtokufu* (Tokyo: Iwanami bunko, 1981), pp. 78–79.

77. Shimada Masarō, "Shinmatsu no gokusei kaikaku to Ogawa Shigejirō," in *Meiji hōseishi seijishi no shomondai*, ed. Tezuka Yutaka kyōju taishoku kinen ronbun shū hansan iinkai (Tokyo: Keiō tsūshin, 1977), pp. 509–26. Ogawa and Nakao, *Gyōkei kaikaikusha*, pp. 124–25, 136–37; Dutton, *Policing and Punishment in China*, pp. 159–61; Dikötter, *Crime, Punishment and the Prison in Modern China*, pp. 50–53; Niida Noboru, *Chūgoku hōsei-shi* (Tokyo: Iwanami shoten, 1952), p. 90.

78. W.E.B. Du Bois, "The Color Line Belts the World," *Collier's Weekly* (October 20, 1906), reprinted in David Levering Lewis, ed., *W.E.B. Du Bois: A Reader* (New York: H. Holt, 1995), pp. 42–43. On the evolution of Du Bois' views on Asia, see Bill V. Mullen, "Du Bois, *Dark Princess*, and the Afro-Asian International," *Positions* 11.1 (spring 2003): 217–40.

79. Cited in Chung, *The Case of Korea*, p. 92. Cf. *New York Times*, July 13, 1919, p. 9.

80. Cited in Chung, *The Case of Korea*, p. 82.

81. For the abolition of flogging in Taiwan, see E. Patricia Tsurumi, *Japanese Colonial Education in Taiwan, 1895–1945* (Cambridge, Mass.: Harvard University Press, 1977), p. 93. For Korea, see Baker, "Role of Legal Reforms," p. 202.

82. Cited in Baker, "Role of Legal Reforms," p. 202.

83. For a critique of the use of flogging in the Kwantung territories in 1936, see Okamoto, "Manshūkoku-jin."

84. Yosaburo Takekoshi, *Self-Portrayal of Japan* (Tokyo: Ritsumeikan Press, 1939), p. 2.

85. Yosaburo Takekoshi, *The Economic Aspect of the History of Japan* (London: George Allen and Unwin, 1930), 3 vols.; Takekoshi, *Self-Portrayal*. See also his *Prince Saionji* (Kyoto: Ritsumeikan, 1936), and *The Story of the Wako: Japanese Pioneers in the Southern Region* (Tokyo: Kenkyusha, 1940). The connections between this last title and Japan's imperial project are, of course, obvious.

86. Takekoshi, *Self-Portrayal*, p. 5.

87. On the concept of "imperial fascism," see Andrew Gordon, *Labor and Imperial Democracy in Prewar Japan* (Berkeley: University of California Press, 1991).

88. See Tsuji Keisuke's introduction in *NKGS* 1:1. Also note the preface by Masaki Tōru, which was cut from later editions. The key term in this and all subsequent discussion of the Stockade is *jiyū kei*, which is a direct translation of the German term *freiheitstrafe*.

89. Ninsoku yoseba kenshōkai, ed., *Ninsoku yoseba shi*.

90. Tsukada, *Mibunsei shakai to shimin shakai*. See also chapter 4.

Bibliography

Gotō Shimpei bunsho, Mizusawa shiritsu Gotō Shimpei kinen kan, Mizusawa
Montague Kirkwood. "Kaakuudo-shi Taiwan ni kansuru oboegaki setsumei
hikki." March 8, 1898.
———. "Taiwan ni kansuru oboegaki." March 8, 1898.
Odate Koretaka. "Chijōkei fukko sono ta ni kan suru iken." July 31, 1903.

Hōsei Shiryōshitsu, Tokyo University
"Rōnai hijiroku."
"Rōya shiki, Asakusa tame, yōjōsho, Shinagawa tame hisho."

Kano bunko, Tōhoku University, Sendai
Nakai Riken, "Jukkei bōgi."

Kyōsei toshokan (Corrections Library), Tokyo
Onoda Motohiro. "Kushiro shūchikan secchi kenpakusho." 1884.

Kyū Bakufu hikitsugi sho, National Diet Library, Tokyo
"Mushuku karikomi ikken." 1839.

Law Faculty Library, Tokyo University
Ogawa Shigejirō. "Chikeiron." R961–2283-T.

Mōri ke monjō, Yamaguchi Prefectural Archive, Yamaguchi
"Zaikasatsu gaki."

National Archive of Japan, Tokyo
"Keibatsu daihiroku." Ca. 1819.
Wei Yuan (Gi Gen). *Amerika sōki.* Translated by Hirose Chikuan. 3 vols. 1854.

Niida bunko, Tōyō bunka kenkyūjo, Tokyo University
Chikeiron. F70/14.

Public Record Office, London
Hall, John Carey. "Mr. Hall's Report." October 20, 1871. Foreign Office 46–142.
Japan correspondence. ff. 204–16.

Rare books collection, Harvard-Yenching Library, Cambridge, Mass.
Wei Yuan (Gi Gen). *Tsūzoku kaikoku zushi Amerika shū no bu.* Translated by
Hirose Chikuan. 5 vols. Osaka: Akitaya Taemon, 1855.

Shizuoka Prefectural Library, Shizuoka.
"Tempō kirei." Ca. 1852.

Tsukigata Kabato Museum, Tsukigata (Hokkaido)
Kaneko Kentarō. "Hokkaidō sanken fukumei sho." 1885.
Tsukigata Kiyoshi. "Hokkai kaiyū ki." 1881.

OTHER WORKS CITED

Abe Akira. *Edo no autorō*. Tokyo: Kōdansha sensho mechie, 1999.

Abe Yoshio. *Meakashi Kinjirō no shōgai*. Tokyo: Chūkō shinsho, 1981.

Alcock, Rutherford. *The Capital of the Tycoon*. 2 vols. New York: Harper and Bros., 1863.

Ambaras, David Richard. "Treasures of the Nation: Juvenile Delinquency, Socialization and Authority in Modern Japan, 1898–1945." Ph.D. dissertation, Princeton University, 1999.

Amino Yoshihiko et al. *Chūsei no tsumi to batsu*. Tokyo: Tokyo Daigaku shuppankai, 1983.

Anderson, Clare. "The Genealogy of the Modern Subject: Indian Convicts in Mauritius, 1814–53." In *Representing Convicts: New Perspectives on Convict Forced Labour Migration*, edited by Ian Duffield and James Bradley, pp. 164–82. London: Leicester University Press, 1997.

Arai Hakuseki. *Lessons from History: The Tokushi Yoron*. Translated by Joyce Ackroyd. St. Lucia: University of Queensland Press, 1982.

Arnold, David. "The Colonial Prison: Power, Knowledge and Penology in Nineteenth Century India." *Subaltern Studies* 8 (1994): 43–77.

Asao Naohiro. "Kinsei no mibun to sono henyō." In *Nihon no Kinsei 7: Mibun to Kakushiki*, edited by Asao Naohiro, pp. 14–34. Tokyo: Chūō kōronsha, 1992.

Backus, Robert L. "The Kansei Prohibition of Heterodoxy and Its Effects on Education." *Harvard Journal of Asiatic Studies* 39.1 (June 1979): 55–106.

Baker, Edward J. "The Role of Legal Reforms in the Japanese Annexation and Rule of Korea, 1905–1919." In *Introduction to the Law and Legal System of Korea*, edited by Sang Hyun Song, pp. 185–212. Seoul: Kyung Mun Sa Publishing, 1983.

Barnett, Suzanne Wilson. "Protestant Expansion and Chinese Views of the West." *Modern Asian Studies* 6.2 (1972): 129–49.

———. "Wei Yüan and the Westerners: Notes on the Sources of the *Hai-kuo t'u chih*." *Ching-shih wen-t'i* 2.4 (November 1970): 1–20.

Beasley, W. G. *The Meiji Restoration*. Stanford: Stanford University Press, 1972.

———. *Select Documents on Japanese Foreign Policy, 1853–1868*. London: Oxford University Press, 1955.

Beattie, J. M. *Crime and the Courts in England, 1660–1800*. Oxford: Clarendon Press, 1986.

Beccaria, Cesare. *On Crimes and Punishments and Other Writings*. Edited by Richard Bellamy. Cambridge: Cambridge University Press, 1995.

Bellah, Robert. *Tokugawa Religion: The Values of Pre-Industrial Japan*. Glencoe, Ill.: Free Press, 1957.

Berry, Katherine. *A Pioneer Doctor in Old Japan*. New York: Fleming H. Revell Co., 1940.

Berry, Mary Elizabeth. *The Culture of Civil War in Kyoto*. Berkeley: University of California Press, 1994.

———. *Hideyoshi*. Cambridge, Mass.: Council on East Asian Studies, Harvard University, 1982.

———. "Public Life in Authoritarian Japan." *Daedalus* 127.3 (summer 1998): 133–65.

Bigelow, Poultney. *Japan and Her Colonies*. London: Edward Arnold, 1923.

Bird, Isabella. *Unbeaten Tracks in Japan*. London: John Murray, 1880.

Bitō Masahide. "Dazai Shundai no hito to shisō." In *Nihon shisō taikei 34: Sorai gakuha*, edited by Rai Tsutomu, pp. 487–514. Tokyo: Iwanami shoten, 1972.

Bix, H. *Peasant Protest in Japan, 1590–1884*. New Haven: Yale University Press, 1986.

Black, J. R. *Young Japan*. Vol. 1. London: Trubner, 1880.

Bodart-Bailey, B. "The Laws of Compassion." *Monumenta Nipponica* 40.2 (summer 1985): 163–89.

Bodde, Derk, and Clarence Morris. *Law in Imperial China Exemplified by 190 Ch'ing Dynasty Cases*. Cambridge, Mass.: Harvard University Press, 1967.

Boissonade, Gustave. *Boasonaado tōmonroku*. Tokyo: Hōsei Daigaku shuppankyoku, 1978.

Bolitho, Harold. "The Tempō Crisis." In Jansen, *The Emergence of Meiji Japan*, pp. 1–52.

————. *Treasures among Men: The Fudai Daimyo in Tokugawa Japan*. New Haven: Yale University Press, 1974.

Borton, H. *Peasant Uprisings in Japan of the Tokugawa Period*. New York: Paragon Book Reprints, 1968.

Botsman, D. V. "Punishment and Power in the Tokugawa Period." *East Asian History* 3 (June 1992): 1–32.

Bowen, Roger W. *Rebellion and Democracy in Meiji Japan*. Berkeley: University of California Press, 1980.

Boxer, C. R. *The Christian Century in Japan: 1549–1650*. Berkeley: University of California Press, 1951.

Braisted, William, trans. and ed. *Meiroku Zasshi: Journal of the Japanese Enlightenment*. Tokyo: University of Tokyo Press, 1976.

Brinkley, F. *A History of the Japanese People*. New York: Encyclopedia Brittanica, 1915.

Brown, Phillip. *Central Authority and Local Autonomy in the Formation of Early Modern Japan*. Stanford: Stanford University Press, 1993.

Burchell, Graham, Colin Gordon, and Peter Miller, eds. *The Foucault Effect: Studies in Governmentality*. Chicago: University of Chicago Press, 1991.

Burns, Susan L. "Tori tsukareta shintai kara kankin sareta shintai e." *Edo no shisō* 6 (May 1997): 48–62.

————. "Contemplating Places: The Hospital as Modern Experience in Meiji Japan." In Hardacre and Kern, *New Directions in the Study of Meiji Japan*, pp. 702–19.

Caron, Francis, and Joost Schorten. *A True Description of the Mighty Kingdoms of Japan and Siam*. Translated by Roger Manley. London: Samuel Brown and John de l'Eclufe, 1663.

Chang, Hsin-pao. *Commissioner Lin and the Opium War*. Cambridge, Mass.: Harvard University Press, 1964.

Charkrabarty, Dipesh. *Provincializing Europe: Postcolonial Thought and Historical Difference*. Princeton: Princeton University Press, 2000.

Chen, Edward I-te. "The Attempt to Integrate the Empire: Legal Perspectives." In Myers and Peattie, *The Japanese Colonial Empire, 1895–1945*, pp. 240–74.

Ch'en, Paul Heng-Chao. *The Formation of the Early Meiji Legal Order: The Japanese Code of 1871 and Its Chinese Foundation.* Oxford: Oxford University Press, 1981.

Chōsenjin kyōsei renkō jittai chōsa hōkokusho henshū iinkai, ed. *Hokkaidō to Chōsenjin rōdōsha.* Ebetsu: Sapporo Gakuin Daigaku seikatsu kyōdō kumiai, 1999.

Chung, Henry. *The Case of Korea.* New York: Fleming H. Revell, 1921.

Clark, Timothy. *Demon of Painting: The Art of Kawanabe Kyōsai.* London: British Museum Press, 1993.

Cooper, Michael, trans. and ed. *They Came to Japan: An Anthology of European Reports on Japan, 1543–1640.* Berkeley: University of California Press, 1965.

Cumings, Bruce. *Korea's Place in the Sun.* New York: W. W. Norton, 1997.

Dazai Shundai. *Keizairoku.* In *Nihon keizai taiten*, vol. 9, edited by Takimoto Seiichi, pp. 492–670. Tokyo: Meiji bunken, 1969.

Dikötter, Frank. *Crime, Punishment and the Prison in Modern China.* New York: Columbia University Press, 2002.

Dore, Ronald P. *Education in Tokugawa Japan.* Berkeley: University of California Press, 1965.

Drake, Fred W. *China Charts the World: Hsu Chi-yü and His Geography of 1848.* Cambridge, Mass.: East Asian Research Center, Harvard University, 1975.

Dudden, Alexis. *Japan's Colonization of Korea: Discourse and Power.* Honolulu: University of Hawai'i Press, forthcoming.

Dutton, Michael R. *Policing and Punishment in China: From Patriarchy to "the People."* Cambridge: Cambridge University Press, 1992.

Elison, George. *Deus Destroyed: The Image of Christianity in Early Modern Japan.* Cambridge, Mass.: Harvard University Press, 1973.

Emsley, Clive. *Crime and Society in England, 1750–1900.* 2nd ed. London: Longman, 1996.

Eskildsen, Robert. "Of Civilization and Savages: The Mimetic Imperialism of Japan's 1874 Expedition to Taiwan." *American Historical Review* 107.2 (April 2002): 388–424.

Fisch, Jörg. *Cheap Lives and Dear Limbs: The British Transformation of Bengal Criminal Law, 1769–1817.* Wiesbaden: Franz Steiner Verlag, 1983.

Fisher, Michael H. "Extraterritoriality: The Concept and Its Application in Princely India." *Indo-British Review* 15.2 (1988): 103–22.

Fletcher, Joseph. "The Heyday of the Qing Order in Mongolia, Sinkiang and Tibet." In *The Cambridge History of China*, edited by Denis Twitchett and John K. Fairbank, 10:351–408. Cambridge: Cambridge University Press, 1978.

Foucault, Michel. *Discipline and Punish: The Birth of the Prison.* Translated by Alan Sheridan. London: Peregrine Books, 1979.

———. "Governmentality." In Burchell, Gordon, and Miller, *The Foucault Effect*, pp. 87–104.

———. *Power/Knowledge: Selected Interviews and Other Writings, 1972–1977.* Edited by Colin Gordon. Sussex: Harvester Press, 1980.

Fraser, Andrew. "Town-Ward Administration in Eighteenth-Century Edo." *Papers in Far Eastern History* 27 (March 1984): 110–45.

Fujimori Terunobu. *Meiji no Tōkyō keikaku.* Tokyo: Iwanami shoten, 1982.

Fujita Satoru. *Tempō no kaikaku.* Tokyo: Yoshikawa kōbunkan, 1999.

———. *Tōyama Kinshirō no jidai.* Tokyo: Azekura shobō, 1992.

Fujitani, Takashi. "*Go for Broke*, the Movie: Japanese-American Soldiers in U.S. National, Military and Racial Discourses." In *Perilous Memories: The Asia-Pacific War(s)*, edited by T. Fujitani, Geoffrey M. White, and Lisa Yoneyama, pp. 239–66. Durham: Duke University Press, 2001.

———. "*Minshūshi* as Critique of Orientalist Knowledges." *positions* 6.2 (fall 1998): 301–22.

———. *Splendid Monarchy: Power and Pageantry in Modern Japan*. Berkeley: University of California Press, 1996.

Fukaya Katsumi. *Hyakusho naritachi*. Tokyo: Hanawa shobō, 1993.

———. "Kōgi to mibunsei." In *Taikei Nihon kokka-shi: Kinsei*, edited by Hora Hidesaburō et al., 3:149–88. Tokyo: Tokyo Daigaku shuppankai, 1975.

Fukuzawa Yukichi, "Kyōto Gakkō no ki." In *Fukuzawa Yukichi on Education*, translated by Eiichi Kiyooka, pp. 73–79. Tokyo: University of Tokyo Press, 1985.

Fukuzawa Yūtarō. "Taiwan kangoku seido ni tai suru gaiken." *Dai Nihon kangoku kyōkai zasshi* 95 (April 25, 1896): 41–44.

Gaimusho chōsabu, ed. *Nihon gaikō monjo*. Vol. 3. Tokyo: Gaimusho, 1919.

Gluck, Carol. "The Invention of Edo." In *Mirrors of Modernity: Invented Traditions of Modern Japan*, edited by Stephen Vlastos, pp. 262–84. Berkeley: University of California Press, 1998.

Gordon, Andrew. *Labor and Imperial Democracy*. Berkeley: University of California Press, 1991.

Griffis, W. E. *The Mikado's Empire*. New York: Harper and Bros., 1890.

Groemer, Gerald. "The Creation of the Edo Outcaste Order." *Journal of Japanese Studies* 27.2 (summer 2001): 263–93.

Haley, John. *Authority without Power: Law and the Japanese Paradox*. Oxford: Oxford University Press, 1991.

Hall, John C. *Japanese Feudal Laws*. Reprint. Washington, D.C.: University Publications of America, 1979.

Hall, John W. "Rule by Status in Tokugawa Japan." *Journal of Japanese Studies* 1.1 (autumn 1974): 39–50.

———. *Tanuma Okitsugu (1719–1788): Forerunner of Modern Japan*. Cambridge, Mass.: Harvard University Press, 1955.

Hara Taneaki and Osatake Takeki, eds. *Edo jidai hanzai keibatsu jireishū*. 1930. Tokyo: Kashiwa shobō, 1982.

Hardacre, Helen, and Adam Kern, eds. *New Directions in the Study of Meiji Japan*. Leiden: Brill, 1997.

Harootunian, H. D. "Late Tokugawa Culture and Thought." In Jansen, *The Emergence of Meiji Japan*, pp. 53–143.

———. *Overcome by Modernity: History, Culture and Community in Interwar Japan*. Princeton: Princeton University Press, 2000.

———. *Things Seen and Unseen: Discourse and Ideology in Tokugawa Nativism*. Chicago: University of Chicago Press, 1988.

———. *Toward Restoration: The Growth of Political Consciousness in Tokugawa Japan*. Berkeley: University of California Press, 1970.

Hasegawa Noboru. *Bakuto to jiyū minken*. Tokyo: Heibonsha Library, 1995.

Hashimoto Tetsuya. "Miike kōzan to shūjin rōdō." *Shakai keizai shigaku* 32.4 (1967): 31–62.

Hatanaka Toshiyuki. "Mibun o koeru toki." In *Mibunteki shūen*, edited by Tsukada Takashi, Yoshida Nobuyuki, and Wakita Osamu, pp. 282–324. Tokyo: Buraku mondai kenkyūjo, 1994.

Hauser, William. *Economic Institutional Change in Tokugawa Japan: Osaka and the Kinai Cotton Trade.* Cambridge: Cambridge University Press, 1974.

Havens, Thomas. *Nishi Amane and Modern Japanese Thought.* Princeton: Princeton University Press, 1970.

Hawks, F. L. *Narrative of the Expedition of an American Squadron to the China Seas and Japan.* Vol. 1. New York, 1857.

Hay, Douglas. "Property, Authority and the Criminal Law." In Hay et al., *Albion's Fatal Tree*, pp. 17–64.

Hay, Douglas, et al., eds. *Albion's Fatal Tree: Crime and Society in Eighteenth-Century England.* London: Peregrine, 1977.

Hayashi Jussai et al., eds. *Kansei chōshū shokafu.* 1812. Vols. 9, 11. Tokyo: Zoku gunshōruijū kanseikai, 1964.

Henderson, Dan Fenno. "Chinese Legal Studies in Early Eighteenth Century Japan: Scholars and Sources." *Journal of Japanese Studies* 30.1 (November 1970): 21–56.

———. *Conciliation and Japanese Law: Tokugawa and Modern.* 2 vols. Seattle: University of Washington Press, 1965.

———. "Introduction to the Kujikata Osadamegaki (1742)." In Hiramatsu, *Hō to keibatsu no rekishiteki kōsatsu*, pp. 489–544.

Hesselink, Reinier H. *Prisoners from Nambu: Reality and Make-Believe in Seventeenth-Century Japanese Diplomacy.* Honolulu: University of Hawai'i Press, 2002.

Hiramatsu Yoshirō. "Bakumatsu ki ni okeru hanzai to keibatsu no jittai." *Kokka gakkai zasshi* 71.3 (March 1957): 76–130.

———. *Edo no tsumi to batsu.* Tokyo: Heibonsha, 1988.

———. "History of Penal Institutions: Japan." *Law in Japan* 6.1 (1973): 1–48.

———. "Keibatsu no rekishi—Nihon." In *Keibatsu no riron to genjitsu*, edited by Shōji Kunio, Hitoshi, Ōtsuka and Hiramatsu Yoshirō, pp. 31–93. Tokyo: Iwanami shoten, 1972.

———. *Kinsei keiji soshō-hō no kenkyū.* Tokyo: Sōbunsha, 1960.

———. "Ninsoku yoseba no seiritsu 1." *Nagoya Daigaku Hōsei Ronshū* 33 (1965): 1–35.

———. "Ninsoku yoseba no seiritsu 2." *Nagoya Daigaku Hōsei Ronshū* 34 (1966): 94–130.

———. "Ninsoku yoseba no seiritsu to hensen." In *Ninsoku yoseba shi*, edited by Ninsoku yoseba kenshōkai, pp. 83–132. Tokyo: Sōbunsha, 1974.

Hiramatsu Yoshirō hakase tsuitō ronbunshū henshū iinkai, ed. *Hō to keibatsu no rekishiteki kōsatsu.* Nagoya: Nagoya Daigaku shuppankai, 1987.

Hirota Masaki. "Bunmei kaika no jendaa: 'Takahashi Oden' monogatari o megutte." *Edo no shisō* 6 (May 1997): 79–95.

———. ed. *Sabetsu no shosō.* Tokyo: Iwanami shoten, 1990.

Hitomi Tonomura. *Community and Commerce in Late Medieval Japan: The Corporate Villages of Tokuchin-ho.* Stanford: Stanford University Press, 1992.

———. "Sexual Violence against Women: Legal and Extralegal Treatment in Premodern Warrior Societies." In Tonomura, Walthall, and Haruko, *Women and Class in Japanese History*, pp. 135–52.

Hiyama Yukio. "Taiwan ni okeru kangoku seido no kakuritsu." In *Taiwan Sōtokufu bunsho mokuroku*, edited by Chūkyō Daigaku shakai kagaku kenkyū jo, pp. 465–516. Tokyo: Yumani shobō, 1993.

Hoare, J. E. *Japan's Treaty Ports and Foreign Settlements*. Sandgate: Japan Library, 1994.

Hobsbawn, E. J. *The Age of Extremes: A History of the World, 1914–1991*. New York: Pantheon, 1994.

———. *Primitive Rebels*. Manchester: Manchester University Press, 1959.

"Hōri enshū kai kiji (Toku ni Taiwan no chikei ni kansuru Hozumi Nobushige hakase no iken)." *Hōgaku kyōkai zasshi* 22.3 (March 1904): 451–54.

Hosokawa Junjirō et al., eds. *Koji ruien hōritsu no bu*. 3 vols. Tokyo: Jingu shichō, 1902.

Howell, David L. *Capitalism from Within: Economy, Society and the State in a Japanese Fishery*. Berkeley: University of California Press, 1995.

———. "Mapping Political Space in the Kantō." Paper presented at the Association of Asian Studies Conference, Washington, D.C., 1988.

———. "Private Violence and Public Virtue in Late Tokugawa Japan." Paper presented at the Princeton University Conference on Premodern Japanese Social History, Princeton, 1995.

———. "Territoriality and Collective Identity in Early Modern Japan." *Daedalus* 12.3 (summer 1998): 105–32.

Hozumi Nobushige. *Hōsō yawa*. Tokyo: Iwanami shoten, 1980.

Huang Zhaotang (Kō Shōdō). *Taiwan sōtokufu*. Tokyo: Iwanami bunko, 1981.

Ignatieff, Michael. *A Just Measure of Pain: The Penitentiary in the Industrial Revolution, 1750–1850*. London: Macmillan, 1978.

Ikegami, Eiko. *The Taming of the Samurai: Honorific Individualism and the Making of Modern Japan*. Cambridge, Mass.: Harvard University Press, 1995.

Imaoka Kentarō. "Meiji jūnen dai no Mokuami—'Shisenryō koban ume no ha' o chūshin ni." *Edo bungaku* 21 (1999): 100–112.

Inagaki Eizō. *Nihon no kindai kenchiku—sono seiritsu katei*. Vol. 1. Tokyo: Kajima shuppansha, 1979.

Innes, Joanna. "Prisons for the Poor: English Bridewells, 1555–1800." In *Labour, Law and Crime in Historical Perspective*, edited by D. Hay and F. Snyder, pp. 42–122. London: Blackwell, 1987.

Innes, Joanna, and John Styles. "The Crime Wave: Recent Writing on Crime and Criminal Justice in Eighteenth Century England." *Journal of British Studies* 25.4 (October 1986): 380–435.

Inoue Kiyoshi. *Jōyaku kaisei: Meiji no minzoku mondai*. Tokyo: Iwanami shoten, 1955.

Inoue Kowashi. "Shihōsho kaikaku iken." In *Inoue Kowashi den shiryō hen*, ed. Inoue Kowashi denki hensan iinkai, 1:54–55. Tokyo: Kokugakuin Daigaku toshokan, 1966.

Ishii Ryōsuke. *Edo no keibatsu*. Tokyo: Chūō kōronsha, 1964.

Ishii Ryōsuke. "Nihon keibatsu shi jō ni okeru ninsoku yoseba no ichi." In Ninsoku, *Ninsoku yoseba shi*, pp. 3–56.

———, ed. *Tokugawa kinreikō (kōshū)*. 4 vols. with 1 appendix vol. Tokyo: Sōbunsha, 1959–61.

———, ed. *Oshioki Reiruishū*. 16 vols. Tokyo: Meicho shuppan, 1971.

———, ed. *Tokugawa kinreikō (zenshū)*. 6 vols. Tokyo: Sōbunsha, 1959–61.

Ishii Ryōsuke and Harafuji Hiroshi, eds. *Bakumatsu ofuregaki shūsei*. Vol. 5. Tokyo: Iwanami shoten, 1992.

Ishii Shirō and Mizubayashi Takeshi, eds. *Hō to chitsujō*. Tokyo: Iwanami shoten, 1992.

Ishii Takashi. "Kōbe jiken." In *Kokushi daijiten*, edited by Kokushi daijiten henshū iinkai, 5:515. Tokyo: Yoshikawa kōbunkan, 1985.

———. *Zōtei Meiji ishin no kokusateki kankyō*. Tokyo: Yoshikawa kōbunkan, 1966.

Ishikawa Junkichi. *Edo jidai daikan seido no kenkyū*. Tokyo: Yoshikawa kōbunkan, 1963.

Iyoku Hideaki. "Fujita Shintarō hen ga 'Tokugawa bakufu keiji zufu' (fukkoku to kaisetsu)." *Meiji daigaku hakubutsukan hōkoku* 4 (March 1999): 49–104.

———, ed. *Hōsei shiryō kenkyū 1*. Tokyo: Gannandō, 1994.

Jansen, Marius B., ed. *The Emergence of Meiji Japan*. Cambridge: Cambridge University Press, 1995.

Johnston, Norman, Kenneth Finkel, and Jeffrey A. Cohen. *Eastern State Penitentiary: Crucible of Good Intentions*. Philadelphia: Philadelphia Museum of Art, 1994.

Jones, F. C. *Extraterritoriality in Japan*. New Haven: Yale University Press, 1931.

Kaempher, Engelbert. *Kaempher's Japan: Tokugawa Culture Observed*. Translated and annotated by Beatrice M. Bodart-Bailey. Honolulu: University of Hawai'i Press, 1999.

Kanzaki Naomi. "Tsuchiura han tokei sho kō." *Kokugakuin Daigaku Nihon bunka kenkyū shohō* 32.3 (September 1995): 3–6.

Kasaya Kazuhiko. "Bushi no mibun to kakushiki." In *Nihon no kinsei 7: Mibun to kakushiki*, edited by Asao Naohiro, pp. 179–224. Tokyo: Chūō kōronsha, 1992.

Katō Hideaki. "Bakumatsu Meiji ryōji saiban ni okeru keibatsu." In Hiramatsu, *Hō to keibatsu no rekishiteki kōsatsu*, pp. 171–94.

Katō Takashi. "Governing Edo." In McClain, Merriman, and Ugawa, *Edo and Paris*, pp. 41–67.

Katō Yasuaki. *Nihon mōnin shakaishi kenkyū*. Tokyo: Miraisha, 1974.

Katō Yōko. *Chōheisei to kindai Nihon*. Tokyo: Yoshikawa kōbunkan, 1996.

Katsu Kokichi. *Musui's Story: The Autobiography of a Tokugawa Samurai*. Translated by Teruko Craig. Tuscon: University of Arizona Press, 1995.

Katsumata Shizuo. "Mimi o kiri, hana o sogu." In *Chūsei no tsumi to batsu*, edited by Amino Yoshihiko et al., pp. 27–42. Tokyo: Tokyo Daigaku shuppankai, 1983.

Kawatake Mokuami. "Shisenryō koban no ume no ha." In *Meisaku kabuki zenshū*, edited by Toita Yasuji et al., 12:65–124. Tokyo: Tōkyō sōgensha, 1970.

Keene, Donald. *The Japanese Discovery of Europe, 1720–1830*. Rev. ed. Stanford: Stanford University Press, 1969.

Keirstead, Thomas. "Inventing Medieval Japan: The History and Politics of National Identity." *Medieval History Journal* 1.1 (January–June 1998): 47–71.

Kelly, William W. *Deference and Defiance in Nineteenth-Century Japan*. Princeton: Princeton University Press, 1985.

———. "Incendiary Actions: Fires and Firefighting in the Shogun's Capital and the People's City." In McClain, Merriman, and Ugawa, *Edo and Paris*, pp. 310–31.

Kikuchi Isao. *Kikin no shakaishi*. Tokyo: Azekura shobō, 1994.

Kikuyama Masaaki. *Meiji kokka no keisei to shihō seido*. Tokyo: Ochanomizu shobō, 1993.

Kinoshita Yasuko, *Kindai Nihon kangoshi*. Tokyo: Meijikaru fuurendo sha, 1974.

Kinsei shiryō kenkyūkai, ed. *Shōhō jiroku*. Vol. 2. Tokyo: Nihon gakujitsu shinkōkai, 1966.

Kobayakawa Kingo. *Meiji hōsei shiron kōhō no bu*. Vol. 2. Tokyo: Ganshodō, 1943.

Kobayashi Ikeda, Masako. "French Legal Advisor in Meiji Japan: Gustave Emile Boissonade de Fontarabie." Ph.D. dissertation, University of Hawai'i, 1996.

Kobayashi Yoshinobu. "Meiji ishin to keihō no sentei." *Hōgaku ronsō* 48.5 (1943): 810–48.

Kobori Kazumasa, Yamanaka Hiroyuki, Kaji Nobuyuki, and Inoue Akihiro. *Sōsho Nihon no shisōka 24: Nakai Chikuzan, Nakai Riken*. Tokyo: Meitoku shuppansha, 1980.

Koike Yoshitaka. *Kusaritsuka: Jiyū minken to shūjin rōdō no kiroku*. Tokyo: Gendaishi shuppankai, 1973.

Komagome Takeshi. *Shokuminchi teikoku Nihon no bunka tōgō*. Tokyo: Iwanami shoten, 1996.

Koo, Vi Kyuin Wellington. *The Status of Aliens in China*. New York: Columbia University Press, 1912.

Kuhn, Philip. *Soulstealers: The Chinese Sorcery Scare of 1768*. Cambridge, Mass.: Harvard University Press, 1990.

Kumagai Masakichi. *Kabato kangoku*. Sapporo: Hokkaidō shimbunsha, 1992.

Kume Kunitake. *Tokumei zenken taishi beiō kairan jikki*. Vol. 1. Tokyo: Iwanami shoten, 1985.

Kuroda Hideo. *Kyōkai no chūsei, shōchō no chūsei*. Tokyo: Tokyo Daigaku shuppankai, 1986.

Kuroda Toshio. *Rekishigaku no saisei: Chūsei shi o kumi naosu*. Tokyo: Azekura shobō, 1983.

Kusaka Genzui. "Shisai takuroku." 1859. In *Sabetsu no shosō*, edited by Hirota Masaki, pp. 431–33. Tokyo: Iwanami shoten, 1991.

Kyū Tōkyō Teikoku Daigaku shidankai, ed. *Kyūjishimonroku*. 1891–92. Reprint. Tokyo: Seiabō, 1998.

Landor, A. H. Savage. *Alone with the Hairy Ainu; Or, 3,800 Miles on a Pack Saddle in Yezo and a Cruise to the Kurile Islands*. London: John Murray, 1893.

Leavell, J. "The Development of the Modern Japanese Police System." Ph.D. dissertation, Duke University, 1975.

———. "The Policing of Society." In *Japan in Transition: Thought and Action in the Meiji Era, 1868–1912*, edited by Hilary Conroy, Sandra T. W. Davis, and Wayne Patterson, pp. 2–49. Rutherford: Fairleigh Dickinson University Press, 1984.

Lee, Chulwoo. "Modernity, Legality, and Power in Korea under Japanese Rule." In *Colonial Modernity in Korea*, edited by Gi-Wook Shin and Michael Robinson, pp. 21–51. Cambridge, Mass.: Harvard University Asia Center, 1999.

Legge, J., trans. *The Chinese Classics*. Vol. 3. Oxford: Oxford University Press, 1895.

——. *The Works of Mencius*. Reprint. New York: Dover Publications, 1970.

Leiter, Samuel L., ed. *Kabuki Encyclopedia*. Westport: Greenwood Press, 1979.

Leonard, Jane Kate. *Wei Yuan and China's Rediscovery of the Maritime World*. Cambridge, Mass.: Council on East Asian Studies, Harvard University, 1984.

Leupp, Gary P. "The Five Men of Naniwa: Gang Violence and Popular Culture in Genroku Osaka." In *Osaka: The Merchants' Capital of Early Modern Japan*, edited by James L. McClain and Wakita Osamu, pp. 125–57. Ithaca: Cornell University Press, 1999.

——. *Servants, Shophands and Laborers in the Cities of Tokugawa Japan*. Princeton: Princeton University Press, 1992.

Lewis, David Levering, ed. *W.E.B. Du Bois: A Reader*. New York: H. Holt, 1995.

Lewis, William S., and Naojiro Murakami, eds. *Ranald MacDonald: The Narrative of His Life, 1824–94*. Portland: Oregon Historical Society, 1990.

Lichtenstein, Alex. *Twice the Work of Free Labor: The Political Economy of Convict Labor in the New South*. London: Verso, 1996.

Lidin, Olof G. *The Life of Ogyū Sorai: A Tokugawa Confucian Philosopher*. Lund: Studentlitteratur, 1973.

Linebaugh, P. *The London Hanged: Crime and Civil Society in the Eighteenth Century*. London: Penguin, 1991.

——. "The Tyburn Riot against the Surgeons." In Hay et al., *Albion's Fatal Tree*, pp. 65–118.

Lone, Stewart. *Japan's First Modern War: Army and Society in the Conflict with China, 1894–95*. New York: St. Martin's Press, 1994.

Lyman, Abbot. "Pictures of the Japanese." *Harper's New Monthly Magazine* 39.231 (August 1869): 305–22.

Mabuchi Miho. "Maruyama Ōkyo hitsu 'Nanfuku zukan' ni tsuite.'" *Bijutsushi* 47.1 (October 1997): 65–81.

Maeda Ai. *Toshi kūkan no naka no bungaku*. Tokyo: Chikuma shobō, 1982.

Maki Kenji. "Higo-han keihō sōsho no seiritsu." *Hōgaku ronsō* 48.5 (1943): 701–47.

Makihara Norio. *Kyakubun to kokumin no aida: Kindai minshū no seiji ishiki*. Tokyo: Yoshikawa kōbunkan, 1998.

Marran, Christine. "'Poison Woman' Takahashi Oden and the Spectacle of Female Deviance in Early Meiji." *U.S.-Japan Women's Journal, English Supplement* 9 (1995): 93–110.

Marshall, P. J., and Glyndwr Williams. *The Great Map of Mankind: British Perceptions of the World in the Age of Enlightenment*. London: J. M. Dent & Sons, 1982.

Maruyama Tadatsuna. "Kayakugata ninsoku yoseba ni tsuite 1." *Hōsei shigaku* 7 (1955): 1–19.

——. "Kayakugata ninsoku yoseba ni tsuite 2." *Hōsei shigaku* 8 (1956): 23–49.

——. "Kayakugata ninsoku yoseba ni tsuite 3." *Hōsei shigaku* 9 (1957): 1–36.

——. "Kayakugata ninsoku yoseba ni tsuite 4." *Hōsei shigaku* 10 (1958): 44–80.

Masuda Wataru. *Japan and China: Mutual Representations in the Modern Era*. Translated by Joshua A. Fogel. Richmond, Surrey: Curzon Press, 2000.

Masur, Louis P. *Rites of Execution: Capital Punishment and the Transformation of American Culture, 1776–1865.* Oxford: Oxford University Press, 1989.

Matano Hansuke. *Etō Nanpaku.* 2 vols. Tokyo: Minyūsha, 1914.

Matsudaira Sadanobu. *Uge no hitogoto, Shūgyōroku.* 1816. Tokyo: Iwanami shoten, 1942.

Matsumoto Ryōta. "Hitoyado." In *Iwanami kōza Nihon tsūshi 15*, edited by Asao Naohiro et al., pp. 315–32. Tokyo: Iwanami shoten, 1995.

Matsura Seizan. *Kasshiyawa.* ca. 1821. Vol. 2. Tokyo: Heibonsha, 1977.

———. *Kasshiyawa zokuhen.* ca. 1832. Vol. 3. Tokyo: Kokusho kankōkai, 1911.

McClain, J., and J. M. Merriman. "Edo and Paris: Cities and Power." In McClain, Merriman, and Ugawa, *Edo and Paris*, pp. 3–40.

McClain, J., J. M. Merriman, and Ugawa Kaoru, eds. *Edo and Paris: Urban Life and the State in the Early Modern Era.* Ithaca: Cornell University Press, 1994.

McClintock, Anne. *Imperial Leather: Race, Gender and Sexuality in the Colonial Contest.* New York: Routledge, 1995.

McEwan, J. R., ed. *The Political Writings of Ogyū Sorai.* Cambridge: Cambridge University Press, 1962.

McGowen, Randall. "Civilizing Punishment: The End of the Public Execution in England." *Journal of British Studies* 33 (July 1994): 257–82.

———. "A Powerful Sympathy: Terror, the Prison, and Humanitarian Reform in Early Nineteenth-Century Britain." *Journal of British Studies* 25.3 (July 1986): 312–34.

McKnight, Brian E. *The Quality of Mercy: Amnesties and Traditional Chinese Justice.* Honolulu: University of Hawai'i Press, 1981.

McNair, J.F.A., and W. D. Bayliss. *Prisoners Their Own Warders: A Record of the Convict Prison at Singapore in the Straits Settlements Established 1825, Discontinued 1873.* Westminster: Archibald Constable, 1899.

Mega Atsuko. *Hankachō no naka no onna tachi.* Tokyo: Heibonsha, 1995.

Mehta, Uday Singh. *Liberalism and Empire: A Study in Nineteenth-Century British Liberal Thought.* Chicago: University of Chicago Press, 1999.

Meranze, Michael. *Laboratories of Virtue: Punishment, Revolution and Authority in Philadelphia, 1760–1835.* Chapel Hill: University of North Carolina Press, 1996.

Mills, D. E. "Kataki-uchi: The Practice of Blood-Revenge in Pre-Modern Japan." *Modern Asian Studies* 10.4 (1976): 525–42.

Minami Denmachō nanushi Takano-ke nikki gonjo no hikae. 1700–1712. Tokyo: Tokyo-to, 1995.

Minami Kazuo. *Edo no shakai kōzō.* Tokyo: Hanawa shobō, 1969.

———. "Takano Chōei no datsugoku." *Nihon rekishi* 244 (September 1968): 128–30.

Minegishi Kentarō. "Edo ni okeru 'hinin' shihai no kakuritsu." *Jinbun gakuhō* 114 (1976): 23–57.

Mishima Masayuki, ed. *Gofunai bikō.* 1846. Vol. 1. Tokyo: Yūzankaku, 1963.

Misu Tatsuo, ed. *Hara Taneaki no Shibecha nikki to sono ashiato.* Kushiro: Kushiro Keimusho, 1998.

Mitamura Engyo. *Engyo Edo bunkō 6: Edo no shiranami.* Edited by Asakura Haruhiko. Tokyo: Chūō kōronsha, 1997.

Mitchell, Richard H. *Janus-Faced Justice: Political Criminals in Imperial Japan*. Honolulu: University of Hawai'i Press, 1992.

Mitchell, Timothy. *Colonizing Egypt*. Berkeley: University of California Press, 1991.

Miura Shūkō. *Hōseishi no kenkyū*. 2 vols. Tokyo: Iwanami shoten, 1919.

Miyamoto Mataji. *Ōsaka*. Tokyo: Shibundō, 1957.

Miyatake Gaikotsu. *Shikei ruisan*. 1922. Reprinted in *Miyatake Gaikotsu chosakushū*, edited by Tanizawa Eiichi and Yoshino Takao, 4:455–606. Tokyo: Kawade shobō shinsho, 1985.

Mizumoto Kunihiko. "Kōgi no saiban to shūdan no okite." In *Saiban to kihan: Nihon no shakaishi 6*, edited by Yamaguchi Keiji, pp. 283–316. Tokyo: Iwanami shoten, 1987.

Montesquieu, Charles de Secondat. *The Spirit of the Laws*. Edited by Anne Cohler, Basia Miller, and Harold Stone. Cambridge: Cambridge University Press, 1995.

Mori Ogai. *The Incident at Sakai and Other Stories: The Historical Fiction of Mori Ogai*. Translated and edited by David Dilworth and J. Thomas Rimer. Honolulu: University of Hawai'i Press, 1977.

Mori Tokujirō. "Chikei ni tsuite." In *Chikeiron*, pp. 1–35. Pamphlet. Niida Bunko, Tōyō bunka kenkyūjo, Tokyo University. No date.

Mōri Toshihiko. *Etō Shimpei*. Tokyo: Chūkō shinsho, 1987.

Morohashi Tetsuji. *Daikanwa jiten*. 13 vols. Tokyo: Taishūkan shoten, 1989–1990.

Morris-Suzuki, Tessa. *Re-Inventing Japan: Time, Space, Nation*. New York: M. E. Sharpe, 1998.

Mullen, Bill V. "Du Bois, *Dark Princess*, and the Afro-Asian International." *Positions* 11.1 (spring 2003): 217–40.

Murai Toshikuni. "'Osorosha' Suzugamori." *Hōgaku seminaa* 527 (November 1998): 90–103.

Muramatsu Teijirō. *Nihon kindai kenchiku gijutsushi*. Tokyo: Shokokusha, 1976.

Myers, Ramon H., and Mark R. Peattie, eds. *The Japanese Colonial Empire, 1895–1945*. Princeton: Princeton University Press, 1984.

Nagahara Keiji. "The Medieval Origins of the *Eta-Hinin*." *Journal of Japanese Studies* 5.2 (summer 1979): 385–403.

Naikaku kiroku kyoku, ed. *Hōki bunrui taizen*. 1890. Tokyo: Hara Shobō, 1980.

Naikaku tōkei kyoku, ed. *Nihon teikoku tōkei nenkan*. Tokyo: Naikaku tōkei kyoku, 1882–.

Najita, Tetsuo. "Ōshio Heihachirō (1793–1837)." In *Personality in Japanese History*, edited by Albert M. Craig and Donald H. Shively, pp. 155–79. Berkeley: University of California Press, 1970.

———. "Political Economism in the Thought of Dazai Shundai (1680–1747)." *Journal of Asian Studies* 31.4 (August 1972): 821–39.

———. *Tokugawa Political Writings*. Cambridge: Cambridge University Press, 1998.

———. *Visions of Virtue in Tokugawa Japan: The Kaitokudō Merchant Academy of Osaka*. Chicago: University of Chicago Press, 1987.

Najita, Tetsuo, and J. Victor Koschmann, eds. *Conflict in Modern Japanese History: The Neglected Tradition*. Princeton: Princeton University Press, 1982.

Najita, Tetsuo, and Irwin Scheiner, eds. *Japanese Thought in the Tokugawa Period, 1600–1868: Methods and Metaphors*. Chicago: University of Chicago Press, 1978.

Nakai, Kate Wildman. *Shogunal Politics: Arai Hakusei and the Premises of Tokugawa Rule.* Cambridge, Mass.: Council on East Asian Studies, Harvard University, 1988.

Nakai Chikuzan. *Sōbō kigen.* In *Nihon keizai taiten,* vol. 23, edited by Takimoto Seiichi, pp. 315–546. Tokyo: Meiji bunken, 1969.

Nakai Riken. *Jukkei bōgi.* In *Nihon keizai taiten,* vol. 23, edited by Takimoto Seiichi, pp. 707–16. Tokyo: Meiji bunken, 1969.

Narusawa Akira. *Gendai Nihon no shakai chitsujo: Rekishiteki kigen o motomete.* Tokyo: Iwanami shoten, 1997.

Nihon keimu kyōkai, ed. *Nihon kinsei gyōkei shikō.* 2 vols. Tokyo: Keimu kyōkai, 1943.

Nihon kōgakkai, ed. *Meiji kōgyō shi: Kenchiku hen.* Tokyo: Meiji kōgyōshi hakkō jo, 1930.

Niida, Noboru. *Chūgoku hōsei shi.* Tokyo: Iwanami shoten, 1952.

———. *Shina mibun hōshi.* Tokyo: Zauko kankōkai, 1943.

Ninsoku yoseba kenshōkai, ed. *Ninsoku yoseba shi.* Tokyo: Sōbusha, 1974.

Nishimura Tokihiko (Tenshū). *Kaitokudōkō.* Ōsaka: Kaitokudō kinenkai, 1925.

Nomura Maki. "'Tsūjin' kara no yuutopia—'Kashō kokuō' Nakai Riken no shisō." *Kokka gakkai zasshi* 107.7–8 (1994): 188–236.

Norman, E. H. *Andō Shōeki and the Anatomy of Japanese Feudalism.* Washington, D.C.: University Publications of America, 1979.

———. *Soldier and Peasant in Japan: The Origins of Conscription.* 1943. Vancouver: University of British Columbia Press, 1965.

Ōba Osamu. *Edo jidai no Nicchū hiwa.* Tokyo: Tōhō shoten, 1980.

Obinata Sumio. *Nihon kindai kokka no seiritsu to keisatsu.* Tokyo: Azekura shobō, 1992.

O'Brien, Patricia. *The Promise of Punishment: Prisons in Nineteenth-Century France.* Princeton: Princeton University Press, 1982.

Ochiai Nobutaka. "Kinsei sonraku ni okeru kaji, nusumi no kenshōken to shinpan no kinō." *Rekishi hyōron* 442 (1987): 63–84.

———. "Mura no keibatsu." In *Kangoku no tanjō: Asahi hyakka rekishi o yominaosu 22,* edited by Yasumaru Yoshio, pp. 30–31. Tokyo: Asahi shimbunsha, 1995.

Ogawa Shigejirō. "Gokusei ron hito han." *Dai Nihon kangoku kyōkai zasshi* 110 (July 1897): 2–10.

———. *Kangokugaku.* Tokyo: Keisatsu kangoku gakkai, 1894.

———. "Taiwan chikei rei ni tsuite (1)." *Hōgaku kyōkai zasshi* 22.4 (April 1904): 511–12.

———. "Taiwan chikei rei ni tsuite (2)." *Hōgaku kyōkai zasshi* 22.5 (May 1904): 697–719.

———. "Taiwan keiritsu no ue ni chijōkei saiyō no gi aru o kikite shoken o nobu." *Kangoku kyōkai zasshi* 17.1 (January 1904): 3–15.

Ogawa Tarō. "Ohara Shigechika." *Keisei* 8.1 (January 1970): 45–58.

Ogawa Tarō and Nakao Bunsaku. *Gyōkei kaikakusha tachi no rirekisho.* Tokyo: Kyōsei kyōkai, 1983.

Ogyū Sorai. *Discourse on Government (Seidan).* Translated by Olof G. Lidin. Wiesbaden: Harrasowitz Verlag, 1999.

Ogyū Sorai. *Seidan*. In *Nihon keizai taiten*, vol. 9, edited by Takimoto Seiichi, pp. 3–196. Tokyo: Meiji bunken, 1969.

Ohara Shigechika. *Dai Nihon gokusei enkakshi*. Tokyo: Kinkōdō, 1880.

———. "Hyōgikai no enzetsu." *Dai Nihon kangoku kyōkai zasshi* 14 (June 1889): 42–6.

———. "Moto genrōin gikan Ohara Shigechika kun kōwa 1." *Dai Nihon kangoku kyōkai zasshi* 41 (September 1891): 37–42.

———. "Moto genrōin gikan Ohara Shigechika kun kōwa 2." *Dai Nihon kangoku kyōkai zasshi* 43 (November 1891): 20–24.

Ohara Shigechika, Amano Mitami, and Kosuke Eishū. *Eikoku saibansho ryakusetsu: Eikoku shikan Jon Hōru kōyaku*. Tokyo: Keibunbō, 1872.

Oka Yoshitake. *Reimeiki no Meiji Nihon*. Tokyo: Miraisha, 1964.

Okamoto Shigeshirō. "Manshūkoku-jin ni chikei o ka suru koto o eru ya." *Hōritsu shimbun* 4003 (July 8, 1936): 2–6.

Okiura Kazumitsu. "Zen Ajia teki shiza kara mibun sabetsu o kangaeru." *Buraku kaihō* 352 (January 1993): 163–79.

Ōkubo Toshitake, ed. *Nihon ni okeru Berii-ō*. Tokyo: Tōkyō hōgakkai, 1930.

Ōkubo Yasuo. *Nihon kindai hō no chichi—Boasonaado*. Tokyo: Iwanami shinsho, 1977.

Ono Takeo, ed. *Edo no keibatsu fūzoku shi*. Tokyo: Tenbōsha, 1998.

Onoda Motohiro. "Kangoku jigyō (2)." *Dai Nihon kangoku kyōkai zasshi* 5 (September 1888): 1–14.

———. *Taisei kangoku mondō roku*. Tokyo: Keishichō, 1889.

Ooms, Herman. *Charismatic Bureaucrat: A Political Biography of Matsudaira Sadanobu*. Chicago: University of Chicago Press, 1975.

———. *Tokugawa Ideology: Early Constructs, 1570–1680*. Princeton: Princeton University Press, 1985.

———. *Tokugawa Village Practice: Class, Status, Power, Law*. Berkeley: University of California University Press, 1996.

Ōsaka-fu shi henshū senmon iinkai, ed. *Ōsaka-fu shi*. Vol. 6. Osaka: Osakafu, 1987.

Ōsaka-shi, ed. *Ōsaka-shi shi*. Vol. 2. Osaka: Osaka-shi, 1965.

Osatake Takeki. *Meiji bunka sōsetsu*. Tokyo: Gakugeisha, 1934.

Oshinsky, David. *Worse Than Slavery: Parchman Farm and the Ordeal of Jim Crow Justice*. New York: Free Press, 1996.

Pasquino, Pasquale. "Theatrum Politicum: The Genealogy of Capital—Police and the State of Prosperity." In Burchell, Gordon, and Miller, *The Foucault Effect*, pp. 105–18.

Peattie, Mark. "Japanese Attitudes toward Colonialism, 1895–1945." In Myers and Peattie, *The Japanese Colonial Empire, 1895–1945*, pp. 80–127.

Perez, Louis G. *Japan Comes of Age: Mutsu Munemitsu and the Revision of the Unequal Treaties*. London: Associated University Presses, 1999.

Pflugfelder, Gregory M. *Cartographies of Desire: Male-Male Sexuality in Japanese Discourse, 1600–1950*. Berkeley: University of California Press, 1999.

Pickering, W. A. *Pioneering in Formosa*. London: Hurst and Blackett, 1898.

Pratt, Edward E. *Japan's Protoindustrial Elite: The Economic Foundations of the Gōnō*. Cambridge, Mass.: Harvard University Asia Center, 1999.

Radcinowicz, Leon. *A History of the English Criminal Law and Its Administration from 1750*. Vol. 1. London: Stevens, 1948.

Ravina, M. *Land and Lordship in Early Modern Japan*. Stanford: Stanford University Press, 1999.

Rejali, Darius. *Torture and Modernity: Self, Society and State in Modern Iran*. Boulder, Colo.: Westview Press, 1994.

Renneville, Constatin de. *Recueil des voyages qui ont servi à l'etablissement et aux progrés de la Compagnie des Indes*. Amsterdam: Aux dépens d'Estienne Roger, 1702–6.

Richie, Donald. *The Japanese Tattoo*. New York: Weatherhill, 1980.

Roberts, Luke S. *Mercantilism in a Japanese Domain: The Merchant Origins of Economic Nationalism in Eighteenth-Century Tosa*. Cambridge: Cambridge University Press, 1998.

"Rōgoku Hiroku." ca. 1800. In *Edo no keibatsu fūzoku shi*, edited by Ono Takeo, pp. 407–81. Tokyo: Tenbōsha, 1998.

Rothman, David. *Discovery of the Asylum: Social Order and Disorder in the New Republic*. 2nd ed. Boston: Little, Brown, 1990.

———. "Perfecting the Prison: United States, 1789–1865." In *The Oxford History of the Prison*, edited by Norval Morris and David J. Rothman, pp. 111–29. New York: Oxford University Press, 1995.

Rozman, Gilbert. "Edo's Importance in Changing Tokugawa Society." *Journal of Japanese Studies* 1.1 (autumn 1974): 91–112.

Rusche, Georg, and Otto Kirchheimer. *Punishment and Social Structure*. New York: Columbia University Press, 1939.

Rutter, Owen. *Through Formosa: An Account of Japan's Island Colony*. London: T. F. Unwin, 1923.

Said, Edward. *Orientalism*. New York: Random House, 1978.

Saikaku Ihara. *Tales of Japanese Justice*. Translated by T. M. Kondo and A. H. Marks. Honolulu: University of Hawai'i Press, 1980.

Saitō Osamu. "The Rural Economy: Commercial Agriculture, By-employment, and Wage Work." In *Japan in Transition: From Meiji to Tokugawa*, edited by Marius Jansen and Gilbert Rozman, pp. 382–430. Princeton: Princeton University Press, 1986.

Sakata, Yoshio, and John W. Hall. "The Motivation of Political Leadership in the Meiji Restoration." *Journal of Asian Studies* 16 (1956): 31–50.

Sakuma Osahiro. *Edo machi bugyō jiseki mondō*. ca. 1890. Tokyo: Jimbutsu Ōraisha, 1967.

———. "Ginmi no kuden." ca. 1890. In Hara Taneaki and Osatake Takeki, *Edo jidai hanzai keibatsu jireishū*, pp. 259–76.

———. "Gōmon jikki." 1893. In Hara Taneaki and Osatake Takeki, *Edo jidai hanzai keibatsu jireishū*, pp. 213–58.

———. "Keizai yōsetsu." 1893. In Hara Taneaki and Osatake Takeki, *Edo jidai hanzai keibatsu jireishū*, pp. 77–130.

Salvatore, Ricardo D., and Carlos Aguirre. *The Birth of the Penitentiary in Latin America*. Austin: University of Texas Press, 1996.

Satow, E. *A Diplomat in Japan*. London: Seeley, Service, 1912.

Schama, Simon. *The Embarrassment of Riches: An Interpretation of Dutch Culture in the Golden Age*. Berkeley: University of California Press, 1988.

Scheiner, Irwin. "Benevolent Lords and Honorable Peasants: Rebellion and Peasant Consciousness in Tokugawa Japan." In Najita and Scheiner, *Japanese Thought in the Tokugawa Period*, pp. 39–62.

Schmid, Andre. "Colonialism and the 'Korea Problem' in the Historiography of Modern Japan." *Journal of Asian Studies* 59.4 (November 2000): 951–76.

Schmidt, Petra. *Capital Punishment in Japan*. Leiden: Brill, 2002.

Sellin, J. T. *Pioneering in Penology: The Amsterdam House of Correction in the Sixteenth and Seventeenth Centuries*. Philadelphia: University of Pennsylvania Press, 1944.

Sen, Satadru. *Disciplining Punishment: Colonialism and Convict Society in the Andaman Islands*. New Dehli: Oxford University Press, 2000.

Sharpe, J. A. *Crime in Early Modern England, 1550–1750*. London: Longman, 1984.

———. *Judicial Punishment in England*. London: Faber and Faber, 1990.

Shaw, A.G.L. *Convicts and Colonies*. Melbourne: Melbourne University Press, 1966.

Shiba Kōkan. "Oranda tsūhaku." 1805. In *Shiba Kōkan zenshū*, vol. 3, edited by Asakura Haruhiko et al., pp. 147–92. Tokyo: Yasaka shobō, 1992.

Shibusawa Eiichi. "Journal of a Voyage to the West." In *The Autobiography of Shibusawa Eiichi*, translated by Teruko Craig, pp. 151–71. Tokyo: University of Tokyo Press, 1994.

Shigematsu Kazuyoshi. "Edo Ōbanya giga kaidai—Kawanabe Kyōsai junan no haikei to banya no jittai." *Kyōsai* 36 (September 1988): 15–16.

———. *Hokkaidō gyōkei shi*. Sapporo: Zufu shuppan, 1970.

———. *Mei tengoku hyōden*. Tokyo: Nihon gyōseishi kenkyūkai, 1984.

———. *Nihon keibatsu shiseki kō*. Tokyo: Seibundō, 1985.

———. "Ninsoku Yoseba to Ishikawajima kangoku." In *Ninsoku Yoseba shi*, edited by Ninsoku Yoseba kenshōkai, pp. 329–44. Tokyo: Sōbunsha, 1974.

———. *Zukan Nihon no kangokushi*. Tokyo: Oyamakaku shuppan, 1985.

Shimada Masarō. "Shinmatsu no gokusei kaikaku to Ogawa Shigejirō." In *Meiji hōseishi seijishi no shomondai*, edited by Tezuka Yutaka kyōju taishoku kinen ronbun shū hansan iinkai, pp. 509–26. Tokyo: Keiō tsūshin, 1977.

Shinagawa machi yakuba, ed. *Shinagawa chōshi*. Tokyo: Shinagawa-machi yakuba, 1932.

Shinoda Kōzō. *Meiji hyakuwa*. 1932. Vol. 1. Tokyo: Iwanami shoten, 1996.

Shirayama Tomomasa. "Ezochi yoseba kō." *Hōseishi kenkyū* 13 (1962): 144–63.

"Shūto kin'en no kekka," *Dai Nihon kangoku kyōkai zasshi* 102 (November 1896): 66.

Smith, George. *Ten Weeks in Japan*. London: Longman, Green, Longman and Roberts, 1861.

Smith, Thomas C. *Native Sources of Japanese Industrialization, 1750–1920*. Berkeley: University of California Press, 1988.

———. "Premodern Economic Growth: Japan and the West." In Smith, *Native Sources of Japanese Industrialization, 1750–1920*, pp. 15–49.

Smits, Gregory. *Visions of Ryukyu: Identity and Ideology in Early Modern Thought and Politics*. Honolulu: University of Hawai'i Press, 1999.

Snodgrass, Judith. "Japan Faces the West: The Representation of Japan at the Columbian Exposition, Chicago 1893." In *Japanese Science, Technology and Economic Growth Down-Under*, edited by Morris Low and Helen Marriott, pp. 5–25. Clayton: Monash Asia Institute, 1996.

Sō Nanshiki. "Kyūbaku jidai taisha iiwatashi no gaikyō." *Keisatsu Kangoku Gakkai Zasshi* 4 (1891): 27–28.

Sone Hiromi. "Prostitution and Public Authority in Early Modern Japan." In Tonomura, Walthall, and Wakita, *Women and Class in Japanese History*, pp. 169–85.

Spierenburg, Pieter. *The Prison Experience: Disciplinary Institutions and Their Inmates in Early Modern Europe*. New Brunswick: Rutgers University Press, 1991.

Stanley, Amy. "Adultery and Punishment in Tokugawa Japan." Senior thesis, Harvard University, 1999.

Sumiya Mikio. *Nihon chin rōdō no shiteki kenkyū*. Tokyo: Ochanomizu shobō, 1976.

Suzuki Ryō. "Nihon kindai shi kenkyū ni okeru buraku mondai no ichi." *Rekishi hyōron* 368 (1980): 1–35.

Suzuki Shōsan. "Roankyō." ca. 1630. In *Suzuki Shōsan dōnin zenshū*, edited by Suzuki Tesshin, pp. 138–284. Tokyo: Sankibo busshorin, 1962.

———. *Selected Writings of Suzuki Shōsan*. Translated by Royall Tyler. Ithaca: Cornell University China-Japan Program, 1977.

Suzuki Sōgen. "Ogawa shi no chikeiron o yomu 1." *Hōgaku kyōkai zasshi* 22.6 (June 1904): 821–36.

———. "Ogawa shi no chikeiron o yomu 2." *Hōgaku kyōkai zasshi* 22.7 (July 1904): 941–59.

———. "Ogawa shi cho chikei ron o yomu 1." *Kangoku kyōkai zasshi* 17.8 (August 1904): 31–35.

———. "Ogawa shi cho chikei ron o yomu 2." *Kangoku kyōkai zasshi* 17.9 (September 1904): 1–7.

———. "Ogawa shi cho chikei ron o yomu 3." *Kangoku kyōkai zasshi* 17.10 (October 1904): 1–8.

———. "Ogawa shi cho chikei ron o yomu 4." *Kangoku kyōkai zasshi* 17.11 (November 1904): 1–7.

———. "Ogawa shi cho chikei ron o yomu 5." *Kangoku kyōkai zasshi* 17.12 (December 1904): 7–12.

"Taihoku kangoku cho zaikansha," *Dai Nihon kangoku kyōkai zasshi* 100 (September 15, 1896): 55–56.

Taiwan Sōtokufu keimukyoku. *Taiwan Sōtokufu keisatsu enkaku shi* 2. Taihoku: Taiwan Sōtokufu keimukyoku, 1942.

Taiwan Sōtokufu Sōtoku kanbō bunsho ka, ed. *Taiwan Sōtokufu tōkei sho*. Taihoku: Sōtoku kanbō bunsho ka, 1900–.

Takahashi Satoshi. *Edo no soshō*. Tokyo: Iwanami Shoten, 1996.

———. *Kunisada Chūji no jidai: Yomi kaki to kenjutsu*. Tokyo: Heibonsha, 1991.

Takano Chōei. "Wasuregatami." ca. 1840. In *Nihon no shisō taikei*, vol. 55, edited by Satō Shōsuke, pp. 174–80. Tokyo: Iwanami shoten, 1971.

Takashio Hiroshi and Kanzaki Naomi. "Kyōsei kyōkai zō 'Yoseba ninsoku kyūki tome.'" *Kokugakuin Daigaku Nihon bunka kenkyū jo kiyō* 76 (September 1995): 143–98.

Takayanagi Kaneyoshi. *Hinin no seikatsu*. Tokyo: Oyamakaku, 1981.

Takayanagi Shinzō. "Tokugawa Bakufu no sharitsu ni tsuite (1)." *Hōgaku* 12.9 (1943): 734–67.

Takayanagi Shinzō and Ishii Ryōsuke. *Ofuregaki Hōreki shūsei*. Tokyo: Iwanami shoten, 1936.

Takayanagi Shinzō and Ishii Ryōsuke. *Ofuregaki Kampō shūsei*. Tokyo: Iwanami shoten, 1935.

———, eds. *Ofuregaki Tempō shūsei*. Tokyo: Iwanami shoten, 1937.

———, eds. *Ofuregaki Tenmei shūsei*. Tokyo: Iwanami shoten, 1936.

Takekoshi, Yosaburo. *The Economic Aspect of the History of Japan*. 3 vols. London: George Allen and Unwin, 1930.

———. *Japanese Rule in Formosa*. London: Longmans, Green and Co., 1907.

———. *Prince Saionji*. Kyoto: Ritsumeikan, 1936.

———. *Self-Portrayal of Japan*. Tokyo: Ritsumeikan Press, 1939.

———. *The Story of the Wako: Japanese Pioneers in the Southern Region*. Tokyo: Kenkyusha, [1940].

———. *Taiwan tōchi shi*. Tokyo: Hakubunkan, 1905.

Takenaka Yasuichi. "Ninsoku yoseba to shingaku." In *Ninsoku yoseba shi*, edited by Ninsoku yoseba kenshōkai, pp. 197–232. Tokyo: Sōbusha, 1974.

Takeuchi Makoto. "Edo tōyō sōdō no seijiteki eikyō." *Tokugawa rinsei shi kenkyū jo kenkyū kiyō* (1977): 259–79.

———. "Kansei kaikaku." In *Iwanami kōza Nihon rekishi 12: Kinsei 4*, edited by Naoki Kōjiro and Asao Naohiro, pp. 1–44. Tokyo: Iwanami shoten, 1976.

———. "Tenmei no Edo uchi kowashi no jittai." *Tokugawa rinsei shi kenkyū jo kenkyū kiyō* (1970): 256–94.

———. "Uchikowashi." In *Edo gaku jiten*, edited by Nishiyama Matsunosuke, p. 584. Tokyo: Kōbundō, 1984.

Takigawa Masajirō. *Hasegawa Heizō—sono shōgai to ninsoku yoseba*. Tokyo: Asahi shimbunsha, 1975.

Tamura Eitarō. *Ikki, kumosuke, bakuto*. Tokyo: Mikasa shobō, 1935.

Tanaka Osamu. *Nihon shihon shugi to Hokkaidō*. Sapporo: Hokkaido Daigaku tosho kankō kai, 1988.

Tanaka Satoshi. *Chizu kara kieta Tōkyō isan*. Tokyo: Shōdensha, 1999.

Tanaka, Stefan. *Japan's Orient: Rendering Pasts into History*. Berkeley: University of California Press, 1993.

Tejima Heijirō. "Taiwan kangoku dan 1." *Kangoku kyōkai zasshi* 18.4 (April 1905): 23–30.

———. "Taiwan kangoku dan 2." *Kangoku kyōkai zasshi* 18.5 (May 1905): 17–26.

Tezuka Yutaka. *Meiji keinō shi no kenkyū*. 3 vols. Tokyo: Keiō Tsūshin, 1985.

Thompson, E. P. "The Moral Economy of the English Crowd in the Eighteenth Century." Reprinted in *Customs in Common*, edited by E. P. Thompson, pp. 185–258. London: Penguin, 1993.

Titsingh, Issac. *Illustrations of Japan*. London: R. Ackermann, 1822.

Toby, Ronald. "Both a Borrower and a Lender Be: From Village Moneylender to Rural Banker in the Tempō Era." *Monumenta Nipponica* 46.4 (winter 1991): 483–512.

———. "Rescuing the Nation from History: The State of the State in Early Modern Japan." *Monumenta Nipponica* 56.2 (spring 2001): 197–237.

———. *State and Diplomacy in Early Modern Japan: Asia in the Development of the Tokugawa Bakufu*. Stanford: Stanford University Press, 1984.

Toby, Ronald, and Kuroda Hideo, eds. *Asahi hyakka rekishi o yominaosu 17: Gyōretsu to misemono*. Tokyo: Asahi shimbunsha, 1994.

Tokyo Daigaku shiryō hensanjo, ed. *Dai Nihon shiryō (Dai Jūni-hen)*. Vol. 44. Tokyo: Tokyo Daigaku shuppankai, 1906.

Tokyo-to. *Ginza renga gai no kensetsu*. Tokyo: Tokyo-to, 1955.

———, ed. *Tōkyō shishi kō: Shigaihen*. 85 vols. Tokyo: Tokyo-to, 1914–.

Tomie Ōhara. *A Woman Called En*. Translated by Kazuko Furuhata and Janet Smith. London: Routledge and Kegan Paul, 1986.

Tonomura, Hitomi. *Community and Commerce in Late Medieval Japan: The Corporate Villages of Tokuchin-ho*. Stanford: Stanford University Press, 1992.

Tonomura, Hitomi, Anne Walthall, and Wakita Haruko, eds. *Women and Class in Japanese History*. Ann Arbor: University of Michigan Center for Japanese Studies, 1999.

Totman, Conrad. *The Collapse of the Tokugawa Bakufu, 1862–1868*. Honolulu: University of Hawai'i Press, 1980.

———. *Early Modern Japan*. Berkeley: University of California Press, 1993.

———. *Politics in the Tokugawa Bakufu, 1600–1843*. 2nd ed. Berkeley: University of California Press, 1988.

Tsuji Tatsuya. *Ōoka Echizen no kami*. Tokyo: Chūō kōronsha, 1964.

Tsukada Takashi. "Edo Asakusa shinchō." In *Nihon toshi nyūmon 2: Chō*, ed Takahashi Yasuo and Yoshida Nobuyuki, pp. 170–71. Tokyo: Tokyo Daigaku shuppankai, 1990.

———. *Kinsei mibunsei to shūen shakai*. Tokyo: Tokyo Daigaku shuppankai, 1997.

———. *Kinsei no toshi shakai-shi*. Tokyo: Aoki shoten, 1996.

———. *Kinsei Nihon mibunsei no kenkyū*. Kōbe: Hyōgo buraku mondai kenkyūjo, 1987.

———. *Mibunsei shakai to shimin shakai*. Tokyo: Kashiwa shobō, 1992.

———. "Shokei to sarashi no ba." In *Asahi hyakka rekishi o yominaosu 17: Gyōretsu to misemono*, edited by Ronald Toby and Kuroda Toshio, pp. 54–55. Tokyo: Asahi shimbunsha, 1994.

Tsukamoto Manabu. *Shōrui o meguru seiji*. Tokyo: Heibonsha, 1983.

Tsunoda Ryūsaku, Wm. Theodore de Bary, and Donald Keene, eds. *Sources of Japanese Tradition*. New York: Columbia University Press, 1964.

Tsurumi, E. Patricia. *Factory Girls: Women in the Thread Mills of Meiji Japan*. Princeton: Princeton University Press, 1990.

———. *Japanese Colonial Education in Taiwan, 1895–1945*. Cambridge, Mass.: Harvard University Press, 1977.

Tsurumi Shunsuke. *Takano Chōei*. Tokyo: Ashai shimbunsha, 1985.

———, ed. *Nihon no hyakunen 9: Waki tatsu minron*. Tokyo: Chikuma shobō, 1967.

Tsurumi Yūsuke. *Gotō Shimpei den*. Vol. 2. Tokyo: Gotō Shimpei-haku denki hensankai, 1937.

Tsutsui Meirin. "Taiwan kangoku keikyō ni tsuite 1." *Kangoku kyōkai zasshi* 14.8 (August 1901): 23–34.

———. "Taiwan kangoku keikyō ni tsuite 2." *Kangoku kyōkai zasshi* 14.9 (September 1901): 16–38.

Ugawa Seisaburō. "Dai Nihon kangoku kyōkai sōsetsu no shui." *Dai Nihon kangoku kyōkai zasshi* 1.1 (May 1889): 1–8.

Ujiie Mikito. *Fugi mittsū: Kinjirareta koi no Edo*. Tokyo: Kodansha, 1996.

———. *Ō Edo shitai kō: Hito kiri Asaemon no jidai*. Tokyo: Heibonsha, 1999.

Ujiie Mikito. *Tonosama to nezumi kozō.* Tokyo: Chūō ōronsha, 1991.

Umemori, Naoyuki. "Modernization through Colonial Mediations: The Establishment of the Police and Prison System in Meiji Japan." Ph.D. dissertation, University of Chicago, 2002.

———. "Shingaku to iu tekunorogii." *Waseda seiji keizai gaku zasshi* 328 (1996): 228–60.

———. "Spatial Configuration and Subject Formation: The Establishment of the Modern Penitentiary System in Meiji Japan." In Hardacre and Kern, *New Directions in the Study of Meiji Japan*, pp. 735–67.

van Dülmen, R. *Theatre of Horror: Crime and Punishment in Early Modern Germany.* Cambridge: Polity Press, 1990.

Vaporis, Constantine Nomikos. *Breaking Barriers: Travel and the State in Early Modern Japan.* Cambridge, Mass.: Council on East Asian Studies, Harvard University, 1994.

Venturi, Franco. *Utopia and Reform in the Enlightenment.* Cambridge: Cambridge University Press, 1971.

Verwayen, F. B. "Tokugawa Translations of Dutch Legal Texts." *Monumenta Nipponica* 53.3 (fall 1998): 335–58.

Vlastos, Stephen. "Opposition Movements in Early Meiji, 1868–1885." In *The Cambridge History of Japan*, edited by Marius B. Jansen, Cambridge: Cambridge University Press, 1989. 5: 267–431.

———. *Peasant Protests and Uprisings in Tokugawa Japan.* Berkeley: University of California Press, 1986.

von Siebold, Phillip Franz. *Manners and Customs of the Japanese in the Nineteenth Century.* 1841. Rutland, Vt.: Charles E. Tuttle, 1973.

Walker, Brett L. *The Conquest of Ainu Lands: Ecology and Culture in Japanese Expansion, 1590–1800.* Berkeley: University of California Press, 2001.

Walthall, Anne, trans. and ed. *Peasant Uprisings in Japan: A Critical Anthology of Peasant Histories.* Chicago: University of Chicago Press, 1991.

———. *Social Protest and Popular Culture in Eighteenth-Century Japan.* Tuscon: University of Arizona Press, 1986.

———. *The Weak Body of a Useless Woman: Matsuo Taseko and the Meiji Restoration.* Chicago: University of Chicago Press, 1998.

Wang, Tay-Sheng. *Legal Reform in Taiwan under Japanese Colonial Rule, 1895–1945.* Seattle: University of Washington Press, 2000.

Washinosu Atsuya. *Taiwan keisatsu shijūnen shiwa.* Taihoku: Washinosu Atsuya, 1938.

Watanabe Hiroshi. "Eta." In *Kokushi daijiten*, edited by Kokushi daijiten henshū iinkai, 2:279. Tokyo: Yoshikawa kōbunkan, 1985.

Wei Yuan. *Haiguo tuzhi.* Edited by Li Julan. Zhengzhou guji chubanshe, 1999.

Westney, D. Eleanor. "The Emulation of Western Organizations in Meiji Japan: The Case of the Paris Prefecture of Police and the Keishi-chō." *Journal of Japanese Studies* 8.2 (summer 1982): 307–42.

White, James W. *Ikki: Social Conflict and Political Protest in Early Modern Japan.* Ithaca: Cornell University Press, 1995.

Wigen, Kären. *The Making of a Japanese Periphery, 1750–1920.* Berkeley: University of California Press, 1995.

Wigmore, John H. *Law and Justice in Tokugawa Japan: Materials for the History of Japanese Law and Justice under the Tokugawa Shogunate, 1603–1867.* Tokyo: Kokusai bunka shinkōkai, 1967.

Wilson, William R., trans. *Hōgen monogatari: Tale of the Disorder in Hōgen.* Tokyo: Sophia University Press, ca. 1971.

Wines, E. C. *The State of Prisons and of Child-Saving Institutions in the Civilised World.* Cambridge, Mass.: John Wilson & Son, 1880.

Wright, Diana E. "Severing the Karmic Ties That Bind: The Divorce Temple Mantokuji." *Monumenta Nipponica* 52.3 (autumn 1997): 357–80.

Wright, Gordon. *Between the Guillotine and Liberty: Two Centuries of the Crime Problem in France.* Oxford: Oxford University Press, 1983.

Yabuta Yutaka. "'Hei' to 'nō' no aida." *Rekishi hyōron* 593 (September 1999): 2–15.

Yamada Hōkoku. "Gokusei kaikaku ikensho." In *Yamada Hōkoku zenshū,* edited by Yamada Jun, pp. 359–61. Okayama: Yamada Hōkoku zenshū kangyōkai, 1951.

Yamada Moritarō. *Nihon shihon shugi bunseki—Nihon shihon shugi ni okeru saiseisan katei haaku.* Tokyo: Iwanami shoten, 1934.

Yamada Yoshio et al., eds. *Konjaku monogatari shū: Nihon koten bungaku taikei.* 5 vols. Tokyo: Iwanami shoten, 1959–63.

Yamamoto Hirofumi. "Edo no tōnin to keibatsu kannen." In *Engyo Edo bunkō 6: Edo no shiranami,* edited by Asakura Haruhiko, pp. 395–411. Tokyo: Chūkō bunkō, 1997.

Yamamura, S. "Politics and Education in Early Meiji Japan: The Modern Military System and the Formation of the 'Gakusei.'" Ph.D. dissertation, University of California at Berkeley, 1978.

Yamashina Tokitsugu. *Tokitsugu kyō ki.* 1527–76. 4 vols. Tokyo: Kokusho kankōkai, 1914–15.

Yamashita, Samuel Hideo. *Master Sorai's Responsals.* Honolulu: University of Hawai'i Press, 1994.

———. "Nature and Artifice in the Writings of Ogyū Sorai (1666–1728)." In *Confucianism and Tokugawa Culture,* edited by Peter Nosco, pp. 138–65. Princeton: Princeton University Press, 1984.

Yasuda Seiichi, ed. *Ōi chō shi.* Tokyo: Ōi chō shi hensan kankōkai, 1923.

Yasumaru Yoshio, ed. *Kangoku no tanjō: Asahi hyakka rekishi o yominaosu 22.* Tokyo: Asahi shimbunsha, 1995.

———. "'Kangoku' no tanjō." In *Bakumatsu Meiji-ki no kokumin kokka keisei to bunka henyō,* edited by Nishikawa Nagao and Matsumiya Hideharu, pp. 279–312. Tokyo: Shinyōsha, 1995.

Yokota Fuyuhiko. "Senshi sareta shokunin shūdan." In *Nihon no shakai shi 6: Shakai-teki sho shūdan,* edited by Asao Naohiro et al., pp. 285–322. Tokyo: Iwanami shoten, 1988.

Yoshida Nobuyuki. "Chōnin to chō." In *Kōza Nihon rekishi 5: Kinsei 1,* edited by Rekishigaku kenkyūkai, pp. 151–88. Tokyo: Tokyo Daigaku shuppankai, 1985.

———. *Kinsei kyodai toshi no shakai kōzō.* Tokyo: Tokyo Daigaku shuppankai, 1991.

———. *Kinsei toshi shakai no mibun kōzō.* Tokyo: Tokyo Daigaku shuppankai, 1998.

Yoshida Shōin. "Edo Gokki." 1855. In *Yoshida Shōin zenshū,* 2nd ed., vol. 2, edited by Yamaguchi-ken kyōikukai, pp. 286–300. Tokyo: Iwanami shoten, 1939.

Yoshida Shōin. "Fukudōsaku." 1855. In *Yoshida Shōin zenshū*, 2nd. ed., vol. 2, edited by Yamaguchi-ken kyōikukai, pp. 163–68. Tokyo: Iwanami shoten, 1939.

———. "Kaikoroku." 1854. In *Yoshida Shōin zenshū*, vol. 7, edited by Yamaguchi-ken kyōikukai, pp. 379–422. Tokyo: Iwanami shoten, 1935.

Yoshimura Shigenori, ed. *Hōgen monogatari shinshaku*. Tokyo: Daidōkan shoten. 1940.

Zinoman, Peter. *The Colonial Bastille: A History of Imprisonment in Vietnam, 1862–1940*. Berkeley: University of California Press, 2001.

Index

Abashiri Prison, 186, 189
Abe Yoshio, 47, 94
Adams, F. O., 149
adultery, 30, 73, 238n.65. *See also* marriage
agriculture, 99, 108, 110, 183. *See also* famine
Aichi Prison, 174
Akitsuki, 172
Alcock, Rutherford, 133
alms, 51, 78
amnesty, 47–49, 58, 89, 90, 201, 204, 243n.28. *See also* pardon
amputation, 90, 91. *See also* mutilation
Amsterdam, 118, 119
animals, 43, 50, 51, 52, 78, 245n.62. *See also* leather work
Aoki Tsutomu, 133
Arai Hakuseki, 31, 43–44, 47–48, 86, 144; *Tokushi yoron*, 43–44
arson, 29, 45, 47, 74, 87, 98, 99, 237n.60, 242n.14, 254n.40
artisans, 51, 59, 99
Asada Gōryū, 117
Asahina Yatarō Yasunari, 76
Asakawa Kan'ichi, 222
Asakusa, 23, 78, 79
Asakusabashi, 20
Asia, 6, 131, 185, 204, 221, 222, 223, 224
assault, 69, 78
Atosanupuri, 185, 192
Auburn State Prison, New York, 122
Australia, 118, 122, 203
authoritarianism, 40
authority, 56, 57, 64, 69–71

Baba Tatsui, 190
Baker, Edward, 212, 220
Bakufu: amnesty by, 48; area controlled by, 15; banishment by, 89; and bannerman, 81; beheading by, 20; benevolence of, 177; bureaucracy of, 70; and Chinese traditions, 144; crucifixion by, 83; and Dutch studies, 117, 119; executions by, 18; and famine, 110; fear of, 46, 49, 91; fiscal fragility of, 178; flogging by, 92;

and Meiji reforms, 141–42, 177–78; national authority of, 80–81; as overseer of public affairs *(kōgi-sama)*, 39; punishment by, 18, 20, 83, 89, 92, 141–42, 201; restrictions on, 177–78; restrictions on Sōroku, 80; and riots, 106; and Sadanobu, 100, 101, 103; and status system, 177; and Stockade for Laborers, 107, 109, 110; tattooing by, 27, 92; and temple as refuge, 47; and unregistereds, 112, 113; and vagrants, 97–100, 112, 113; vengeance registration with, 30–31; warlords' permission from, 81–82, 83; and Western imperialism, 115; and Western studies, 119; and Yamada's reforms, 126. *See also* Tokugawa government
Bakumatsu Japan: and death of Shimazu Seiji, 136; modern prisons in, 127; prison reform in, 123, 125, 126; social disorder in, 127–28. *See also* Meiji government
Bandit Punishment Ordinance, 206, 207, 219
banditry, 108, 206
banishment: abolition of, 88–89, 91, 92, 143–44, 160; by Bakufu, 89; by bannermen, 81, 89; as cause of crime, 88–89, 93, 107–8; of commoners, 77–78, 92; and Edo Stockade, 112; for gambling, 72; by governor of accounts, 70; to *hinin* groups, 77–78; long-term jail as alternative to, 97; and Meiji government, 160, 175–76, 177; and mercy pleas, 48; in murder cases, 30; with mutilation, 15; and Ohara, 146; penal servitude as replacement for, 146; for rape, 30; Riken's critique of, 92–93, 96; for robbery of shogun, 33; Shundai's critique of, 91; and social order, 89; Sorai's critique of, 88–89; to Stockade for Laborers, 107, 108, 109, 110, 112, 113; and stockades, 111; with tattooing, 28; of unregistereds, 103; by village headman, 69; by warlords, 89, 91; in Warring States period, 88; under Yoshimune, 91, 92. *See also* exile
bannermen, 81, 89